Ninth International Workshop on Natural Language Processing for Social Media (SocialNLP 2021)

Online
10 June 2021

ISBN: 978-1-7138-3030-6

Printed from e-media with permission by:

Curran Associates, Inc.
57 Morehouse Lane
Red Hook, NY 12571

Some format issues inherent in the e-media version may also appear in this print version.

Printed with permission by Curran Associates, Inc. (2021)

For permission requests, please contact the Association for Computational Linguistics at the address below.

Association for Computational Linguistics
209 N. Eighth Street
Stroudsburg, Pennsylvania 18360

Phone: 1-570-476-8006
Fax: 1-570-476-0860

acl@aclweb.org

Additional copies of this publication are available from:

Curran Associates, Inc.
57 Morehouse Lane
Red Hook, NY 12571 USA
Phone: 845-758-0400
Fax: 845-758-2633
Email: curran@proceedings.com
Web: www.proceedings.com

SocialNLP 2021

The Ninth International Workshop on Natural Language Processing for Social Media

Proceedings of the Workshop

June 10, 2021

SocialNLP 2021@NAACL Chairs' Welcome

It is our great pleasure to welcome you to the Ninth Workshop on Natural Language Processing for Social Media-SocialNLP 2021, associated with NAACL 2021. SocialNLP is an inter-disciplinary area of natural language processing (NLP) and social computing. We hold SocialNLP twice a year: one in the NLP venue, the other in the associated venue such as those for web technology or artificial intelligence. This year the other version has been successfully held in conjunction with TheWebConf 2021 (formerly WWW), and we are very happily looking forward the NLP version in NAACL 2021. We are very glad that the number of submissions to this year's workshop keeps increasing this year, and the submissions themselves were still of high quality with the accepted threshold 3.33 (maximum 5), which again leads to a competitive selection process. We received submissions from Asia, Europe, and the United States. Considering the review process is rigorous and we want to encourage authors to participate the online workshop, we accepted 16 oral papers and thus the acceptance rate was 55 percent. These exciting papers include novel and practical topics for researchers working on NLP for social media, such as bias mitigation, domain transfer, and dataset constructed for the newly emerged research problems. We believe they will benefit our research community.

Besides the main workshop, we are having this year a new EmotionX challenge, Fake-EmoReact. At the time we compose this proceedings, we already have 20 international teams registered and the challenge is still ongoing. We have a special session for this challenge to exchange related ideas and experience in the workshop. We hope this challenge series can bring participants from the research problem to the real solution.

This year we are excited to have Prof. Dan Goldwasser from Purdue University and Prof. Tim Weninger from University of Notre Dame as our keynote speakers. As one of our beautiful tradition, all the authors provide their poster in gather.town. We encourage attendees to (virtually) attend our keynote speech, oral sessions as well as the poster session to have more discussions with outstanding researchers.

Putting together SocialNLP 2021 was a team effort. We first thank the authors for providing the quality content of the program. We are grateful to the program committee members, who worked very hard in reviewing papers and providing feedback to authors. For a lot of tedious work coming from the challenge, we thank the challenge co-chairs Prof Hon-Han Shuai and Dr. Ming Sun for their great effort. We also thank Mr. Chien-Kun Huang and Mr. Yi-Ting Chang for their assistance on the challenge website. Finally, we especially thank the NAACL Workshop chairs Prof. Bhavana Dalvi, Prof. Mamoru Komachi, and Prof. Michel Galley for helping us on all the complicated logistics for this year's online version.

We hope you enjoy the workshop!

Organizers
Lun-Wei Ku, Academia Sincia, Taiwan
Cheng-Te Li, National Cheng Kung University, Taiwan

Challenge Organizers
Lun-Wei Ku, Academia Sincia, Taiwan
Hong-Han Shuai, National Yang Ming Chiao Tung University, Taiwan
Ming Sun, Facebook

Organizers:

Lun-Wei Ku, National Yang Ming Chiao Tung University
Chenge-Te Li, National Cheng Kung University

Organizers of Fake-EmoReact Challenge:

Lun-Wei Ku, Academia Sinica
Hong-Han Shuai, Academia Sinica
Ming Sun, Facebook

Program Committee:

Khalid Al Khatib, Leipzig University
Milad Alshomary, Paderborn University
Silvio Amir, Northeastern University
Guozhen An, City University of New York
Sabine Bergler, Concordia University
Laura Biester, University of Michigan
Victoria Bobicev, Technical University of Moldova
Caroline Brun, Institut NeuroMyoGène, Lyon
Erik Cambria, Nanyang Technological University
Paula Carvalho, UT Austin, Portugal CoLab
Yung-Chun Chang, Taipei Medical University
Yue Chen, Indiana University
Zhuang Chen, WuHan University
Hai Leong Chieu, DSO National Laboratories
Patricia Chiril, Paul Sabatier University
Oana Cocarascu, King's College London
Danilo Croce, University of Roma, Tor Vergata
Lei Cui, Microsoft Research
Daniel Dakota, Uppsala University
Pradipto Das, Rakuten USA
MeiXing Dong, University of Michigan
Rory Duthie, University of Dundee
Wassim El-Hajj, American University of Beirut
Elisabetta Fersini, University of Milano-Bicocca
Lucie Flek, Philipps University of Marburg, TU Darmstadt
Andrea Galassi, Università di Bologna
Aparna Garimella, Adobe Inc
Alexander Gelbukh, Instituto Politécnico Nacional
Marco Guerini, Fondazione Bruno Kessler
Tunga Güngör, Bogazici University
Loitongbam Gyanendro Singh, IIT Guwahati
Hatem Haddad, iCompass
Chenyang Huang, University of Alberta
Hen-Hsen Huang, National Chengchi University
Kokil Jaidka, National University of Singapore
Charles Jochim, IBM Research - Europe
Xincheng Ju, Soochow University
Pallika Kanani, Oracle Labs

Tsung-Ting Kuo, University of California San Diego
Yang Li, Northwestern Polytechnical University
Yingjie Li, University of Illinois at Chicago
Yang Li, Northeast Electric Power University
Peiqin Lin, Sun Yat-sen University
Chuan-Jie Lin, National Taiwan Ocean University
Marco Lippi, Università di Modena e Reggio Emilia
Pengfei Liu, SpeechX Limited
Avinash Madasu, Samsung R & D Institute Bangalore
Eugenio Martínez-Cámara, Universidad de Granada
Bruno Martins, University of Lisbon
Sahisnu Mazumder, University of Illinois at Chicago
Manuel Montes, INAOE, Mexico
Véronique MORICEAU, IRIT, Université de Toulouse
Hamdy Mubarak, Qatar Computing Research Institute QCRI
Nona Naderi, Bibliomics and Text Mining Group
Jose Ochoa-Luna, Universidad Catolica San Pablo
Endang Wahyu Pamungkas, Universita Degli Studi di Torino
Haris Papageorgiou, ATHENA Research and Innovation Center
Georgios Petasis, National Center for Scientific Research Demokritos
Omid Rohanian, University of Oxford
Mohammad Salameh, University of Alberta
Annika Marie Schoene, University of Manchester
Boaz Shmueli, National Tsing Hua University and Institute of Information Science, Academia Sinica
Abu Awal Md Shoeb, Rutgers University
Priyanka Sinha, Tata Consultancy Services
Irena Spasic, Cardiff University
Xavier Tannier, Sorbonne Université, INSERM, LIMICS
Paolo Torroni, University of Bologna
Amine Trabelsi, University of Alberta
Enrica Troiano, University of Stuttgart
Paola Velardi, Sapienza University of Roma
Jingjing Wang, Tsinghua University
Hao Wang, Southwest Jiaotong University
Ingmar Weber, Qatar Computing Research Institute QCRI
Steven Wilson, The University of Edinburgh
Zhen Wu, Nanjing University
Shih-Hung Wu, Chaoyang University of Technology
Frank Xing, Nanyang Technological University
Lu Xu, Singapore University of Technology and Design
Jun Yang, Nanjing University
Zixiaofan Yang, Columbia University
Diyi Yang, Georgia Institute of Technology
Liang-Chih Yu, Yuan Ze University
Zhe Zhang, IBM
Lei Zhang, University of Illinois at Chicago
Bowen Zhang, Harbin Institute of Technology
Dongyu Zhang, Dalian University of Technology
Qi Zhang, Fudan University
Fei Zhao, Nanjing University

Table of Contents

Analysis of Nuanced Stances and Sentiment Towards Entities of US Politicians through the Lens of Moral Foundation Theory
Shamik Roy and Dan Goldwasser 1

Content-based Stance Classification of Tweets about the 2020 Italian Constitutional Referendum
Marco Di Giovanni and Marco Brambilla 14

A Case Study of In-House Competition for Ranking Constructive Comments in a News Service
Hayato Kobayashi, Hiroaki Taguchi, Yoshimune Tabuchi, Chahine Koleejan, Ken Kobayashi, Soichiro Fujita, Kazuma Murao, Takeshi Masuyama, Taichi Yatsuka, Manabu Okumura and Satoshi Sekine .. 24

Quantifying the Effects of COVID-19 on Restaurant Reviews
Ivy Cao, Zizhou Liu, Giannis Karamanolakis, Daniel Hsu and Luis Gravano 36

Assessing Cognitive Linguistic Influences in the Assignment of Blame
Karen Zhou, Ana Smith and Lillian Lee 61

Evaluating Deception Detection Model Robustness To Linguistic Variation
Maria Glenski, Ellyn Ayton, Robin Cosbey, Dustin Arendt and Svitlana Volkova 70

Reconsidering Annotator Disagreement about Racist Language: Noise or Signal?
Savannah Larimore, Ian Kennedy, Breon Haskett and Alina Arseniev-Koehler 81

Understanding and Interpreting the Impact of User Context in Hate Speech Detection
Edoardo Mosca, Maximilian Wich and Georg Groh 91

Self-Contextualized Attention for Abusive Language Identification
Horacio Jarquín-Vásquez, Hugo Jair Escalante and Manuel Montes 103

Unsupervised Domain Adaptation in Cross-corpora Abusive Language Detection
Tulika Bose, Irina Illina and Dominique Fohr 113

Using Noisy Self-Reports to Predict Twitter User Demographics
Zach Wood-Doughty, Paiheng Xu, Xiao Liu and Mark Dredze 123

PANDORA Talks: Personality and Demographics on Reddit
Matej Gjurković, Mladen Karan, Iva Vukojević, Mihaela Bošnjak and Jan Snajder 138

Room to Grow: Understanding Personal Characteristics Behind Self Improvement Using Social Media
MeiXing Dong, Xueming Xu, Yiwei Zhang, Ian Stewart and Rada Mihalcea 153

Mitigating Temporal-Drift: A Simple Approach to Keep NER Models Crisp
Shuguang Chen, Leonardo Neves and Thamar Solorio 163

Jujeop: Korean Puns for K-pop Stars on Social Media
Soyoung Oh, JISU KIM, Seungpeel Lee and Eunil Park 170

Identifying Distributional Perspectives from Colingual Groups
Yufei Tian, Tuhin Chakrabarty, Fred Morstatter and Nanyun Peng 178

Workshop Program

June 10, 2021

9:00–9:10 ***Opening***

9:10–10:00 *Keynote Speech 1*
Dan Goldwasser (Purdue University)

10:00–10:10 Coffee Break

10:10–11:10 Technical Session 1: Sentiment, Reviews and Comments

Analysis of Nuanced Stances and Sentiment Towards Entities of US Politicians through the Lens of Moral Foundation Theory
Shamik Roy and Dan Goldwasser

Content-based Stance Classification of Tweets about the 2020 Italian Constitutional Referendum
Marco Di Giovanni and Marco Brambilla

A Case Study of In-House Competition for Ranking Constructive Comments in a News Service
Hayato Kobayashi, Hiroaki Taguchi, Yoshimune Tabuchi, Chahine Koleejan, Ken Kobayashi, Soichiro Fujita, Kazuma Murao, Takeshi Masuyama, Taichi Yatsuka, Manabu Okumura and Satoshi Sekine

Quantifying the Effects of COVID-19 on Restaurant Reviews
Ivy Cao, Zizhou Liu, Giannis Karamanolakis, Daniel Hsu and Luis Gravano

June 10, 2021 (continued)

11:10–11:40 Technical Session 2: Inappropriate Language (1)

Assessing Cognitive Linguistic Influences in the Assignment of Blame
Karen Zhou, Ana Smith and Lillian Lee

Evaluating Deception Detection Model Robustness To Linguistic Variation
Maria Glenski, Ellyn Ayton, Robin Cosbey, Dustin Arendt and Svitlana Volkova

11:40–12:40 Lunch Break, Poster and Fake-EmoReact Challenge

12:40–13:40 *Keynote Speech 2*
Tim Weninger (University of Notre Dame)

13:40–14:40 Technical Session 3: Inappropriate Language (2)

Reconsidering Annotator Disagreement about Racist Language: Noise or Signal?
Savannah Larimore, Ian Kennedy, Breon Haskett and Alina Arseniev-Koehler

Understanding and Interpreting the Impact of User Context in Hate Speech Detection
Edoardo Mosca, Maximilian Wich and Georg Groh

Self-Contextualized Attention for Abusive Language Identification
Horacio Jarquín-Vásquez, Hugo Jair Escalante and Manuel Montes

Unsupervised Domain Adaptation in Cross-corpora Abusive Language Detection
Tulika Bose, Irina Illina and Dominique Fohr

June 10, 2021 (continued)

14:40–14:50 Coffee Break

14:50–15:35 Technical Session 4: Personality and Demographics

Using Noisy Self-Reports to Predict Twitter User Demographics
Zach Wood-Doughty, Paiheng Xu, Xiao Liu and Mark Dredze

PANDORA Talks: Personality and Demographics on Reddit
Matej Gjurković, Mladen Karan, Iva Vukojević, Mihaela Bošnjak and Jan Snajder

Room to Grow: Understanding Personal Characteristics Behind Self Improvement Using Social Media
MeiXing Dong, Xueming Xu, Yiwei Zhang, Ian Stewart and Rada Mihalcea

15:35–16:20 Technical Session 5: Contexts and Perspectives

Mitigating Temporal-Drift: A Simple Approach to Keep NER Models Crisp
Shuguang Chen, Leonardo Neves and Thamar Solorio

Jujeop: Korean Puns for K-pop Stars on Social Media
Soyoung Oh, JISU KIM, Seungpeel Lee and Eunil Park

Identifying Distributional Perspectives from Colingual Groups
Yufei Tian, Tuhin Chakrabarty, Fred Morstatter and Nanyun Peng

16:20–16:30 *Closing*

Analysis of Nuanced Stances and Sentiment Towards Entities of US Politicians through the Lens of Moral Foundation Theory

Shamik Roy
Department of Computer Science
Purdue University, USA
roy98@purdue.edu

Dan Goldwasser
Department of Computer Science
Purdue University, USA
dgolwas@purdue.edu

Abstract

The Moral Foundation Theory suggests five moral foundations that can capture the view of a user on a particular issue. It is widely used to identify sentence-level sentiment. In this paper, we study the nuanced stances and partisan sentiment towards entities of US politicians using Moral Foundation Theory, on two politically divisive issues - *Gun Control* and *Immigration*. We define the nuanced stances of the US politicians on these two topics by the grades given by related organizations to the politicians. To conduct this study, we first filter out 74k and 87k tweets on the topics *Gun Control* and *Immigration*, respectively, from an existing tweet corpus authored by US parliament members. Then, we identify moral foundations in these tweets using deep relational learning. Finally, doing qualitative and quantitative evaluations on this dataset, we found out that there is a strong correlation between moral foundation usage and politicians' nuanced stances on a particular topic. We also found notable differences in moral foundation usage by different political parties when they address different entities.

1 Introduction

Over the last decade political discourse has shifted from traditional news outlet to social media. These platforms give politicians the means to interact with their supporters and explain their political perspectives and policy decisions. While formulating policies and passing legislation are complex processes which require reasoning over the pros and cons of different alternatives, *gathering support* for these policies often relies on appealing to peoples' "gut feeling" and invoking an emotional response (Haidt, 2001).

Moral Foundation Theory (MFT) provides a theoretical framework for analyzing the use of moral sentiment in text. The theory (Haidt and Joseph, 2004; Haidt and Graham, 2007) suggests that there are a small number of moral values, emerging from evolutionary, cultural and social reasons, which humans support. These are referred to as the moral foundations (MF) and include Care/Harm, Fairness/Cheating, Loyalty/Betrayal, Authority/Subversion, and Purity/Degradation. This theory was used to explain differences between political ideologies, as each side places more or less value on different moral foundations (Graham et al., 2009). Liberals tend to emphasize the *Fairness* moral foundation, for example, consider the following tweet discussing the 2021 mass shooting event in Colorado, focusing on how the race of the shooter changes the coverage of the event.

Liberal Gun Control tweet. **Fairness**

@IlhanMN The shooter's race or ethnicity seems front and center when they aren't white. Otherwise, it's just a mentally ill young man having a bad day.

On the other hand, conservatives tend to place more value on *Loyalty*. The following tweet discusses the same event, emphasizing solidarity with the families of victims and the broader community.

Conservative Gun Control tweet. **Loyalty**

@RepKenBuck My prayers are with the families of the victims of today's tragedy in Boulder. I join the entire community of Boulder in grieving the senseless loss of life. I am grateful for the officers who responded to the scene within minutes. You are true heroes.

In this paper, we study the relationship between moral foundation usage by politicians on social media and the stances they take on two policy issues, *Gun Control* and *Immigration*. We use the dataset provided by (Johnson and Goldwasser, 2018) for training a model for automatically identifying moral foundations in tweets. We then apply the model to a collection of 74k and 87k congressional tweets discussing the two issues - *Gun Control* and *Immigration*, respectively. Our analysis goes beyond binary liberal-conservative ideological labels (Preoţiuc-Pietro et al., 2017). We use a scale of 5 letter grades assigned to politicians by

Proceedings of the Ninth International Workshop on Natural Language Processing for Social Media, pages 1–13
Online Workshop, June 10, 2021.

relevant policy watchdog groups, based on their votes on legislation pertaining to the specific policy issue. We analyze the tweets associated with the members of each group. Furthermore, we hypothesize that even when different groups use similar moral foundation, they aim to invoke different feelings in the readers. To capture these differences, we analyze the targets of the moral tweets by different groups. Our analysis captures several interesting trends. First, the proportion of *non-moral* tweets on both issues decreases as grades move from A (most conservative) to F (most liberal), while for the topic of Gun Control (Immigration), the proportion of *Harm* (*Loyalty*) tweets increases. Second, even when using the same moral foundation, their targets differ. For example, when discussing Gun Control, using the *Loyalty* moral foundation, liberal mostly mention *march life, Gabby Gifford*, while conservatives mention *gun owner, Texas*.

2 Related Works

The Moral Foundation Theory (MFT) (Haidt and Joseph, 2004; Haidt and Graham, 2007) has been proven to be useful in explaining social behaviour of humans (Mooijman et al., 2018; Hoover et al., 2018; Dehghani et al., 2016; Brady et al., 2017; Hoover et al., 2020). Recent works have shown that political discourse can also be explained using MFT (Dehghani et al., 2014; Johnson and Goldwasser, 2018, 2019). Existing works explain the political discourse mostly at issue and sentence level (Fulgoni et al., 2016; Garten et al., 2016; Lin et al., 2018; Xie et al., 2019) and at left-right polar domains of politics.

Several works have looked at analyzing political ideologies, beyond the left and right divide, using text (Sim et al., 2013; Preoţiuc-Pietro et al., 2017), and specifically using Twitter data (Conover et al., 2011; Johnson and Goldwasser, 2016; Mohammad et al., 2016; Demszky et al., 2019). To the best of our knowledge, this is the first work that studies whether MFT can be used to explain nuanced political standpoints of the US politicians, breaking the left/right political spectrum to nuanced standpoints. We also study the correlation between entity mentions and moral foundation usage by different groups, which helps pave the way to analyze partisan sentiment towards entities using MFT. In that sense, our work is broadly related to entity-centric affective analysis (Deng and Wiebe, 2015; Field and Tsvetkov, 2019; Park et al., 2020).

We use a deep structured prediction approach (Pacheco and Goldwasser, 2021) to identify moral foundations in tweets by being motivated from the works that combine structured prediction with deep neural networks in NLP tasks (Niculae et al., 2017; Han et al., 2019; Liu et al., 2019; Widmoser et al., 2021).

3 Dataset

In this section, we describe the data collection process to analyze the US politicians' stances and sentiment towards entities on the topics - *Immigration* and *Gun Control*. First, we discuss existing datasets. Then, we create a topic specific lexicon from existing resource to identify topics in new data. Finally, we collect a large tweet corpus on the two topics using a lexicon matching approach.

3.1 Candidate Datasets

To study the nuanced stances and sentiment towards entities of politicians using MFT on the text they use, ideally, we need a text dataset annotated for moral foundations from US politicians with known political bias. To the best of our knowledge there are two existing Twitter datasets that are annotated for moral foundations - (1) The Moral Foundations Twitter Corpus (MFTC) by Hoover et al. (2020), and (2) The tweets by US politicians by Johnson and Goldwasser (2018). In MFTC, the moral foundation annotation is done in 35k Tweets on 7 distinct domains, some of which are not related to politics (e.g. Hurricane Sandy) and the political affiliations of the authors of the tweets are not known. The dataset proposed by Johnson and Goldwasser (2018) contains 93K tweets by US politicians in the years 2016 and 2017. 2050 of the tweets are annotated for moral foundations, policy frames (Boydstun et al., 2014) and topics. The dataset contains 6 topics including *Gun Control* and *Immigration*. We extend this dataset for these two topics by collecting more tweets from US Congress members using a lexicon matching approach, described in the next section.

3.2 Building Topic Indicator Lexicon

To build a topic indicator lexicon, we take the dataset proposed by Johnson and Goldwasser (2018). We build topic indicator lexicons for each of the 6 topics comprised of n-grams ($n \leq 5$) using Pointwise Mutual Information (PMI) scores (Church and Hanks, 1990). For an n-gram, w we calculate the pointwise mutual information (PMI) with topic t, $I(w,t)$ using the following formula.

$$I(w,t) = \log \frac{P(w|t)}{P(w)}$$

Where $P(w|t)$ is computed by taking all tweets with topic t and computing $\frac{count(w)}{count(allngrams)}$ and similarly, $P(w)$ is computed by counting n-gram w over the set of tweets with any topic. Now, we rank n-grams for each topic based on their PMI scores. We assign one n-gram to its highest PMI topic only. Then for each topic we manually go through the n-gram lexicon and omit any n-gram that is not related to the topic. In this manner, we found an indicator lexicon for each topic. The lexicons for the topics *Gun Control* and *Immigration* can be found in Appendix A. Note that, as a pre-processing step, n-grams were stemmed and singularized.

3.3 Tweet Collection

We use the large number of unlabeled tweets from US Congress members, written between 2017 and February, 2021[1]. We detect tweets related to the topics *Gun Control* and *Immigration* using lexicon matching. If a tweet contains any n-gram from the topic lexicons, we label the tweet with the corresponding topic. We take only the tweets on topics *Gun Control* and *Immigration* from the Democrat and Republican US Congress members for our study. Given the political affiliation of the authors of the tweets, this dataset is readily useful for the analysis of political stance and partisan sentiment. The details of the dataset is presented in Table 1.

	Gun Control			Immigration		
	Dem	Rep	Total	Dem	Rep	Total
# of politicians	350	377	727	349	364	713
# of Twitter acc.	644	641	1,285	621	606	1,227
# of tweets	53,793	20,424	74,217	65,671	21,407	87,078

Table 1: Dataset summary. Here, 'Dem' and 'Rep' represent 'Democrat' and 'Republican', respectively. The number of politicians and the number of Twitter accounts differs as politicians often have multiple accounts (e.g. personal account, campaign account, etc.).

4 Identification of Moral Foundation in Tweets

To identify moral foundations in the collected dataset, we rely on a supervised approach using a deep relational learning framework. In this section, we first describe the model we use for the supervised classification. Then, we describe our training procedure and analyze the performance of our model on a held out set. Finally, we describe the procedure to infer moral foundations in the collected dataset using our model.

4.1 Deep Relational Learning For Moral Foundation (MF) Identification

For the identification of moral foundation (MF) in tweets, Johnson and Goldwasser (2018) rely on linguistic cues such as - political slogans, Policy Frames, Annotator's Rationale; along with party affiliation, topic and so on, while Johnson and Goldwasser (2019) models the behavioural aspects of the politicians in MF identification. In both of the works they use Probabilistic Soft Logic for modeling. Some of the features used by Johnson and Goldwasser (2018) and Johnson and Goldwasser (2019) are hard to get for a large corpus and some require human annotation. Note that, in this section, our goal is not to outperform the state-of-the-art MF classification results, rather we want to identify MFs in the large corpus where only limited information is available. So, to identify MFs in our corpus we mostly rely on text and the information available with the unlabeled corpus such as, topics, authors' political affiliations and time of the tweets. We jointly model all of these features using DRaiL, a declarative framework for deep structured prediction proposed by Pacheco and Goldwasser (2021) which is described below.

Modeling Features and Dependencies In DRaiL, we can explicitly model features such as - tweet text, authors' political affiliations and topics using *base rules* as follows.

$r_1 : \texttt{Tweet(t)} \Rightarrow \texttt{HasMF(t,m)}$

$r_2 : \texttt{Tweet(t)} \wedge \texttt{HasIdeology(t,i)} \Rightarrow \texttt{HasMF(t,m)}$

$r_2 : \texttt{Tweet(t)} \wedge \texttt{HasTopic(t,k)} \Rightarrow \texttt{HasMF(t,m)}$

These rules correspond to base classifiers that map features in the left hand side of the $\Rightarrow$ to the predicted output in the right hand side. For example, the rule, r_2 translates as "A tweet, t with authors' political affiliation, i has moral foundation label, m". We can also model the temporal dependency between two classification decisions using a second kind of rule, namely *constraint* as follows.

$$c : \texttt{SameIdeology}(\texttt{t}_1,\texttt{t}_2) \wedge \texttt{SameTopic}(\texttt{t}_1,\texttt{t}_2) \wedge \texttt{SameTime}(\texttt{t}_1,\texttt{t}_2) \wedge \texttt{HasMF}(\texttt{t}_1,\texttt{m}) \Rightarrow \texttt{HasMF}(\texttt{t}_2,\texttt{m})$$

[1]https://github.com/alexlitel/congresstweets

This constraint translates as "If two tweets have the same topic, are from the authors of the same political affiliation and are published nearly at the same time, then they have the same moral foundation". This constraint is inspired from the experiments done by Johnson and Goldwasser (2019). In DRaiL, rules can be weighted or unweighted. We consider weighted version of the rules, making constraint c a soft-constraint as it is not guaranteed to be true all of the time. In DRaiL, the global decision is made considering all rules. It transforms rules into linear inequalities and MAP inference is then defined as an integer linear program:

$$\begin{aligned} {}_{\boldsymbol{y}\in\{0,1\}^n} P(\boldsymbol{y}|\boldsymbol{x}) \equiv_{\boldsymbol{y}\in\{0,1\}^n} \sum_{\psi_{r,t}\in\Psi} w_r\, \psi_r(\boldsymbol{x_r}, \boldsymbol{y_r}) \\ s.t.\ c(\boldsymbol{x_c}, \boldsymbol{y_c}) \leq 0;\ \ \forall c \in C \end{aligned} \quad (1)$$

Here, rule grounding, r, generated from template, t, with input features, $\boldsymbol{x_r}$ and predicted variables, $\boldsymbol{y_r}$ defines the potential, $\psi_r(\boldsymbol{x_r}, \boldsymbol{y_r})$ where weights, w_r are learned using neural networks defined over parameter set, $\boldsymbol{\theta}$. The parameters can be learned by training each rule individually (*locally*), or by using inference to ensure that the scoring functions for all rules result in a globally consistent decision (*globally*) using the structured hinge loss:

$$\max_{\hat{\mathbf{y}}\in Y}(\Delta(\hat{\mathbf{y}}, \mathbf{y}) + \sum_{\psi_r\in\Psi} \Phi_t(\boldsymbol{x_r}, \hat{\boldsymbol{y}}_{\boldsymbol{r}}; \theta^t)) - \sum_{\psi_r\in\Psi} \Phi_t(\boldsymbol{x_r}, \boldsymbol{y_r}; \theta^t)$$

Here, t is rule template, Φ_t is the associated neural network, and θ^t is the parameter set. $\mathbf{y}$ and $\hat{\mathbf{y}}$ are gold assignments and predictions resulting from the MAP inference, respectively.

Neural Architectures Each base rule and the soft-constraint is associated with a neural architecture which serve as weighting functions for the rules and constraints. For rules, r_1, r_2 and r_3, we use BERT (Devlin et al., 2019) to encode the tweet text. In rules r_2 and r_3, we encode ideology and topic with a feed-forward neural network over their one-hot encoded form and we concatenate the encoded features with BERT representation of tweets to get a final representation for the rule. In all of the rules we use a classifier on top of the final representation that maps the features to labels. For the soft-constraint c, we encode the ideologies and topics in the left hand side of the constraint similarly and concatenate them and pass through a classifier to predict if the constraint holds or not.

4.2 Experimental Evaluation

We use the dataset proposed by Johnson and Goldwasser (2018) for this experiment.[2] We perform a 5-fold cross validation on 2050 tweets annotated for moral foundations. This is a 11 class classification task where there is one additional class, 'Non-moral' apart from the 10 moral classes. We experiment with the global learning of DRaiL using rules r_1, r_2, r_3 and soft constraint c. For the BERT (base-uncased) classifiers we use a learning rate of $2e^{-5}$, batch size of 32, patience 10 and AdamW as optimizer. All of the tweets were truncated to a length of 100 tokens before passing through BERT. For constraint c we consider two tweets to be at the same time if they are published on the same day. All of the one-hot representations are mapped to a 100 dimensional space and ReLU and Softmax activation functions are used in all hidden and output neural units, respectively. The hyper-parameters are determined empirically.[3] We compare our model with two baselines as follows.

(1) Lexicon matching with Moral Foundations Dictionary (MFD) This approach does not have a training phase. Rather we use the Moral Foundation Dictionary (Graham et al., 2009) and identify moral foundation in a tweet using unigram matching from the MFD. A tweet having no dictionary matching is labeled as 'Non-moral'.

(2) Bidirectional-LSTM We run a bidirectional LSTM (Hochreiter and Schmidhuber, 1997) over the Glove (Pennington et al., 2014) word embeddings of the words of the tweets. We concatenate the hidden states of the two opposite directional LSTMs to get representation over one timestamp and average the representations of all time stamps to get the final representation of a tweet. We map each tweet to a 128-d space using Bi-LSTM and use this representation for moral foundation classification using a fully connected output layer. We use the same folds as the DRaiL experiments.

The classification results are summarized in Table 2. We can see that the DRaiL model combining all base rules and the soft-constraint performs best. This indicates that combining other features with

[2]More details on dataset can be found in the original paper.

[3]Dataset and codes can be found at `https://github.com/ShamikRoy/MF-Prediction`.

	Models	Average Macro F1	Weighted F1
Baselines	MFD matching	15.93	18.38
	Bi-LSTM	42.59	50.43
DRaiL	r_1 (BERT only)	49.01	57.96
	$r_1 + r_2$	50.54	58.90
	$r_1 + r_2 + r_3$	51.49	60.02
	$r_1 + r_2 + r_3 + c$	**52.14**	**60.24**

Table 2: Moral Foundation classification results.

BERT and modeling the dependencies among multiple decisions help in prediction. This encourages us to experiment with other linguistic features (e.g. policy frames) and dependencies as a future work.

Morals	Prec.	Rec.	F1	Support
Care	53.18	62.02	57.26	337
Harm	52.01	56.35	54.10	252
Fairness	67.93	59.24	63.29	211
Cheating	27.27	16.98	20.93	53
Loyalty	52.63	56.60	54.55	212
Betrayal	60.00	31.58	41.38	19
Authority	40.17	41.59	40.87	113
Subversion	68.55	71.23	69.86	358
Purity	67.20	64.62	65.88	130
Degradation	53.85	22.58	31.82	31
Non-moral	77.48	70.06	73.58	334
Accuracy			60.39	2050
Avg. Mac.	56.39	50.26	52.14	2050
Weighted	60.72	60.39	60.24	2050

Table 3: Per class Moral Foundation classification results for the best model in Table 2

We present the per class statistics of the prediction of the best model in Table 3. We can see that mostly the classes with lower number of examples are harder to classify for the model (e.g. *Cheating*, *Degradation*). So, annotating more tweets on the low frequency classes may improve the overall performance of the model.

4.3 Inference on the Collected Corpus

Now, we train our best model (combining all base rules and the constraint in DRaiL) using the dataset we experiment with in Section 4.2. We, held out 10% of the data as validation set selected by the random seed of 42. We train the model using the hyper-parameters described in Section 4.2 and predict moral foundations in the tweets of the large corpus we annotated for the topics *Gun Control* and *Immigration* in Section 3. The validation macro F1 score and weighted F1 scores of the model were 49.44% and 58.30%, respectively. We use this annotated dataset to study nuanced stances and partisan sentiment towards entities of the US politicians.

5 Analysis of Politicians' Nuanced Stances

In this section, we analyze the nuanced stances of US politicians on the topics *Gun Control* and *Immigration*, using Moral Foundation Theory. First, we define nuanced political stances. Then we study the correlation between the moral foundation usage and nuanced political stances.

5.1 Nuanced Political Stance

Despite of being highly polarized, US politicians show mixed stances on different topics. For example, a politician may be supportive of gun prevention laws to some extent despite their party affiliation of the Republican Party. So, we hypothesize that the political stance is more nuanced than binary, left and right. We define the nuanced political stances of the politicians as the grades assigned to them by the *National Rifle Association (NRA)*[4] on *Gun Control* and by *NumbersUSA*[5] on *Immigration*. The politicians are graded in range (A+, A, ..., F, F-) based on candidate questionnaire and their voting records by both of the organizations in the two different topics where A+ indicates most anti-immigration/pro-gun and F or F- indicates the most pro-immigration/anti-gun. In other words, A+ means extreme right and F/F- means extreme left and the other grades fall in between. We convert these letter grades in 5 categories: A, B, C, D, F. Here, A+, A and A- grades are combined in A and so on. We define these grades as nuanced stances of the politicians on the two topics.

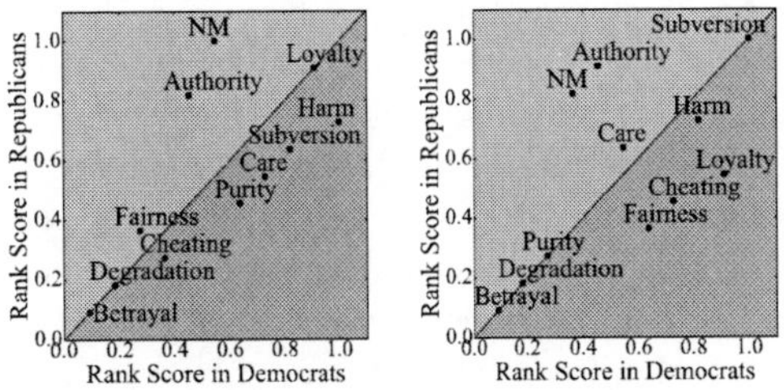

(a) Gun Control (b) Immigration

Figure 1: Polarization in Moral Foundation usage. Here, NM stands for 'Non-moral'.

5.2 Moral Foundation Usage

In this section, first, we study the political polarization, similar to Roy and Goldwasser (2020), in

[4]Collected from everytown.org

[5]Collected from numbersusa.com

moral foundation usage by Democrats and Republicans on the two topics. Therefore, we rank the moral foundations by the frequency of usage inside each party. Then we plot the rank score of each moral foundation in Democrats and Republicans in x and y axes, respectively, where the most used moral foundation gets the highest rank score. Any moral foundation falling in the diagonal is not polarized and as far we go away from the diagonal it becomes more polarized. We show the polarization graphs for the two topics in Figure 1. It can be seen that the parties are polarized in moral foundation usage. The Republicans use 'Non-moral' and 'Authority' moral foundations in both of the topics. On the other hand, Democrats use 'Subversion' and 'Harm' on *Gun Control* and 'Loyalty' and 'Cheating' on *Immigration.*

Now, we examine the moral foundation usage by the politicians from each of the grade categories. For that, we match the politicians with grades with our dataset and consider politicians tweeting at least 100 times on each topic. The statistics of politicians and corresponding tweets found for each grade is presented in Table 4. Now, to compare

GRADES	GUN CONTROL		IMMIGRATION	
	# POLITICIANS	# TWEETS	# POLITICIANS	# TWEETS
A	31	6,822	25	5,592
B	5	1,236	11	2,177
C	7	908	3	679
D	9	1,340	14	4,691
F	128	33,792	123	38,102

Table 4: Distribution of number of Politicians and tweets over the letter grades.

the moral foundation usage by each of the grade classes, we rank the moral foundations based on their usage inside each grade. Then we compare the rank of each grade class with the two opposite extremes (grades A and F) using Spearman's Rank Correlation Coefficient (Zar, 2005) where coefficient 1 means perfect correlation. As the grades B, C, D have fewer tweets, we sub-sample 500 tweets from each class and do the analysis on them. We repeat this process 10 times with 10 different random seeds and plot the average correlations in Figure 2.[6]

It can be seen from the figures that the the correlations follow a progressive trend with the extreme left while moving from grade A to grade F and the trend is opposite with the extreme right, for both of the topics. This indicates that there is a correlation

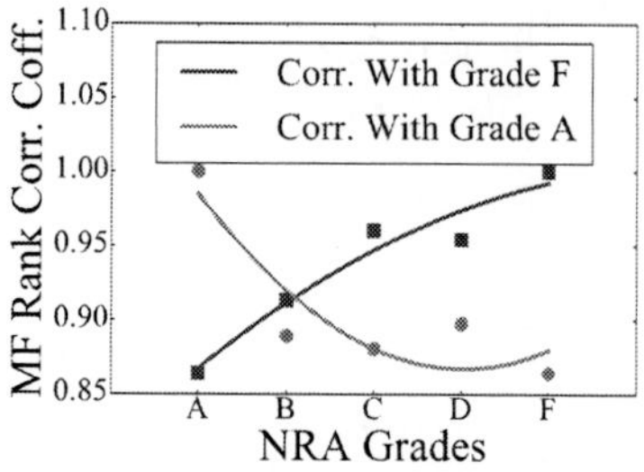

(a) Gun Control

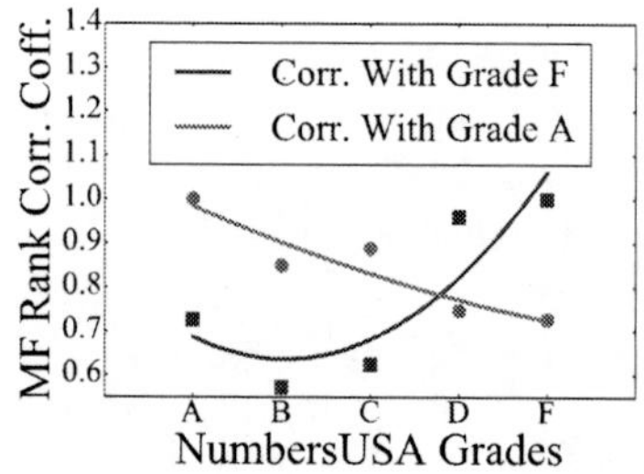

(b) Immigration

Figure 2: Correlation of moral foundation usage with NRA and NumbersUSA grades of politicians on the topics *Gun Control* and *Immigration*, respectively.

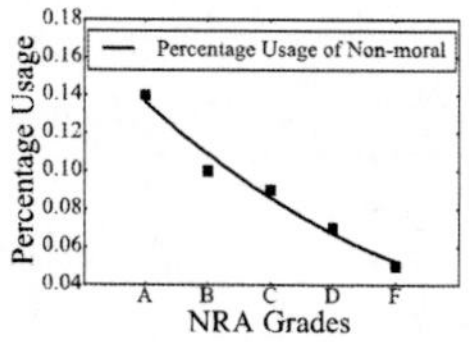

(a) Usage of **'Non-moral'** on **Gun Control**

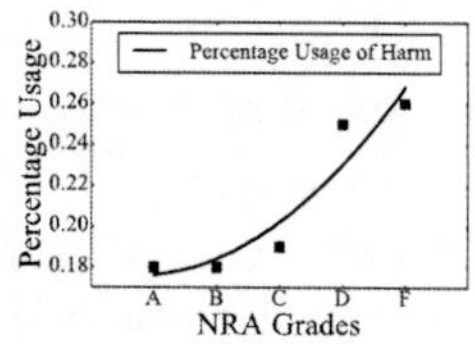

(b) Usage of **'Harm'** on **Gun Control**

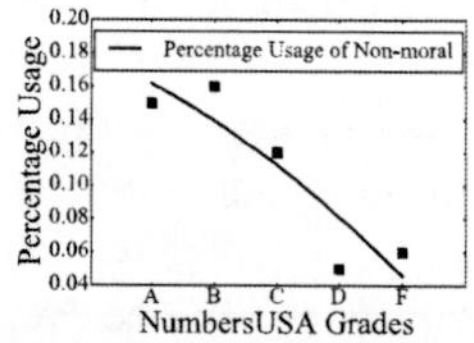

(c) Usage of **'Non-moral'** on **Immigration**

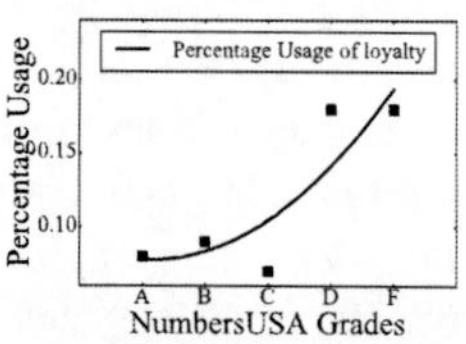

(d) Usage of **'Loyalty'** on **Immigration**

Figure 3: Moral Foundation distribution over politicians' grades.

between the MF usage and politicians' nuanced stances. To further analyze which moral foundations most correlate with the nuanced stances, we plot the percentage of usage of the most polar moral foundations from Figure 1, inside each grade class. We found good correlations in case of the usage of 'Non-moral' and 'Harm' on *Gun Control*; in usage of 'Non-moral' and 'Loyalty' on *Immigration.* The distributions are shown in Figure 3. Distribution plots for the other moral foundations can be found

[6]Standard Deviations can be found in Appendix B.

Morals	Gun Control: High PMI Entities by Democrats	Gun Control: High PMI Entities by Republicans	Immigration: High PMI Entities by Democrats	Immigration: High PMI Entities by Republicans
Care	community safe, gun violence prevention, assault weapon	law enforcement, bipartisan bill, health care	protect dreamer, immigration status, young people	build wall, immigration law, border patrol
Harm	mass shooting, innocent life, school shooting	police officer, mexico, texas	detention facility, detention center, migrant child	illegal alien, build wall, illegal immigrant
Fairness	gun sale, universal background check, gun owner	gun owner, amendment, nra	immigration status, dream promise, dream	illegal immigrant, illegal alien, american citizen
Cheating	bump stock, nra, black	gun owner, gun control, amendment	citizenship question, muslim, american value	illegal immigrant, illegal alien, illegal immigration
Loyalty	march life, gabby gifford, young people	gun owner, texas, charleston	protect dream, defend daca, dream promise act	border patrol, southern border, american people
Betrayal	congress, gun	gun	human right, refugee, american citizen	illegal alien, illegal immigrant, sanctuary city
Authority	bipartisan background check, american people, house judiciary	gun, american people	circuit judge, comprehensive immigration reform, supreme court	circuit judge, circuit court, senate
Subversion	house gop, republican, gun lobby	gun control, dem, medicare	trump shutdown, national emergency, border wall	illegal immigrant, illegal immigration, sanctuary city
Purity	pulse, tragic shooting, honor action	tragic shooting, police officer, las vegas	refugee, america, american value	american citizen, circuit court, illegal alien
Degradation	el paso, nra, republican	orlando, texas, black	muslim, usc, daca	muslim, human right, fema
Non-moral	town hall, medicare, shannon r watt	amendment, gun, charleston	medicare, usc, house judiciary	government shutdown, border security, homeland

Table 5: Top-3 high PMI entities for each moral foundation by each party.

in Appendix C. It can be seen from the figures that, as we move from grade A to F, the usage of 'Non-moral' decreases for both of the topics, indicating - the more conservative a politician is, they discuss the issues from a more 'Non-moral' perspective. On the other hand, more usage of 'Harm' and 'Loyalty' indicates more liberal stances on *Gun Control* and *Immigration*, respectively.

6 Analysis of Partisan Sentiment Towards Entities

In this section, we study the partisan sentiment towards entities by examining the usage of moral foundations while discussing the entities. First, we extract entities from the tweets, then we analyze the usage of moral foundations in the context of those entities by the two opposite parties.

6.1 Entity Extraction from Tweets

To study partisan sentiment towards entities we first identify entities mentioned in the tweets. We hypothesize entities to be noun phrases. So, we use an off-the-shelf noun phrase extractor[7] and extract noun phrases from the tweets. We filter out noun phrases occurring less than 100 times. Then we manually filter out noun phrases that are irrelevant to the topics (e.g. COVID-19). In this manner, we found 64 and 79 unique noun phrases for *Gun Control* and *Immigration*, respectively. We treat these noun phrases as entities and run our analysis using these entities. The complete list of entities can be found in Appendix D

6.2 MF Usage in the Context of Entities

In this section, we analyze the partisan sentiment towards entities by looking at the moral foundation usage trend of the parties when discussing the entities related to the topics. For each party and each moral foundation we calculate the PMI score with each entity. We create 22 classes comprised of the 2 party affiliations and 11 moral foundation classes (e.g. Democrat-Care, Republican-Care and so on) and calculate the PMI scores as described in Section 3. We list the top-3 highest PMI entities for each moral foundation and each party in Table 5. We can see notable difference in moral foundation usage in the context of different entities by the two parties. For example, on the issue *Immigration*, the Democrats use 'Care' when addressing 'dreamers' and 'young people'. On the other hand, the Republicans use care in the context of 'border wall' and 'border patrol'. On the

[7]https://textblob.readthedocs.io/

ID	Party	Topic	Entities	Predicted MF	Tweet Text
(1)	Democrat	Immigration	Migrant Child; Trump Administration	Harm	How many more **migrant children** must die under the **Trump administration** until something changes?
(2)	Democrat	Immigration	Migrant Child; Detention Facility	Harm	12,800! That's how many **migrant CHILDREN** are locked up in **detention facilities** in America. How can this be happening?
(3)	Republican	Gun Control	Police Officer	Harm	A Charleston **police officer** has been shot in the face.
(4)	Republican	Gun Control	Police Officer; Communities; Families	Care	North Carolina **police officers** protect our **communities**, keep our **families** safe, and have earned our support.
(5)	Democrat	Gun Control	Tragic Shooting	Purity	Our thoughts and prayers are with the victims of the **tragic shooting** in Las Vegas. Look forward to a full investigation to give us answers.
(6)	Republican	Gun Control	Tragic Shooting	Purity	Praying for the families of victims of **tragic shooting** in Vegas. Time to transcend politics and pray for God's healing for those affected.
(7)	Republican	Gun Control	Gun Owner	Fairness	Law-abiding **gun owners** deserve the full protection of the U.S. Constitution when exercising their right to carry a concealed weapon – and that right should not end at a state line.
(8)	Democrat	Gun Control	Gun Owner	Fairness	I am a hunter who believes in protecting the rights of law abiding **gun owners**. I am also a father of two young boys who believes there need to be changes in our gun laws.

Table 6: Qualitative evaluation of Moral Foundation usage in the context of entities.

issue *Gun Control*, when talking about 'NRA' the Democrats associate 'Cheating' and 'Degradation', while the Republicans use 'Fairness'. These imply high polarization in partisan sentiment towards entities. We can see some interesting cases as well. For example, on *Guns*, the Republicans use 'Harm' with the entity 'police officer' and on *Immigration*, the Democrats use 'Harm' with 'migrant child'. On *Guns*, democrats and republicans sometimes use the same moral foundation in the context of the same entity. For example, both Democrats and Republicans use 'Fairness' in the context of 'Gun Owner' and 'Purity' in the context of 'tragic shooting'. So, we take a closer look at the usage of MFs in the context of these entities and list a few tweets discussing each of these entities in Table 6.

We can see that on *Immigration*, for Democrats, 'migrant child' is target of harm while 'detention facility' and 'Trump administration' are the entities posing the harm (examples (1), (2) in Table 6). So, even if the high-level moral foundation is the same, different participating entities in the text may have different partisan sentiments towards them.

On *Guns*, although the entity 'police officer' carries a positive sentiment for the Republicans across different moral foundations, the fine-grained sentiment towards this entity is different in the case of different moral foundations. For example, 'police officer' is the target of harm and is the entity providing care for the Republicans when used in the context of 'Harm' and 'Care', respectively (examples (3), (4) in Table 6). So, moral foundation can explain the sentiment towards entities beyond positive and negative categories.

In the context of 'Gun Owner', both of the parties use 'Fairness' in support of gun owners' rights, but they frame the issue differently - Democrats, by focusing on the need for more restrictions while preserving gun rights (example (8)) and Republicans, by focusing on the violation of constitutional rights if more restrictions are applied (example (7)). So, even if the moral foundation usage is the same, there is a framing effect to establish the corresponding partisan stances. While using 'Purity' in the context of 'tragic shooting', we found that both of the parties express their prayers for the shooting victims (example (5), (6)).

Now, we find out the entities with highest disagreement between parties in moral foundation usage in context. To calculate the disagreement we rank the moral foundations based on frequency in usage by each party in the context of each entity. Then we calculate the Spearman's Rank Correlation Coefficient between these two rankings for each entity and list the top-10 entities with the highest disagreement in Table 7. Then we show the polarity graphs for one entity from each topic list in Figure 4. We can see that, on *Gun*, while discussing 'Amendment' the Republicans use 'Loyalty', although 'Loyalty' is not polarized towards the Republicans in aggregate (Figure 1). On the other hand, the Democrats use 'Cheating' in the context of 'Amendment'. Similarly, while discussing 'Donald Trump' on *Immigration*, the Democrats use 'Cheating' more, while the Republicans use 'Care' and 'Authority'. These analyses indicate that moral foundation analysis can be a useful tool to analyze partisan sentiment towards entities.

TOPICS	ENTITIES WITH HIGHEST DISAGREEMENT IN MF USAGE IN CONTEXT BETWEEN DEMOCRATS AND REPUBLICANS
GUN CONTROL	Amendment, background check, gun, gun control, NRA, gun violence, violence, Congress, gun owner, high school
IMMIGRATION	immigration policy, Donald Trump, America, DHS Gov, Supreme Court, legal immigration, Mexico, immigration system, DHS, ICE

Table 7: Top-10 entities with highest disagreement in MF usage in context between Democrats and Republicans (in descending order of agreement).

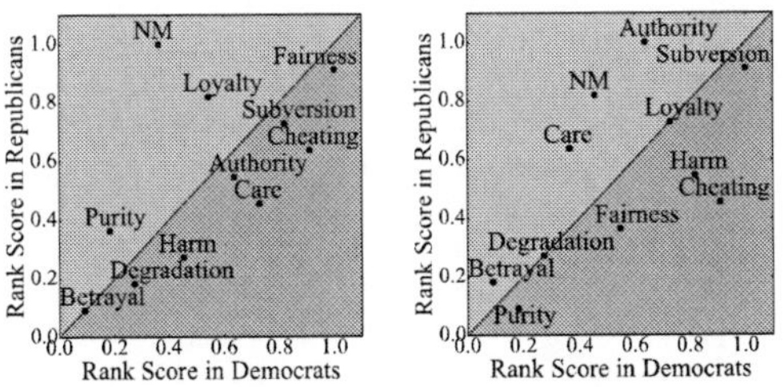

(a) Polarization while discussing **'Amendment'** on topic **Gun Control**.

(b) Polarization while discussing **'Donald Trump'** on topic **Immigration**.

Figure 4: Polarization in entity discussion.

7 Future Work

In this section, we discuss some potential research directions that our analyses may lead to and their application in understanding political discourse.

Our experiments in Section 4 show that joint modeling of multiple aspects of the dataset (e.g. text, issue, and political affiliation) and the dependency among multiple decisions (e.g. temporal dependency), helps in classification. Incorporating other information such as linguistic cues, behavioural aspects, and so on, has the potential to improve the prediction furthermore. In general, incorporating information from multiple sources (e.g. social, textual) and modeling dependencies among decisions is an interesting future work that can help in the identification of the underlying intent of the text. So, this framework may be extended to similar tasks, such as political framing analysis, misinformation analysis, propaganda detection, and so on.

In Section 5, we found out that moral foundation usage can be useful in explaining the nuanced political stances of politicians beyond the left/right discreet categories. We observed that usage of some moral foundations strongly correlates with the nuanced stances of the politicians. While the stances of the extreme left (grade F) and extreme right (grade A) politicians are easy to explain, what are the stances of the politicians in the middle (grades B to D), is yet to be investigated qualitatively. This line of research would help in understanding the stance of the politicians at **individual** levels and has real-life implications. For example, understanding politicians' individual stances would help determine their future vote on legislative decisions and to identify the aisle-crossing politicians.

In Section 6, we found out clear cases where sentiment towards entities can be explained by grounding the Moral Foundation Theory at the entity level. This is an interesting direction where we can seek answers to several research questions, such as, (r1) What are the dimensions in a moral foundation category along which the sentiment towards the entities can be explained?; (r2) Can sentiment towards entities, inspired from moral foundations, explain political discourse?; (r3) Do the sentiment towards entities change over time and in response to real-life events? We believe our analyses will help advance the research in this direction.

8 Summary

In this paper, we study how Moral Foundation Theory (MFT) can explain nuanced political stances of US politicians and take the first step towards partisan sentiment analysis targeting different entities using MFT. We collect a dataset of 161k tweets authored by US politicians, on two politically divisive issues, *Gun Control* and *Immigration*. We use a deep relational learning approach to predict the moral foundations in the tweets, that models tweet text, topic, author's ideology, and captures temporal dependencies based on publication time. Finally, we analyze the politicians' nuanced standpoints and partisan sentiment towards entities using MFT. Our analyses show that both phenomena can be explained well using MFT, which we hope will help motivate further research in this area.

9 Ethical Considerations

To the best of our knowledge no code of ethics was violated throughout the experiments and data collection done in this paper. We presented the detailed data collection procedure and cited relevant papers and websites from which we collected the data. We provided all implementation details and hyper-parameter settings for reproducibility. Any qualitative result we report is outcome from machine learning models and doesn't represent the authors' personal views, nor the official stances of the political parties analyzed.

Acknowledgements

We gratefully acknowledge Maria Leonor Pacheco for helping in setting up the deep relational learning task using DRaiL and the anonymous reviewers for their insightful comments. We also acknowledge Nikhil Mehta for his useful feedback on the writing.

References

Amber Boydstun, Dallas Card, Justin H. Gross, Philip Resnik, and Noah A. Smith. 2014. Tracking the development of media frames within and across policy issues.

William J Brady, Julian A Wills, John T Jost, Joshua A Tucker, and Jay J Van Bavel. 2017. Emotion shapes the diffusion of moralized content in social networks. *Proceedings of the National Academy of Sciences*, 114(28):7313–7318.

Kenneth Ward Church and Patrick Hanks. 1990. Word association norms, mutual information, and lexicography. *Computational Linguistics*, 16(1):22–29.

Michael D Conover, Bruno Gonçalves, Jacob Ratkiewicz, Alessandro Flammini, and Filippo Menczer. 2011. Predicting the political alignment of twitter users. In *2011 IEEE third international conference on privacy, security, risk and trust and 2011 IEEE third international conference on social computing*, pages 192–199. IEEE.

Morteza Dehghani, Kate Johnson, Joe Hoover, Eyal Sagi, Justin Garten, Niki Jitendra Parmar, Stephen Vaisey, Rumen Iliev, and Jesse Graham. 2016. Purity homophily in social networks. *Journal of Experimental Psychology: General*, 145(3):366.

Morteza Dehghani, Kenji Sagae, Sonya Sachdeva, and Jonathan Gratch. 2014. Analyzing political rhetoric in conservative and liberal weblogs related to the construction of the "ground zero mosque". *Journal of Information Technology & Politics*, 11(1):1–14.

Dorottya Demszky, Nikhil Garg, Rob Voigt, James Zou, Jesse Shapiro, Matthew Gentzkow, and Dan Jurafsky. 2019. Analyzing polarization in social media: Method and application to tweets on 21 mass shootings. In *Proceedings of the 2019 Conference of the North American Chapter of the Association for Computational Linguistics: Human Language Technologies, Volume 1 (Long and Short Papers)*, pages 2970–3005.

Lingjia Deng and Janyce Wiebe. 2015. Joint prediction for entity/event-level sentiment analysis using probabilistic soft logic models. In *Proceedings of the 2015 Conference on Empirical Methods in Natural Language Processing*, pages 179–189, Lisbon, Portugal. Association for Computational Linguistics.

Jacob Devlin, Ming-Wei Chang, Kenton Lee, and Kristina Toutanova. 2019. BERT: Pre-training of deep bidirectional transformers for language understanding. In *Proceedings of the 2019 Conference of the North American Chapter of the Association for Computational Linguistics: Human Language Technologies, Volume 1 (Long and Short Papers)*, pages 4171–4186, Minneapolis, Minnesota. Association for Computational Linguistics.

Anjalie Field and Yulia Tsvetkov. 2019. Entity-centric contextual affective analysis. *arXiv preprint arXiv:1906.01762*.

Dean Fulgoni, Jordan Carpenter, Lyle Ungar, and Daniel Preoţiuc-Pietro. 2016. An empirical exploration of moral foundations theory in partisan news sources. In *Proceedings of the Tenth International Conference on Language Resources and Evaluation (LREC'16)*, pages 3730–3736, Portorož, Slovenia. European Language Resources Association (ELRA).

Justin Garten, Reihane Boghrati, Joe Hoover, Kate M Johnson, and Morteza Dehghani. 2016. Morality between the lines: Detecting moral sentiment in text. In *Proceedings of IJCAI 2016 workshop on Computational Modeling of Attitudes*.

Jesse Graham, Jonathan Haidt, and Brian A Nosek. 2009. Liberals and conservatives rely on different sets of moral foundations. *Journal of personality and social psychology*, 96(5):1029.

Jonathan Haidt. 2001. The emotional dog and its rational tail: a social intuitionist approach to moral judgment. *Psychological review*, 108(4):814.

Jonathan Haidt and Jesse Graham. 2007. When morality opposes justice: Conservatives have moral intuitions that liberals may not recognize. *Social Justice Research*, 20(1):98–116.

Jonathan Haidt and Craig Joseph. 2004. Intuitive ethics: How innately prepared intuitions generate culturally variable virtues. *Daedalus*, 133(4):55–66.

Rujun Han, Qiang Ning, and Nanyun Peng. 2019. Joint event and temporal relation extraction with shared representations and structured prediction. In *Proceedings of the 2019 Conference on Empirical Methods in Natural Language Processing and the 9th International Joint Conference on Natural Language Processing (EMNLP-IJCNLP)*, pages 434–444, Hong Kong, China. Association for Computational Linguistics.

Sepp Hochreiter and Jürgen Schmidhuber. 1997. Long short-term memory. *Neural computation*, 9(8):1735–1780.

Joe Hoover, Kate Johnson, Reihane Boghrati, Jesse Graham, Morteza Dehghani, and M Brent Donnellan. 2018. Moral framing and charitable donation: Integrating exploratory social media analyses and confirmatory experimentation. *Collabra: Psychology*, 4(1).

Joe Hoover, Gwenyth Portillo-Wightman, Leigh Yeh, Shreya Havaldar, Aida Mostafazadeh Davani, Ying Lin, Brendan Kennedy, Mohammad Atari, Zahra Kamel, Madelyn Mendlen, et al. 2020. Moral foundations twitter corpus: A collection of 35k tweets annotated for moral sentiment. *Social Psychological and Personality Science*, 11(8):1057–1071.

Kristen Johnson and Dan Goldwasser. 2016. Identifying stance by analyzing political discourse on twitter. In *Proceedings of the First Workshop on NLP and Computational Social Science*, pages 66–75.

Kristen Johnson and Dan Goldwasser. 2018. Classification of moral foundations in microblog political discourse. In *Proceedings of the 56th Annual Meeting of the Association for Computational Linguistics (Volume 1: Long Papers)*, pages 720–730, Melbourne, Australia. Association for Computational Linguistics.

Kristen Johnson and Dan Goldwasser. 2019. Modeling behavioral aspects of social media discourse for moral classification. In *Proceedings of the Third Workshop on Natural Language Processing and Computational Social Science*, pages 100–109.

Ying Lin, Joe Hoover, Gwenyth Portillo-Wightman, Christina Park, Morteza Dehghani, and Heng Ji. 2018. Acquiring background knowledge to improve moral value prediction. In *2018 ieee/acm international conference on advances in social networks analysis and mining (asonam)*, pages 552–559. IEEE.

Jiangming Liu, Shay B. Cohen, and Mirella Lapata. 2019. Discourse representation parsing for sentences and documents. In *Proceedings of the 57th Annual Meeting of the Association for Computational Linguistics*, pages 6248–6262, Florence, Italy. Association for Computational Linguistics.

Saif Mohammad, Svetlana Kiritchenko, Parinaz Sobhani, Xiaodan Zhu, and Colin Cherry. 2016. A dataset for detecting stance in tweets. In *Proceedings of the Tenth International Conference on Language Resources and Evaluation (LREC'16)*, pages 3945–3952.

Marlon Mooijman, Joe Hoover, Ying Lin, Heng Ji, and Morteza Dehghani. 2018. Moralization in social networks and the emergence of violence during protests. *Nature human behaviour*, 2(6):389–396.

Vlad Niculae, Joonsuk Park, and Claire Cardie. 2017. Argument mining with structured SVMs and RNNs. In *Proceedings of the 55th Annual Meeting of the Association for Computational Linguistics (Volume 1: Long Papers)*, pages 985–995, Vancouver, Canada. Association for Computational Linguistics.

Maria Leonor Pacheco and Dan Goldwasser. 2021. Modeling Content and Context with Deep Relational Learning. *Transactions of the Association for Computational Linguistics*, 9:100–119.

Chan Young Park, Xinru Yan, Anjalie Field, and Yulia Tsvetkov. 2020. Multilingual contextual affective analysis of lgbt people portrayals in wikipedia. *arXiv preprint arXiv:2010.10820*.

Jeffrey Pennington, Richard Socher, and Christopher D Manning. 2014. Glove: Global vectors for word representation. In *Proceedings of the 2014 conference on empirical methods in natural language processing (EMNLP)*, pages 1532–1543.

Daniel Preoţiuc-Pietro, Ye Liu, Daniel Hopkins, and Lyle Ungar. 2017. Beyond binary labels: political ideology prediction of twitter users. In *Proceedings of the 55th Annual Meeting of the Association for Computational Linguistics (Volume 1: Long Papers)*, pages 729–740.

Shamik Roy and Dan Goldwasser. 2020. Weakly supervised learning of nuanced frames for analyzing polarization in news media. In *Proceedings of the 2020 Conference on Empirical Methods in Natural Language Processing (EMNLP)*, pages 7698–7716.

Yanchuan Sim, Brice DL Acree, Justin H Gross, and Noah A Smith. 2013. Measuring ideological proportions in political speeches. In *Proceedings of the 2013 conference on empirical methods in natural language processing*, pages 91–101.

Manuel Widmoser, Maria Leonor Pacheco, Jean Honorio, and Dan Goldwasser. 2021. Randomized deep structured prediction for discourse-level processing. *Computing Research Repository*, arxiv:2101.10435.

Jing Yi Xie, Renato Ferreira Pinto Junior, Graeme Hirst, and Yang Xu. 2019. Text-based inference of moral sentiment change. In *Proceedings of the 2019 Conference on Empirical Methods in Natural Language Processing and the 9th International Joint Conference on Natural Language Processing (EMNLP-IJCNLP)*, pages 4646–4655.

Jerrold H Zar. 2005. Spearman rank correlation. *Encyclopedia of Biostatistics*, 7.

A Topic Indicator Lexicon

A.1 Topic Indicators for Gun Control

'reduce gun', 'orlando shooting', 'terrorism watch', 'keep gun', 'terrorist watch', 'orlandounited', 'violence nobillnobreak', 'noflynobuy loophole', 'disarmhate', 'shooting', 'firearm', 'end gun', 'mas shooting', 'gun violence', 'sanbernadino', 'keeping gun', 'watch list', 'gun reform', 'hate crime', 'nobillnobreak', 'charleston9', 'gun safety', 'prevention legislation', 'gun owner', 'reducing gun', 'orlando terrorist', 'address gun', '2nd amendment', 'gun show', 'tragic shooting', 'gun law', 'notonemore', 'ending gun', 'nomoresilence', 'closing terror', 'buy gun', 'nra', 'massacre', 'amendment right', 'reckles gun', 'endgunviolence', 'orlando terror', 'stopgunviolence', 'prevent gun', 'buying gun', 'gun loophole', 'gun legislation', 'massacred', 'sensible gun', 'sense gun', 'gun control', 'gun', 'terror watch', 'noflynobuy', 'standwithorlando', '2a', 'charleston', 'gunviolence', 'background check', 'commonsense gun', 'guncontrol'

A.2 Topic Indicators for Immigration

'fight for family', 'illegal immigrant', 'immigrant', 'granting amnesty', 'migration', 'asylum', 'dreamer', 'deportation', 'immigration action', 'homeland security', 'daca', 'fightforfamily', 'detain', 'borderwall', 'immigrationaction', 'border protection', 'daca work', 'sanctuarycity', 'sanctuary city', 'immigration detention', 'immigration system', 'immigration policy', 'illegal immigration', 'immigration', 'dacawork', 'detention', 'immigration reform', 'dhsgov', 'immigration law', 'executive amnesty', 'deport', 'dapa', 'immigration executive', 'refugee', 'border security', 'border wall', 'border sec', 'cir', 'comprehensive immigration', 'detained', 'detainee', 'amnesty', 'borderprotection', 'grant amnesty', 'deportee', 'immigr'

B Numeric Data of the Figure 2

The numeric values of each point in Figure 2 are as follows with standard deviations in brackets.

- Points fitting the red line in Figure 2(a): 1.0 (0), 0.889 (0.02), 0.880 (0.04), 0.897 (0.05), 0.864 (0.05)
- Points fitting the blue line in Figure 2(a): 0.864 (0.05), 0.913 (0.05), 0.960 (0.02), 0.954 (0.03), 1.0 (0)
- Points fitting the red line in Figure 2(b): 1.0 (0), 0.849 (0.02), 0.887 (0.03), 0.746 (0.03), 0.727 (0.04)
- Points fitting the blue line in Figure 2(b): 0.727 (0.04), 0.571 (0.04), 0.623 (0.03), 0.960 (0.01), 1.0 (0)

C Distribution of Most Polar Moral Foundation Usage over Grades

The distributions for the topics *Gun Control* and *Immigration* can be found in Figure 5 and Figure 6, respectively.

D Entities

D.1 Entities related to Gun Control

'amendment', 'assault weapon ban', 'gun safety legislation', 'mexico', 'innocent life', 'gun sale', 'law enforcement', 'mass shooting', 'senseless gun violence', 'house judiciary', 'march life', 'young people', 'common sense gun reform', 'gun violence prevention', 'house gop', 'honor action', 'bump stock', 'wear orange', 'gun violence', 'assault weapon', 'republican', 'parkland', 'address gun violence', 'gun safety', 'gabby gifford', 'gun owner', 'las vegas', 'gun law', 'senate gop', 'mom demand', 'black', 'gun reform', 'tragic shooting', 'texas', 'dem', 'gun violence epidemic', 'congress', 'nra', 'police officer', 'town hall', 'virginia', 'bipartisan bill', 'pulse', 'universal background check', 'bipartisan background check', 'america', 'orlando', 'shannon r watt', 'end gun violence', 'school shooting', 'gun control', 'violence', 'american people', 'gun', 'community safe', 'el paso', 'high school', 'medicare', 'sandy hook', 'charleston', 'health care', 'gun lobby', 'background check', 'house democrat'

D.2 Entities related to Immigration

'white house', 'hhs gov', 'republican', 'house judiciary', 'family', 'mexico', 'wall', 'refugee', 'supreme court', 'immigrant', 'protect dream', 'immigrant community', 'border patrol', 'dream act', 'protect dreamer', 'build wall', 'senate', 'american value', 'fema', 'human right', 'dreamer', 'save tps', 'asylum seeker', 'usc', 'illegal alien', 'hispanic caucus', 'immigration status', 'migrant child', 'ice', 'family separation', 'trump shutdown', 'detention facility', 'american citizen', 'homeland', 'real donald trump', 'ice gov', 'comprehensive immigration reform', 'dhs', 'illegal immigrant', 'defend daca',

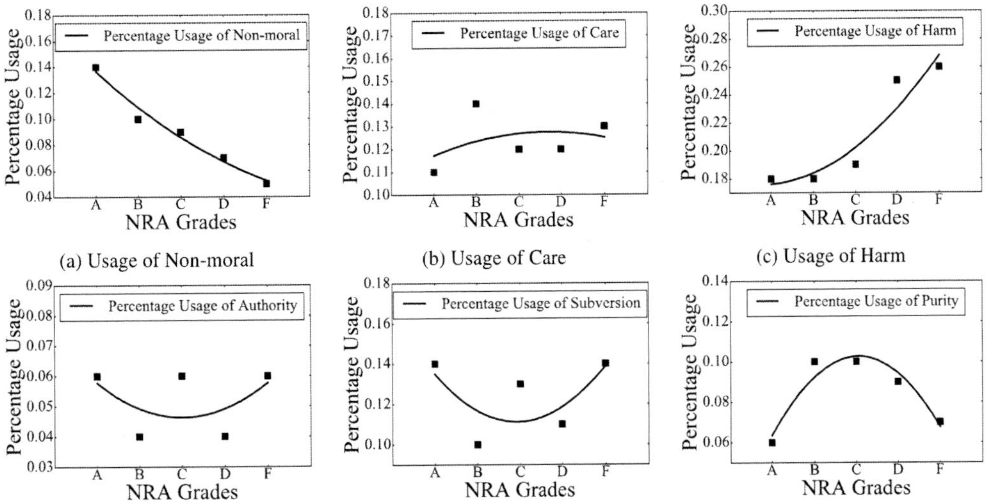

(a) Usage of Non-moral (b) Usage of Care (c) Usage of Harm

(d) Usage of Authority (e) Usage of Subversion (f) Usage of Purity

Figure 5: Moral Foundation distributions over NRA grades on Gun Control.

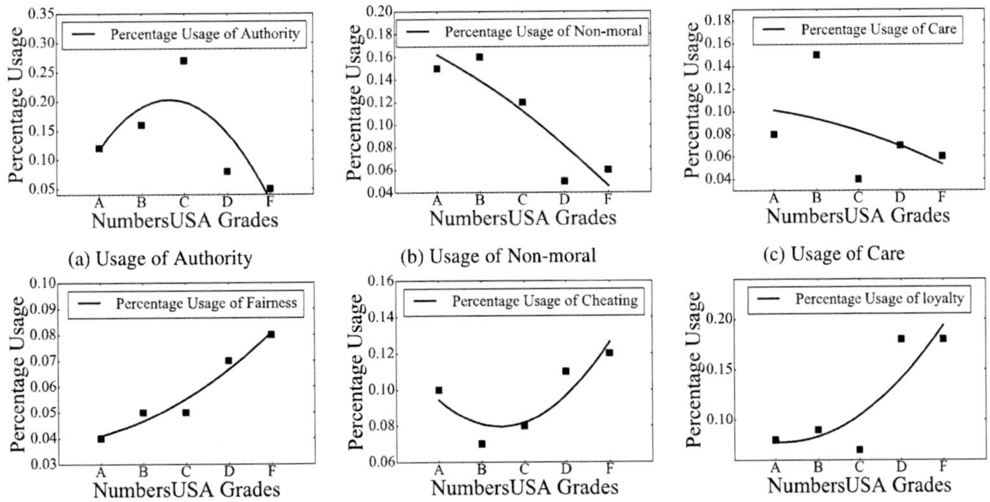

(a) Usage of Authority (b) Usage of Non-moral (c) Usage of Care

(d) Usage of Fairness (e) Usage of Cheating (f) Usage of Loyalty

Figure 6: Moral Foundation distribution over NumbersUSA grades on Immigration.

'family belong together', 'legal immigration', 'scotus', 'congress', 'daca', 'circuit court', 'government shutdown', 'muslim', 'dhs gov', 'immigration', 'national emergency', 'immigration system', 'immigration reform', 'border security', 'immigration law', 'immigrant family', 'anti immigrant agenda', 'house floor', 'america', 'c bp', 'sanctuary city', 'latino', 'humanitarian crisis', 'national security', 'dream promise', 'citizenship question', 'immigration policy', 'american people', 'border wall', 'detention center', 'dream promise act', 'southern border', 'immigrant child', 'medicare', 'keep family together', 'illegal immigration', 'dream', 'circuit judge', 'young people'

Content-based Stance Classification of Tweets about the 2020 Italian Constitutional Referendum

Marco Di Giovanni
Politecnico di Milano, Milan, Italy
Università di Bologna, Bologna, Italy
marco.digiovanni@polimi.it

Marco Brambilla
Politecnico di Milano, Milan, Italy
marco.brambilla@polimi.it

Abstract

On September 2020 a constitutional referendum was held in Italy. In this work we collect a dataset of $1.2M$ tweets related to this event, with particular interest to the textual content shared, and we design a hashtag-based semi-automatic approach to label them as Supporters or Against the referendum. We use the labelled dataset to train a classifier based on transformers, unsupervisedly pre-trained on Italian corpora. Our model generalizes well on tweets that cannot be labeled by the hashtag-based approach. We check that no length-, lexicon- and sentiment-biases are present to affect the performance of the classifier. Finally, we discuss the discrepancy between the magnitudes of tweets expressing a specific stance, obtained using both the hashtag-based approach and our trained classifier, and the real outcome of the referendum: the referendum was approved by 70% of the voters, while the number of tweets against the referendum is four times greater than the number of tweets supporting it. We conclude that the 2020 Italian constitutional referendum was an example of event where the minority was very loud on social media, highly influencing the perception of the event. Based on our findings, we suggest that drawing conclusion following only social media analysis should be performed carefully since it can lead to extremely wrong forecasts.

1 Introduction

On September 20 and 21, 2020, a constitutional referendum was held in Italy to reduce the number of parliamentarians (from 630 to 400). 69.96% of the voters approved it, with a voter turnout of about 51%[1]. Since the main Italian political parties supported the referendum, at first the outcome was obvious, but, through a huge activity on social media, opposers unsuccessfully tried to overturn the result. The referendum was a *confirmatory* referendum: voters were asked to approve a law. Thus, we refer to people that voted "yes", agreeing with the introduction of the new law that reduces the number of parliamentarians, as Supporters, and we refer to people that voted "no", against the introduction of the new law, as Opposers.

Since an always greater number of people share their thoughts online, social network analysis helps understanding the causes and forecasting the outcomes of political events, in parallel with already widely used approaches such as surveys and pools (Callegaro and Yang, 2018). Like surveys, *selection biases* are hard to remove. Social media users and citizens have different demographic distributions, resulting in under-represented categories of people (e.g., elderly people) (Mislove et al., 2011)[2]. Moreover, social media are also populated by bots, softwares that run accounts and automatically share content, introducing noise and bias in the collected data (Ferrara et al., 2016). These accounts are not run by real people and the data shared by them should not be included to perform analysis and statistics. However, a big advantage of the analysis of social media data is the higher magnitude of available data, easy to collect and process. It is often less expensive to collect content from social media than using classical approaches.

In this study we collect and analyze Twitter data about the Italian referendum in 2020. Our contributions can be summarized as follows:

- We collect and publicly share a corpus of $1.2M$ tweets about the Italian referendum in 2020. This is a rare and fundamental resource for NLP analysis, expecially stance detection, for non-English texts[3];

[1] https://en.wikipedia.org/wiki/2020_Italian_constitutional_referendum

[2] https://www.statista.com/statistics/283119/age-distribution-of-global-twitter-users/

[3] The dataset is publicly available at https://github.com/marco-digio/italian-referendum-2020

Proceedings of the Ninth International Workshop on Natural Language Processing for Social Media, pages 14–23
Online Workshop, June 10, 2021.

- We design a content-based, semi-automatic, approach to label big magnitudes of textual data through hashtags. We obtain a set of $85k$ cleaned labeled texts with low human effort;
- We fine-tune an accurate text classifier to detect the stance of tweets (Support or Against the referendum). We also successfully apply it to classify tweets that the semi-automatic approach *cannot* label;
- We inspect three common text biases (length-bias, lexical-bias and sentiment-bias), observing that our dataset does not suffer from them;
- We discuss the discrepancy between the collected data from Twitter and the real outcome of the referendum, including possible further investigation essential to understand the phenomenon.

2 Related Works

Numerous published works correlate social media data with elections or referendums. The main and most studied recent event is the Brexit referendum, largely investigated from many different points of view (Howard and Kollanyi, 2016; Grčar et al., 2017; Del Vicario et al., 2017; Mora-Cantallops et al., 2019; Lopez et al., 2017; Llewellyn and Cram, 2016), but many other political events have been analyzed from a social media perspective (Tumasjan et al., 2010; Sobhani et al., 2017; Darwish et al., 2017; Pierri et al., 2020; Vicario et al., 2017).

A general approach to quantify controversy in social media has been proposed by Garimella et al. (2018), designing a graph-based approach using solely on the underneath social graphs. This approach is language independent, relying solely on the social structure of communities of users, but computational expensive. Another approach has been proposed, that includes the content of texts to make more precise and fast computations (de Zarate et al., 2020).

We investigate this event from a content-based *stance detection* perspective (Küçük and Can, 2020), analyzing only user-generated content to detect the inclination about the referendum in Italy. There are few works about stance detection with non-English tweets (Vamvas and Sennrich, 2020). Lai et al. (2018) collect a similar dataset for the Italian referendum in 2016. They tackle the stance detection task by adding to simple NLP approaches, such as bag of hashtags, bag of mentions or bag of replies, network based features obtained by clustering the retweet/quote/reply networks with Louvain Modularity algorithm. They also analyze the datasets from a diachronic perspective by splitting the time window into four sections based on the dates of referendum-related events. Other works focus on the Italian political situation of Twitter users with content-based approaches (Ramponi et al., 2019, 2020; Di Giovanni et al., 2018). They collect tweets shared by politicians and their followers, and train accurate classifiers that predict the political inclination of users, without considering the social interactions: the content shared contains enough information to successfully perform classification of political inclination.

iovoto*	parlamentari	iovoto*taglioparlamentari
voto*	vota_efaivotare*	tagliodeiparlamentari
vota*	referendum	referendum2020_iovoto*
votare*	referendum2020	iovoto*_referendum2020
unitiperil*	maratonaperil*	cittadiniperil*

Table 1: List of keywords used to filter relevant tweets. They refer to *vote*, *parliamentarians*, *cuts* and *referendum*. We substitute * with no, si and sì (*yes* in Italian).

Similar tasks have been proposed at SemEval 2016 (Mohammad et al., 2016b), IberEval 2017 (Taulé et al., 2017), IberEval 2018 (Taulé et al., 2018) and finally at EVALITA 2020 (Cignarella et al., 2020), where teams were challenged to detect stances of manually labeled Italian Tweets about the Sardine Movement. We remark the difficulty of such tasks by looking at the performance of the best team (Giorgioni et al., 2020), that fine-tuned an Italian pre-trained BERT model (Devlin et al., 2019) and augmented the data with results from three auxiliary tasks.

A comparative study (Ghosh et al., 2019) shows that for stance-detection datasets of English texts from Web and Social Media, BERT model achieves the best performance, but there is still much room for improvements.

3 Data Collection, Description and Labeling

The dataset is collected from **Twitter**[4], a microblogging platform widely used to discuss trending topics, whose official API allows a fast and comprehensive implementation. On Twitter, users share *tweets*, small texts (up to 280 characters) that can

[4]https://twitter.com

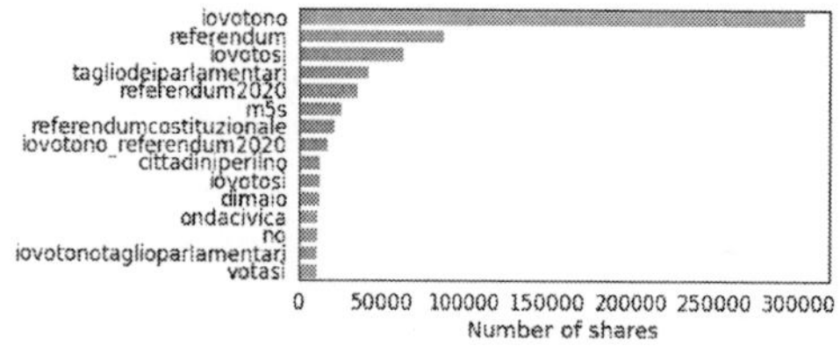

Figure 1: Mostly shared hashtags in the dataset.

be enriched with images, videos or URLs. Other users can *quote* (or *retweet*) another tweet by sharing it with (or without) a personal comment. A user can also *follow* other users to get a notification when they tweet (retweet or quote), and can be followed by other users.

We query data about the referendum held in Italy in September 2020 by searching Italian tweets, containing at least one of the keywords reported in Table 1, usually used as hashtags, but not always. In total we collected $1.2M$ Italian tweets posted between 01/08/2020 and 01/10/2020 by about $111k$ users.

The keywords are refined and validated iteratively. Starting from three keywords (referendum, iovotosì - IVoteYes, iovotono - IVoteNo), we inspect the most frequent hashtags and, if related to the topic, we add them to the query. In Figure 1 we show the most used hashtags in our complete dataset. Many frequent hashtags have no clear and safe connection with the referendum, thus we do not select them as keywords during the collection step, such surnames of politicians ("dimaio") and political parties ("m5s").

3.1 Hashtag-based Semi-automatic Labeling

Manually labeling big data sets is an expensive and not-scalable approach. Usually more than one annotator, fluent in the selected language, is required to produce a reliable label, and the time and cost to obtain a data set large enough to train an accurate classifier is usually high.

Graph-based approaches have obtained impressive results when applied to detect stances in controversial debates (Garimella et al., 2018; Cossard et al., 2020). These approaches are mainly used to label user by looking at the nearest community in the social graph. They firstly define the graph structure, e.g. retweet graph, and then they apply community detection algorithms to partition the bigger connected component of the graph.

We design a content-based approach to semi-automatically label large sets of tweets. Different from the graph-based approaches, we label *single* tweets, while the graph approaches work at the user-level. The approach is based on *hashtags*, often used to express the inclination of users about a topic (Mohammad et al., 2016a). Trending hashtags attract audience and get the attention of other users in the social network[5].

We pick two main classes: in *Support* of the referendum and *Against* the referendum. We define as *Gold hashtags* the hashtags that clearly state a side in the vaccine debate. We plan to collect two sets of Gold hashtags, one for each side of the debate. If a tweet contains at least one of the Gold hashtags, we define its stance as the stance of the hashtag. Tweets containing at least one Gold hashtag from both sides are discarded. Firstly, we select two Gold hashtags, one for each side: #iovotosì (I Vote Yes) for the Support class and #iovotono (I Vote No) for the Against class. Note that in Italian the word *yes* is translated as *sì*, with the grave accent that is often omitted in informal texts, such as tweets. Thus, in the whole paper, every time we refer to the word *sì*, we include also the word *si*, without the accent. Two annotators manually validate this initial selection by inspecting 100 tweets for each class and finding only 4 tweets that clearly belongs to the opposite stance. They were used to attract the attention of the other side or to delegitimise a specific hashtag., e.g. "I cannot understand people that write #IVoteYes". However, our validation process confirms that these tweets are rare and introduce little noise to the data set.

We iteratively add new hashtags by inspecting the most frequent co-occurring ones and manually selecting the most pertinent ones, basing the selection on their meaning. An example of discarded hashtags is #conte (the surname of the Prime Minister of Italy at the time of the Referendum), highly co-occuring with #iovotono, since we cannot safely assume that it was used only by users Against the referendum. We also discard hashtags that co-occur with hashtags from both sides in similar percentages. An example is #referendum, obviously frequently used by both sides of the debate. Finally, after each iteration two annotators manually validate the selected hashtags, as previously described for the initial Gold hashtags. An hashtag passes the validation if the percentage of tweets that is

[5]Twitter has a specific section for trending hashtags and keywords `https://twitter.com/explore/tabs/trending`

	Tweets using both #IoVotoSì and #IoVotoNo
A	In a few days we will meet at the ballot boxes to express our preference about the #CutOfParliamentarians. While waiting, let's retrace the most famous referendums in the history of the Republic. #Referendum2020 #IVoteYes #IVoteNo
B	Let's dismantle some lies about #IVoteNO. The #CutOfParliamentarians is a reform that fixes the Italian distortion of having a very big number of elected people. Who talks about dictatorship is only using the usual fear strategy to keep a useless privilege. #IVoteYes

Table 2: Translated examples of tweets containing both the Gold hashtag #iovoto and #iovotosì. (A) shows a neutral tweet, (B) shows a Supporter attacking the point of view of people Against the referendum.

classified by at least one annotator as belonging to the opposite class is lower than 10%. We finally obtain two final sets of **Support Gold hashtags** and **Against Gold hashtags**, that allows us to get about $450k$ labeled tweets by manually labeling *few hundreds*. The selected Gold hashtags are the keywords reported in Table 1 that contains the * symbol. The symbol is substituted with the corresponding stance ("sì" or "no"). For example, #referendum2020_iovotono is a Gold hashtag for Against class, while #referendum2020_iovotosì (and #referendum2020_iovotosi) is a Gold hashtag for Support class. Since no other hashtag among the 50 most-frequent ones passes the full validation procedure, we end the labeling phase.

Note that we label tweets containing at least one hashtag from a single set in the corresponding class, while tweets with at least one hashtag from both sets as Both and tweets without any hashtag from both sets as Unknown. We remark that Both and Unknown tweets cannot be safely considered *neutral* since they can express a stance without explicitly using one of the selected hashtags, or using both of them (Table 2 reports an example of a neutral tweet labeled as *Both* (A) and a Support tweet labeled as *Both* (B). This is the main limitation of this semi-automatic labeling procedure: no neutral class can be safely defined, thus we can only train a binary-classifier, leaving for future works the design of a three-classes stance detector.

We label *retweets* by looking at the hashtags in the original tweet, we label *quotes* by only looking at the hashtags in the quote itself, not at the quoted hashtags. In Table 3 we report the statistics of the obtained labeled dataset. Original tweets are tweets that are neither retweets nor quotes of other tweets, nor replies to other tweets.

Label	Tweets	Original	Retweets	Quotes	Replies
Support	93149	74086	2890	10572	5665
Against	364865	291185	15368	34559	24145
Both	4224	2796	145	246	1042
Unknown	353033	236743	16600	53119	47059
Total	815271	604810	35003	98496	77911

Table 3: Tweets Statistics.

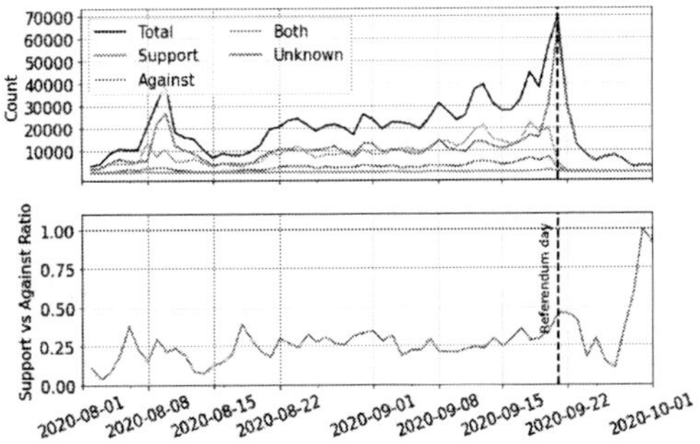

Figure 2: *Top*: Number of daily shared tweets, grouped by stance. *Bottom*: Daily Support vs Against Ratio. The higher the ratio, the greater the number of tweet Against the referendum. The red line (1) sets the value of equal number of Support and Against tweets.

3.2 Temporal Analysis

In Figure 2 (top) we show the distribution of tweets, grouped by their stance, during the time window selected, highlighting the referendum day. We notice a first peak around the August 8, due to an unrelated event about parliamentarians, that we accidentally included, since we used *parliamentarians* as a keyword to filter tweets. To remove noise and unrelated data, we discard all tweets posted before August 15 in the following analyses.

We also notice a huge peak of Unknown tweets during the referendum days, probably because users switched from the old hashtags *#IVoteYes* and *#IVoteNo* to their past tense versions (*#IVotedYes* and *#IVotedNo*). Thus, we discard tweets posted after September 19. Moreover, we do not want to influence our stance classification with tweets posted after the referendum.

In Figure 2 (bottom) we show how the ratio between Support and Against tweets evolves during the time window, observing constant values around 0.25 from August 15 to September 19. Thus, the daily number of tweets Against the referendum is four times bigger than the number of tweets Supporting it, further confirmed in Table 3, where the total number of Support tweets is four times smaller than the total number of tweets Against the referendum. We also notice big peaks and valleys outside the selected time window, caused by the low number of daily posted tweets.

4 Data Analysis

In this section we describe the cleaning process, the stance classifiers and their results on the collected dataset.

4.1 Data Cleaning

Before training a stance classifier, we clean the text of tweets through the following procedure.

Texts are lowercased, URLs are removed and spaces are standardized. **We remove Gold hashtags** (see Table 1) since they were used to automatically label tweets and users, thus maintaining them will introduce a strong bias in the trained models. We keep the other hashtags since they could encode useful information and are not a clear source of bias. Tweets containing at least half of the characters as hashtags are also removed, since they are too noisy. They are usually used by bots to collect the daily trending hashtags. To prevent overfitting we remove duplicate texts, including retweets. We also remove texts shorter than 20 characters, that usually comment URLs or other tweets, being difficult to understand and contextualize. We keep emoji as they include useful information, e.g., the scissor emoji was mainly used by Supporters of the referendum since they want to *cut* the number of parliamentarians. We select only tweets shared after 15/08/2020 and before 20/09/2020, the first referendum day.

4.2 Stance classification

We analyze the dataset from a stance classification perspective.

Due to the impossibility to interpret the tweets labeled as Both or Unknown, we formulate the tweet stance classification task as a binary classification problem: the two classes represent tweets Supporting or Against the referendum. We obtain an unbalanced clean datasets: $85k$ tweets, of which 80% Against the referendum. To obtain a balanced dataset, over-sampling the *Support* class leads to slightly better results in the Validation dataset, but worse results on the Test set, probably due to overfitting, while under-sampling the *Against* class leads to worse results due to the removal of 60% of the original dataset.

We select three models (one baseline and two commonly used architectures):

	Validation			Test		
Model	AUROC	$F1_w$	$F1_s$	AUROC	$F1_w$	$F1_s$
Baseline	0.50	0.78	0	0.50	0.52	0
FastText	0.74	**0.89**	0.56	0.65	0.59	0.18
BERT	**0.88**	0.86	**0.63**	**0.78**	**0.71**	**0.5**

Table 4: Area under ROC (AUROC), weighted F1 score ($F1_w$) and F1 score of the Supporters ($F1_s$) of the three models, as 5-fold Cross Validation on the training set (left) and on the Test Sets of 227 randomly selected and manually evaluated texts.

- Majority classifier (Baseline);
- FastText (Joulin et al., 2017), a fast approach widely used for text classification. Its architecture is similar to the CBOW model in Word2Vec (Mikolov et al., 2013): a look-up table of words is used to generate word representations, that are averaged and fed into a linear classifier. A softmax function is used to compute the probability distribution over the classes. To include the local order of words, n-grams are used as additional features, with the *hashing trick* to keep the approach fast and memory efficient. FastText is known to reach performances on par with some deep learning methods, while being much faster;
- BERT (Devlin et al., 2019), a Transformer-based model (Vaswani et al., 2017) that reaches state-of-the-art performances on many heterogeneous benchmark tasks. The model is pre-trained on large corpora of unsupervised texts using two self-supervised techniques: Masked Language Models (MLM) task and Next Sentence Prediction (NSP) task. Pre-trained weights are available on the Huggingface models repository (Wolf et al., 2020). We select a model pre-trained on a concatenation of Italian Wikipedia texts, OPUS corpora (Tiedemann, 2012) and OSCAR corpus (Ortiz Suárez et al., 2019), performed by MDZ Digital Library[6]. We fine-tune the model on our data[7].

4.3 Results

In Table 4 (left) we report the results of a 5-fold cross validation process. We select Area Under

[6]`https://huggingface.co/dbmdz/bert-base-italian-xxl-uncased`

[7]Fine-tuning performed on a single NVIDIA Tesla P100, for 5 epochs. Best weights selected by minimizing the evaluation loss. Learning rate (10^{-5}) set through grid search.

the ROC curve (Fawcett, 2006), weighted F1-score (the F1 score for the classes are weighted by the support, i.e., the number of true instances for each class) and $F1_s$, the F1 score on the Support class (the under-represented class, that, by definition, a Majority classifier cannot detect).

Both FastText model and BERT outperform the Random Baseline approach, the latter obtaining higher AUROC and $F1_s$.

However, our goal is to predict the stance of tweets that do *not* share a Gold Hashtag. We use these models, trained on the big dataset labeled using Gold hashtags, to predict tweets that do not contain Gold Hashtags, thus tweets that, with the previously described automatic approach, were labeled as Unknown. Two human annotators manually labeled 500 randomly sampled tweets. After removing neutral and incomprehensible texts, we obtain a dataset of 227 tweets, of which 78 labeled as Supporters. We test our models on this dataset, the results are reported in Table 4 (right), confirming that even if there is a gap among the Validation performances and the Test performances, BERT did not strongly overfit the Training data.

Finally, we obtain an approximate statistic of the total number of tweets Supporting and Against the referendum by predicting the stance of every tweet previously labeled as Unknown ($110k$ tweets). It results in about 20% of Unknown tweets classified as Supporters, confirming the general number of tweets Against the referendum is four times bigger that the number of shared tweets Supporting it. However, we cannot validate this result since we do not have manually labeled the full dataset.

5 Biases analysis

In this section we inspect three common biases that often affect the accuracies of classifiers: Length of texts, Lexicon and Sentiment.

5.1 Length Analysis

The length of sentences, defined as the number of characters or tokens, often influences the prediction of a model, acting as a bias. In Figure 3 we plot the distribution of lengths of tweets calculated as the number of characters, after the cleaning procedure (there are no tweets shorter than 20 characters). There is no evident difference between the distribution of the number of characters in tweets labeled as Support or Against, suggesting that no length-bias is present in our dataset.

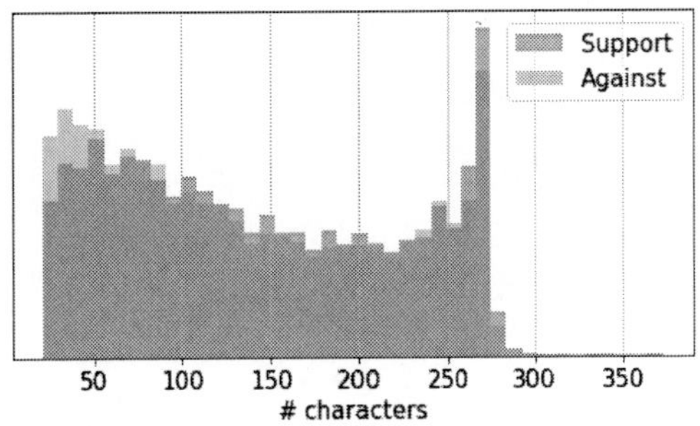

Figure 3: Length distribution of generated tweets grouped by stance. There is no significant difference in the normalized distributions.

5.2 Lexicon analysis

We check if tweets in different stances use similar lexicons. A big lexicon overlap in the dataset results in an accurate classifier that must learn the *meaning* of sentences, while a small lexicon overlap in the dataset allows the detection of specific words to be sufficient to make a prediction, neglecting the real meaning of the texts. We quantify the lexicon difference by computing the Pointwise Mutual Information (PMI) between words and classes (Gururangan et al., 2018).

A high PMI score of a word in a class is obtained when the word is used mainly in tweets belonging to that class. For this analysis, we discard Italian stop words collected from the NLTK library (Bird et al., 2009).

We report in Table 5 the first five words for each class, sorted by PMI score and the proportion of texts in each class containing each word. The frequency of words with higher PMI is low, thus we conclude that the two stances use mostly similar lexicons. A classifier cannot safely rely on the presence of specific words since the most indicative ones (higher PMI score) are not frequent enough. For example, the most frequent word among the top-5 is orgoglio5stelle, a keyword used by Supporters of the Referendum stating that they are proud of their party (5 stars) because the referendum was held by them. However, only 3% of the Supporter texts include this word.

5.3 Sentiment analysis

We distinguish between sentiment classification and stance classification by searching for a correlation between sentiment and stance in the datasets. Our goal is to have a stance classifier that does not

Support	%	Against	%
orgoglio5stelle	3.0	ondacivica	2.2
scissors emoji	0.3	30giorni_iovotono	0.5
laricchiapresidente	0.9	iostoconsalvini	0.5
pugliafutura	0.5	noino	0.4
rotolidistampaigienica	0.3	darevocealreferendum	0.4

Table 5: Top 5 tokens ranked by PMI (Pointwise Mutual Information) scores and the proportion of texts in each class containing each word.

rely on the sentiment of tweets to make a prediction. If Support and Against tweets are unbalanced in the Positive and Negative sentiment classes, the dataset contains a sentiment-bias.

We compute the sentiment scores of tweets and users using Neuraly's "Bert-italian-cased-sentiment" model[8] hosted by Huggingface (Wolf et al., 2019). It is a BERT base model trained from an instance of "bert-base-italian-cased"[9] and fine-tuned on an Italian dataset of $45k$ tweets on a 3-classes sentiment analysis task (negative, neutral and positive) from SENTIPOLC task at EVALITA 2016 (Barbieri et al., 2016), obtaining 82% test accuracy.

In Figure 4 we show the Kernel Density Estimation plot of positive and negative sentiment of tweets grouped by stance. The probability of being neutral is not shown as it can be obtained with $1 - p('positive') - p('negative')$. Since the distributions of the sentiments largely overlap, we conclude that there is no sentiment-bias in our datasets. It is further confirmed by looking at the actual predictions: for both Support and Against texts, 63% of them are classified as Negative, 25% as Neutral and 15% as Positive .

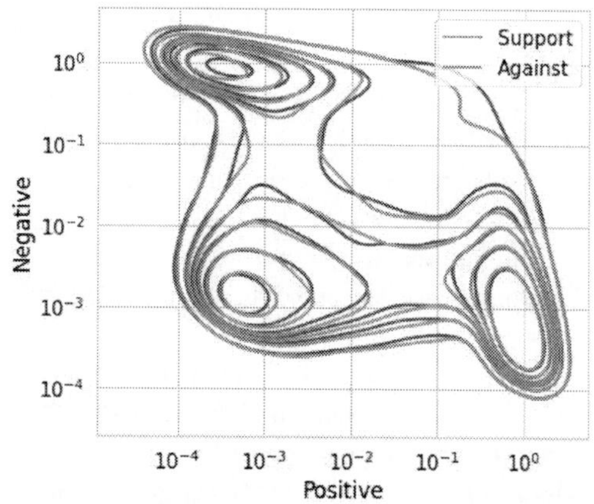

Figure 4: Sentiment distribution of generated tweets grouped by stance. There is no evident difference in the distributions. To improve the visualization, we use the same number of data points for both stances, downsampling the texts Against the referendum.

6 Discussion

6.1 Discrepancy between Twitter activity and the Referendum outcome

We notice a huge discrepancy between what users posted on Twitter and what citizens voted. The fraction of tweets and users that explicitly state their stance (and our prediction of tweets and users that do not) is very different from the final outcome of the referendum (69.96% of the voters approved it): the number of tweets with a Gold Hashtag Against the referendum is 4 times higher than the number of tweets with a Supporter Gold Hashtag, and the number of Unknown tweets that our best classifier predicts as Support or Against the referendum follows the same proportion. By looking only at what is shared online, we could have easily guessed that the Opposers won the referendum, while the real outcome is the opposite.

To further understand this discrepancy, we briefly inspect the differences in social characteristics of users. We label users as Support (Against) if they share only tweets previously labeled as Support (Against) the referendum. Figure 5 shows the normalized distribution of number of *followers* and number of *following* of users Supporting and Against the referendum. No difference in shape proves that the social audience of the two sides of users is quantitatively similar (the tails of the figures are cut for visualization purposes). Inspecting the most followed and following users (long tail of the distribution), we notice that among the top-10, exactly half of them are Supporters and half are Against the referendum, confirming our finding. Thus we conclude that Supporters won the referendum, not because they tweeted more than Opposers (they actually tweeted 4 times less than the people against the referendum), neither because they have more audience (the distributions of number of followers and following people is similar). We leave for future works the inspection of more detailed graph-related quantities, such as centrality of users in the network and topological measures to describe the graph structure.

[8]https://huggingface.co/neuraly/bert-base-italian-cased-sentiment

[9]https://huggingface.co/dbmdz/bert-base-italian-cased

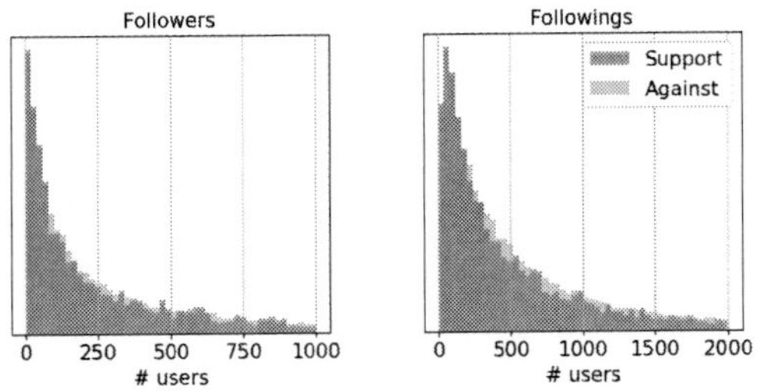

Figure 5: Distribution of followers (left) and following (right) users of users Supporting and Against the referendum.

We observed an event where the majority of voters were silent, or not even present on Social Media, while the minority was loud. This phenomenon implies not only that restricting the focus on social media to fully analyze an event could lead to extremely wrong forecasts, but also that the user perception of the general political situation can be influenced by an unrealistic image of the public opinion on social media that does not match the real sentiment towards the topic.

6.2 Ethical Considerations

Political inclinations of people is a sensitive topic. This work is meant to be a exploration on how to apply state-of-the-art NLP techniques to predict the stance of tweets about a political event, and whether they can help to perform more accurate forecasts of the outcome of a political event. Due to privacy issues, we do not share the trained model nor the obtained labels of tweets. However, we share the dehydrated collected tweets and the set of keywords to obtain the gold labels. These data allow researchers to reproduce the results but do not contain sensitive information, meeting the Twitter's Terms of Service[10]. In this study we prove that the political inclination of users can be detected by modern NLP approaches, *even if no evident hashtags of keywords are shared in a tweet.* Thus, we suggest a thoughtful and appropriate usage of social networks in order to keep private sensitive information.

7 Conclusion

Thanks to the last referendum in Italy, we collected a big Italian stance detection user-generated dataset. The dataset consists in $1.2M$ tweets, of which $85k$ are cleaned and labeled as Supporters or Against the referendum. The designed hashtag-based semi-automatic labeling approach allows us to train an accurate classifier that generalizes well also on tweets that do not contain Gold hashtags. We considered three common dataset biases (length-bias, lexicon-bias and sentiment-bias), confirming no significant dangers. Finally, we investigated the discrepancy between the fraction of collected tweets labeled by stance and the real outcome of the referendum, observing no clues that explain this difference. Based on our findings, we suggest that drawing conclusions following social media analysis should be performed carefully, and the results should be integrated with other other classical approaches such as surveys.

In future works, we aim to build a three-classes stance classifier, that can also predict *neutral* texts, since we observed big magnitudes of data that does not explicitly state a stance. We will also move the focus from tweets to users, detecting their inclination by looking at the history of shared tweets. We believe that the investigation of users that *changed* stance during the time window could help us understand how people opinions are influenced by social media. Finally, we observe that our classifier do not generalize well on other Italian stance-detection data sets, due to the high specificity of the task: the model learned the debate about the 2020 Italian constitutional referendum and its actors' inclination, but the knowledge obtained is not adequate to perform zero-shot transfer to other data sets. However, we plan to investigate if we can obtain boosts of performances in a multi-task and multi-source context, training a model on multiple similar tasks and data at the same time.

[10] `https://twitter.com/en/privacy`

References

Francesco Barbieri, Valerio Basile, Danilo Croce, Malvina Nissim, Nicole Novielli, and Viviana Patti. 2016. *Overview of the Evalita 2016 SENTIment POLarity Classification Task*, pages 146–155.

Steven Bird, Ewan Klein, and Edward Loper. 2009. *Natural Language Processing with Python*, 1st edition. O'Reilly Media, Inc.

Mario Callegaro and Yongwei Yang. 2018. *The Role of Surveys in the Era of "Big Data"*, pages 175–192. Springer International Publishing, Cham.

Alessandra Cignarella, Mirko Lai, Cristina Bosco, Viviana Patti, and Paolo Rosso. 2020. Sardistance @ evalita2020: Overview of the task on stance detection in italian tweets.

Alessandro Cossard, Gianmarco De Francisci Morales, Kyriaki Kalimeri, Yelena Mejova, Daniela Paolotti, and Michele Starnini. 2020. Falling into the echo chamber: The italian vaccination debate on twitter. *Proceedings of the International AAAI Conference on Web and Social Media*, 14(1):130–140.

Kareem Darwish, Walid Magdy, and Tahar Zanouda. 2017. Trump vs. hillary: What went viral during the 2016 us presidential election. In *Social Informatics*, pages 143–161, Cham. Springer International Publishing.

Juan Manuel Ortiz de Zarate, Marco Di Giovanni, Esteban Zindel Feuerstein, and Marco Brambilla. 2020. Measuring controversy in social networks through nlp. In *String Processing and Information Retrieval*, pages 194–209, Cham. Springer International Publishing.

Michela Del Vicario, Fabiana Zollo, Guido Caldarelli, Antonio Scala, and Walter Quattrociocchi. 2017. Mapping social dynamics on facebook: The brexit debate. *Social Networks*, 50:6–16.

Jacob Devlin, Ming-Wei Chang, Kenton Lee, and Kristina Toutanova. 2019. BERT: Pre-training of deep bidirectional transformers for language understanding. In *Proceedings of the 2019 Conference of the North American Chapter of the Association for Computational Linguistics: Human Language Technologies, Volume 1 (Long and Short Papers)*, pages 4171–4186, Minneapolis, Minnesota. Association for Computational Linguistics.

M. Di Giovanni, M. Brambilla, S. Ceri, F. Daniel, and G. Ramponi. 2018. Content-based classification of political inclinations of twitter users. In *2018 IEEE International Conference on Big Data (Big Data)*, pages 4321–4327.

Tom Fawcett. 2006. An introduction to roc analysis. *Pattern Recogn. Lett.*, 27(8):861–874.

Emilio Ferrara, Onur Varol, Clayton Davis, Filippo Menczer, and Alessandro Flammini. 2016. The rise of social bots. *Commun. ACM*, 59(7):96–104.

Kiran Garimella, Gianmarco De Francisci Morales, Aristides Gionis, and Michael Mathioudakis. 2018. Quantifying controversy on social media. *Trans. Soc. Comput.*, 1(1).

Shalmoli Ghosh, Prajwal Singhania, Siddharth Singh, Koustav Rudra, and Saptarshi Ghosh. 2019. Stance detection in web and social media: A comparative study. In *Experimental IR Meets Multilinguality, Multimodality, and Interaction*, pages 75–87, Cham. Springer International Publishing.

Simone Giorgioni, Marcello Politi, Samir Salman, R. Basili, and Danilo Croce. 2020. Unitor @ sardistance2020: Combining transformer-based architectures and transfer learning for robust stance detection. In *EVALITA*.

Miha Grčar, Darko Cherepnalkoski, Igor Mozetič, and Petra Kralj Novak. 2017. Stance and influence of twitter users regarding the brexit referendum. *Computational Social Networks*, 4.

Suchin Gururangan, Swabha Swayamdipta, Omer Levy, Roy Schwartz, Samuel R. Bowman, and Noah A. Smith. 2018. Annotation artifacts in natural language inference data. In *Short Papers*, NAACL HLT 2018 - 2018 Conference of the North American Chapter of the Association for Computational Linguistics: Human Language Technologies - Proceedings of the Conference, pages 107–112. Association for Computational Linguistics (ACL).

Philip N. Howard and Bence Kollanyi. 2016. Bots, #strongerin, and #brexit: Computational propaganda during the uk-eu referendum.

Armand Joulin, Edouard Grave, Piotr Bojanowski, and Tomas Mikolov. 2017. Bag of tricks for efficient text classification. In *Proceedings of the 15th Conference of the European Chapter of the Association for Computational Linguistics: Volume 2, Short Papers*, pages 427–431, Valencia, Spain. Association for Computational Linguistics.

Dilek Küçük and Fazli Can. 2020. Stance detection: A survey. *ACM Comput. Surv.*, 53(1).

Mirko Lai, Viviana Patti, Giancarlo Ruffo, and Paolo Rosso. 2018. Stance evolution and twitter interactions in an italian political debate. In *Natural Language Processing and Information Systems*, pages 15–27, Cham. Springer International Publishing.

C. Llewellyn and L. Cram. 2016. Brexit? analyzing opinion on the uk-eu referendum within twitter. In *ICWSM*.

Julio Lopez, Sofia Collignon-Delmar, Kenneth Benoit, and Akitaka Matsuo. 2017. Predicting the brexit vote by tracking and classifying public opinion using twitter data. *Statistics, Politics and Policy*, 8.

Tomás Mikolov, Kai Chen, Greg Corrado, and Jeffrey Dean. 2013. Efficient estimation of word representations in vector space. In *1st International Conference on Learning Representations, ICLR 2013, Scottsdale, Arizona, USA, May 2-4, 2013, Workshop Track Proceedings*.

Alan Mislove, Sune Lehmann, Yong-Yeol Ahn, Jukka-Pekka Onnela, and (James) Rosenquist. 2011. Understanding the demographics of twitter users. volume 11.

Saif Mohammad, Svetlana Kiritchenko, Parinaz Sobhani, Xiaodan Zhu, and Colin Cherry. 2016a. A dataset for detecting stance in tweets. In *Proceedings of the Tenth International Conference on Language Resources and Evaluation (LREC'16)*, pages 3945–3952, Portorož, Slovenia. European Language Resources Association (ELRA).

Saif Mohammad, Svetlana Kiritchenko, Parinaz Sobhani, Xiaodan Zhu, and Colin Cherry. 2016b. SemEval-2016 task 6: Detecting stance in tweets. In *Proceedings of the 10th International Workshop on Semantic Evaluation (SemEval-2016)*, pages 31–41, San Diego, California. Association for Computational Linguistics.

Marçal Mora-Cantallops, Salvador Sánchez-Alonso, and Anna Visvizi. 2019. The influence of external political events on social networks: the case of the brexit twitter network. *Journal of Ambient Intelligence and Humanized Computing*.

Pedro Javier Ortiz Suárez, Benoît Sagot, and Laurent Romary. 2019. Asynchronous pipelines for processing huge corpora on medium to low resource infrastructures. Proceedings of the Workshop on Challenges in the Management of Large Corpora (CMLC-7) 2019. Cardiff, 22nd July 2019, pages 9 – 16, Mannheim. Leibniz-Institut für Deutsche Sprache.

Francesco Pierri, Alessandro Artoni, and Stefano Ceri. 2020. Investigating italian disinformation spreading on twitter in the context of 2019 european elections. *PLOS ONE*, 15(1):1–23.

Giorgia Ramponi, Marco Brambilla, Stefano Ceri, Florian Daniel, and Marco Di Giovanni. 2019. Vocabulary-based community detection and characterization. In *Proceedings of the 34th ACM/SIGAPP Symposium on Applied Computing*, SAC '19, page 1043–1050, New York, NY, USA. Association for Computing Machinery.

Giorgia Ramponi, Marco Brambilla, Stefano Ceri, Florian Daniel, and Marco Di Giovanni. 2020. Content-based characterization of online social communities. *Information Processing & Management*, 57(6):102133.

Parinaz Sobhani, Diana Inkpen, and Xiaodan Zhu. 2017. A dataset for multi-target stance detection. In *Proceedings of the 15th Conference of the European Chapter of the Association for Computational Linguistics: Volume 2, Short Papers*, pages 551–557, Valencia, Spain. Association for Computational Linguistics.

M. Taulé, M. Martí, Francisco M. Rangel Pardo, P. Rosso, C. Bosco, and V. Patti. 2017. Overview of the task on stance and gender detection in tweets on catalan independence. In *IberEval@SEPLN*.

M. Taulé, Francisco M. Rangel Pardo, M. Martí, and P. Rosso. 2018. Overview of the task on multimodal stance detection in tweets on catalan #1oct referendum. In *IberEval@SEPLN*.

Jörg Tiedemann. 2012. Parallel data, tools and interfaces in OPUS. In *Proceedings of the Eighth International Conference on Language Resources and Evaluation (LREC'12)*, pages 2214–2218, Istanbul, Turkey. European Language Resources Association (ELRA).

Andranik Tumasjan, Timm Sprenger, Philipp Sandner, and Isabell Welpe. 2010. Predicting elections with twitter: What 140 characters reveal about political sentiment. volume 10.

Jannis Vamvas and Rico Sennrich. 2020. X-stance: A multilingual multi-target dataset for stance detection.

Ashish Vaswani, Noam Shazeer, Niki Parmar, Jakob Uszkoreit, Llion Jones, Aidan N. Gomez, Lukasz Kaiser, and Illia Polosukhin. 2017. Attention is all you need.

M. D. Vicario, S. Gaito, W. Quattrociocchi, M. Zignani, and F. Zollo. 2017. News consumption during the italian referendum: A cross-platform analysis on facebook and twitter. In *2017 IEEE International Conference on Data Science and Advanced Analytics (DSAA)*, pages 648–657.

Thomas Wolf, Lysandre Debut, Victor Sanh, Julien Chaumond, Clement Delangue, Anthony Moi, Pierric Cistac, Tim Rault, R'emi Louf, Morgan Funtowicz, and Jamie Brew. 2019. Huggingface's transformers: State-of-the-art natural language processing. *ArXiv*, abs/1910.03771.

Thomas Wolf, Lysandre Debut, Victor Sanh, Julien Chaumond, Clement Delangue, Anthony Moi, Pierric Cistac, Tim Rault, Rémi Louf, Morgan Funtowicz, Joe Davison, Sam Shleifer, Patrick von Platen, Clara Ma, Yacine Jernite, Julien Plu, Canwen Xu, Teven Le Scao, Sylvain Gugger, Mariama Drame, Quentin Lhoest, and Alexander M. Rush. 2020. Transformers: State-of-the-art natural language processing. In *Proceedings of the 2020 Conference on Empirical Methods in Natural Language Processing: System Demonstrations*, pages 38–45, Online. Association for Computational Linguistics.

A Case Study of In-House Competition for Ranking Constructive Comments in a News Service

Hayato Kobayashi[1*] **Hiroaki Taguchi**[1*] **Yoshimune Tabuchi**[1] **Chahine Koleejan**[1]
Ken Kobayashi[1] **Soichiro Fujita**[2] **Kazuma Murao**[3] **Takeshi Masuyama**[1]
Taichi Yatsuka[1] **Manabu Okumura**[2] **Satoshi Sekine**[4]
[1]Yahoo Japan Corporation [2]Tokyo Institute of Technology [3]VISITS Technologies Inc. [4]RIKEN
{hakobaya, htaguchi, yotabuch, ckoleeja, kenkoba, tamasuya, tyatsuka}@yahoo-corp.jp
{fujiso@lr., oku@}pi.titech.ac.jp murao@vis-its.com satoshi.sekine@riken.jp

Abstract

Ranking the user comments posted on a news article is important for online news services because comment visibility directly affects the user experience. Research on ranking comments with different metrics to measure the comment quality has shown "constructiveness" used in argument analysis is promising from a practical standpoint. In this paper, we report a case study in which this constructiveness is examined in the real world. Specifically, we examine an in-house competition to improve the performance of ranking constructive comments and demonstrate the effectiveness of the best obtained model for a commercial service.

1 Introduction

In online news services, the user comments posted on news articles function as a type of useful content known as user-generated content (UGC). Figure 1 shows examples of comments posted on Yahoo! JAPAN News, a Japanese news portal.[1] By reading these comments along with the article, users can obtain supplementary information such as other users' opinions, experiences, and simplified explanations of the article. There is a limit, however, on the number of comments that can be displayed on a page, and as users typically do not have the time or inclination to read through all the comments, ideally they should be ranked in some way. Prioritizing the comments for display is directly linked to user satisfaction, so improving this ranking is an important issue for such services.

There have already been multiple studies on comment ranking in online news services and discussion forums (Hsu et al., 2009; Das Sarma et al., 2010; Brand and Van Der Merwe, 2014; Wei et al., 2016). All of these studies have utilized user feedback (e.g., "Like"-button clicks in Figure 1) as their ranking metrics. Although such user feedback is

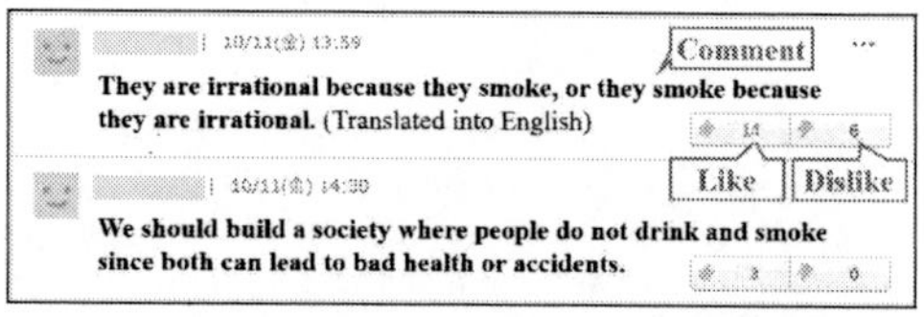

Figure 1: Comments on Yahoo! JAPAN News for article "Lifting the ban on drinking/smoking at 18."

easy to obtain, this type of measurement has two drawbacks: (i) user feedback does not always satisfy the service provider's needs, such as to create a fair place (i.e., a news space that is neutral), and (ii) user feedback will be biased by where comments appear in a comment thread (also known as "position bias" (Craswell et al., 2008)). A typical example for (i) can be seen in political comments, where the "goodness" of the comment tends to be decided on the basis of the political views of the majority of the users rather than on its quality. A typical example of (ii) can be illustrated by a case where earlier comments tend to receive more feedback since they are displayed at the top of the page, which implies later comments will be ignored irrespective of their quality. To resolve this issue, Fujita et al. (2019) introduced a metric representing a comment's constructiveness (see Section 2 for details), which has also been studied in argument analysis (Kolhatkar and Taboada, 2017a; Napoles et al., 2017a). Interestingly, they found empirical evidence that the constructiveness has no correlation with the user feedback, which has been commonly used for ranking comments. This implies that we need to consider the constructiveness rather than the user feedback to avoid unfavorable situations (i) and (ii) in real services.

In this paper, we take their study one step further towards practical application. Specifically, in collaboration with Yahoo! JAPAN News, we report a case study of deploying a model that ranks constructive comments in a commercial service. The

*Equal contribution.

[1]https://news.yahoo.co.jp/

Proceedings of the Ninth International Workshop on Natural Language Processing for Social Media, pages 24–35
Online Workshop, June 10, 2021.

characteristic unique point of our study is that we aim to improve the ranking quality through an in-house competition. As represented by Kaggle (Kaggle, 2020), the machine learning competition platform, it has become common to improve a model's performance through a competition format. This kind of experiment has also been conducted in various research areas through shared-task workshops, with the WMT translation task (Barrault et al., 2019), TAC text analysis task (Demner-Fushman et al., 2018), and NTCIR information retrieval task (Kato and Liu, 2019) being well-known examples. Following this trend, we also aim to improve the ranking performance through a competition format. As this kind of work conducted within a company towards a commercial service is rarely released in the form of an academic paper, we expect our findings to become valuable knowledge for practitioners in the field. We clarify the novelty of our study against other previous studies in Section 7.

Our main contributions are as follows:

- We report the details of the in-house competition (i.e., constructive comment ranking task) conducted in a commercial news service, Yahoo! JAPAN News, where we obtained a new model with a 2.73% improvement in performance (NDCG) compared to the baseline (Section 3). We also administer a participant survey and discuss positive and negative opinions relating to this competition (Section 6).
- We consider several ensembles of the submitted models and show that the best one performed better than the best single model (Section 4). Nevertheless, the service does not find it reasonable for practical use considering the need for maintainability and low latency against the performance increase (0.62%). This suggests that while an ensemble of various models submitted in the competition is promising in an academic sense, it still has challenges in an industrial sense. We believe that this will open a new direction for the ensemble research field to solve such challenges.
- We demonstrate that the high-performance models in the competition are practically useful in the real world with a service perspective evaluation (Section 5), and in fact, the service decided to introduce the best single model.
- We will release the 59K labeled dataset and the models submitted in the competition for future research.[2]

[2]https://research-lab.yahoo.co.jp/en/software/

Precondition	• Related to article and not libelous
Main conditions	• Intended to stimulate discussions • Objective and supported by fact • New idea, solution, or insight • User's unique experience

Table 1: Conditions for constructive comments.

2 Preliminaries

Constructiveness: We use the concept of constructiveness to prioritize comments that provide insight and encourage healthy discussion. According to the dictionary (Oxford, 2020), the term "constructive" is defined as *"having or intended to have a useful or beneficial purpose."* However, this dictionary definition is a bit too generic to determine whether a comment is constructive or not. To avoid individual variation as much as possible, we need a more specific definition for our task. Thus, we follow a previous study (Kolhatkar and Taboada, 2017a) on constructiveness, where a questionnaire administered to 100 people clarified the detailed conditions for constructive comments. Table 1 shows a summarized version of the conditions, which was also used by Fujita et al. (2019). The conditions consist of one precondition for maintaining decency and relevance and four main conditions for representing typical cases of being constructive. Specifically, a constructive comment is defined as one that satisfies the precondition and at least one of the main conditions.

YJCCR Dataset: We use (part of) the YJ Constructive Comment Ranking (YJCCR) Dataset, which was created by Fujita et al. (2019). The YJCCR dataset consists of more than 100K Japanese comments labelled with a **constructiveness score (C-score)**, which is a graded numeric score representing the level of constructiveness for ranking comments. The C-score was defined as the number of crowdsourced workers who judged a comment as constructive in response to a yes-or-no (binary) question. As a consequence, the C-score indicates how many people think that a comment is constructive with the goal of sufficiently satisfying as many users as possible.

The detailed settings of the crowdsourcing were as follows. The task was prepared with questions referencing a news article and its comments extracted from Yahoo! JAPAN News and conducted on a crowdsourcing service. The workers were asked to read the definition of constructiveness and then judge whether each comment was constructive. To ensure reliability, only the results of serious workers who correctly answered quality-control questions that were randomly included in each task were kept. Ten workers were used for each comment in the dataset, so a C-score of 8, for example, means that eight workers judged a comment as constructive. The reliability of this annotation was confirmed with Krippendorff's alpha, which was "moderate agreement."

The comments in Figure 1 are actual ones in the YJCCR dataset. The lower comment has a high score (9) because it includes a constructive opinion with some reasoning, whereas the upper comment has a low score (0) since it includes offensive content (see Appendix C for more examples).

3 In-House Competition

Task: The competition task consisted of ranking comments based on their degree of constructiveness, that is, the **C-score** defined in Section 2. Specifically, given that we have training data with triples $\{(a, x, y)\}$ consisting of a news article a, a comment x on the article, and its corresponding C-score y, the task is to predict the ranking of comments for every article in the test dataset $\{(a, x)\}$, where the C-scores are unknown. The goal of this task is to create a model that predicts the correct ranking from the training data as closely as possible.

The competition was held for about six weeks (Dec. 13, 2018 – Jan. 23, 2019), and a dozen employees related to the comment ranking service were made aware of it. The information shared among them included not only the dataset but also sample code consisting of a simple feature extraction, model creation, and evaluation pipeline in order to reduce the burden on the participants. We also prepared a leaderboard to display the latest evaluation results for submitted models. The participants reported their evaluation results on the leaderboard and were able to update them any number of times during the competition period.

Dataset: The training dataset consisted of a combination of the above-mentioned public dataset YJCCR and a new dataset of long comments created for this study. We used 49,215 comments (9,845 articles with five comments each) from the YJCCR dataset, each comment having a C-score assigned by crowdsourcing. While this dataset only contained comments up to 125 characters in length, we noticed in our preliminary experiments that long

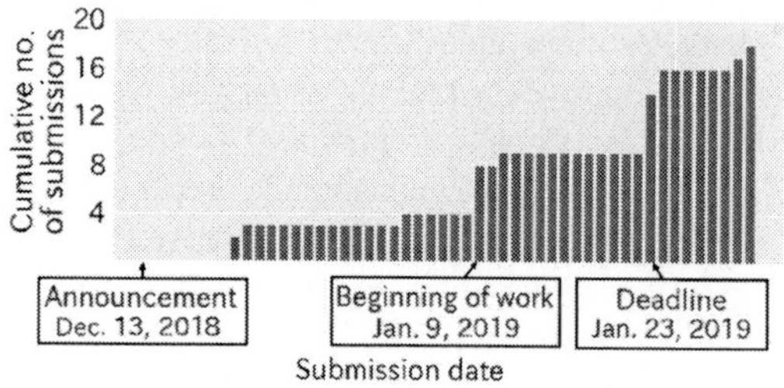

Figure 2: Cumulative number of submissions over the competition period.

comments tended to be incorrectly determined as constructive despite having a bigger impact on visibility than short ones. For that reason, we additionally extracted long comments (from 126 up to the maximum of 400 characters) posted to the articles in YJCCR and created a long comment dataset with C-scores assigned by crowdsourcing in the same way as for YJCCR, as described in Section 2. The resulting combination of the above two datasets yielded 59,120 comments (9,845 articles with an average of six comments). We split it into 80% training data, 10% validation data, and 10% test data to form the competition dataset.

Evaluation: We used Normalized Discounted Cumulative Gain (NDCG) (Burges et al., 2005), which is a widely used evaluation measure for ranking tasks. In this competition, we adopted a variant defined as $\text{NDCG@}k = Z_k \sum_{i=1}^{k} \frac{2^{r_i}-1}{\log_2(i+1)}$, which was also used in the Yahoo! Learning to Rank Challenge (Chapelle and Chang, 2011). This NDCG@k computes how close the top k comments predicted by a model are to the correct ranking, where r_i is the true C-score of the comment with predicted rank i, and Z_k is a normalization term.

To simplify the evaluation process, we set the average value of NDCG@k, i.e., $\frac{1}{K} \sum_{k=1}^{K} \text{NDCG@}k$, as the main measure in the competition, where K is the number of comments included in the article. Furthermore, to particularly encourage the performance improvement for long comments, we extracted a dataset consisting of only long comments (305 articles, 917 comments) from the test data and used its NDCG@k value as a supplementary measure. This was meant to reduce the effect of submitting sloppy methods that merely determined long comments to be constructive. From here on we call the normal measure NDCG and the one for long comments NDCG-L.

Submitted Models: Eight individuals participated in the competition and submitted 14 models during the competition period (before the deadline). Figure 2 shows the total number of submissions across the competition period. We can see that the number of submissions was low during the initial period of the competition but increased significantly at the start of the year (beginning of work), a period where time is relatively more available (Jan. 9, 2019), and on the day of the deadline (Jan. 23, 2019). Moreover, after the submission deadline had passed, several participants continued to work on the task and created an additional four models. We included these additional models when carrying out our analysis, although only the models submitted before the deadline were eligible for internal awards. We obtained a wide variety of models created by the participants' trials and errors, but due to space limitations, we only discuss in detail the four highest-performing models, which were `Model-4`, `Model-11`, `Model-14`, and `Model-17`. The following list includes the summary of each model with its detailed settings and features (see Appendix A for their hyperparameter settings).

- `Model-4`: The model with the highest NDCG (before the deadline). It is a gradient boosting model (pairwise learning) with features based on pretrained word embeddings.
  Model: The model was a LambdaMART model (Burges, 2010), which is a boosted tree variant of LambdaRank (Burges et al., 2007) extended from RankNet (Burges et al., 2005). It was trained using RankLib (ver. 2.1) (Lemur Project, 2020), a library of "learning to rank" algorithms.
  Features: The features were based on pretrained word embeddings trained with fastText (ver. 0.2.0) (Facebook, 2020), an open-source library,that includes a subword-based extension (Bojanowski et al., 2017) of the skip-gram model (Mikolov et al., 2013). The training dataset consisted of 100M news articles in the service, and they were split into words using MeCab (ver. 0.996), a Japanese morphological analyzer (Kudo et al., 2004; Kudo, 2020a), with IPADIC (ver. 2.7.0). Finally, the features of each comment were set to the average vector of the pretrained word embeddings for the words in the comment.
- `Model-11`: The model with the highest sum of NDCG and NDCG-L. It is a linear rankSVM (Lee and Lin, 2014) model (pairwise learning) with features based on C-score prediction and the distance between an article and its comment, where this setting is a kind of stacking ensemble.
  Model: The model was an L2-regularized L2-loss linear rankSVM model that was implemented as an instance of the well-known SVM tool LIBLINEAR (ver. 2.1.1) (Lin, 2020). The cost parameter C was determined from $\{2^{-13}, \ldots, 2^{1}\}$ on the basis of the performance on the validation set.
  Features: The features consisted of two factors. The first was the expected C-score, which was determined by first computing the probabilities of C-scores (considered as classes) using the open-source library fastText (ver. 0.2.0) (Joulin et al., 2017; Facebook, 2020)[2] with word embeddings trained on news articles and then calculating their expected value. The second feature was the Euclidean distance between the comment and title vectors, each of which consisted of the frequencies of words.
- `Model-14`: The model with the highest NDCG-L. It is a gradient boosting model (pointwise learning) with features based on maximal substrings and words.
  Model: The model was based on LightGBM (ver. 2.2.1) (Microsoft, 2020; Ke et al., 2017), a tree-based gradient boosting framework. The parameters were hand-tuned with a tuning guide (LightGBM Doc., 2020).
  Features: The features were based on a combination of maximal substrings and words, where a maximal substring is a substring s whose superstring never occurs at the same frequency as s. The features of the maximal substrings were the number of unique substrings, the frequencies of substrings, and the tf-idf values of substrings in the character-based maximal substrings in each comment (see Appendix A for how to extract maximal substrings). The features of words were the frequencies of words, which were extracted by MeCab (ver. 0.996), a Japanese morphological analyzer, with IPADIC (ver. 2.7.0). Finally, those two kinds of feature were combined and scaled to the range of $[-1, 1]$ using svm-scale in LIBLINEAR (ver. 2.1.1), a feature-scaling library.
- `Model-17`: The model with the highest NDCG (after the deadline). It is a variant of the RankNet model (pointwise and listwise learning) with features based on subwords.
  Model: The model was a variant of RankNet,

which has an encoder-scorer structure consisting of BiLSTMs and Gated CNNs (see Appendix A for the detailed model structure). C-score was predicted by (a) extracting the representations of the input subwords, (b) obtaining one vector averaging their representations, (c) estimating the classification probabilities, regarding the prediction problem of the C-score (0–10) as an 11-class classification problem, and (d) calculating the expected C-score with the probabilities. The loss was a combination of a pointwise loss, i.e., cross entropy loss for C-score probabilities, and a listwise loss, i.e., permutation probability loss for comment lists (Cao et al., 2007). The optimizer was Adam (Kingma and Ba, 2015) with parameters ($\alpha = 10^{-3}, \beta_1 = 0.9, \beta_2 = 0.999, \epsilon = 10^{-8}$), and the training was done in ten epochs with early stopping after random initialization in the range of $[-0.01, 0.01]$, where the batch size was 32 and the dropout rate was 0.3.
Features: The features (input) were a sequence of subwords based on SentencePiece (ver. 0.1.8) (Kudo and Richardson, 2018; Kudo, 2020b), where the subword model was trained with the training data using the unigram language model algorithm with the vocabulary size of 5,000.

Comparison with Baseline: We analyzed how well the submitted models performed compared to the baseline described below.

- `Baseline`: A linear rankSVM model (pairwise learning) with features based on term-frequency vectors. It was almost the same as the model in the previous study (Fujita et al., 2019) but was tuned for this competition.
Model: The model was an L2-regularized L2-loss linear rankSVM model, which was implemented in LIBLINEAR (ver. 2.1.1). The cost parameter C was determined from $\{2^{-13}, \ldots, 2^{1}\}$ on the basis of the performance on the validation set.
Features: The features consisted of the frequencies of words in each comment. Note that this setting performed better than the one-hot representations, the fractions (normalized frequencies) of the words, the number of distinct words, the tf-idf values, and any combinations thereof. They were scaled to the range of $[-1, 1]$ by using svm-scale in LIBLINEAR.

Figure 3 shows the performance increase (%) in NDCG and NDCG-L for the submitted models compared to `Baseline`. Note that decreases are not shown. As we can see, many models performed better than `Baseline`. Interestingly, a high NDCG score did not necessarily correspond to a high NDCG-L score, and in fact, `Model-4` with a high NDCG in particular had a lower NDCG-L than `Baseline`. The use of the leaderboard had a positive effect for participants submitting high-performance models for both measures in the latter half of the competition (right sides of the graphs). In the end, the highest performance increase was 2.73% by `Model-17` for NDCG and 2.34% by `Model-14` for NDCG-L.

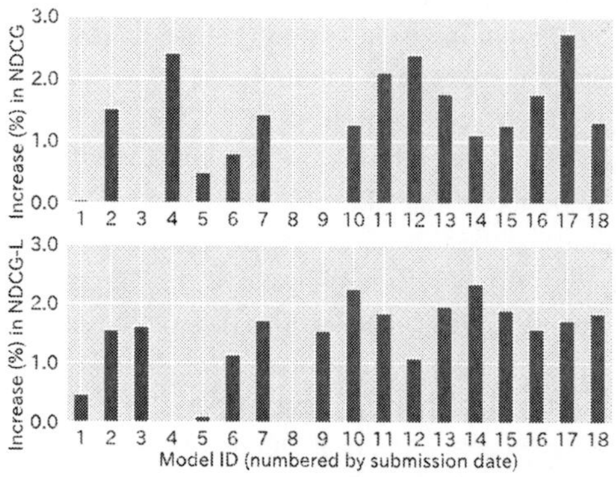

Figure 3: Increase (%) in NDCG (top) and NDCG-L (bottom) for each model compared to `Baseline`.

4 Model Ensemble

To further improve the performance, we considered using an ensemble of the models submitted in the competition. For ease of implementation, we focused on unsupervised ensemble methods that combine predicted scores. Assuming practical use, we only used the models that could accurately (or stably) reproduce their leaderboard performance, resulting in ensembles of 12 models.
Ensemble Methods: We prepared various ensemble methods covering both commonly used and recently proposed ones as follows.

- `ScoreAve`: Use the average of the predicted scores of all models as an ensemble score.
- `NormAve`: Use `ScoreAve` after normalizing the scores (Burges et al., 2011). We treated the predicted scores for all comments in each article as a vector v and applied the L2 norm, i.e., $v/||v||_2$.
- `RankAve`: Use the inverse of the averaged rank after ranking all comments with each model.
- `TopkAve`: Use `ScoreAve` only for the top-k ranked comments by each model (Cormack et al.,

	NDCG	NDCG-L	NDCG@3	Prec@3
Baseline	81.63	86.74	81.09	73.30
Model-4	83.60	82.15	82.79	73.98
Model-11	83.35	88.34	82.93	73.20
Model-14	82.53	**88.77**	81.83	72.86
Model-17	83.86	88.24	83.27	72.01
ScoreAve	83.85	86.66	83.20	73.40
NormAve	84.33	88.41	84.01	**74.11**
RankAve	83.46	88.25	82.92	73.30
TopkAve	84.35	88.35	83.31	73.54
PostEval	84.32	88.64	83.88	73.91
WeightEval	**84.38**	88.30	**84.18**	74.04

Table 2: NDCG variants (%) and precision (%) for (a part of) the submitted models and their ensembles.

2009), where k was chosen with the validation set.

- PostEval: Select the most promising output (or model) per article with a continuous version of majority voting (Kobayashi, 2018), where the similarity of two outputs was calculated with NDCG.
- WeightEval: Use the weighted average of the top-k promising outputs (Fujita et al., 2020), where k was chosen with the validation set. This method is a hybrid of output selection (PostEval) and output average (NormAve), where NDCG was used as a similarity function for selecting and weighting.

Evaluation Measures: Along with NDCG and NDCG-L, we used NDCG@3 and Prec@3 as supplementary measures, since only the top three comments are displayed first on each article page in the actual service, although users can read all comments on the next comment list page. Prec@3 is defined as the proportion of the predicted top-3 comments being in the correct top-3. Note that Järvelin and Kekäläinen (2002) reported that NDCG is more suitable than precision for graded scores like in our setting.

Results: Table 2 lists the results of the four high-performance models in Section 3 and the six ensembles of submitted models. Looking at the ensemble models, we can see that the recently proposed WeightEval performed the best for the main measure NDCG, and NormAve also performed competitively despite its simplicity. ScoreAve and RankAve did not perform as well as NormAve, as ScoreAve did not adjust outputs with different scales and RankAve failed when trying to adjust them, ignoring score shapes. These results imply that score adjustment (NormAve, TopkAve) and model selection (PostEval, WeightEval) contributed to the performance improvement. As a whole, NormAve is the most promising for practical use, since TopkAve and WeightEval need parameter tuning. Looking at single models, all the models performed better than Baseline for the main measure NDCG, and Model-17 performed the best overall. The differences between Baseline and Model-17 and between Model-17 and NormAve for the main measure NDCG were statistically significant in a Wilcoxon signed-rank test ($p < 0.05$). The high NDCG-L of Model-14 seems to be related to how to make the features. Model-14 used maximal substrings, including longer text spans than ordinary words. This implies that Model-14 can successfully characterize long comments, even if it might be harmful for short ones. We may need to consider this effect for other tasks including only long texts, although it was not effective for the main measure NDCG of our task since most comments are short.

5 Towards Practical Use

To determine if the submitted models can be used in the running service, we carried out a qualitative evaluation from the perspective of service, not just constructiveness. Specifically, we prepared the comment lists ranked by candidate models for each news article and asked three experts in the comment service to rank them. We instructed the experts to evaluate them on the basis of "which list should be provided as a service" rather than "which list is constructive," as the goal of this evaluation was to improve the service quality. As an evaluation measure, we calculated the micro-average of the ranks by the experts over the evaluation data prepared separately from the competition data. We used 104 articles (each having 3,406 comments on average) for the first evaluation and 66 articles (each having 3,888 comments on average) for the second evaluation.[3]

Baseline vs. Naive Methods: We first examined whether the constructiveness ranking model Baseline is useful compared to other naive methods, which was confirmed by Fujita et al. (2019) in terms of automatic evaluation (NDCG) only. Specifically, we compared the four models described below in terms of human evaluation.

- Feedback: A model ranking basically in descending/ascending order of the number of

[3]We reduced the number of articles in the second round because the evaluation cost was too high.

	Average Rank
Feedback	2.61
Latest	3.42
Length	2.20
Baseline (C-score)	**1.77**

Table 3: Qualitative evaluation results of Baseline and naive methods (lower ranks are better).

	Average Rank
Baseline	3.86
Model-4	3.64
Model-11	3.63
Model-14	3.41
Model-17	**3.11**

Table 4: Qualitative evaluation results of submitted models and Baseline (lower ranks are better).

Likes/Dislikes. This model has been used in the service.

- Latest: A model ranking in descending order of comment date. This model is a naive method used when user feedback and constructiveness scores are not available.
- Length: A model ranking in descending order of comment length. This model is a naive method based on the rule of thumb that long comments tend to be constructive.
- Baseline: A model ranking in descending order of predicted C-score, which is almost the same as the model in the previous study (Fujita et al., 2019) but has been tuned to this competition.

Table 3 shows the results of the qualitative evaluation. We can see that Baseline clearly performed better than the other models. The differences between Baseline and Feedback and between Baseline and Length were statistically significant in a Wilcoxon signed-rank test ($p < 0.05$). These results mean that the finding in the previous paper holds true even in human evaluation.

Baseline vs. Submitted Models: We prepared the four high-performance single models in Table 2 (excluding ensemble models) for comparison with Baseline. We also suggested introducing the most promising ensemble model, NormAve, but the service preferred not to because it would be unreasonable to maintain 12 different models and to re-normalize the scores every time a comment was posted, where static scores must be stored in the DB due to the low latency constraint.

Table 4 lists the results of the qualitative evaluation. As shown, the best single model for NDCG, Model-17, also had the best (lowest) average rank. The difference between Baseline and Model-17 was statistically significant in a Wilcoxon signed-rank test ($p < 0.05$). This implies that a competition format is effective in terms of obtaining an improved model even when we consider service-level judgment. As a result, the service introduced Model-17 into its comment ranking module.

One of the reasons Model-17 performed better than the others seems to be related to the fact that it had a full neural structure (as explained in Section 3), which implies "robustness" (or expressiveness of the model) thanks to a lot of parameters, as in Neyshabur et al. (2017)'s study. In fact, the evaluators reported that Model-17 had few critical errors compared to the other models. Although Model-4 and Model-11 performed well in Table 2 (automatic evaluation), we will have to consider the robustness (or the number of critical errors) from a practical point of view. Note that the detailed investigation of these factors is beyond the scope of this study.

6 Participant Survey and Future Issues

After the competition, we collected opinions from the participants through an optional survey. We discuss certain positive and negative opinions in detail below (see Appendix B for other opinions).

Positive Opinions: The most popular opinion was that the number of model submissions was greater than initially expected. According to the participants, this was mainly due to the game element of the competition, i.e., publicly competing against other participants. In other words, the fun of the task was an implicit incentive to encourage submissions. As a result, we were able to use a wide variety of models for the ensemble experiment (Section 4), which seems to have contributed to the performance improvement. Another interesting opinion was about disclosure of the modeling methods. In this competition, the participants were encouraged to include model descriptions such as structures and features when reporting their evaluation results on the leaderboard. This information helped the participants make improved models, which contributed to the best performance of single models (Section 3). Other positive opinions were related to the improved knowledge and skills acquired by the participants.

Negative Opinions: One major negative opinion

was about the leaderboard system, where the participants individually posted their own results pertaining to the evaluation tool and test data. This setting allowed the participants to purposefully design models effective only on the test data, although we confirmed that they actually used the validation data for fine-tuning. To hold a competition on a larger scale, we should prepare an automatic evaluation system with private test data. Such a setting is relatively common in strict competitions such as Kaggle, while most test datasets tend to be publicly available in research communities (under research ethics). Another insightful opinion was to make an incentive for exploring new directions, since it is valuable to obtain findings in unknown/rare directions, even if the results are not superior. In addition, model diversity can contribute to the ensemble performance, as discussed above. We suggest preparing a special prize for novelty in order to encourage exploring different directions.

7 Related Work

Constructiveness: Analyzing the comments on online news services or discussion forums has been extensively studied (Wanas et al., 2008; Ma et al., 2012; Llewellyn et al., 2016; Shi and Lam, 2018). In this line of research, many studies have focused on ranking comments (Hsu et al., 2009; Das Sarma et al., 2010; Brand and Van Der Merwe, 2014; Wei et al., 2016). However, the prior approaches have been based on user feedback, which is completely different from constructiveness.

Constructiveness has been introduced in argument analysis frameworks (Napoles et al., 2017a,b; Kolhatkar and Taboada, 2017a,b; Kolhatkar et al., 2020). The purpose of these studies was to classify constructive comments, whereas Fujita et al. (2019) recently expanded their tasks to a ranking one. They created a new dataset for ranking constructive comments on a news service and showed that the commonly used method that ranks comments by user feedback does not contribute to constructiveness in terms of automatic evaluation (NDCG). Our study has value as a deployment report of their approach, and we also confirmed that constructiveness performed better than user feedback for ranking comments in terms of human evaluation by experts.

Aside from constructiveness and user feedback, we may consider hate speech detection (Kwok and Wang, 2013; Nobata et al., 2016; Davidson et al., 2017) and sentiment analysis (Fan and Sun, 2010; Siersdorfer et al., 2014) as alternative approaches for analyzing the quality of comments on the basis of their content. Although these approaches are useful for other tasks, they do not directly solve our task, namely, ranking constructive comments. For example, the simple comment "Great!" is positive and is not hate speech, but it is not suitable as a top-ranked comment in our task.

Shared Tasks and Competitions: There have been many competitions in various research areas through shared-task workshops, such as the WMT translation task (Barrault et al., 2019), TAC text analysis task (Demner-Fushman et al., 2018), and NTCIR information retrieval task (Kato and Liu, 2019). Their purpose to find good models for a specific task is almost the same as ours, and the main difference (ignoring the task) is that the competition in our work was conducted within a company. As this kind of work towards a commercial service is rarely released in the form of an academic paper, we expect that our findings will become valuable knowledge for practitioners in this field.

As for "learning to rank" tasks, there have also been several competitions such as the Internet Mathematics 2009 (Yandex, 2020), the Yahoo! Learning to Rank Challenge (Chapelle and Chang, 2011), and the Personalized Web Search Challenge (Kharitonov and Serdyukov, 2020). Their tasks are basically to rank pages in terms of relevance to a search query, which is common in the information retrieval field. In contrast, our task is to rank comments in terms of constructiveness. It has value in the sense of applying the concept of argument analysis in the real world.

A unique aspect of our work is the ensemble of submitted models in the competition. Although there have been many studies on model ensembles (Hoi and Jin, 2008; Cormack et al., 2009; Burges et al., 2011), the models for prior ensemble experiments were basically prepared by either random initialization or a researcher's preference, which is different from our competition setting. The most closely related study involves the concept of "Resource by Collaborative Contribution (RbCC)" (Sekine et al., 2019), which collaboratively creates a large-scale dataset for named entity recognition by using the predicted labels of submitted models in a shared task, although their purpose and task were completely different from ours. We believe our findings in a commercial service will be useful for future ensemble studies.

8 Conclusion

We reported a case study of an in-house competition for ranking constructive comments. Our experimental results showed that the competition format is effective for testing various model structures, and that ensembling submitted models can further improve the ranking performance. Moreover, we confirmed that the submitted models were practically useful in a service perspective evaluation.

Acknowledgements

We would like to thank the comment service team in Yahoo! JAPAN News for their continued support of our research. We would also like to thank the anonymous reviewers for their constructive comments.

References

Alfred V. Aho and Margaret J. Corasick. 1975. Efficient String Matching: An Aid to Bibliographic Search. *Communications of the ACM*, 18(6):333–340.

Shunsuke Aihara. 2020. pykwic. https://github.com/shunsukeaihara/pykwic. Accessed: Apr. 1, 2020.

Loïc Barrault, Ondřej Bojar, Marta R. Costa-jussà, Christian Federmann, Mark Fishel, Yvette Graham, Barry Haddow, Matthias Huck, Philipp Koehn, Shervin Malmasi, Christof Monz, Mathias Müller, Santanu Pal, Matt Post, and Marcos Zampieri. 2019. Findings of the 2019 Conference on Machine Translation (WMT19). In *Proceedings of the Fourth Conference on Machine Translation (WMT 2019)*, pages 1–61. Association for Computational Linguistics.

Piotr Bojanowski, Edouard Grave, Armand Joulin, and Tomas Mikolov. 2017. Enriching Word Vectors with Subword Information. *Transactions of the Association for Computational Linguistics*, 5:135–146.

Dirk Brand and Brink Van Der Merwe. 2014. Comment Classification for an Online News Domain. In *Proceedings of the First International Conference on the Use of Mobile Informations and Communication Technology in Africa*, pages 50–55. Stellenbosch University.

Christopher J. C. Burges. 2010. From RankNet to LambdaRank to LambdaMART: An Overview. Technical Report MSR-TR-2010-82, Microsoft.

Christopher J. C. Burges, Robert Ragno, and Quoc V. Le. 2007. Learning to Rank with Nonsmooth Cost Functions. In *Advances in Neural Information Processing Systems 19 (NIPS 2007)*, pages 193–200. MIT Press.

Christopher J. C. Burges, Tal Shaked, Erin Renshaw, Ari Lazier, Matt Deeds, Nicole Hamilton, and Greg Hullender. 2005. Learning to Rank Using Gradient Descent. In *Proceedings of the 22nd International Conference on Machine Learning (ICML 2005)*, pages 89–96. ACM.

Christopher J. C. Burges, Krysta Svore, Paul Bennett, Andrzej Pastusiak, and Qiang Wu. 2011. Learning to Rank Using an Ensemble of Lambda-Gradient Models. In *Proceedings of the Learning to Rank Challenge*, pages 25–35.

Zhe Cao, Tao Qin, Tie-Yan Liu, Ming-Feng Tsai, and Hang Li. 2007. Learning to Rank: From Pairwise Approach to Listwise Approach. In *Proceedings of the 24th International Conference on Machine Learning (ICML 2007)*, pages 129–136. ACM.

Olivier Chapelle and Yi Chang. 2011. Yahoo! Learning to Rank Challenge Overview. In *Proceedings of the Learning to Rank Challenge*, pages 1–24. PMLR.

Gordon V. Cormack, Charles L A Clarke, and Stefan Buettcher. 2009. Reciprocal Rank Fusion Outperforms Condorcet and Individual Rank Learning Methods. In *Proceedings of the 32Nd International ACM SIGIR Conference on Research and Development in Information Retrieval (SIGIR 2009)*, pages 758–759. ACM.

Nick Craswell, Onno Zoeter, Michael Taylor, and Bill Ramsey. 2008. An Experimental Comparison of Click Position-Bias Models. In *Proceedings of the 2008 International Conference on Web Search and Data Mining (WSDM 2008)*, pages 87–94. Association for Computing Machinery.

Anish Das Sarma, Atish Das Sarma, Sreenivas Gollapudi, and Rina Panigrahy. 2010. Ranking Mechanisms in Twitter-like Forums. In *Proceedings of the Third ACM International Conference on Web Search and Data Mining (WSDM 2010)*, pages 21–30. ACM.

Thomas Davidson, Dana Warmsley, Michael Macy, and Ingmar Weber. 2017. Automated Hate Speech Detection and the Problem of Offensive Language. In *Proceedings of the Eleventh International AAAI Conference on Web and Social Media (ICWSM 2017)*, pages 512–515. AAAI Press.

Dina Demner-Fushman, Kin Wah Fung, Phong Do, Richard D. Boyce, and Travis Goodwin. 2018. Overview of the TAC 2018 Drug-Drug Interaction Extraction from Drug Labels Track. In *Proceedings of the 2018 Text Analysis Conference (TAC 2018)*.

Facebook. 2020. fastText. https://github.com/facebookresearch/fastText. Accessed: Apr. 1, 2020.

Wen Fan and Shutao Sun. 2010. Sentiment classification for online comments on Chinese news. In *Proceedings of the 2010 International Conference on Computer Application and System Modeling (ICCASM 2010)*, volume 4, pages V4–740–V4–745. IEEE.

Jerome H. Friedman. 2000. Greedy Function Approximation: A Gradient Boosting Machine. *Annals of Statistics*, 29:1189–1232.

Soichiro Fujita, Hayato Kobayashi, and Manabu Okumura. 2019. Dataset Creation for Ranking Constructive News Comments. In *Proceedings of the 57th Annual Meeting of the Association for Computational Linguistics (ACL 2019)*, pages 2619–2626. Association for Computational Linguistics.

Soichiro Fujita, Hayato Kobayashi, and Manabu Okumura. 2020. Unsupervised Ensemble of Ranking Models for News Comments Using Pseudo Answers. In *Proceedings of the 42nd European Conference on Information Retrieval (ECIR 2020)*, pages 133–140. Springer International Publishing.

Steven C. H. Hoi and Rong Jin. 2008. Semi-supervised Ensemble Ranking. In *Proceedings of the 23rd National Conference on Artificial Intelligence (AAAI 2008)*, pages 634–639. AAAI Press.

Chiao-Fang Hsu, Elham Khabiri, and James Caverlee. 2009. Ranking Comments on the Social Web. In *Proceedings of the 2009 International Conference on Computational Science and Engineering (CSE 2009)*, volume 4, pages 90–97. IEEE.

Kalervo Järvelin and Jaana Kekäläinen. 2002. Cumulated Gain-based Evaluation of IR Techniques. *ACM Transactions on Information Systems (TOIS)*, 20(4):422–446.

Armand Joulin, Edouard Grave, Piotr Bojanowski, and Tomas Mikolov. 2017. Bag of Tricks for Efficient Text Classification. In *Proceedings of the 15th Conference of the European Chapter of the Association for Computational Linguistics (EACL 2017)*, pages 427–431. Association for Computational Linguistics.

Kaggle. 2020. Kaggle: Your Home for Data Science. https://www.kaggle.com/. Accessed: Apr. 1, 2020.

Makoto P. Kato and Yiqun Liu. 2019. Overview of NTCIR-14. In *Proceedings of the 14th NTCIR Conference (NTCIR 2019)*.

Guolin Ke, Qi Meng, Thomas Finley, Taifeng Wang, Wei Chen, Weidong Ma, Qiwei Ye, and Tie-Yan Liu. 2017. LightGBM: A Highly Efficient Gradient Boosting Decision Tree. In *Advances in Neural Information Processing Systems 30 (NIPS 2017)*, pages 3146–3154. Curran Associates, Inc.

Eugene Kharitonov and Pavel Serdyukov. 2020. Personalized Web Search Challenge. https://www.kaggle.com/c/yandex-personalized-web-search-challenge/overview/description. Accessed: Apr. 1, 2020.

Diederik P. Kingma and Jimmy Ba. 2015. Adam: A Method for Stochastic Optimization. In *Proceedings of the 3rd International Conference on Learning Representations (ICLR 2015)*.

Hayato Kobayashi. 2018. Frustratingly Easy Model Ensemble for Abstractive Summarization. In *Proceedings of the 2018 Conference on Empirical Methods in Natural Language Processing (EMNLP 2018)*, pages 4165–4176. Association for Computational Linguistics.

Varada Kolhatkar and Maite Taboada. 2017a. Constructive Language in News Comments. In *Proceedings of the First Workshop on Abusive Language Online*, pages 11–17. Association for Computational Linguistics.

Varada Kolhatkar and Maite Taboada. 2017b. Using New York Times Picks to Identify Constructive Comments. In *Proceedings of the 2017 EMNLP Workshop: Natural Language Processing meets Journalism*, pages 100–105. Association for Computational Linguistics.

Varada Kolhatkar, Nithum Thain, Jeffrey Scott Sorensen, Lucas Dixon, and Maite Taboada. 2020. Classifying Constructive Comments. *arXiv*, abs/2004.05476.

Taku Kudo. 2020a. MeCab: Yet Another Part-of-Speech and Morphological Analyzer . https://taku910.github.io/mecab/. Accessed: Apr. 1, 2020.

Taku Kudo. 2020b. SentencePiece. https://github.com/google/sentencepiece. Accessed: Apr. 1, 2020.

Taku Kudo and John Richardson. 2018. SentencePiece: A simple and language independent subword tokenizer and detokenizer for Neural Text Processing. In *Proceedings of the 2018 Conference on Empirical Methods in Natural Language Processing (EMNLP 2018)*, pages 66–71. Association for Computational Linguistics.

Taku Kudo, Kaoru Yamamoto, and Yuji Matsumoto. 2004. Applying conditional random fields to japanese morphological analysis. In *Proceedings of EMNLP 2004*, pages 230–237, Barcelona, Spain. Association for Computational Linguistics.

Irene Kwok and Yuzhou Wang. 2013. Locate the Hate: Detecting Tweets Against Blacks. In *Proceedings of the Twenty-Seventh AAAI Conference on Artificial Intelligence (AAAI 2013)*, pages 1621–1622. AAAI Press.

Ching-Pei Lee and Chih-Jen Lin. 2014. Large-scale Linear RankSVM. *Neural Computation*, 26(4):781–817.

Lemur Project. 2020. RankLib. https://sourceforge.net/p/lemur/wiki/RankLib/. Accessed: Apr. 1, 2020.

LightGBM Doc. 2020. LightGBM Parameters Tuning. https://lightgbm.readthedocs.io/en/latest/Parameters-Tuning.html. Accessed: Apr. 1, 2020.

Chih-Jen Lin. 2020. LIBLINEAR. https://www.csie.ntu.edu.tw/~cjlin/liblinear/. Accessed: Apr. 1, 2020.

Clare Llewellyn, Claire Grover, and Jon Oberlander. 2016. Improving Topic Model Clustering of Newspaper Comments for Summarisation. In *Proceedings of the ACL 2016 Student Research Workshop*, pages 43–50. Association for Computational Linguistics.

Zongyang Ma, Aixin Sun, Quan Yuan, and Gao Cong. 2012. Topic-driven Reader Comments Summarization. In *Proceedings of the 21st ACM International Conference on Information and Knowledge Management (CIKM 2012)*, pages 265–274. ACM.

Microsoft. 2020. LightGBM. https://github.com/microsoft/LightGBM. Accessed: Apr. 1, 2020.

Tomas Mikolov, Ilya Sutskever, Kai Chen, Greg S Corrado, and Jeff Dean. 2013. Distributed Representations of Words and Phrases and their Compositionality. In *Advances in Neural Information Processing Systems 26*, pages 3111–3119. Curran Associates, Inc.

Wojciech Muła. 2020. pyachocorasick. https://pypi.org/project/pyahocorasick/. Accessed: Apr. 1, 2020.

Courtney Napoles, Aasish Pappu, and Joel R Tetreault. 2017a. Automatically Identifying Good Conversations Online (Yes, They Do Exist!). In *Proceedings of the Eleventh International AAAI Conference on Web and Social Media (ICWSM 2017)*, pages 628–631. AAAI Press.

Courtney Napoles, Joel Tetreault, Aasish Pappu, Enrica Rosato, and Brian Provenzale. 2017b. Finding Good Conversations Online: The Yahoo News Annotated Comments Corpus. In *Proceedings of the 11th Linguistic Annotation Workshop*, pages 13–23. Association for Computational Linguistics.

Behnam Neyshabur, Srinadh Bhojanapalli, David Mcallester, and Nati Srebro. 2017. Exploring Generalization in Deep Learning. In *Advances in Neural Information Processing Systems 30 (NIPS 2017)*, pages 5947–5956. Curran Associates, Inc.

Chikashi Nobata, Joel Tetreault, Achint Thomas, Yashar Mehdad, and Yi Chang. 2016. Abusive Language Detection in Online User Content. In *Proceedings of the 25th International Conference on World Wide Web (WWW 2016)*, pages 145–153. International World Wide Web Conferences Steering Committee.

Daisuke Okanohara and Jun'ichi Tsujii. 2009. Text Categorization with All Substring Features. In *Proceedings of the SIAM International Conference on Data Mining (SDM 2009)*, pages 838–846. SIAM.

Oxford. 2020. Definition of Constructive by Oxford Dictionary. https://www.lexico.com/definition/constructive. Accessed: Jun. 17, 2020.

Satoshi Sekine, Akio Kobayashi, and Kouta Nakayama. 2019. SHINRA: Structuring Wikipedia by Collaborative Contribution. In *Proceedings of the 1st International Conference on Automated Knowledge Base Construction (AKBC 2019)*.

Bei Shi and Wai Lam. 2018. Reader Comment Digest Through Latent Event Facets and News Specificity. *IEEE Transactions on Knowledge and Data Engineering*.

Stefan Siersdorfer, Sergiu Chelaru, Jose San Pedro, Ismail Sengor Altingovde, and Wolfgang Nejdl. 2014. Analyzing and Mining Comments and Comment Ratings on the Social Web. *ACM Transactions on the Web (TWEB)*, 8(3):17:1–17:39.

Nayer Wanas, Motaz El-Saban, Heba Ashour, and Waleed Ammar. 2008. Automatic Scoring of Online Discussion Posts. In *Proceedings of the Second ACM Workshop on Information Credibility on the Web*, pages 19–26. ACM.

Zhongyu Wei, Yang Liu, and Yi Li. 2016. Is This Post Persuasive? Ranking Argumentative Comments in Online Forum. In *Proceedings of the 54th Annual Meeting of the Association for Computational Linguistics (ACL 2016)*, pages 195–200. Association for Computational Linguistics.

Yandex. 2020. Internet Mathematics 2009. https://academy.yandex.ru/events/data_analysis/grant2009. Accessed: Apr. 1, 2020.

A Details of Model Settings

The following list shows the detailed settings for the submitted models. Figure 4 shows the model structure of `Model-17`.

- Parameters of LambdaMART for `Model-4`: number of trees ('tree') = 1000, number of leaves for each tree ('leaf') = 10, learning rate ('shrinkage') = 0.1, number of threshold candidates for tree splitting ('tc') = 256, minimum number of samples each leaf has to contain ('mls') = 1, number of rounds for early stopping ('estop') = 100 (stopping early when no improvement is observed on the validation set over 100 rounds), and metric to optimize on the training data ('metric2t') = NDCG@100.
- Parameters of fastText for `Model-4` and `Model-11`: learning rate ('lr') = 0.1, update rate for the learning rate ('lrUpdateRate') = 100, dimension size of word embeddings ('dim') = 100, size of the context window ('ws') = 5, number of epochs ('epoch') = 5, number of negative

samples ('neg') = 5, and loss function ('loss') = 'softmax'.

- Parameters of LightGBM for `Model-14`: boosting type ('boosting_type') = Gradient Boosting Decision Tree (Friedman, 2000) ('gbdt'), objective function ('objective') = L2-loss ('regression'), evaluation metric ('metric') = L2-loss ('l2'), maximum number of leaves in one tree ('num_leaves') = 128, learning rate ('learning_rate') = 0.1, fraction to randomly select part of features on each iteration or tree ('feature_fraction') = 0.9, fraction to randomly select part of data without resampling ('bagging_fraction') = 0.8, frequency for bagging ('bagging_freq') = 5 (every 5 iterations), maximum number of bins that feature values are bucketed in ('max_bin') = 1000, number of iterations ('num_iteration') = 1000, and number of rounds for early stopping ('early_stopping_rounds') = 10 (stop if a validation metric does not improve in last 10 rounds).
- Feature construction for NDCG-L. The substrings were extracted by making a dictionary of maximal substrings (whose frequencies were more than 2) from all the comments by using a suffix tree-based extraction algorithm (Okanohara and Tsujii, 2009) with pykwic (ver. 0.1.5), a Python library (Aihara, 2020), and searching for maximal substrings in each comment by using the Eho-Chorasic dictionary-matching algorithm (Aho and Corasick, 1975) with pyachocorasick (ver. 1.4.0), another Python library (Muła, 2020).

B Details of Participant Survey

Table 5 shows the details of the participant survey (translated fromJapanese to English).

C Examples of Scored Comments

Table 6 shows examples of scored comments (translated into English) in the YJCCR dataset. Ex. 1 has a high score because it includes a constructive opinion with some reasoning. Ex. 2 has a middle score because the judgement, e.g., whether the comment is a new idea, depends on each worker's background knowledge. Ex. 3 has a low score since it includes offensive content.

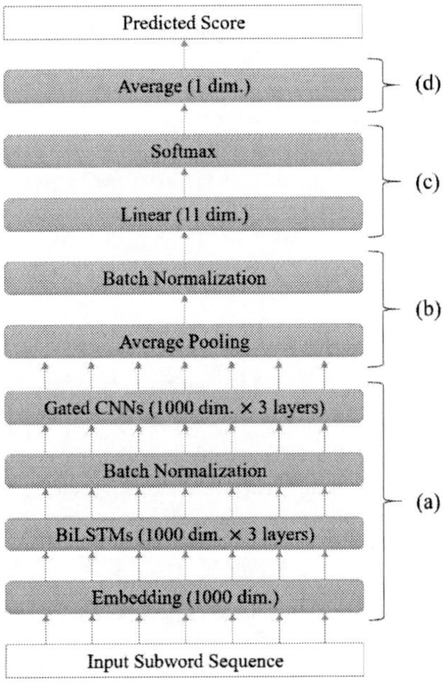

Figure 4: Structure of `Model-17`.

	Opinion
+	There were more participants than initially expected and a wide variety of models were submitted, so it turned out to be a good competition.
+	Since the participants disclosed their modeling methods, there were cases where one participant adopted the methods of other participants, which had a positive effect on improving the model's performance.
+	Although I did not understand much about the work I was not in charge of, my participation in this competition deepened my understanding of the task and made it easier to participate in discussions during meetings.
+	I managed to learn a lot through trial and error in the competition.
–	It would be better to have a system that automatically evaluates predictions upon submission.
–	It would be better to not publicly disclose the test data.
–	When we were able to create a model with a high performance, we could not share detailed knowledge such as what kind of library was used, so it seems like there is room for improvement in the knowledge sharing system.
–	It would be good to have a system that rewards not only an increase in performance but also trying out new methods.

Table 5: Summary of the survey results (translated from Japanese to English).

Comment	Score
We should build a society where people do not drink and smoke since both can lead to bad health or accidents.	9
If we give freedom, punishment should also be strictly given.	6
They are irrational because they smoke, or they smoke because they are irrational.	0

Table 6: Examples of comments and scores for article "Lifting the ban on drinking and smoking at 18."

Quantifying the Effects of COVID-19 on Restaurant Reviews

Ivy Cao, Zizhou Liu, Giannis Karamanolakis, Daniel Hsu, Luis Gravano
Columbia University, New York, NY 10027, USA
`{ic2502,zl2889}@columbia.edu`, `{gkaraman,djhsu,gravano}@cs.columbia.edu`

Abstract

The COVID-19 pandemic has implications beyond physical health, affecting society and economies. Government efforts to slow down the spread of the virus have had a severe impact on many businesses, including restaurants. Mandatory policies such as restaurant closures, bans on social gatherings, and social distancing restrictions have affected restaurant operations as well as customer preferences (e.g., prompting a demand for stricter hygiene standards). As of now, however, it is not clear how and to what extent the pandemic has affected restaurant reviews, an analysis of which could potentially inform policies for addressing this ongoing situation.

In this work, we present our efforts to understand the effects of COVID-19 on restaurant reviews, with a focus on Yelp reviews produced during the pandemic for New York City and Los Angeles County restaurants. Overall, we make the following contributions. First, we assemble a dataset of 600 reviews with manual annotations of fine-grained COVID-19 aspects related to restaurants (e.g., hygiene practices, service changes, sympathy and support for local businesses). Second, we address COVID-19 aspect detection using supervised classifiers, weakly-supervised approaches based on keywords, and unsupervised topic modeling approaches, and experimentally show that classifiers based on pretrained BERT representations achieve the best performance (F1=0.79). Third, we analyze the number and evolution of COVID-related aspects over time and show that the resulting time series have substantial correlation (Spearman's ρ=0.84) with critical statistics related to the COVID-19 pandemic, including the number of new COVID-19 cases. To our knowledge, this is the first work analyzing the effects of COVID-19 on Yelp restaurant reviews and could potentially inform policies by public health departments, for example, to cover resource utilization.

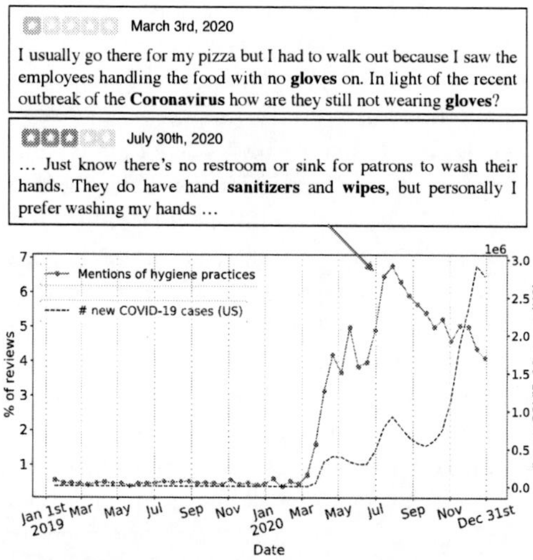

Figure 1: Top: Examples of Yelp restaurant reviews discussing hygiene practices. Bottom: Time series showing the number of reviews discussing hygiene practices and also the number of new COVID-19 cases in the US.

1 Introduction

The outbreak of the SARS-CoV-2 virus in December of 2019 and its evolution to the COVID-19 pandemic have had many devastating consequences in society. Restaurants have been among the hardest-hit businesses during the pandemic.[1] Yelp data (as of September 2020) shows that out of the 32,109 restaurant closures in the U.S., 61% have been permanent, and a greater impact is observed in local businesses in larger metropolitan areas, such as New York City and Los Angeles County, on which we focus in this paper.

Restaurants operate under great uncertainty during this ongoing situation and, therefore, it is critical to understand how the pandemic has affected public attitude towards restaurants. The disruption in daily routines as well as fear and anxiety due

[1] `https://www.yelpeconomicaverage.com/business-closures-update-sep-2020.html`

Proceedings of the Ninth International Workshop on Natural Language Processing for Social Media, pages 36–60
Online Workshop, June 10, 2021.

to the pandemic have been shown to affect eating habits (Naja and Hamadeh, 2020; Di Renzo et al., 2020). The pandemic may have also affected customers' preferences, such as changes in cuisine types, or higher expectations of hygiene and social distancing practices followed by restaurants.

In this paper, we present our efforts to understand the effects of COVID-19 on restaurant reviews. Reviewers provide ratings and free-form text to express their opinions and experiences about restaurants and we argue that the pandemic has affected such reviews. As an example, Figure 1 shows a Yelp review discussing the hygiene practices of a restaurant, including a mention of "coronavirus" and associated concerns. To understand more broadly the effect of the pandemic on restaurant reviews, we analyze 3 million Yelp reviews published before and during the pandemic, for restaurants in two large metropolitan areas, namely, New York City and Los Angeles County. We measure changes in user activity, ratings, and restaurant type preferences using the corresponding metadata, and quantify changes in written text using relevant extraction and classification techniques.

Overall, we make the following contributions.

Creation of a dataset with fine-grained COVID-19 aspect annotations. To facilitate text analysis, we create a dataset of 600 Yelp restaurant reviews with manual annotations of fine-grained COVID-19 aspects discussed in the reviews, such as hygiene practices, concerns of virus transmission, and sympathy and support messages. Our annotations can support detailed review analyses beyond simple mentions of COVID in text.[2]

Evaluation of COVID-19 aspect extraction techniques. We use our dataset to evaluate several techniques for COVID-19 aspect extraction from the review text, including unsupervised topic modeling (Blei et al., 2003), weakly-supervised classification based on COVID-related keywords (Karamanolakis et al., 2019), and (fully) supervised classification.

Analysis of the correlation between Yelp reviews and critical COVID-19 statistics over time. We analyze the distribution and evolution of the extracted COVID-19 aspects and other review metadata over time, capturing the period before and during the pandemic. We observe revealing trends, such as increased interest in fast food restaurants compared to traditional American-food restaurants (including brunch restaurants), increased mentions of hygienic practices of restaurants (Figure 1), service changes, racist and xenophobic attacks against the Asian American community, and sympathy and support messages expressed especially for local businesses. Crucially, we show that the resulting time series have substantial correlation (Spearman's ρ=0.84, p<0.01) with critical statistics and milestones related to the pandemic, such as the number of COVID-19 cases in the U.S. While our findings do not necessarily imply that the observed trends are caused by the pandemic, they may provide useful insights for restaurant owners, customers, public health officials, and the broad research community.

This paper is organized as follows. Section 2 reviews related work. Section 3 describes the Yelp data collection and annotation procedures. Section 4 outlines the techniques for data analysis. Section 5 summarizes our findings. Finally, Section 6 concludes the paper and suggests future work.

2 Related Work

The natural language processing community has been increasingly pushing efforts towards the better understanding and management of the pandemic. Valuable insight can be extracted from text data, including the COVID-19 scientific literature (Wang et al., 2020; Gutierrez et al., 2020), and web search data (Effenberger et al., 2020; Rovetta and Bhagavathula, 2020). Below, we review related work on the analysis of online user-generated reviews and posts on social media.

Social media reflects public attitudes during the pandemic (Chen et al., 2020). Existing work on sentiment or emotion analysis has considered Twitter (Drias and Drias, 2020; Nemes and Kiss, 2020; Li et al., 2020a; Samuel et al., 2020), Reddit (Biester et al., 2020), Weibo (Li et al., 2020b), and other platforms (Kleinberg et al., 2020). For example, Biester et al. (2020) analyzed how the pandemic has influenced the online behavior of Reddit users and found an increase in posts expressing mental health concerns, including anxiety and concerns for health and family. Beyond sentiment analysis, existing work has considered deep learning techniques for the identification of informative

[2]Our annotations are available at the following link: `https://drive.google.com/drive/folders/1PwYGO68fDjpjRgKN6rry-P9ji57OIa-r`.

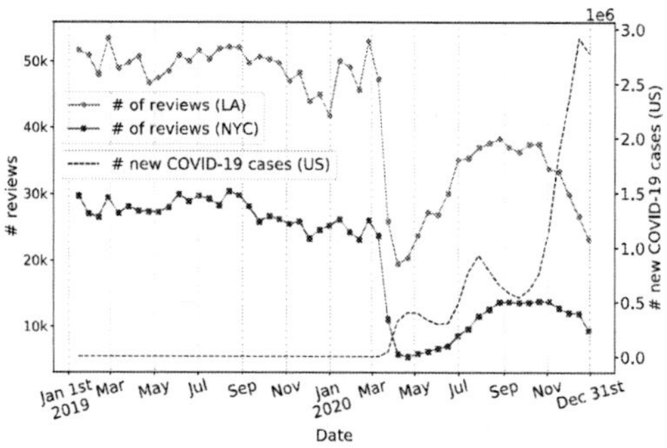

Figure 2: Total number of reviews for New York City and Los Angeles County over January 1, 2019 - December 31, 2020.

tweets that contain information relevant to the pandemic (Nguyen et al., 2020; Laxmi et al., 2020; Verspoor et al., 2020). To our knowledge, our work is the first that analyzes the effects of COVID-19 on restaurant reviews. To perform this analysis, we extract fine-grained COVID-19 aspects related to restaurants (e.g., hygiene practices, sympathy and support, social distancing, etc.).

Other work has studied nutrition during the pandemic by conducting surveys (Di Renzo et al., 2020) or by analyzing Twitter (Van et al., 2020). Van et al. (2020) observe a shift from mentions of healthy to unhealthy foods. Naja and Hamadeh (2020) propose a framework for action to maintain optimal nutrition during the pandemic. As part of our work, we show trends in restaurant preferences, such as increased interest in fast food restaurants compared to traditional American-food restaurants.

While prior work demonstrates changes in public attitude and nutrition during the pandemic, it is not clear how and to what extent restaurant reviews have changed during the pandemic. Yelp has introduced special COVID-19 review guidelines, and subsequently removed more than 4,000 reviews that violated those guidelines.[3] Our work demonstrates that many aspects of the review content and metadata have changed during the pandemic.

3 Data

We now describe our procedure for Yelp data collection (Section 3.1) and COVID-19 aspect annotation (Section 3.2).

[3]https://blog.yelp.com/2021/01/yelp-will-display-user-feedback-on-health-and-safety-practices

Aspect	Star Rating					ALL
	1	2	3	4	5	
Hygiene	103	21	16	25	78	**243**
Non-COVID	39	13	14	28	117	**211**
Service	21	4	8	9	41	**83**
Social Distancing	9	2	8	8	40	**67**
Sympathy & Support	8	1	3	1	28	**41**
Transmission	26	6	4	1	2	**39**
Racism	30	1	0	0	2	**33**
Other	14	1	3	0	3	**21**

Table 1: Aspect- and rating-related statistics for the 600 labeled Yelp reviews: ALL reports the number of reviews for each COVID aspect; the other columns report the number of reviews for the different star ratings. Out of the 600 reviews, 81 reviews were annotated with more than one aspect.

3.1 Yelp Data Collection

We consider Yelp reviews for New York City (NYC) and Los Angeles County (LA) restaurants uploaded over January 1, 2019 - December 31, 2020. Our dataset overalls consists of 1 million reviews for NYC and 2.1 million reviews for LA.

Figure 2 plots the number of reviews across time as well as the number of new COVID-19 cases in the U.S. For both NYC and LA, the number of reviews decreases significantly after January 2020, especially in March and April 2020: shutdowns and more stringent guidelines were put into effect starting in March. Such restrictions were only lifted in July 2020 and a second peak in the number of reviews is observed during September 2020.

3.2 COVID-19 Aspect Annotation

We manually labeled 600 reviews published after March 2020 with annotations relevant to COVID-19. In particular, we aimed to understand what aspects of restaurant operations are discussed in reviews referring to the pandemic. We will use these labels in Section 4.1 to train and evaluate classifiers for COVID aspect detection. For annotation, we considered 600 Yelp reviews posted after March 1, 2020, selected as follows. First, we considered all reviews after March 1, 2020 that contain COVID-related keywords[4] and selected 400 reviews uniformly at random among them. Second, we selected 200 reviews uniformly at random from

[4]We consider the following COVID-related keywords (case insensitive; adopted from Biester et al. (2020)): "corona," "outbreak," "pandemic," "virus," "sars-cov-2," "coronavirus," "wuhan," "2019ncov," "2019-ncov," "wuflu," "covid-19," "covid19," "covid," "sars," and "mers."

all reviews after March 1, 2020 that do not contain such keywords. We considered the following aspects related to COVID-19:

1. Hygiene: hygiene conditions of restaurants and protective equipment (e.g., *"Just know there's no restroom or sink for patrons to wash their hands. They do have hand sanitizers and wipes, but personally I prefer washing my hands."*).
2. Transmission: concern of virus transmission (e.g., *"All the whole coughing without covering his mouth"*).
3. Social Distancing: social distancing measures (e.g., *"The tables are set far apart – a more than acceptable social distance"*).
4. Racism: racism experiences (e.g., *"She was the only one waiting at the register but no one came to ring her up. She waited for a while but decided to leave after realizing she was ignored because of her race."*).
5. Sympathy and Support: messages of solidarity, for example, towards local businesses (e.g., *"Help support your Chinatown restaurants who are deeply hurting from the stigma around corona virus."*).
6. Service: service changes during the pandemic (e.g., *"Not sure if the restaurant was empty because of the coronavirus scare but the food came out suuuuper fast..."*).
7. Other: aspects that are related to COVID but that do not fall under any of the above categories (e.g., *"Shame on management for taking advantage of people trying to keep safe from coronavirus during a NY state of emergency."*).

We annotated each review with a COVID-related aspect if at least a sentence of the review discusses such aspect. A single review can be annotated with more than one distinct aspect. In cases where a review did not contain any sentences that were deemed relevant to any of the seven COVID-related aspects, then it received the "Non-COVID" aspect.

Table 1 shows annotation statistics. (We discuss review ratings later.) Most reviews discuss hygiene conditions of restaurants, and many reviews discuss social distance measures as well as changes in the restaurant service related to COVID.

4 Methodology

We now describe the techniques that we apply to the 3.1 million Yelp reviews from Section 3 for COVID-19 aspect analysis (Section 4.1) and time series analysis (Section 4.2), leveraging the labeled reviews of Section 3.2.

4.1 COVID-19 Aspect Analysis

First, we extract topics from reviews using unsupervised topic modeling. We train Latent Dirichlet Allocation (LDA) topic models (Blei et al., 2003) with different numbers of topics (5, 10, 25, 50, 100). Then, we manually annotate the obtained topics with descriptive labels by examining the highest-probability words for each topic. We noticed that it is hard to align the topics discovered by LDA with the COVID aspects of interest (Section 3.2) and, therefore, we experiment with supervised and weakly-supervised techniques, as discussed next.

We use our annotated dataset from Section 3.2 to train and evaluate review classifiers (via 5-fold cross-validation) for multi-class COVID-19 aspect classification. We consider two alternative training procedures: fully-supervised classification using labeled training data, and weakly-supervised classification using a small number of indicative keywords per class. The fully-supervised approaches are standard and listed at the end of this subsection.

The weakly-supervised approach we use is the co-training method of Karamanolakis et al. (2019), which works as follows. First, we manually define a small number of keywords or key phrases for each COVID-19 aspect.[5] Then, we employ a teacher-student architecture, where the teacher classifier considers keywords to annotate unlabeled reviews with aspects and the teacher-labeled reviews are used to train a student classifier. The teacher classifier does not require training and instead predicts aspect probabilities proportionally to keyword counts for each aspect. If no keywords appear in a review, then the teacher predicts the "Non-COVID" aspect. The student classifier can be any classifier, and here we consider both stan-

[5]**Hygiene:** "masks," "gloves," "mask," "glove," "shield," "sanitize," "sanitizer," "sanitizing," "disinfect," "disinfecting," "face cover," "covering face," "face covers," "wipe," "wiping," and "wipes." **Transmission:** "cough," "spread," "infected," "cautious," "potential germs," "concerning," "worried," "covid test," "tested positive," and "asymptomatic." **Social Distancing:** "social distance," "social distancing," "six feet," "6 feet," "spaced out," "6ft," and "distanced." **Racism:** "racist," "xenophobia," "racism," "race," "xenophobic," "asian," and "asians." **Sympathy and Support:** "small business," "local business," "struggling," "support," "stress," "stressful," "suffer," "sympathy," and "stressed." **Service:** "takeout," "outdoor dining," "take out," "re-stocked," "restocked," "curbside pickup," "online order," "rude," and "service." **Other:** "covid," "pandemic," "quarantine," "covid19," "lockdown," "shutdown," and "cdc."

dard bag-of-words classifiers and classifiers based on pre-trained BERT representations (Devlin et al., 2019). Note that the student is trained using the teacher's predictions and no manually annotated reviews; in contrast to the teacher, which only considers keywords, the student can identify aspects even if no keywords appear in a review. As labeled data are expensive to obtain, such a weakly-supervised technique is promising to scale classification by leveraging unlabeled reviews (and keywords) for training (Karamanolakis et al., 2019).

Overall, we consider the following approaches:

1. Random: assigns reviews to a random aspect.
2. Majority: assigns all reviews to the "Non-COVID" aspect.
3. Supervised bag-of-words (BoW) classifiers: represents each review as a bag of words, where words can be unigrams and bigrams. We evaluate logistic regression (LogReg) and Support Vector Machines (SVM).
4. Supervised BERT: fine-tunes pre-trained BERT (Devlin et al., 2019) for supervised aspect classification.
5. Weakly-supervised Teacher: classifies a review solely based on keywords (Teacher in Karamanolakis et al. (2019)).
6. Weakly-supervised Student: is trained using Teacher's predictions on unlabeled data (Student in Karamanolakis et al. (2019)). We evaluate different modeling approaches for Student, namely, BoW-LogReg, BoW-SVM, and BERT.

The above techniques classify Yelp reviews into COVID aspects using either labeled data (supervised approach) or COVID-related keywords (weakly-supervised approach) for training. In addition to COVID aspect classification, we conduct time series analysis to understand how COVID aspects evolve over time, as discussed next.

4.2 Time Series Analysis

To understand how reviews have changed during the pandemic, we extract time series from the text of the reviews. For a given aspect (e.g., Hygiene), the corresponding time series is computed as the percentage of the reviews at each point in time that contain at least one aspect-specific keyword (see Section 4.1). We consider two approaches: time-series cross-correlation and time-series intervention analysis, as discussed next.

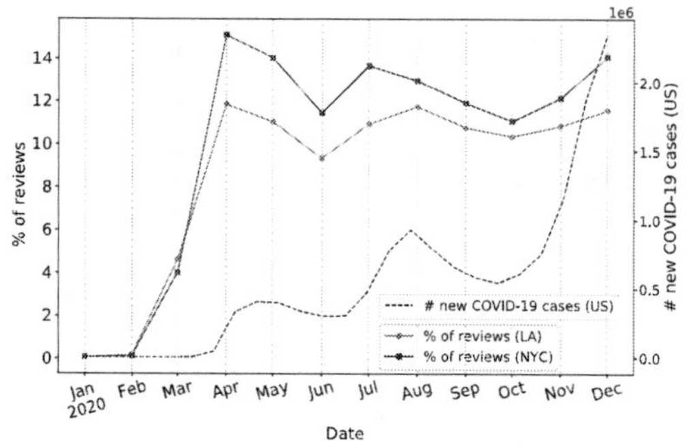

Figure 3: Percentage of reviews containing COVID-related keywords.

As a first approach, we measure the correlation between the Yelp review time series and important statistics related to COVID-19, such as the number of new COVID-19 cases in the U.S or the new COVID-19 cases in NYC and LA individually. As we do not expect Yelp review time series to have a linear relationship with COVID-19 time series, we compute the Spearman's correlation metric, which only assumes a monotonic but possibly non-linear relationship between the two time series. We also measure the Pearson's correlation metric as a robustness check.

As a second approach, we consider a time series intervention analysis. First, we train a time-series model on the observations before COVID-19 (i.e., on reviews posted before March 1, 2020) and then we compare the model's predictions against the observations during COVID-19 (i.e., on reviews posted on March 1, 2020 or later). Similar to Biester et al. (2020), we consider the Prophet time-series forecasting model (Taylor and Letham, 2018), an additive regression model that has been shown to forecast social media time series effectively. After training Prophet on the pre-pandemic data, we check to what degree its forecasts for during COVID-19 differed from the actual values. Specifically, we compute the proportion of observations outside the 95% prediction uncertainty interval produced by Prophet after March 1, 2020.

By constructing Yelp review time series and comparing them to statistics related to COVID-19, we find interesting trends in reviews during the pandemic, as discussed next.

5 Findings

We use the methodology from Section 4 to address various questions on the 3.1 million-review

Topic label (manually assigned)	10 highest-probability words
Protective equipment and social distancing	covid, mask, masks, people, customers, staff, social, wearing, distancing, pandemic
Outdoor seating	outdoor, seating, dining, ramen, good, tables, covid, outside, really, place

Table 2: The two (out of 25 LDA) topics that we identified as relevant to COVID-19, along with manually assigned topic labels and the 10 highest probability words for each topic. (All topics are reported in Table 7 in the Appendix.)

Method	Binary F1	Multi-Class F1
Random	0.459	0.115
Majority	0.346	0.070
Methods below are fully supervised		
BoW-LogReg	0.741	0.481
BoW-SVM	0.739	0.422
BERT	**0.786**	**0.522**
Methods below are weakly supervised		
Teacher	0.605	0.270
Student-BERT	**0.657**	**0.407**

Table 3: F1 values for binary (left) and multi-class (right) COVID-19 aspect classification. Classifiers based on pre-trained BERT representations outperform simpler bag-of-words classifiers.

dataset from Section 3. First, we analyze the text of the Yelp reviews (Section 5.1), and then we use both the metadata and the text to create time series and evaluate their correlation with the number of COVID-19 cases (Section 5.2).

5.1 COVID-19 Aspect Analysis

In this section, we analyze the text of the Yelp reviews and evaluate the performance of several methods for COVID aspect classification on our manually annotated dataset from Section 3.2.

Number of reviews with COVID-related keywords: Figure 3 shows the percentage of reviews that contain COVID-related keywords. Interestingly, after March 2020, more than 10% of the reviews contain COVID-related keywords: thousands of restaurant reviews per week discuss aspects related to the pandemic.

Topics discussed in reviews: We apply topic modeling on all Yelp reviews after March 1, 2020. Table 2 shows the two (out of the 25) topics that we identified as relevant to COVID-19. The first topic is related to protective equipment and social distancing, while the second topic is related to outdoor seating. The remaining 23 topics did not contain any COVID-related keywords among the 10 highest-probability words: it is hard to align the topics discovered by LDA with the fine-grained COVID aspects of Section 3.2, so we consider aspect classification approaches, as discussed next.

COVID aspect classification: We evaluate supervised and weakly-supervised approaches for COVID aspect classification via cross-validation using the 600 manually annotated reviews (Section 4.1). Table 3 shows the cross-validation results for binary (COVID vs. Not COVID) and multi-class aspect classification. Table 8 in the Appendix reports additional metrics. The fully supervised BERT-based classifier outperforms BoW-* classifiers on both binary and multi-class classification. The weakly-supervised Teacher that classifies aspects using keywords and no labeled data (Section 4.1) leads to a more accurate Student-BERT classifier: weakly-supervised co-training with keywords leads to substantially better performance than Random. The weakly-supervised Student-BERT has lower F1 score than the fully supervised BERT, which was expected because Student-BERT does not consider labeled reviews for training but instead uses Teacher's predictions on unlabeled reviews as weak supervision.

5.2 Time-series Construction

In this section, we analyze how reviews have changed during the pandemic by extracting time series from metadata (star ratings, cuisine types) and the text of the reviews (see Section 4.2).

Star ratings: Figure 4 shows the average star rating over time for NYC and LA. For both time series, there is a sharp decrease in average rating starting in March 2020 and an increasing trend after June 2020. Figure 5 shows the number of star ratings across time for NYC. The trends are similar for LA (Figure 9b in the Appendix). For the first time after 2019, the percentage of 1-star ratings in NYC surpassed the percentage of 4-star ratings. Interestingly, for both NYC and LA, a peak in the number of new COVID-19 cases (April 2020 for NYC and July 2020 for LA) coincides with a peak in the percentage of 1-star ratings. Also, after September 2020, there is a decreasing trend in the number of 1-star ratings and an increasing trend in the number

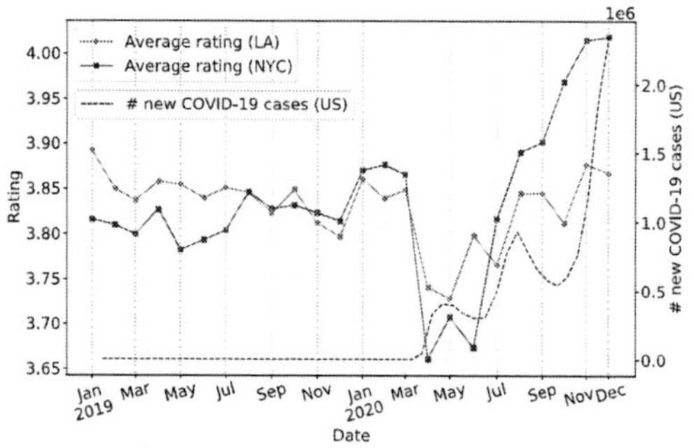

Figure 4: Average star rating across all reviews in NYC and LA over January 1, 2019 - December 31, 2020.

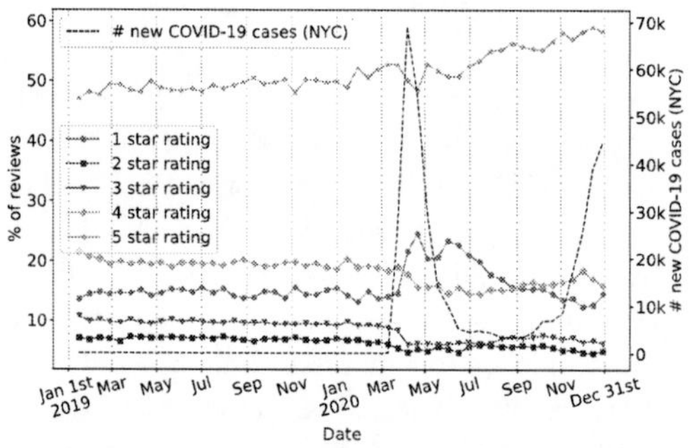

Figure 5: Percentage of reviews for each star rating in NYC over January 1, 2019 - December 31, 2020.

of 5-star ratings. We conclude that, during the first months of the pandemic, users' ratings shifted to extremely positive (5 star) or extremely negative (1 star) values, but after September 2020, users posted increasingly more 5-star rating reviews, leading to a total increase in average rating.

Types of cuisine: Restaurant metadata include tags that indicate the cuisine types, such as "Italian" and "sandwich." Figure 6 shows the percentage of reviews for selected groups of cuisine type over time.Such time series are relatively stable during 2019 but change significantly during 2020. "American" substantially dropped at the beginning of the pandemic (March) and rose again after indoor dining re-opened (July). The drop in "American" coincided with the increase of "Fast Food." "Asian Food" also dropped sharply in March but recovered quickly within 2 weeks. These trends indicate important changes in user activity during the pandemic that affect specific cuisine types, which could be supported by previous observations of nutrition changes (Van et al., 2020).

Time Series (NYC)	**NYC Cases**	**US Cases**
Social Distancing	0.768***	0.836***
Hygiene	0.765***	0.822***
Transmission	0.816***	0.804***
Sympathy & Support	0.822***	0.755***
Service	0.772***	0.736***
Racism	0.293**	0.237*
Time Series (LA)	**LA Cases**	**US Cases**
Service	0.536***	0.644***
Sympathy & Support	0.490***	0.551***
Hygiene	0.395***	0.538***
Transmission	0.409***	0.522***
Social Distancing	0.347**	0.513***
Racism	-0.006	-0.019

Table 4: Spearman correlation results from comparing COVID aspects and the number of COVID cases in NYC (top) and LA (bottom), sorted in decreasing order by correlation compared with the number of new US cases. Results are marked as statistically significant at the p<0.1*, p<0.05**, and p<0.01*** levels.

Evolution of restaurant review aspects over time: Figure 7 shows the evolution of aspects over time for NYC. Aspects for LA reviews follow similar trends (see Table 12 in the Appendix). Aspects such as "Hygiene," and "Social Distancing" have been discussed more frequently after March 2020, covering up to 8% of the restaurant reviews: reviewers discuss such aspects during the pandemic more than before the pandemic. Interestingly, while "Hygiene" peaked during July 2020 (during restaurant re-opening) for both cities and since then keeps decreasing, "Sympathy & Support" peaked during Spring 2020, then decreased, and follows an increasing trend after November 2020.

Correlation of aspects with COVID-19 statistics: We now consider our first approach for time series analysis from Section 4.2 and measure the correlation between Yelp review time series and COVID-19 statistics. Table 4 reports the Spearman correlation between time series constructed from restaurant reviews and the number of new COVID-19 cases. For Pearson correlation results, see Tables 9 and 10 in the Appendix. For both NYC and LA, there is significant correlation between restaurant review aspects and new cases of COVID-19, reaching up to Spearman's ρ=0.84 for the Hygiene aspect. For LA, COVID aspects have higher absolute correlation to the number of US

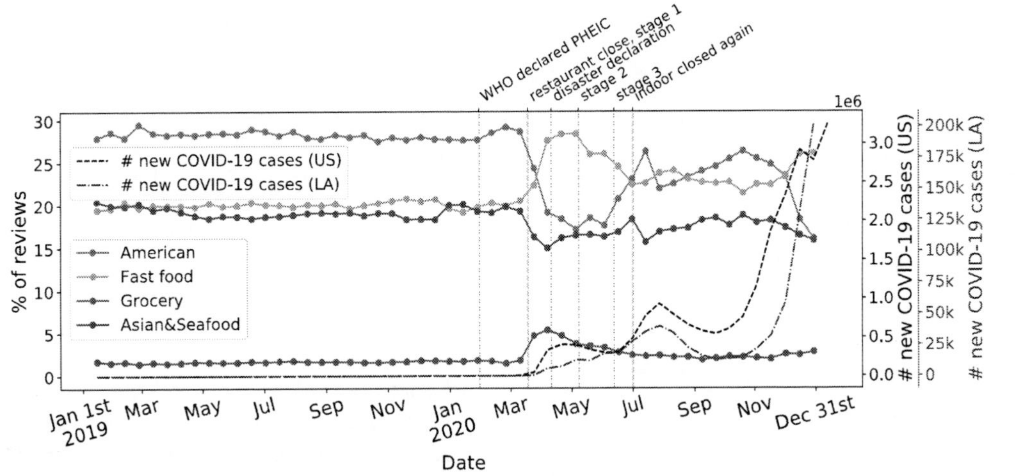

Figure 6: Evolution of cuisine types over time for LA. For each time series, we compute the percentage of reviews that include at least one tag from a predefined tag list: "American": ["steak", "cocktailbars", "bars", "breakfast brunch", "newamerican", "tradamerican"], "Fast Food": ["sandwiches", "pizza", "hotdogs", "chicken wings", "thai"], "Groceries": ["grocery"], "Deserts&Drinks": ['juicebars,' 'bubbletea,' 'icecream,' 'desserts,' 'bakeries'], "Asian&Seafood": ["sushi", "japanese", "seafood", "asianfusion", "korean"]. Tags within each category follow similar trends, which we individually report in the Appendix.

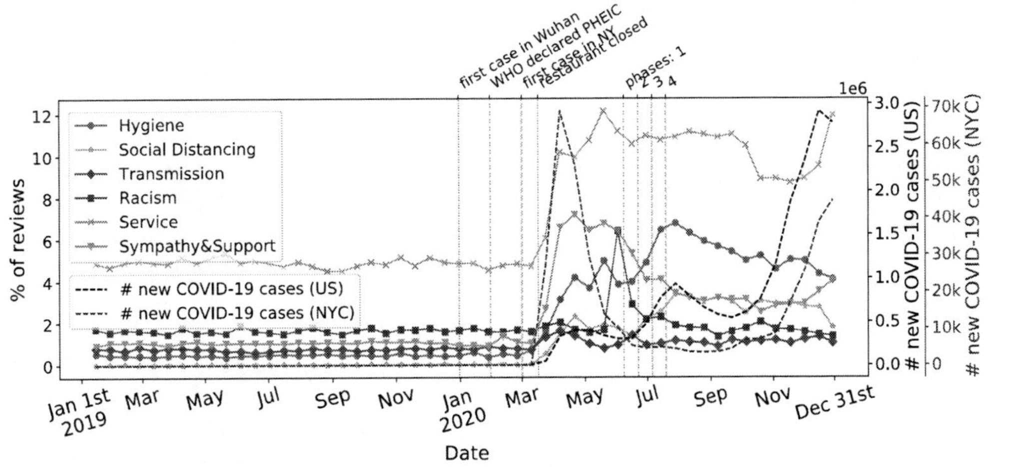

Figure 7: COVID aspects for NYC restaurants over January 1, 2019 - December 31, 2020.

cases compared to the number of LA cases. For NYC, most aspects present higher correlation with the number of NYC cases compared to the number of US cases. Even though we cannot draw causal conclusions from these correlations, our results highlight interesting trends of Yelp reviews during the pandemic.

Time-series intervention analysis: Here, we consider our second approach for time series analysis (Section 4.2) and compare time series constructed from the metadata of Yelp reviews to the corresponding Prophet forecasts. Figure 8 shows the evolution of the "pizza" tag (left) and "seafood" tag (right) over time and the Prophet forecasts. During COVID-19 (i.e., on March 1, 2020 or later), most true values for "pizza" were higher than forecasts while most true values for "seafood" were lower than Prophet forecasts. The Appendix reports forecasts for more cuisine tags. The difference between Prophet's forecasts and true values indicates that user activity has shifted towards specific types of businesses, as we further discuss next.

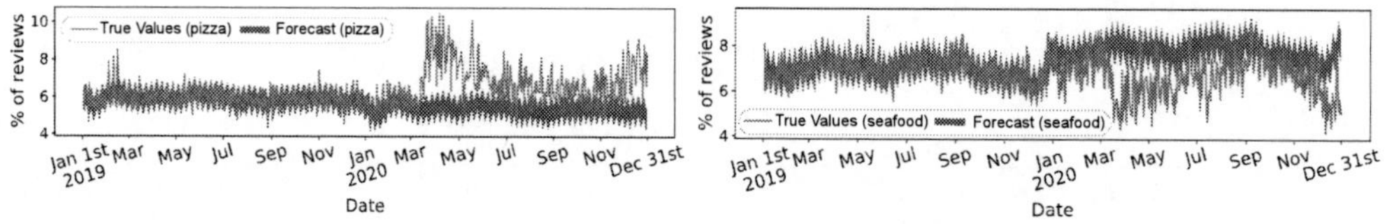

(a) "Pizza" business tag. (b) "Seafood" business tag.

Figure 8: Evolution of business tags and the corresponding Prophet forecasts over time for LA. The red line is the true value and the blue line is the Prophet forecast. After March 1, 2020, most true values for "pizza" restaurants (left) were higher than Prophet forecasts, while most true values for "seafood" restaurants (right) were lower than Prophet forecasts. The Appendix reports all forecasts of Prophet.

Time Series	% of outliers	
	LA	NYC
1 star rating	62.28 ↑	69.55 ↑
2 star rating	55.36 ↓	91.35 ↓
3 star rating	83.04 ↓	47.75 ↓
4 star rating	61.94 ↓	61.24 ↓
5 star rating	88.24 ↑	50.17 ↑
Grocery	82.35 ↑	96.54 ↑
Chicken Wings	64.36 ↑	92.73 ↑
Sandwiches	95.50 ↑	75.78 ↑
Thai	69.20 ↑	68.86 ↑
Bakeries	47.06 ↑	66.78 ↑
Hotdogs	77.85 ↑	65.05 ↑
Pizza	89.96 ↑	56.75 ↑
Ice Cream	71.28 ↑	56.40 ↑
Breakfast&Brunch	81.31 ↓	53.98 ↓
Sushi	41.52 ↓	55.01 ↓
Steak	84.78 ↓	58.48 ↓
Cocktail Bars	99.31 ↓	58.82 ↓
Trad American	93.08 ↓	58.82 ↓
Bars	69.90 ↓	59.86 ↓
Japanese	40.83 ↓	61.24 ↓
Asian Fusion	41.87 ↓	76.47 ↓
New American	89.62 ↓	91.70 ↓

Table 5: Percentage of outliers (observations outside Prophet's 95% uncertainty interval) for LA and NYC reviews posted after March 1, 2020. Arrows indicate whether the mean value of the outliers is higher (up) or lower (down) than the mean of Prophet's predictions.

Table 5 reports the percentage of outliers (i.e., true values outside of Prophet's 95% uncertainty interval) for star ratings (top) and some of the most frequent business tags (bottom). For tags such as "Grocery," "Chicken Wings," and "Sandwiches," upwards pointing arrows indicate that the mean value of outliers is higher than the mean of Prophet's predictions. In contrast, for tags such as "New American," "Asian Fusion," and "Japanese," downwards pointing arrows indicate that the mean value of outliers is lower than the mean of Prophet's predictions. The Appendix reports all forecasts of Prophet. The direction arrows in Table 5 support our previous observations about the corresponding changes of cuisine types and star ratings during the pandemic.

6 Conclusions and Future Work

We presented our effort to understand the effects of COVID-19 on restaurant reviews. We created a dataset with fine-grained COVID-19 aspect annotations, evaluated fully- and weakly-supervised techniques for COVID aspect detection, and showed that BERT-based classifiers outperform bag-of-words classifiers. We observed changes in restaurant reviews (e.g., increased discussions of hygiene practices and messages of solidarity), and showed that they correlate with critical COVID-19 statistics. We found a shift of ratings towards extreme values (1 and 5 stars) and shifts of user activity towards specific types of cuisines. Our insights could potentially be interesting for restaurant owners, customers, and public health officials.

In future work, we plan to expand the regional coverage of our analysis to reveal distinct patterns across cities. It would also be interesting to improve aspect-based sentiment analysis approaches (Pontiki et al., 2016) by considering the new aspects explored in this work.

Acknowledgments

We thank the anonymous reviewers for their constructive feedback. This material is based upon work supported by the National Science Foundation under Grant No. IIS-15-63785.

References

Laura Biester, Katie Matton, Janarthanan Rajendran, Emily Mower Provost, and Rada Mihalcea. 2020. Quantifying the effects of covid-19 on mental health support forums. In *Proceedings of the 1st Workshop on NLP for COVID-19 (Part 2) at EMNLP 2020*.

David M Blei, Andrew Y Ng, and Michael I Jordan. 2003. Latent dirichlet allocation. *Journal of Machine Learning Research*, 3(Jan):993–1022.

Emily Chen, Kristina Lerman, and Emilio Ferrara. 2020. Tracking social media discourse about the covid-19 pandemic: Development of a public coronavirus Twitter data set. *JMIR Public Health and Surveillance*, 6(2):e19273.

Jacob Devlin, Ming-Wei Chang, Kenton Lee, and Kristina Toutanova. 2019. Bert: Pre-training of deep bidirectional transformers for language understanding. In *NAACL-HLT (1)*.

Laura Di Renzo, Paola Gualtieri, Francesca Pivari, Laura Soldati, Alda Attinà, Giulia Cinelli, Claudia Leggeri, Giovanna Caparello, Luigi Barrea, Francesco Scerbo, et al. 2020. Eating habits and lifestyle changes during covid-19 lockdown: an Italian survey. *Journal of translational medicine*, 18:1–15.

Habiba H Drias and Yassine Drias. 2020. Mining Twitter data on covid-19 for sentiment analysis and frequent patterns discovery. *medRxiv*.

Maria Effenberger, Andreas Kronbichler, Jae Il Shin, Gert Mayer, Herbert Tilg, and Paul Perco. 2020. Association of the covid-19 pandemic with internet search volumes: a google trendsTM analysis. *International Journal of Infectious Diseases*, 95:192–197.

Bernal Jimenez Gutierrez, Jucheng Zeng, Dongdong Zhang, Ping Zhang, and Yu Su. 2020. Document classification for covid-19 literature. In *Proceedings of the 2020 Conference on Empirical Methods in Natural Language Processing: Findings*, pages 3715–3722.

Giannis Karamanolakis, Daniel Hsu, and Luis Gravano. 2019. Leveraging just a few keywords for fine-grained aspect detection through weakly supervised co-training. In *Proceedings of the 2019 Conference on Empirical Methods in Natural Language Processing and the 9th International Joint Conference on Natural Language Processing (EMNLP-IJCNLP)*, pages 4603–4613.

Bennett Kleinberg, Isabelle van der Vegt, and Maximilian Mozes. 2020. Measuring emotions in the covid-19 real world worry dataset. In *Proceedings of the 1st Workshop on NLP for COVID-19 at ACL 2020*.

Sirigireddy Dhana Laxmi, Rohit Agarwal, and Aman Sinha. 2020. DSC-IIT ISM at WNUT-2020 Task 2: Detection of covid-19 informative tweets using RoBERTa. In *Proceedings of the Sixth Workshop on Noisy User-generated Text (W-NUT 2020)*, pages 409–413.

Irene Li, Yixin Li, Tianxiao Li, Sergio Alvarez-Napagao, Dario Garcia-Gasulla, and Toyotaro Suzumura. 2020a. What are we depressed about when we talk about covid-19: Mental health analysis on tweets using natural language processing. In *International Conference on Innovative Techniques and Applications of Artificial Intelligence*, pages 358–370. Springer.

Xiaoya Li, Mingxin Zhou, Jiawei Wu, Arianna Yuan, Fei Wu, and Jiwei Li. 2020b. Analyzing covid-19 on online social media: Trends, sentiments and emotions. *arXiv preprint arXiv:2005.14464*.

Farah Naja and Rena Hamadeh. 2020. Nutrition amid the covid-19 pandemic: A multi-level framework for action. *European Journal of Clinical Nutrition*, 74(8):1117–1121.

László Nemes and Attila Kiss. 2020. Social media sentiment analysis based on covid-19. *Journal of Information and Telecommunication*, pages 1–15.

Dat Quoc Nguyen, Thanh Vu, Afshin Rahimi, Mai Hoang Dao, Long Doan, et al. 2020. Wnut-2020 task 2: Identification of informative covid-19 English tweets. In *Proceedings of the Sixth Workshop on Noisy User-generated Text (W-NUT 2020)*, pages 314–318.

Maria Pontiki, Dimitrios Galanis, Haris Papageorgiou, Ion Androutsopoulos, Suresh Manandhar, Mohammad Al-Smadi, Mahmoud Al-Ayyoub, Yanyan Zhao, Bing Qin, Orphée De Clercq, et al. 2016. Semeval-2016 task 5: Aspect based sentiment analysis. In *International Workshop on Semantic Evaluation*, pages 19–30.

Alessandro Rovetta and Akshaya Srikanth Bhagavathula. 2020. Global infodemiology of covid-19: analysis of Google web searches and Instagram hashtags. *Journal of medical Internet research*, 22(8):e20673.

Jim Samuel, GG Ali, Md Rahman, Ek Esawi, Yana Samuel, et al. 2020. Covid-19 public sentiment insights and machine learning for tweets classification. *Information*, 11(6):314.

Sean J Taylor and Benjamin Letham. 2018. Forecasting at scale. *The American Statistician*, 72(1):37–45.

Hoang Van, Ahmad Musa, Mihai Surdeanu, and Stephen Kobourov. 2020. The language of food during the pandemic: Hints about the dietary effects of covid-19. *arXiv preprint arXiv:2010.07466*.

Karin Verspoor, Kevin Bretonnel Cohen, Michael Conway, Berry de Bruijn, Mark Dredze, Rada Mihalcea, and Byron Wallace, editors. 2020. *Proceedings of the 1st Workshop on NLP for COVID-19 (Part 2) at*

EMNLP 2020. Association for Computational Linguistics, Online.

Lucy Lu Wang, Kyle Lo, Yoganand Chandrasekhar, Russell Reas, Jiangjiang Yang, Doug Burdick, Darrin Eide, Kathryn Funk, Yannis Katsis, Rodney Michael Kinney, et al. 2020. Cord-19: The covid-19 open research dataset. In *Proceedings of the 1st Workshop on NLP for COVID-19 at ACL 2020*.

A Appendix

Here, we provide detailed information on our dataset (Section A.1), topic modeling and aspect classification results (Section A.2), time series plots (Section A.3), correlation analysis results A.4, and time-series intervention analysis results (Section A.5).

A.1 Yelp Review Dataset

Table 6 shows more statistics for our dataset. Our COVID aspect annotations for the 600 Yelp reviews are available at the following link: `https://drive.google.com/drive/folders/1PwYGO68fDjpjRgKN6rry-P9ji57OIa-r`.

A.2 Topic Modeling and COVID Aspect Classification

Table 7 shows the 25 LDA topics obtained from all reviews posted after March 1, 2020. Table 8 reports detailed evaluation results for COVID aspect classification.

A.3 Time Series Plots

Star ratings: Figure 9 shows the number of star ratings across time for NYC and LA.

Cuisine types: Figure 10 shows the percentage of reviews in NYC (top) and (LA) over time for each selected group of cuisine types. Figure 11 shows the percentage of reviews over time for each individual business tag in our selected groups of cuisine types.

COVID-19 aspects: Figure 12 shows the percentage of reviews over time for each individual business tag in our selected groups of cuisine types.

A.4 Correlation Analysis

Tables 9 and 10 report correlation results between time series constructed from restaurant reviews and the number of new COVID-19 cases for NYC and LA, respectively. Tables 11 and 12 show correlation results between each individual business tag and the number of new COVID-19 cases for NYC and LA, respectively.

A.5 Time-series Intervention Analysis

Table 13 reports the percentage of outliers (according to Prophet's predictions) for time series constructed from the text and metadata of Yelp reviews. Figures 13-74 plot Prophet's forecasts for each individual time series.

	NYC	LA County
# Restaurants	55K	65K
# Users	344K	710K
# Reviews	1.0M	2.1M

Table 6: Statistics for our Yelp dataset collected during January 1, 2019 - December 31, 2020.

Topic Label	High Probability Words
Fast food	chicken, fries, burger, wings, sauce, fried, ordered, good, got, food
PPE and social distancing	covid, mask, masks, people, customers, staff, social, wearing, distancing, pandemic
Bakery	cake, chocolate, bakery, cookies, cakes, delicious, flavors, ve, sweet, best
Pizza and pie	pizza, slice, pie, best, good, crust, cheese, sauce, place, new
Service and Environment	great, place, food, staff, friendly, service, love, coffee, amazing, best
Mexican food	tacos, bagel, taco, bagels, mexican, good, chips, burrito, guacamole, delicious
Dinner meals	pasta, steak, good, ordered, sauce, delicious, dish, got, salad, dinner
Savory food	rice, pork, soup, noodles, chicken, thai, good, spicy, fried, beef
Sandwiches and salad	sandwich, cheese, bread, salad, good, egg, sandwiches, bowl, bacon, meat
Ice cream	cream, ice, ordered, like, cold, dessert, tasted, got, came, didn
Sushi	sushi, fish, roll, ordered, shrimp, fresh, good, salmon, rolls, food
Ordering	like, just, don, know, didn, place, people, want, said, order
Delivery service	order, delivery, food, ordered, time, ordering, pick, delicious, great, ve
Brunch	brunch, good, chocolate, eggs, toast, got, really, french, sweet, pancakes
Food quality	food, place, good, love, try, amazing, best, restaurant, really, delicious
Outdoor seating	outdoor, seating, dining, ramen, good, tables, covid, outside, really, place
Business	food, store, don, place, time, ve, years, money, just, business
Milk tea and boba	tea, milk, drink, sugar, drinks, sweet, like, bubble, boba, matcha
Indian and Korean cuisine	food, dishes, restaurant, like, dish, menu, meal, indian, korean, ve
Food and service quality	great, food, service, amazing, place, delicious, definitely, recommend, drinks, restaurant
Service wait time	food, table, came, minutes, wait, time, service, got, drinks, order
Food quality and price	food, good, prices, price, place, great, service, quality, pretty, nice
Service	order, said, told, service, asked, called, customer, manager, restaurant, food
Bars	free, promoter, door, issues, text, entry, drinks, table, vip, nyc
Bars	bar, wine, beer, card, like, bartender, night, drink, credit, place

Table 7: 25 LDA topics with manually assigned topic labels and the 10 highest probability words for each topic.

	Binary			Multi-Class		
Method	**Accuracy**	**Precision**	**Recall**	**Accuracy**	**Precision**	**Recall**
Random	0.467	0.459	0.459	0.132	0.118	0.112
Majority	0.533	0.267	0.500	0.373	0.048	0.129
Methods below are fully supervised						
BoW-LogReg	0.742	0.741	0.742	0.622	0.501	0.462
BoW-SVM	0.737	0.737	0.740	0.605	0.486	0.419
BERT	0.787	0.785	0.786	0.652	0.542	0.503
Methods below are weakly supervised						
Teacher	0.560	0.610	0.600	0.360	0.334	0.268
Student-LogReg	0.545	0.636	0.511	0.393	0.320	0.389
Student-SVM	0.538	0.568	0.506	0.397	0.321	0.396
Student-BERT	0.603	0.767	0.574	0.472	0.383	0.434

Table 8: Results for binary (left) and multi-class (right) COVID-19 aspect classification.

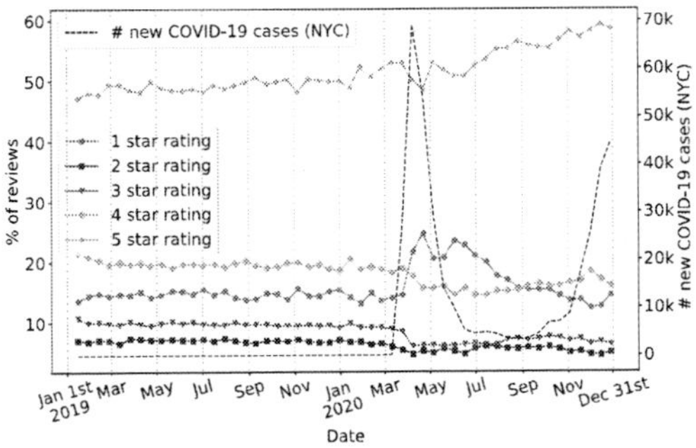

(a) New York City.

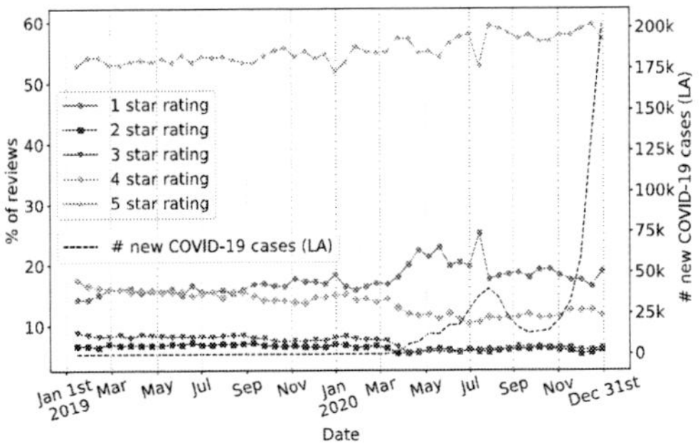

(b) Los Angeles County.

Figure 9: Percentage of reviews for each individual star rating in NYC (top) and LA (bottom) over January 1, 2019 - December 31, 2020.

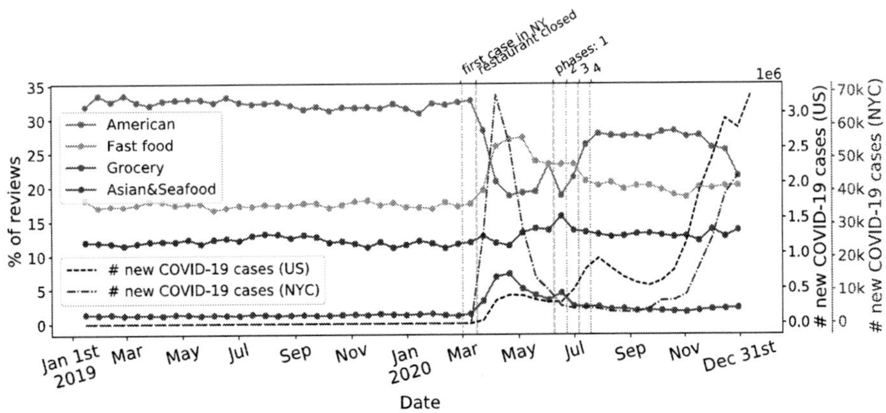

(a) NYC.

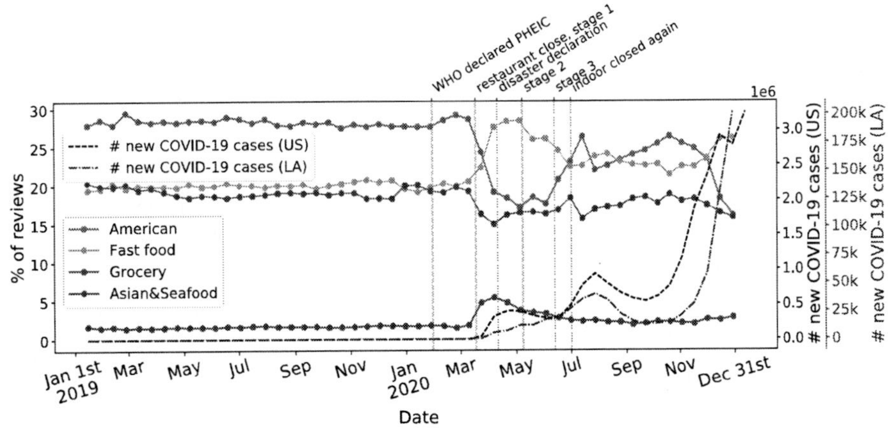

(b) LA.

Figure 10: Evolution of cuisine types over time for NYC (top) and LA (bottom).

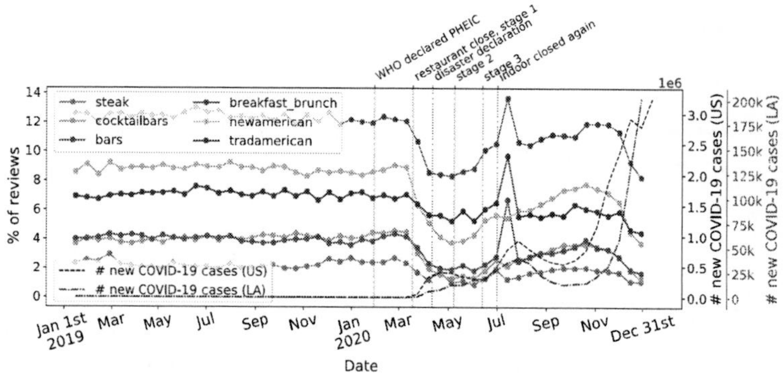

(a) American.

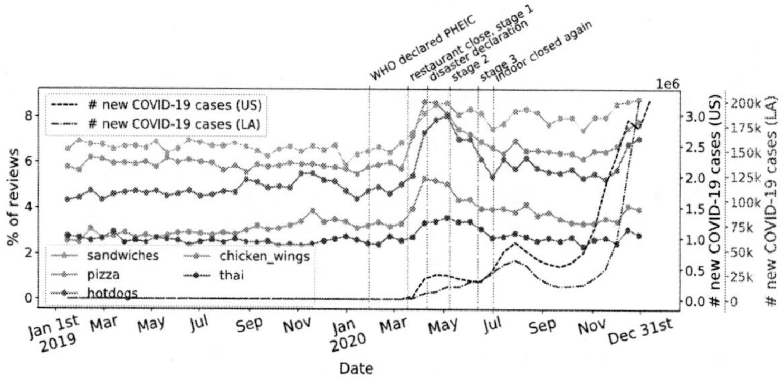

(b) Fast food.

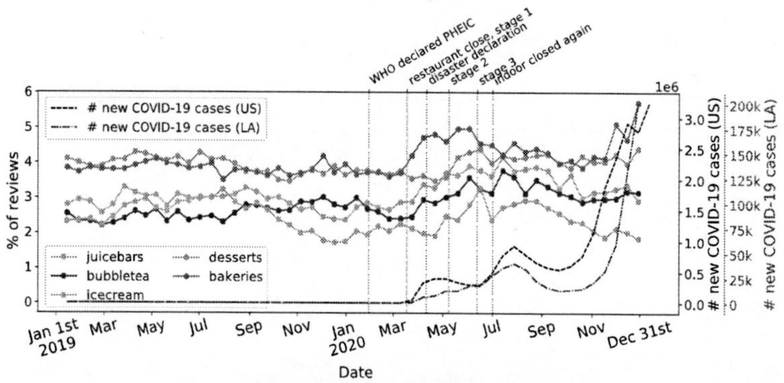

(c) Beverages & Desserts.

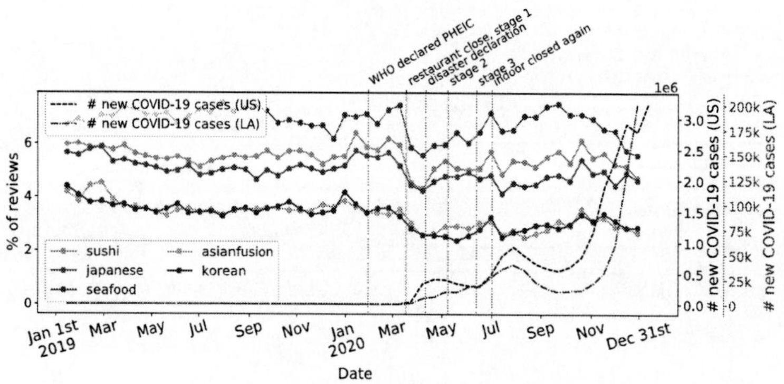

(d) Asian & Seafood.

Figure 11: Time-series of individual tags for each group of cuisine types defined in the main paper.

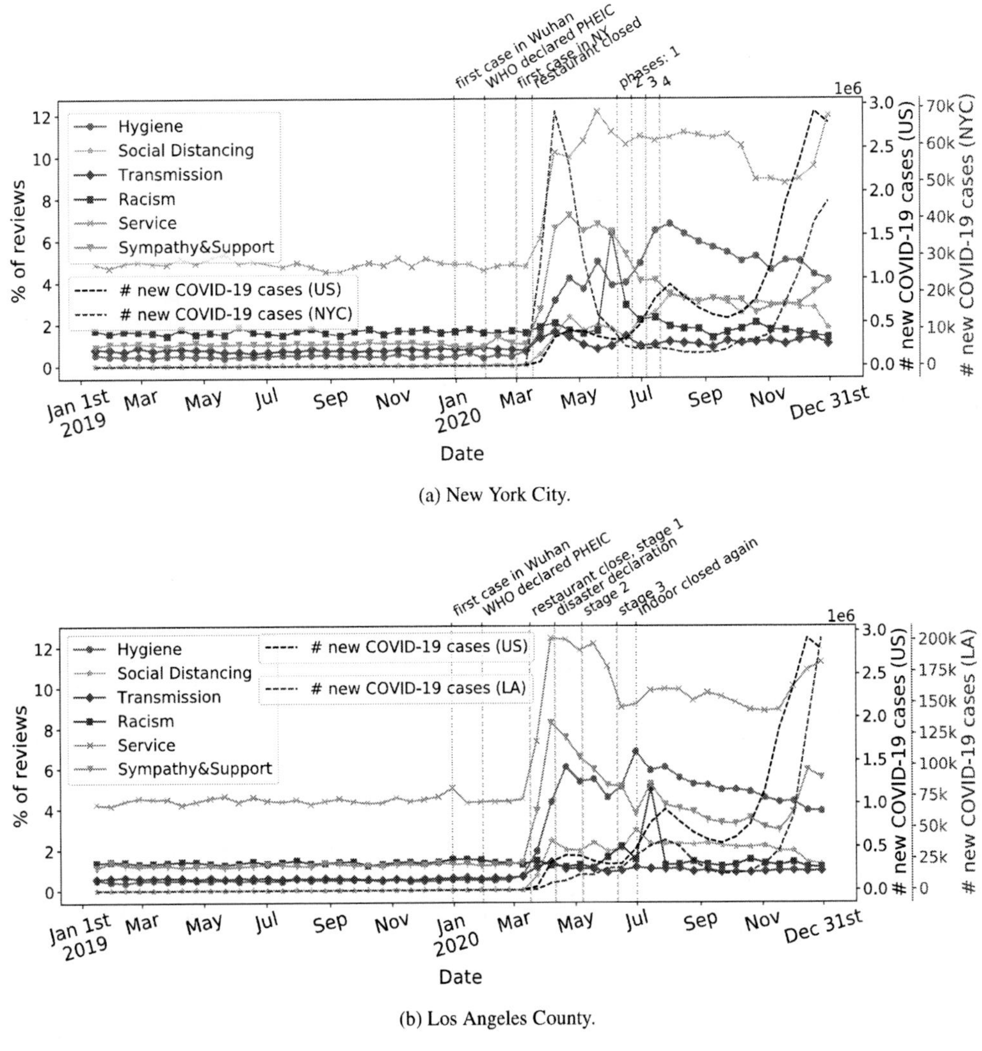

(a) New York City.

(b) Los Angeles County.

Figure 12: COVID aspects for New York City restaurants (top) and Los Angeles County restaurants (top) over January 1, 2019 - December 31, 2020.

Time Series	NYC Cases	US Cases
Results below are Pearson correlations.		
Hygiene	0.412***	0.612***
Transmission Case	0.708***	0.532***
Social Distancing	0.427***	0.650***
Racism	0.036	-0.025
Sympathy & Support	0.683***	0.407***
Service	0.566***	0.630***
Other	0.590***	0.652***
1 star rating	0.337**	-0.088
2 star rating	-0.724***	-0.712***
3 star rating	-0.624***	-0.619***
4 star rating	-0.384***	-0.476***
5 star rating	0.411***	0.813***
American	-0.731***	-0.541***
Fast Food	0.698***	0.341**
Grocery	0.713***	0.159
Beverages & Desserts	0.221	0.426***
Asian & Seafood	-0.594***	-0.083
Results below are Spearman correlations.		
Hygiene	0.765***	0.822***
Transmission Case	0.816***	0.804***
Social Distancing	0.768***	0.836***
Racism	0.293**	0.237*
Sympathy & Support	0.822***	0.755***
Service	0.772***	0.736***
Other	0.827***	0.808***
1 star rating	0.242***	0.118
2 star rating	-0.882***	-0.859***
3 star rating	-0.855***	-0.833***
4 star rating	-0.770***	-0.825***
5 star rating	0.705***	0.862***
American	-0.830***	-0.750***
Fast Food	0.832***	0.745***
Grocery	0.850***	0.751***
Beverages & Desserts	0.545***	0.524***
Asian & Seafood	-0.463***	-0.238*

Table 9: Correlation results from comparing NYC review statistics and the number of COVID cases in NYC (left) and US (right), sorted in decreasing order by correlation compared with the number of new US cases. Results marked as statistically significant at the p<0.1*, p<0.05**, and p<0.01*** levels.

Time Series	LA Cases	US Cases
Results below are Pearson correlations.		
Hygiene	0.395***	0.538***
Transmission Case	0.409***	0.522***
Social Distancing	0.347**	0.513***
Racism	-0.006	-0.019
Sympathy & Support	0.490***	0.551***
Service	0.536***	0.644***
Other	0.527***	0.671***
1 star rating	0.244*	0.289**
2 star rating	-0.416***	-0.571***
3 star rating	-0.429***	-0.559***
4 star rating	-0.402***	-0.513***
5 star rating	0.445***	0.608***
American	-0.654***	-0.656***
Fast Food	0.529***	0.577***
Grocery	0.214	0.251*
Beverages & Desserts	0.504***	0.524***
Asian & Seafood	-0.514***	-0.542***
Results below are Spearman correlations.		
Hygiene	0.814***	0.808***
Transmission Case	0.810***	0.779***
Social Distancing	0.773***	0.767***
Racism	-0.235*	-0.291**
Sympathy & Support	0.817***	0.788***
Service	0.812***	0.771***
Other	0.836***	0.811***
1 star rating	0.724***	0.705***
2 star rating	-0.831***	-0.839***
3 star rating	-0.811***	-0.798***
4 star rating	-0.818***	-0.822***
5 star rating	0.730***	0.762***
American	-0.804***	-0.753***
Fast Food	0.822***	0.785***
Grocery	0.801***	0.784***
Beverages & Desserts	0.725***	0.607***
Asian & Seafood	-0.760***	-0.701***

Table 10: Correlation results from comparing LA review statistics and the number of COVID cases in NYC (left) and US (right), sorted in decreasing order by correlation compared with the number of new US cases. Results marked as statistically significant at the p<0.1*, p<0.05**, and p<0.01*** levels.

Time Series	NYC Cases	US Cases
Results below are Pearson correlations.		
Bakeries	0.684***	0.710***
Thai	0.445***	0.616***
Sandwiches	0.636***	0.466***
Sushi	-0.080	0.450***
Bubble tea	-0.142	0.277**
Grocery	0.713***	0.159***
Pizza	0.698***	0.156
Chicken Wings	0.596***	0.156
Hotdogs	0.518***	0.113
Korean	0.007	0.065
Juice Bars	0.001	0.051
Japanese	-0.427***	0.048
Desserts	-0.164	0.026
Ice Cream	-0.250*	-0.210
Cocktail Bars	-0.635***	-0.229
Asian Fusion	-0.534***	-0.340**
Steak	-0.495***	-0.347**
Seafood	-0.744***	-0.381***
Breakfast & Brunch	-0.667***	-0.469***
New American	-0.614***	-0.528***
Bars	-0.698***	-0.592***
Trad American	-0.639***	-0.658***
Results below are Spearman correlations.		
Thai	0.718***	0.790***
Bakeries	0.864***	0.785***
Grocery	0.850***	0.751***
Chicken Wings	0.798***	0.691***
Pizza	0.761***	0.658***
Hotdogs	0.571***	0.402***
Bubble tea	0.153	0.287**
Sushi	0.029	0.185
Juice Bars	0.203	0.127
Ice Cream	-0.112	-0.114
Seafood	-0.374***	-0.143
Desserts	-0.087	-0.145
Cocktail Bars	-0.438***	-0.179
Korean	-0.290**	-0.252*
Japanese	-0.394***	-0.290**
Asian Fusion	-0.678***	-0.566***
Steak	-0.739***	-0.614***
Bars	-0.778***	-0.730***
New American	-0.816***	-0.732***
Sandwiches	0.844***	-0.736***
Breakfast & Brunch	-0.842***	-0.811***
Trad American	-0.851***	-0.832***

Table 11: Correlation results for individual business tags in NYC. Results marked as statistically significant at the p<0.1*, p<0.05**, and p<0.01*** levels.

Time Series	LA Cases	US Cases
Results below are Pearson correlations.		
Sandwiches	0.644***	0.747***
Bakeries	0.702***	0.704***
Pizza	0.536***	0.557***
Hotdogs	0.500***	0.523***
Bubble tea	0.465***	0.519***
Desserts	0.414***	0.394***
Chicken Wings	0.340*****	0.381***
Sushi	-0.390***	0.357***
Juice Bars	0.202	0.292**
Grocery	0.214***	0.251*
Thai	0.221***	0.225***
Ice Cream	-0.250*	-0.298**
Japanese	-0.309**	-0.378***
Korean	-0.362***	-0.423***
Bars	-0.451***	-0.456***
Breakfast & Brunch	-0.512***	-0.489***
Asian Fusion	-0.432***	-0.506***
Trad American	-0.485***	-0.535***
Seafood	-0.574***	-0.543***
Steak	-0.590***	-0.605***
Cocktail Bars	-0.620***	-0.612***
New American	-0.632***	-0.643***
Results below are Spearman correlations.		
Sandwiches	0.859***	0.807***
Grocery	0.801***	0.784***
Hotdogs	0.799***	0.766***
Pizza	0.779***	0.753***
Chicken Wings	0.743***	0.734***
Bubble tea	0.772***	0.714***
Bakeries	0.795***	0.714***
Juice Bars	0.685***	0.605***
Thai	0.513***	0.454***
Desserts	0.374***	0.267
Ice Cream	-0.118	-0.232*
Seafood	-0.424***	-0.383***
Sushi	-0.522***	-0.427***
Japanese	-0.680***	-0.602***
Bars	-0.699***	-0.645***
Breakfast & Brunch	-0.711***	-0.705***
Cocktail Bars	-0.803***	-0.706***
Steak	-0.793***	-0.708***
Korean	-0.794***	-0.763***
Trad American	-0.746***	-0.765***
New American	-0.810***	-0.767***
Asian Fusion	-0.801***	-0.816***

Table 12: Correlation results for individual business tags in LA. Results marked as statistically significant at the p<0.1*, p<0.05**, and p<0.01*** levels.

Time Series	% of outliers	
	LA	**NYC**
1 star rating	62.28 ↑	69.55 ↑
2 star rating	55.36 ↓	91.35 ↓
3 star rating	83.04 ↓	47.75 ↓
4 star rating	61.94 ↓	61.24 ↓
5 star rating	88.24 ↑	50.17 ↑
Fast food	95.85 ↑	96.88 ↑
Beverages&Desserts	51.56 ↑	83.04 ↑
Grocery	96.54 ↑	82.35 ↑
Asian&Seafood	52.94 ↓	87.89 ↓
American	76.47 ↓	92.73 ↓
Grocery	82.35 ↑	96.54↑
Chicken Wings	64.36↑	92.73↑
Sandwiches	95.50↑	75.78 ↑
Thai	69.20 ↑	68.86↑
Bakeries	47.06 ↑	66.78 ↑
Hotdogs	77.85↑	65.05↑
Pizza	89.96↑	56.75↑
Ice Cream	71.28↑	56.40 ↑
Seafood	77.51 ↓	53.28 ↑
Korean	56.40 ↓	32.87↑
Juice Bars	76.12 ↑	50.52 ↓
Desserts	80.62↑	51.90↓
Breakfast&Brunch	81.31↓	53.98 ↓
Sushi	41.52 ↓	55.01 ↓
Bubble tea	56.06 ↑	54.67 ↓
Steak	84.78↓	58.48↓
Cocktail Bars	99.31 ↓	58.82↓
Trad American	93.08 ↓	58.82↓
Bars	69.90 ↓	59.86↓
Japanese	40.83 ↓	61.24 ↓
Asian Fusion	41.87 ↓	76.47↓
New American	89.62 ↓	91.70↓

Table 13: Percentage of outliers (observations outside Prophet's 95% uncertainty interval) for LA and NYC reviews posted after March 1, 2020. Arrows indicate whether the mean value of the outliers is higher (up) or lower (down) than the mean of Prophet's predictions.

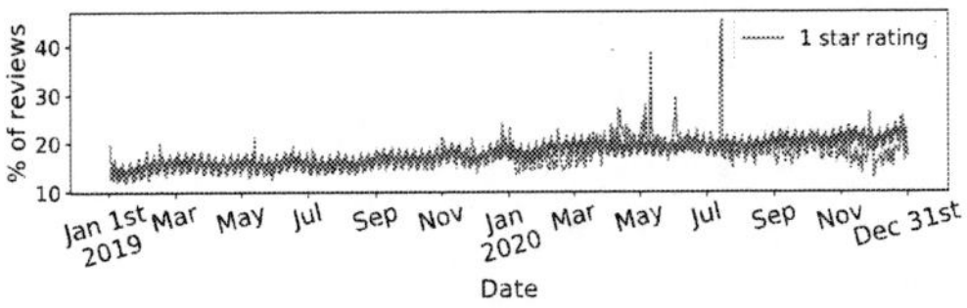

Figure 13: Prophet forecast for 1 star rating (LA)

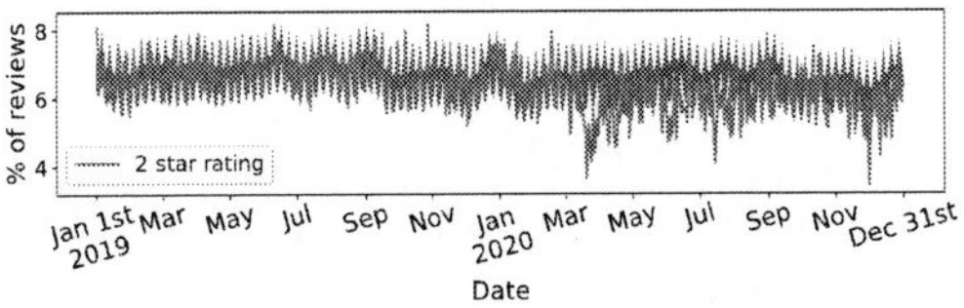

Figure 14: Prophet forecast for 2 star rating (LA)

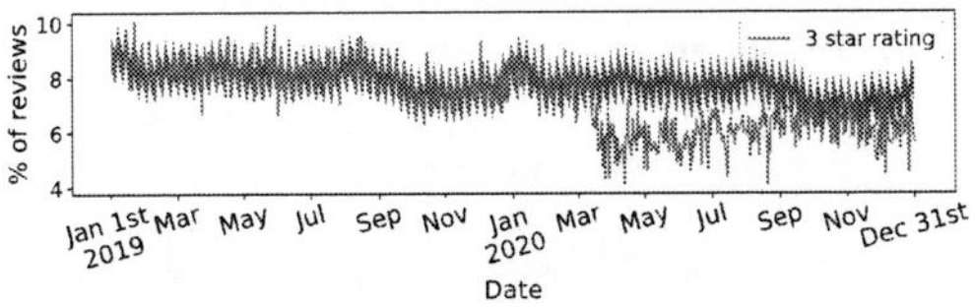

Figure 15: Prophet forecast for 3 star rating (LA)

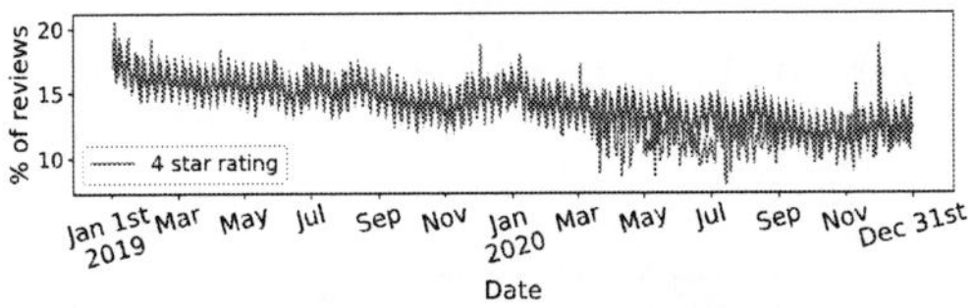

Figure 16: Prophet forecast for 4 star rating (LA)

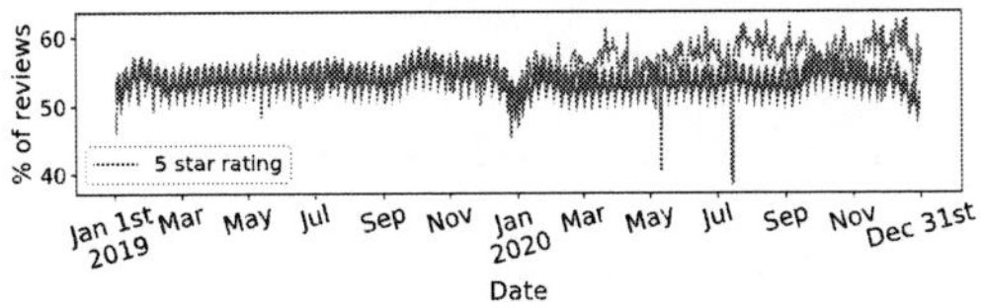

Figure 17: Prophet forecast for 5 star rating (LA)

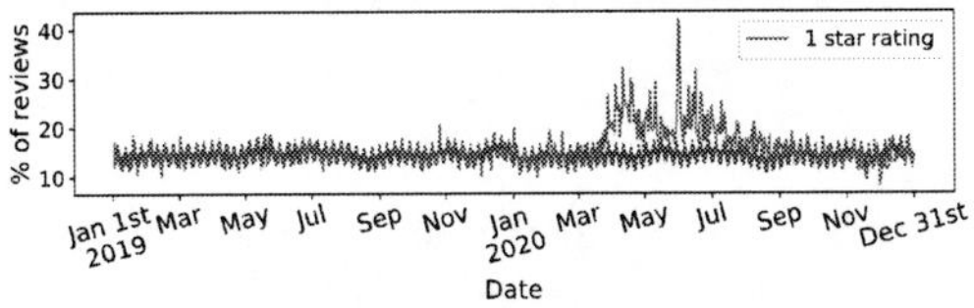

Figure 18: Prophet forecast for 1 star rating (NYC)

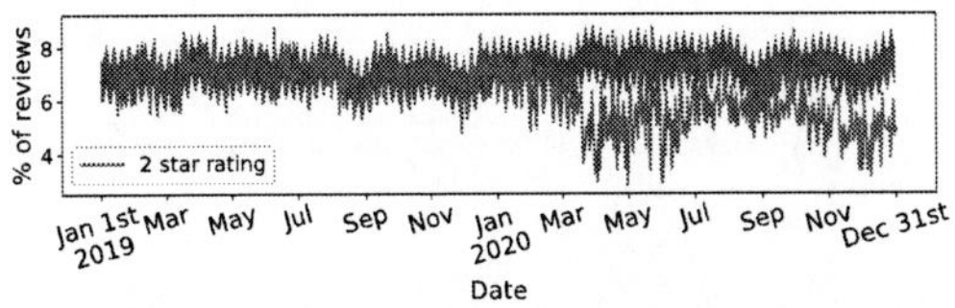

Figure 19: Prophet forecast for 2 star rating (NYC)

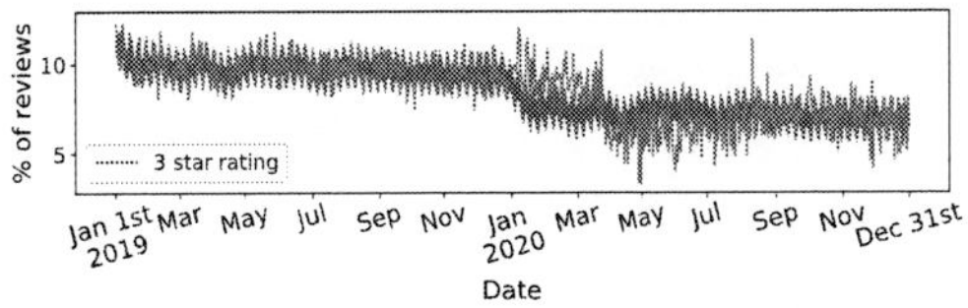

Figure 20: Prophet forecast for 3 star rating (NYC)

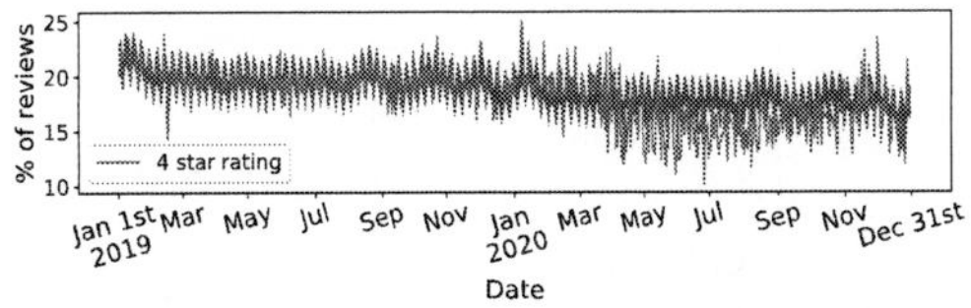

Figure 21: Prophet forecast for 4 star rating (NYC)

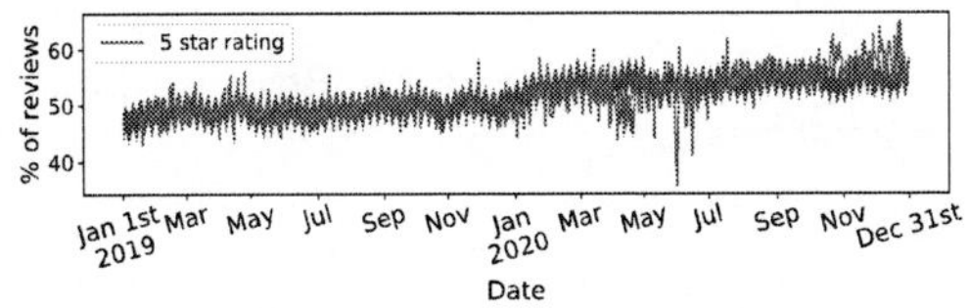

Figure 22: Prophet forecast for 5 star rating (NYC)

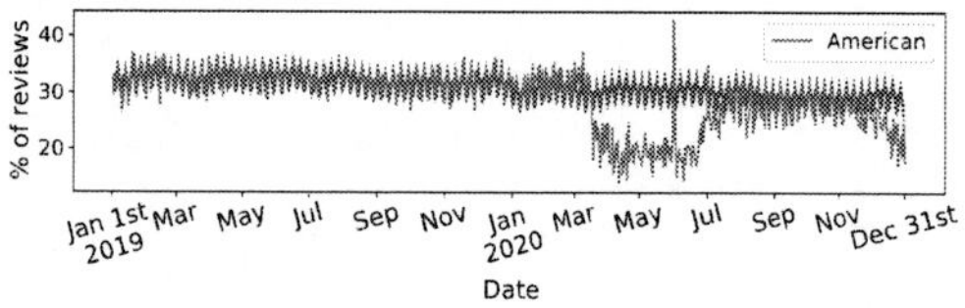

Figure 23: Prophet forecast for "American" group of business tags (LA)

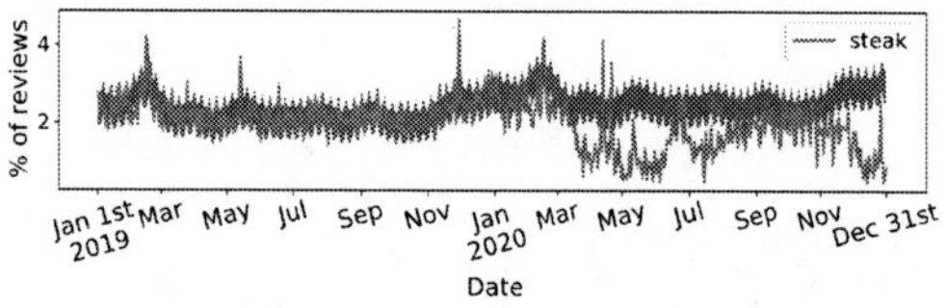

Figure 24: Prophet forecast for "Steak" business tag (LA)

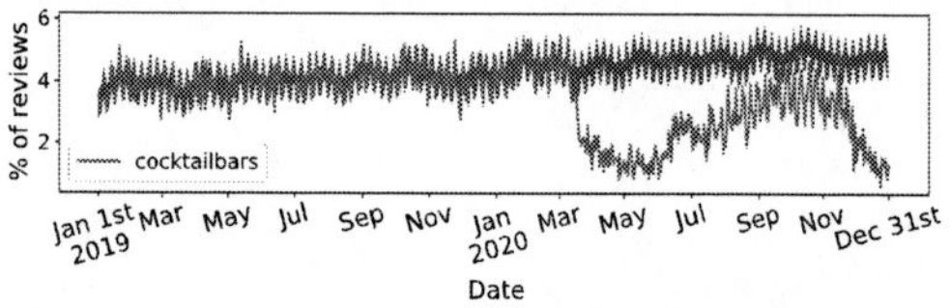

Figure 25: Prophet forecast for "Cocktail Bars" business tag (LA)

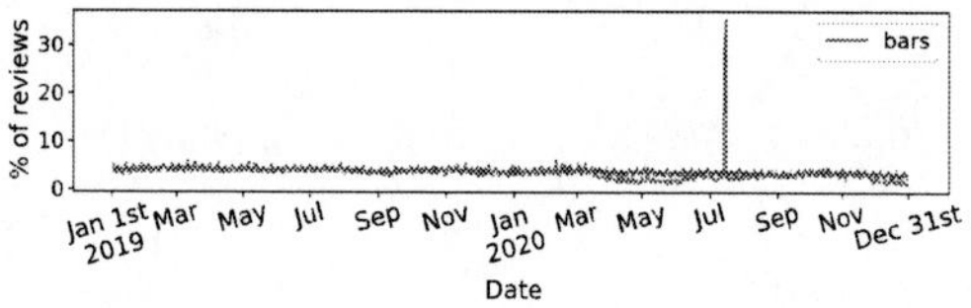

Figure 26: Prophet forecast for "Bars" business tag (LA)

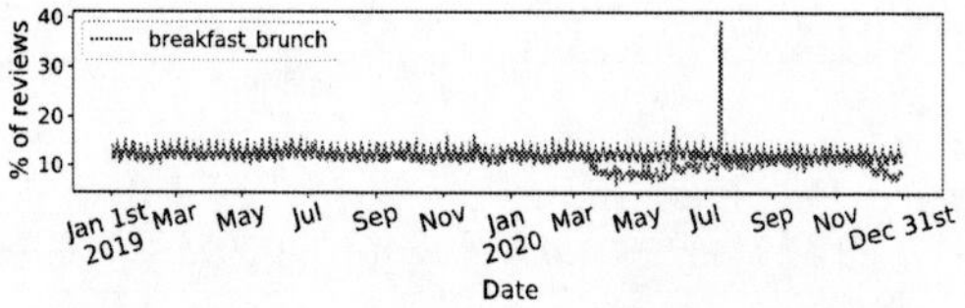

Figure 27: Prophet forecast for "Breakfast&Brunch" business tag (LA)

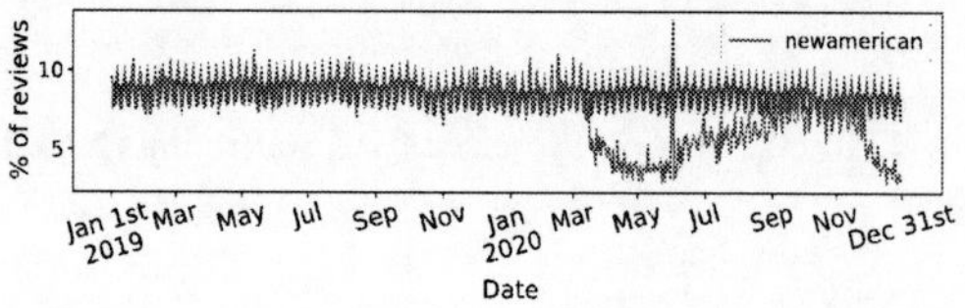

Figure 28: Prophet forecast for "New American" business tag (LA)

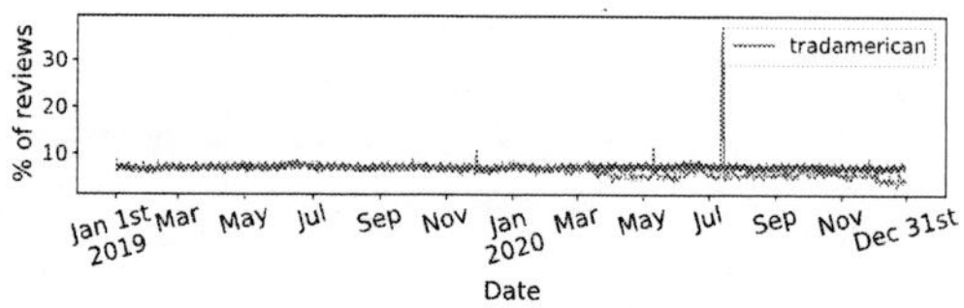

Figure 29: Prophet forecast for "Traditional American" business tag (LA)

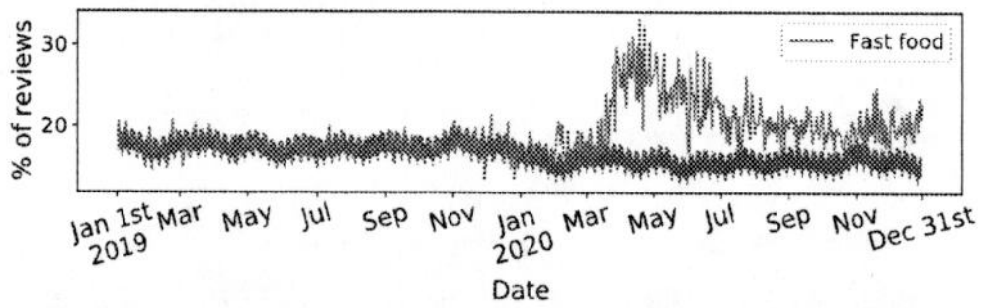

Figure 30: Prophet forecast for "Fast Food" group of business tags (LA)

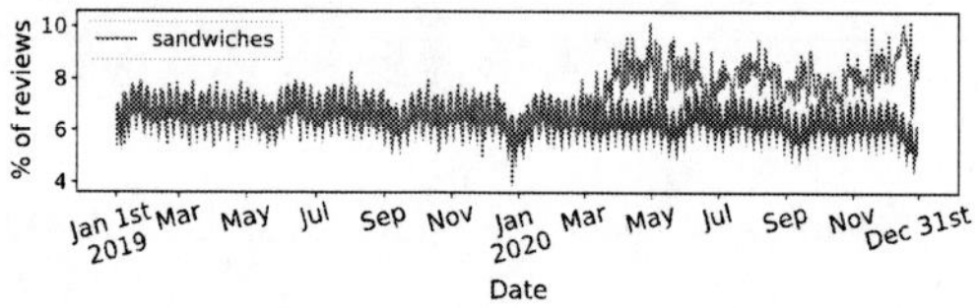

Figure 31: Prophet forecast for "Sandwich" business tag (LA)

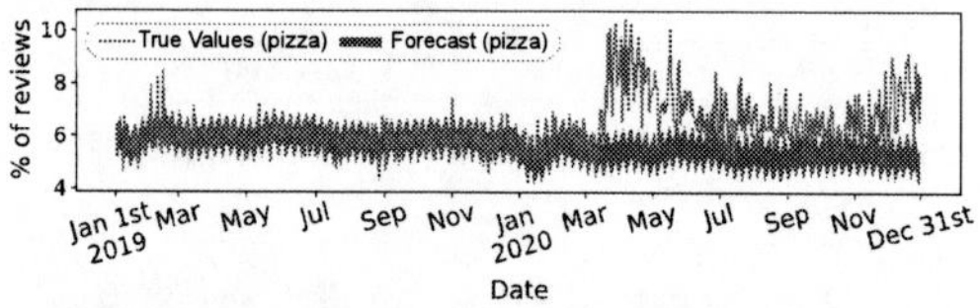

Figure 32: Prophet forecast for "Pizza" business tag (LA)

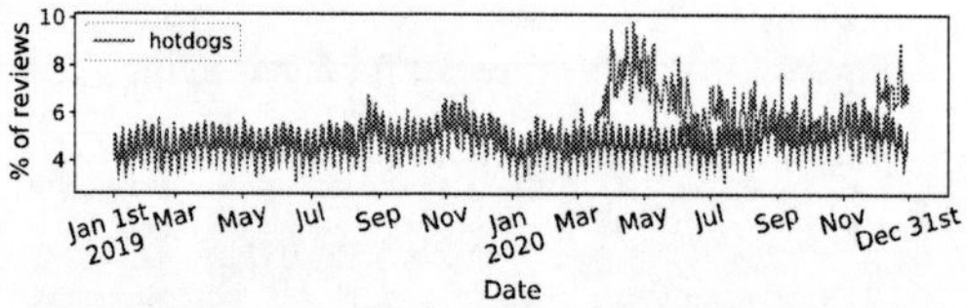

Figure 33: Prophet forecast for "Hot Dog" business tag (LA)

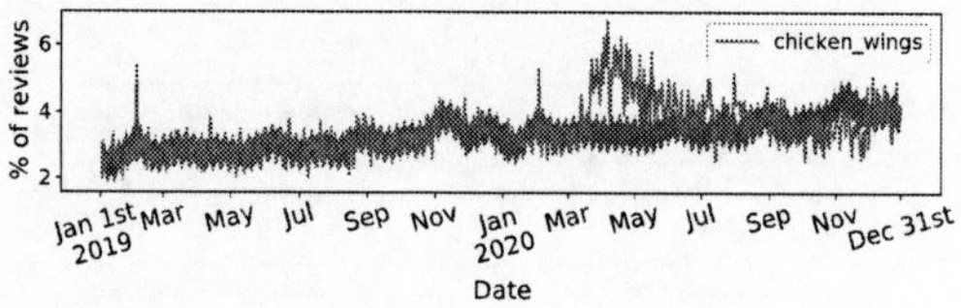

Figure 34: Prophet forecast for "Chicken Wings" business tag (LA)

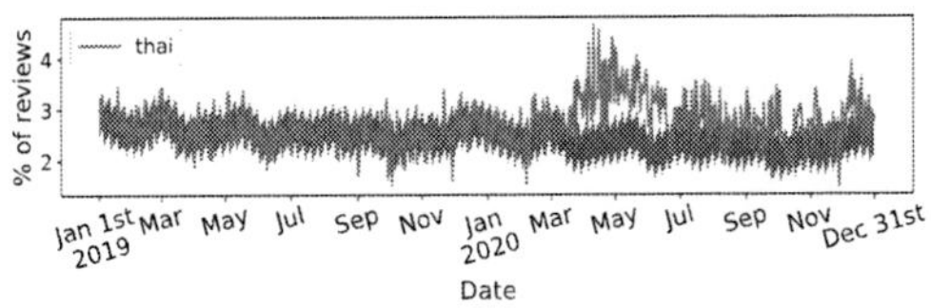

Figure 35: Prophet forecast for "Thai" business tag (LA)

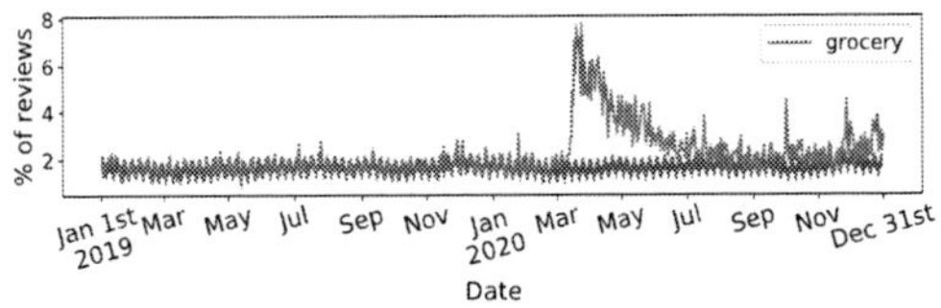

Figure 36: Prophet forecast for "Grocery" business tag (LA)

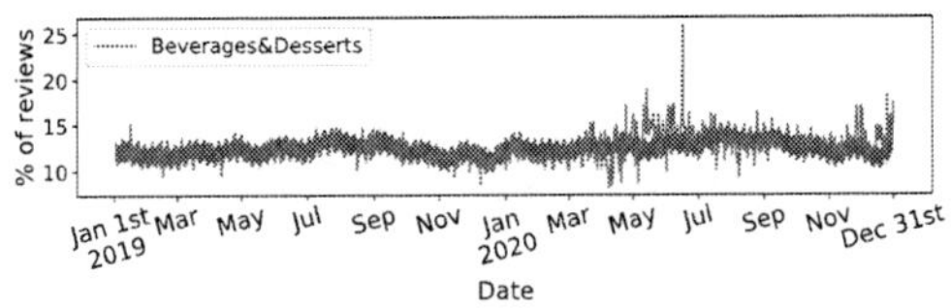

Figure 37: Prophet forecast for "Beverages&Desserts" group of business tags (LA)

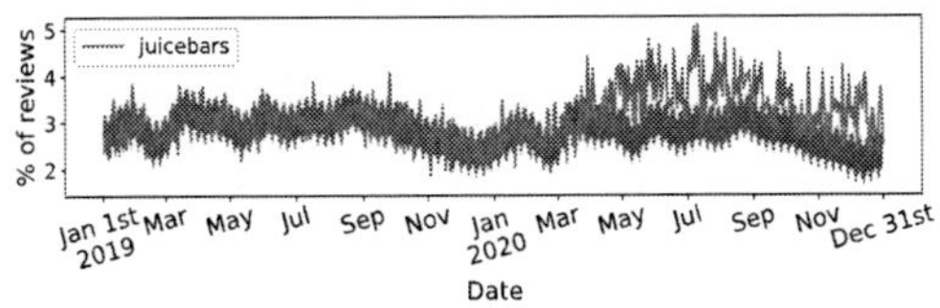

Figure 38: Prophet forecast for "Juice Bars" business tag (LA)

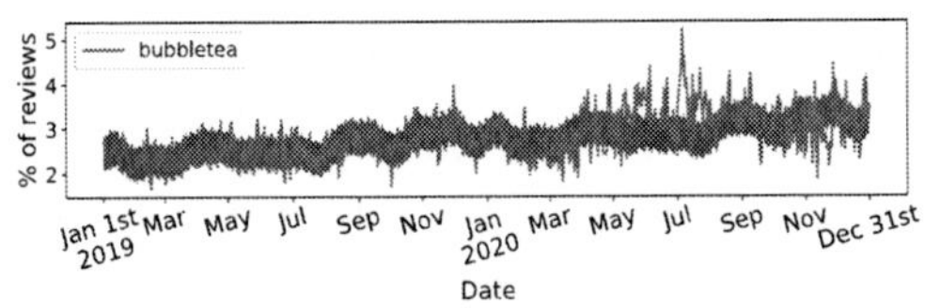

Figure 39: Prophet forecast for “Bubble Tea” business tag (LA)

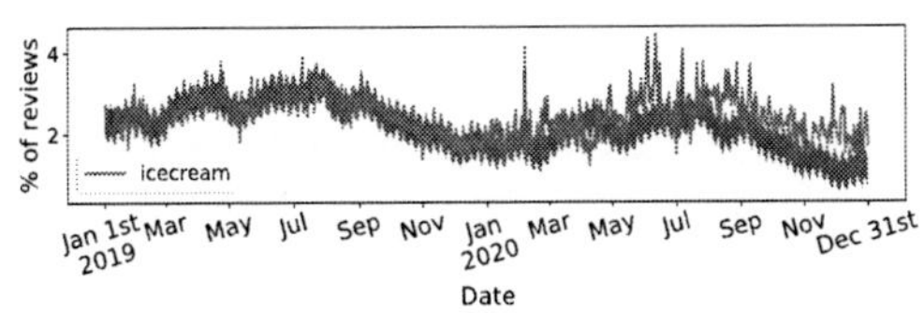

Figure 40: Prophet forecast for “Ice Cream” business tag (LA)

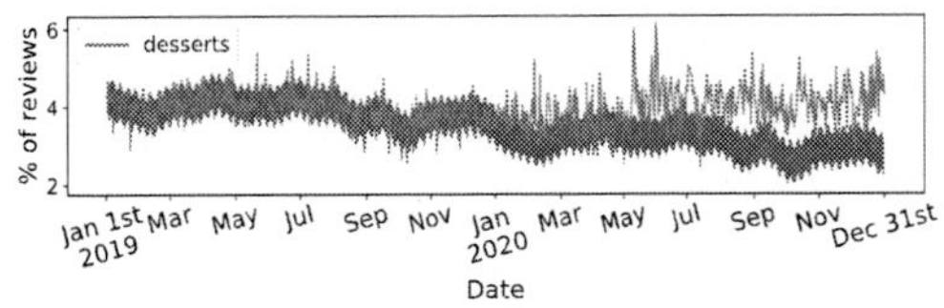

Figure 41: Prophet forecast for “Desserts” business tag (LA)

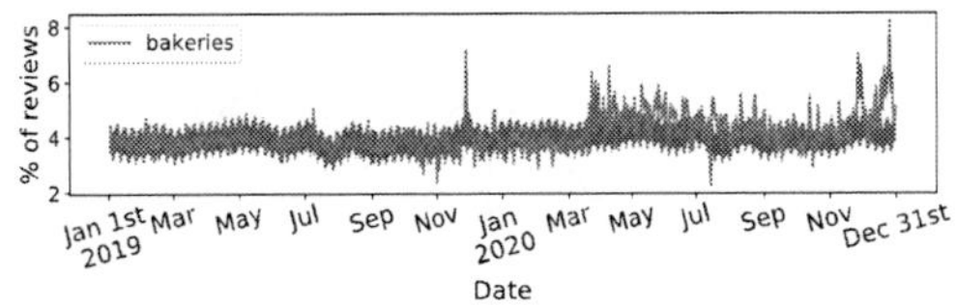

Figure 42: Prophet forecast for “Bakeries” business tag(LA)

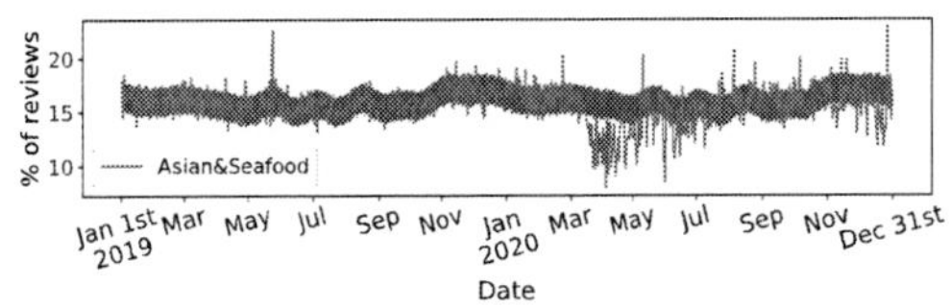

Figure 43: Prophet forecast for “Asian&Seafood” group of business tags (LA)

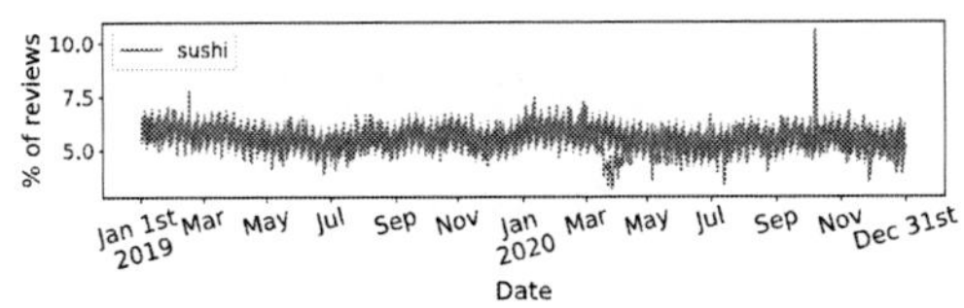

Figure 44: Prophet forecast for "Sushi" business tag (LA)

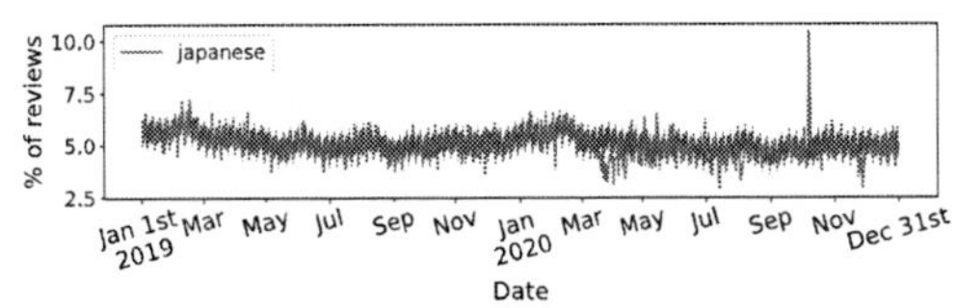

Figure 45: Prophet forecast for "Japanese" business tag (LA)

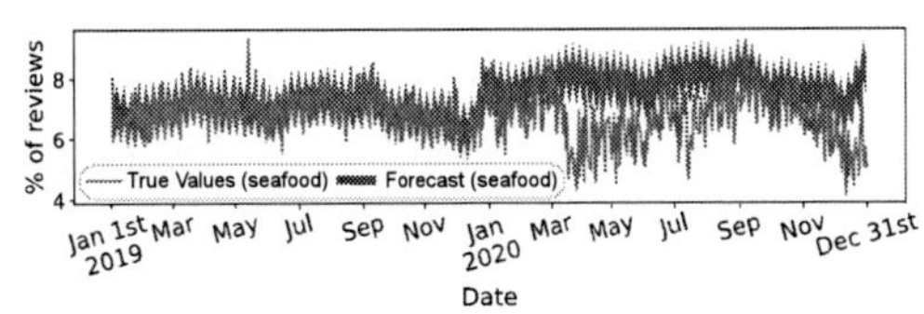

Figure 46: Prophet forecast for "Seafood" business tag (LA)

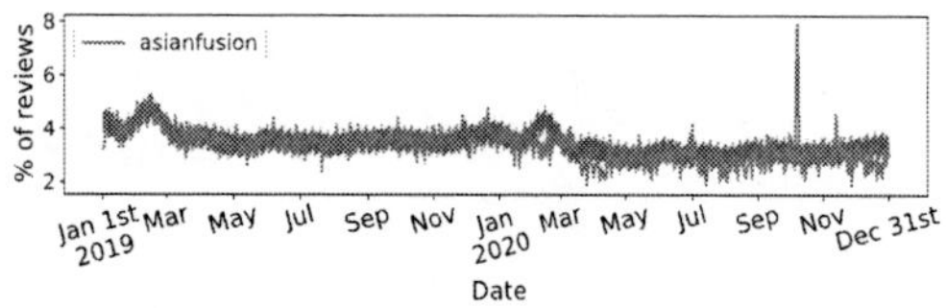

Figure 47: Prophet forecast for "Asian Fusion" business tag (LA)

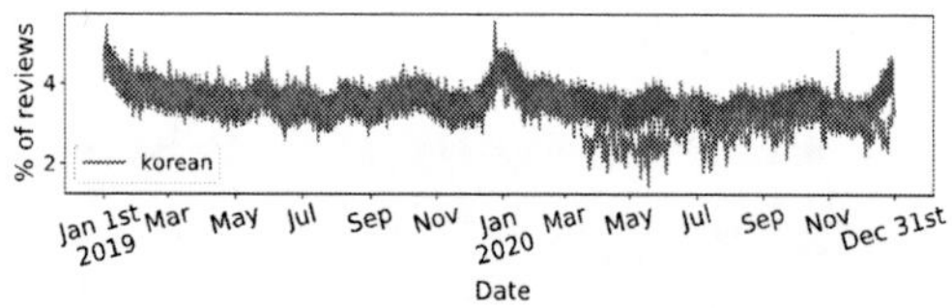

Figure 48: Prophet forecast for "Korean" business tag (LA)

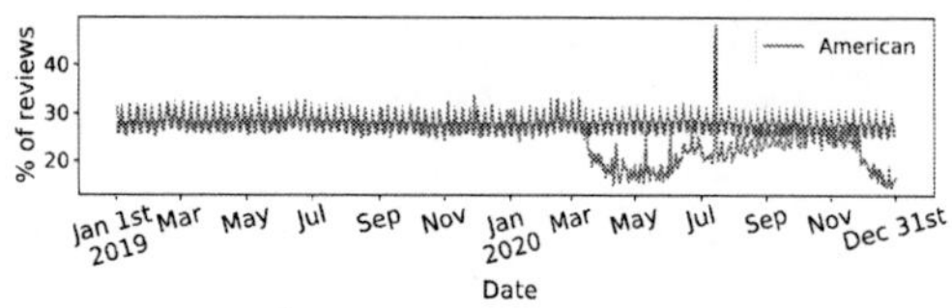

Figure 49: Prophet forecast for "American" group of business tags (NYC)

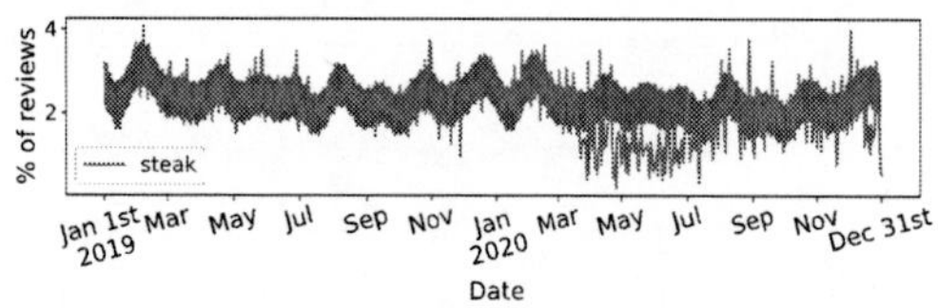

Figure 50: Prophet forecast for "Steak" business tag (NYC)

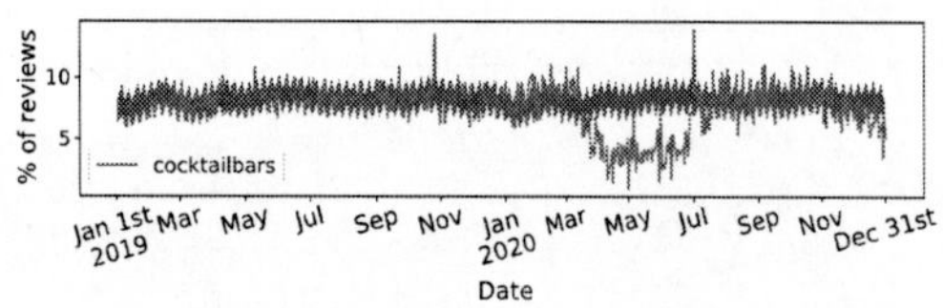

Figure 51: Prophet forecast for "Cocktail Bars" business tag (NYC)

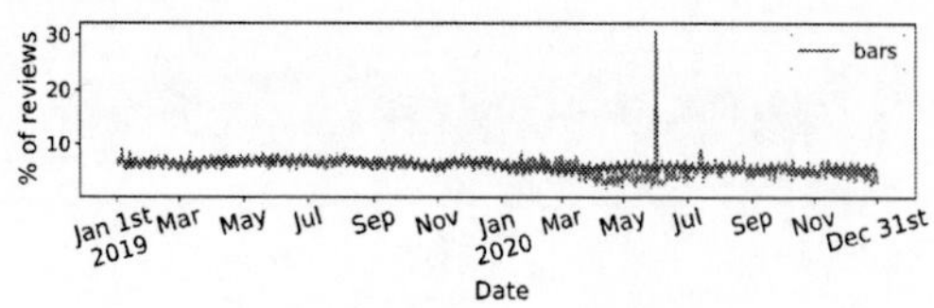

Figure 52: Prophet forecast for "Bars" business tag (NYC)

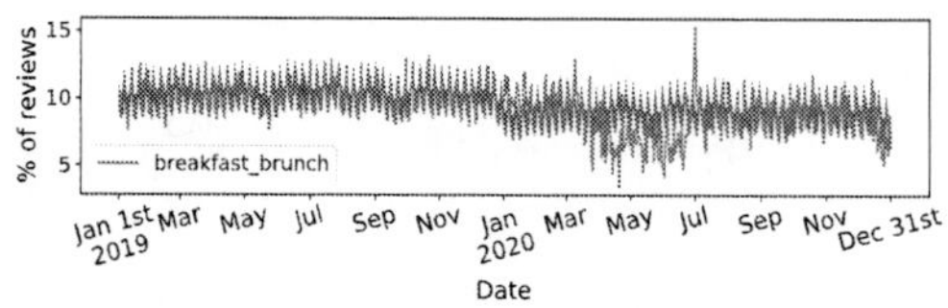

Figure 53: Prophet forecast for "Breakfast&Brunch" business tag (NYC)

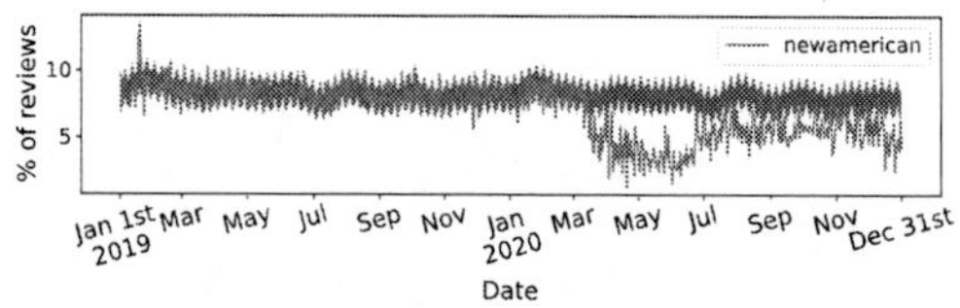

Figure 54: Prophet forecast for "New American" business tag (NYC)

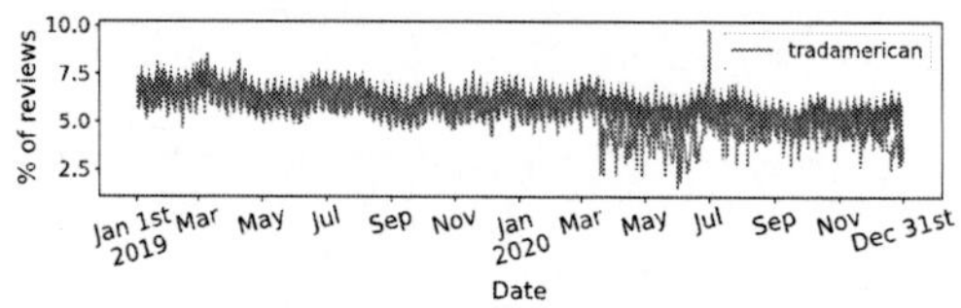

Figure 55: Prophet forecast for "Traditional American" business tag (NYC)

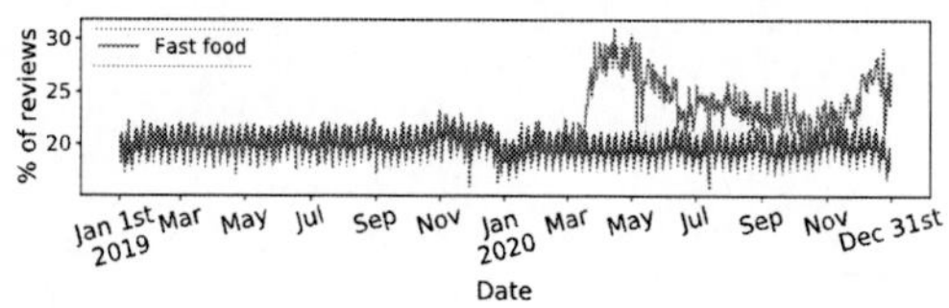

Figure 56: Prophet forecast for "Fast food" group of business tags (NYC)

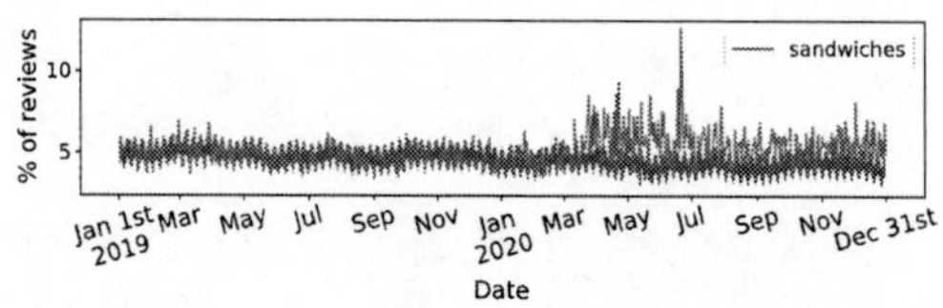

Figure 57: Prophet forecast for "Sandwich" business tag (NYC)

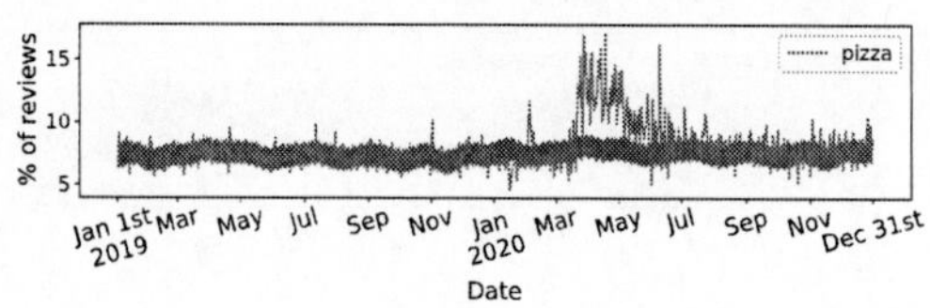

Figure 58: Prophet forecast for "Pizza" business tag (NYC)

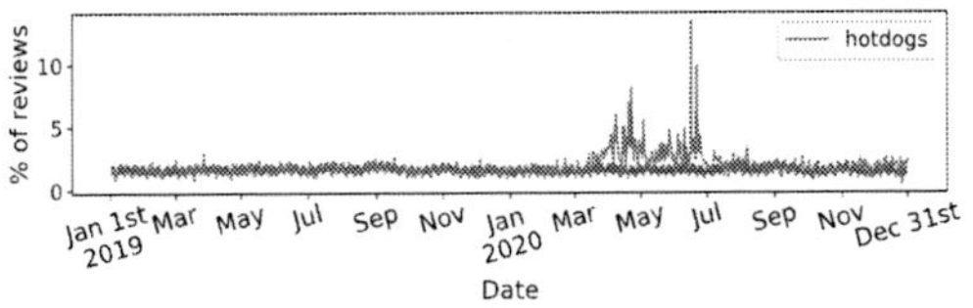

Figure 59: Prophet forecast for "Hot Dog" business tag (NYC)

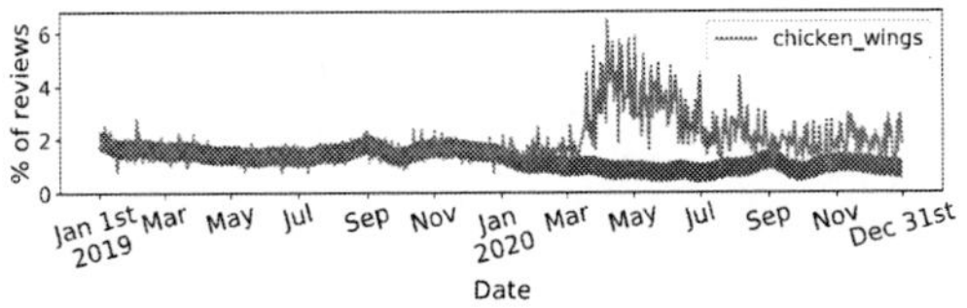

Figure 60: Prophet forecast for "Chicken Wings" business tag (NYC)

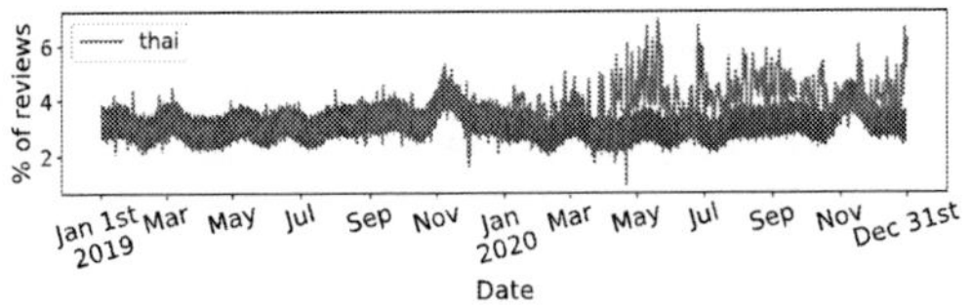

Figure 61: Prophet forecast for "Thai" business tag (NYC)

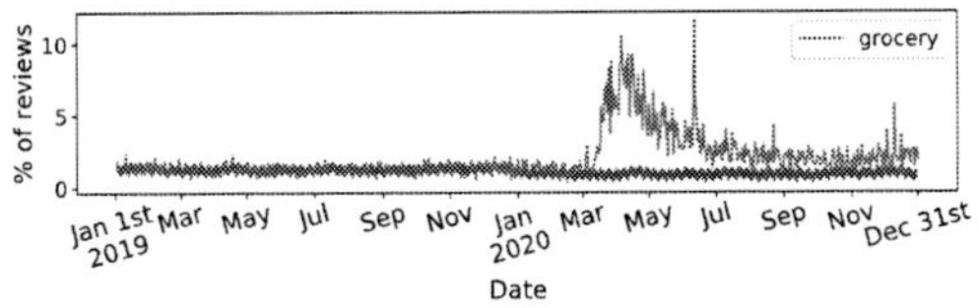

Figure 62: Prophet forecast for "Grocery" business tag (NYC)

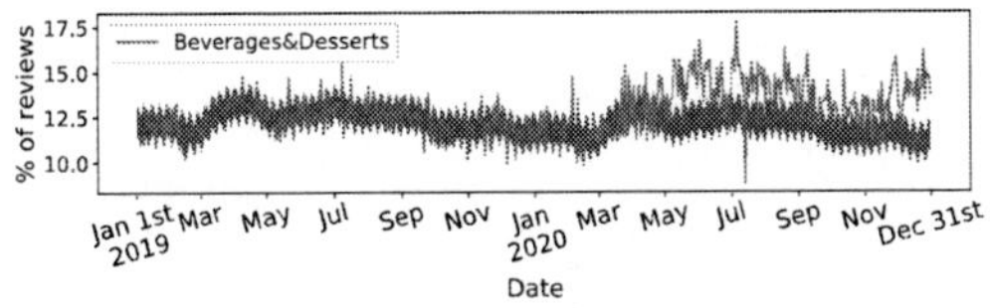

Figure 63: Prophet forecast for Beverages&Desserts group of business tags (NYC)

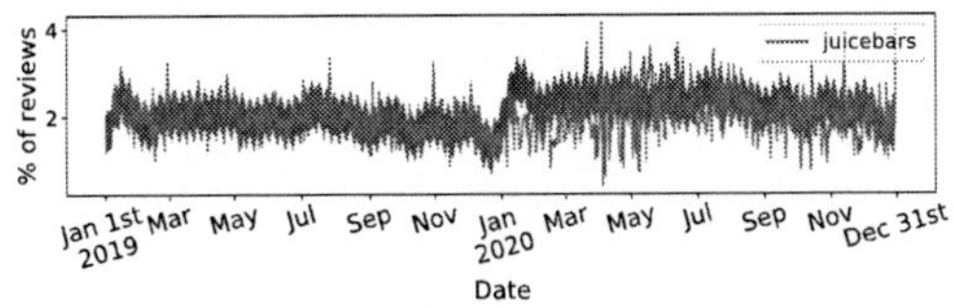

Figure 64: Prophet forecast for "Juice Bars" business tag (NYC)

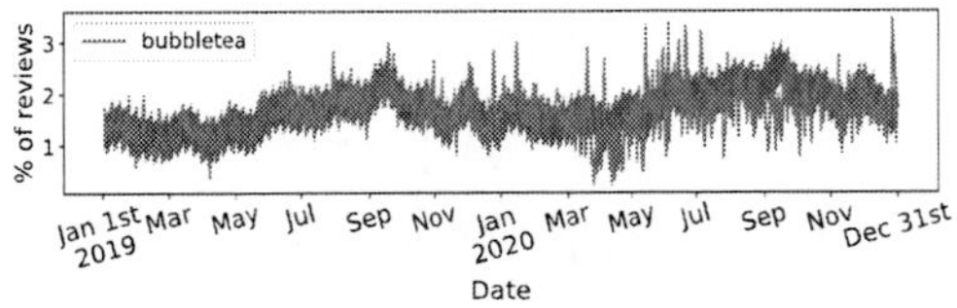

Figure 65: Prophet forecast for "Bubble Tea" business tag (NYC)

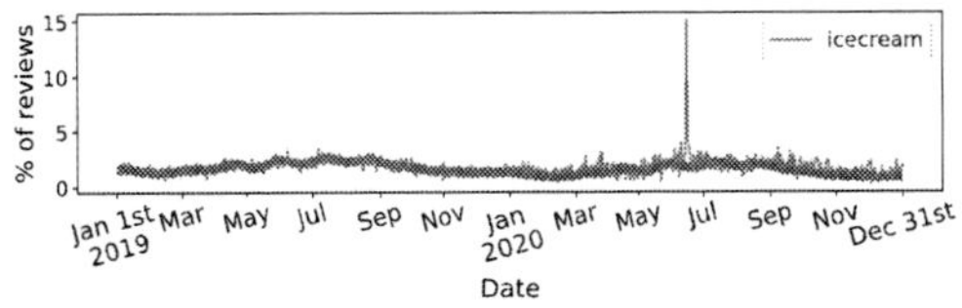

Figure 66: Prophet forecast for "Ice Cream" business tag (NYC)

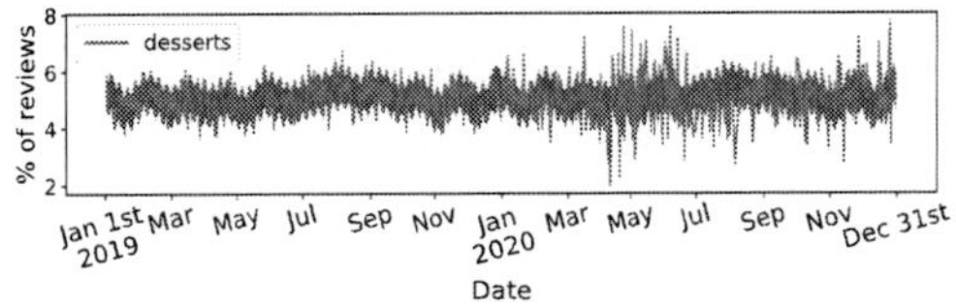

Figure 67: Prophet forecast for "Desserts" business tag (NYC)

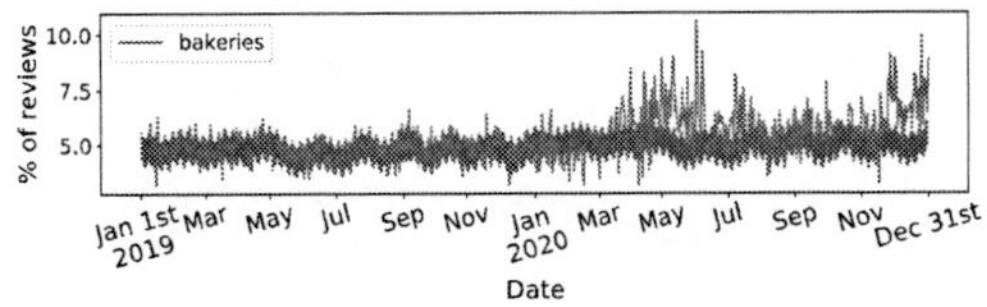

Figure 68: Prophet forecast for "Bakeries" business tag (NYC)

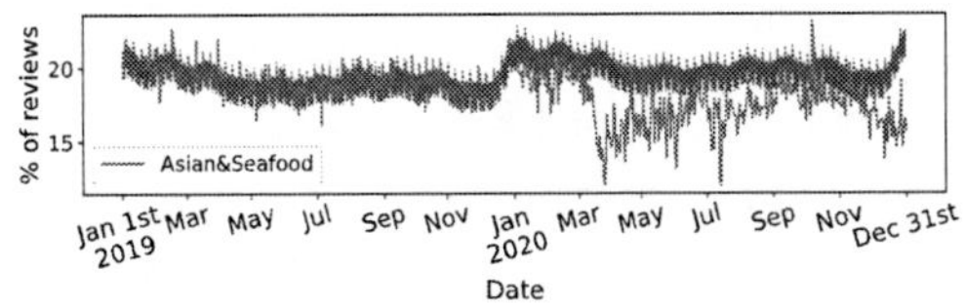

Figure 69: Prophet forecast for "Asian&Seafood" group of business tags (NYC)

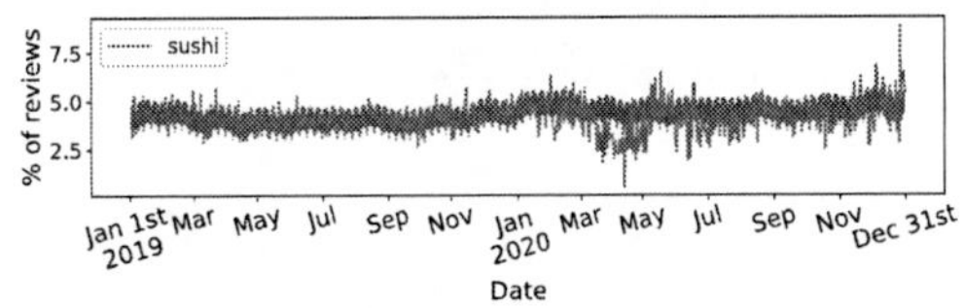

Figure 70: Prophet forecast for "Sushi" business tag (NYC)

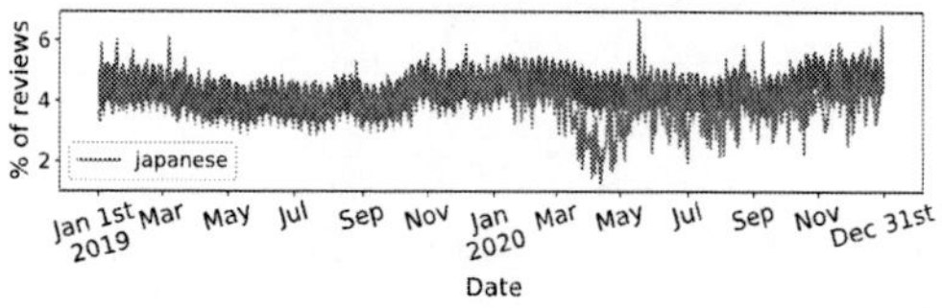

Figure 71: Prophet forecast for "Japanese" business tag (NYC)

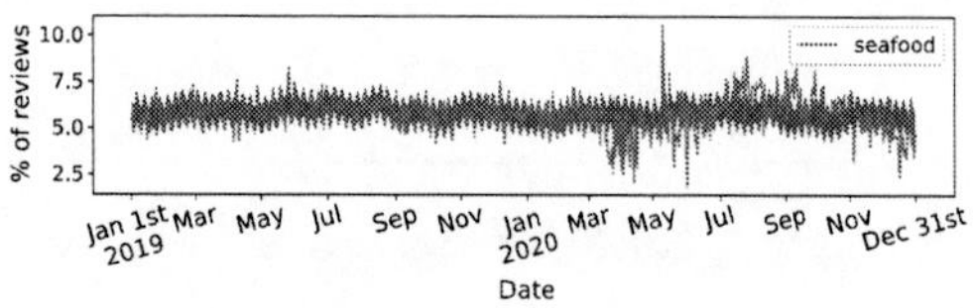

Figure 72: Prophet forecast for "Seafood" business tag (NYC)

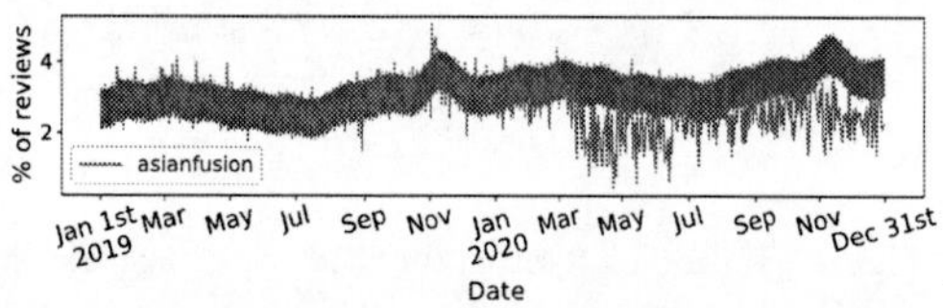

Figure 73: Prophet forecast for "Asian Fusion" business tag (NYC)

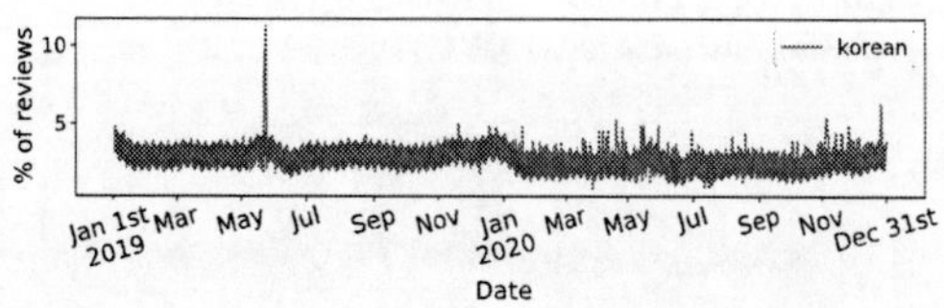

Figure 74: Prophet forecast for "Korean" business tag (NYC)

Assessing Cognitive Linguistic Influences in the Assignment of Blame

Karen Zhou and **Ana Smith** and **Lillian Lee**
Cornell University, Ithaca, NY
`{kz265, als476}@cornell.edu, llee@cs.cornell.edu`

Abstract

Lab studies in cognition and the psychology of morality have proposed some thematic and linguistic factors that influence moral reasoning. This paper assesses how well the findings of these studies generalize to a large corpus of over 22,000 descriptions of fraught situations posted to a dedicated forum. At this social-media site, users judge whether or not an author is in the wrong with respect to the event that the author described. We find that, consistent with lab studies, there are statistically significant differences in usage of first-person passive voice, as well as first-person agents and patients, between descriptions of situations that receive different blame judgments. These features also aid performance in the task of predicting the eventual collective verdicts.

1 Introduction

Dyadic morality theory proposes that the harm one party causes another is an important component in how other people form judgments of the two parties as acting morally or not. Under this framework, perpetrators (agents) are perceived as blameworthy, whereas victims (patients) are not (Gray and Wegner, 2009; Schein et al., 2015). This effect appears to transfer to how active (agentive) a party is described to be, even if the activity was in the past — a phenomenon described by Gray and Wegner's (2011) paper titled, "To Escape Blame, Don't be a Hero — Be a Victim".

The online forum `https://reddit.com/r/AmItheAsshole` collects first-person descriptions of (purportedly) real-life situations, together with commentary from other users as to who is blameworthy in the situation described; two examples are shown in Figure 1. (Additional examples may be found in Appendix A.) This data allows us to evaluate findings from dyadic morality theory on a corpus involving over 22,000 events and 685,000 passed judgments.

The research questions we address with this data in this paper include:

(1) Do authors refer to themselves in passive voice more often in descriptions of situations where they are judged to be morally incorrect?

(2) How does an author's framing of themselves as an "agent" or "patient" in describing a moral situation affect the judgments they receive?

The first question is motivated by Bohner (2002), who found that using passive voice, by placing someone who was actually a victim in subject position (e.g., "X was threatened by Y"), causes the victim to seem more responsible for the event. (See also Niemi and Young (2016) on the effect of syntactic-subject position for perpetrator vs. victim descriptions.) Importantly, our two questions *together* separate passive voice from agentiveness.

We find that while the agentive aspect of dyadic morality theory is upheld in our data, passive voice theory does not align empirically. We also incorporate these theories as features in a verdict prediction task.

2 Data

The subreddit from which we draw our data is self-described as follows:

> A catharsis for the frustrated moral philosopher in all of us, and a place to finally find out if you were wrong in an argument that's been bothering you. Tell us about any non-violent conflict you have experienced; give us both sides of the story, and find out if you're right, or you're the [jerk].

It has served as the basis of prior computational analysis of moral judgment by Botzer et al. (2021) and Lourie et al. (2021). (The Moral Stories dataset

Proceedings of the Ninth International Workshop on Natural Language Processing for Social Media, pages 61–69
Online Workshop, June 10, 2021. ©2021 Association for Computational Linguistics

Title: AITA for telling a kid to shut up on a plane

Situation: I was on a trip to Michigan a yearback and some kid was crying on the plane for 30 minutes. I yelled for the kid to shut up and the kid quieted down but the parents started freaking out.

Top verdict: YTA, call the flight attendant if this is going on. You yelling for a child to shut up is only going to escalate tensions and, like exactly what happened, get the parents pissed off at you and start freaking out.

(a)

Title: WIBTA if I had someone's car towed?

Situation: My building has pretty limited parking and we've been having an issue with people who don't live here taking up all the parking. I asked one guy if he lived here, and when he said he didn't I told him he couldn't park there. His car is back again, WIBTA if I had him towed without a warning?

Top verdict: NTA. Resident parking is included in what you pay towards rent, typically - it helps keep insurance lower than having to park on the street or away from the complex.
You gave him fair warning. If he wants to visit, he needs to find guest parking or park on the street himself.

(b)

Figure 1: Two example situations and the top-rated comment attached to each. Other comments are omitted for space. (a) In this case, the top-rated comment starts with **YTA** ("You're the [jerk]"), indicating a judgment that the post author is at fault, and no other participant is. (b) In this case, the top-rated comment starts with **NTA** ("You're not the [jerk]"), indicating a judgment that the post author is not at fault, but rather the other party is. (In the post title, "WIBTA" stands for "Would I be the [jerk]".)

(Emelin et al., 2020) would have been an interesting alternative corpus to work with. It also draws some of its situations from the same subreddit.)

Since the SCRUPLES dataset (Lourie et al., 2021), also based on the aforementioned subreddit, does not include corresponding full comments, which we wanted to have as an additional source of analysis,[1] we scraped the subreddit ourselves. Our dataset (henceforth AITA) includes posts from the same timeframe as SCRUPLES: November 2018-April 2019.

The winning verdict of each post is determined, according to the subreddit's rules, by the verdict espoused by the top-voted comment 18 hours after submission. We aim to only include posts with meaningful content, so we discard posts with fewer than 20 comments and fewer than 6 words in the body, as manual appraisal revealed that these were often uninformative (e.g., body is "As described in the title").

For simplicity, we only consider situations with the YTA (author in the wrong, other party in the right) and NTA (author in the right, other party in the wrong) verdicts, although other verdicts (such as "everyone is in the wrong", and "no one is in the wrong") are possible. We still use over 75% of the data since these are the most prevalent outcomes on the forum, and the theories we assess align with having binary outcomes (comparing victim vs. perpetrator responsibility). This selection results in 22,795 posts, fewer than the over 32,000 in SCRUPLES (Lourie et al., 2021). The corpus contains more NTA posts, which are longer in word length on average (see Table 1).

Verdict	Average post length	Class proportion
YTA	333 tokens	40.3%
NTA	384 tokens	59.7%

Table 1: AITA corpus statistics.

3 Methodology

Passive subject identification To model the use of passive voice in moral situations, a dependency parser is used to match spans of passive subjects in sentences. We use spaCy's Matcher object to extract tokens tagged `nsubjpass`. Cases where the extracted passive subject is in first person (1P) are also tracked, as indication of the author being referred to passively. Some examples include:

[1] For each post, up to 100 of the most "upvoted" comments were also retrieved; these were not used here but could be useful for further cognitive theory reinforcement or nuanced controversy analysis.

- 1P passive subject: **I** was asked to be a bridesmaid and then she changed her mind last minute and **I** was removed from the bridal party in favor of one of her husbands cousins.
- Other passive subject: She obliged but **she** was pissed off the rest of the night.

For manual evaluation, we randomly selected 500 posts, containing a total of 675 uses of passive voice. The tagger achieved 0.984 precision on these posts. Among the 199 first-person passive subjects tagged, the precision achieved was 0.971.

Because Niemi and Young (2016) and Bohner (2002) find that passive voice is associated with greater perception of victims' causal responsibility, we hypothesize that situations with the YTA verdict may have higher rates of 1P passive subject usage.

Thematic role identification To approximate moral agents vs. patients, Semantic Role Labelling (SRL) is used to extract agents and patients. Semantic, or thematic, roles express the roles taken by arguments of a predicate in an event; an agent is the volitional causer of the event, while the theme or patient is most affected by the event (Jurafsky and Martin, 2019). The AllenNLP BERT-based Semantic Role Labeller (Gardner et al., 2017; Shi and Lin, 2019) is employed to extract spans that are tagged `ARG0` for agents and `ARG1` for patients. We also tag uses of 1P- agents and patients. Here are two examples:

- 1P agent: **I** don't want my fiance to take care these freeloaders anymore.
- 1P patient: He called **me** names, threatened divorce, and told me he's a saint for staying married to me.

As a sanity check, we manually evaluated a subset of 579 verb frames, corresponding to 15 posts, identified by the SRL tagger. The tagger achieved a precision of 0.934 on all verb frames. The precision on the 193 verb frames in this subset that contained a first-person `ARG0` or `ARG1` was 0.891. Examples where the tagger failed include sentence fragments (e.g. "Made my MMA debut today.") and use of first-person pronouns to describe other parties (e.g. "Everyone we know").

Gray and Wegner (2011) concluded that "it pays to be a [patient] when trying to escape blame. [Agents],... depending on the situation, may actually earn increased blame." Thus, we hypothesize that NTA may be associated with higher 1P-patient usage and YTA with higher 1P-agent usage.

4 Statistical Analysis

Due to the post length discrepancy between verdicts, we attempt to control for length in the analysis by assessing significance at the sentence level. While NTA posts average approximately 50 words more than YTA posts, sentences from NTA posts average only 0.5 words more than YTA sentences (17.0 vs. 16.6 words respectively).

We assess statistical significance as follows. We use a simple binomial test: let r be the rate of the given feature of interest (say, 1P-passive voice) over the entire collection of posts. We then compute the probability according to the r-induced binomial distribution — i.e., the null hypothesis that there is no difference between the YTA posts and the body of posts overall — of the observed number of occurrences of the feature in just the YTA posts. Similarly, we compute this probability for just the NTA posts.

4.1 Passive Subject Identification

We find that NTA situations have a higher rate of 1P passive subject usage than YTA situations, and that the deviation of both the rate in the YTA posts and in the NTA posts from the overall data is statistically significant. As shown in Table 2, 45.8% of NTA posts' passive voice uses are 1P, while 37.4% of YTA posts' passive voice uses are 1P.

The rate difference across verdicts is significant, with NTA posts having a higher 1P-passive rate (see Table 2). This could account for the 0.5-words-longer sentence average of NTA posts; since, for example, "I hit John" is shorter than its passive counterpart, "John was hit by me." This contradicts our hypothesis, as we expected higher 1P-passive rates for YTA posts.

We do not discount a possible explanation for this differing result being that the cognitive researchers had better control over narrative structure, content of their situations, and participants that provided judgment. On the other hand, it is also possible that the forum setting is, at least in certain respects, more natural (and definitely larger-scale) than the lab setting in which the original experiments took place.

Verdict	Rate	Binomial Significance Test
YTA	0.374	$p = 2.14\text{e-}22$
NTA	0.458	$p = 2.42\text{e-}15$
Overall	0.424	

Table 2: Rate of 1P-passive voice use, i.e. where the author is the passive subject.

	YTA	NTA	Overall
# Agents	32.1	37.8	35.5
1P-Agent Rate	**0.502**	0.482	0.492
# Patients	35.9	42.5	39.8
1P-Patient Rate	0.232	**0.238**	0.235
Verbs per Post	47.3	55.9	52.5

Table 3: SRL post average semantic role usage. Higher rates per row are bolded. Recall that on average, NTA posts are longer than YTA posts.

4.2 Thematic Role Identification

The NTA posts use more agents and patients by raw count and also have more verbs per post, since they are generally longer than YTA posts (see Table 3). When we examine proportions of uses, we find that the NTA posts have a higher rate of 1P-patient usage, while YTA posts have a higher rate of 1P-agent usage.

While the verdicts do not differ significantly in overall agent and patient usage, there are significant differences in rates of 1P (see Table 4). The rate of 1P-patient usage in NTA posts is significantly higher than that of YTA posts ($p < 0.005$), while the rate of 1P-agent usage in YTA posts is significantly higher than that of NTA posts ($p < 0.001$). These results seem to align with our hypothesis based on Gray and Wegner (2011)'s findings.

5 Verdict prediction task

In the previous section, we examined statistical correlations between features of interest in the previous literature to the verdicts presented in our data.

	YTA	NTA
Agent/Verbs	$p = 0.06$	$p = 0.15$
1P/Agent	$p = 1.70\text{e-}26$	$p = 7.54\text{e-}16$
Patient/Verbs	$p = 0.965$	$p = 0.972$
1P/Patient	$p = 1.06\text{e-}4$	$p = 3.49\text{e-}3$

Table 4: SRL sentence-level binomial significance tests. The differences for first-person/agent and first-person/patient rates of usage are noticeable.

Title: AITA for telling a kid to shut up on a plane

Situation: I was on a trip to Michigan a yearback and some kid was crying on the plane for 30 minutes. I yelled for the kid to shut up and the kid quieted down but the parents started freaking out.

Features:

```
{
  'text.word_length': 41,                          LENGTH
  'text.passive_fp_i': 0,
  'text.passive_fp_we': 0,
  'text.passive_fp': 0,                            +PASSIVE
  'text.passive_total': 0,
  'text.passive_fp_rate': 0,
  'text.unqiue_passive_subjs': 0,
  'text.srl_num_sents': 2,
  'text.srl_avg_verbs_per_sents': 3.0,
  'text.srl_arg0_fp': 1,
  'text.srl_arg1_fp': 0,                           +SRL
  'text.srl_unique_arg0': 5,
  'text.srl_unique_arg1': 5,
  'text.srl_unique_verbs': 6
}
```

Figure 2: Features extracted for a sample post. The verbs identified by the tagger are highlighted in yellow, and the 1P ARG0 is highlighted in cyan. Note that the +Passive features are very sparse. First-person "me" and "us" were not added as +Passive features, as their inclusion yielded about 1% worse performance (likely since they added additional noise).

In this section, we turn to prediction as another way to examine the magnitude of potential linkages between these features and judgments of blame. In particular, we see how incorporating these quite small set of features compares against a baseline classifier that has access to many more (lexical-based) features, but where these features are not explicitly cognitively motivated.

Specifically, to analyze the significance of passive voice and thematic roles as features in making moral judgments, we model the task of predicting the verdict of a situation as binary classification (YTA or NTA). We compare the performance of a linear and non-linear model.

We stress that we are *not* striving to build the most accurate judgment predictor for moral-scenario descriptions, nor arguing the utility or importance of such a classification task. Rather, we are using prediction as a further mechanism for answering the research questions we delineated in the introduction to this paper. We do not use BERT since it is pre-trained, possibly containing encoded biases, and is not as interpretable as simpler models.

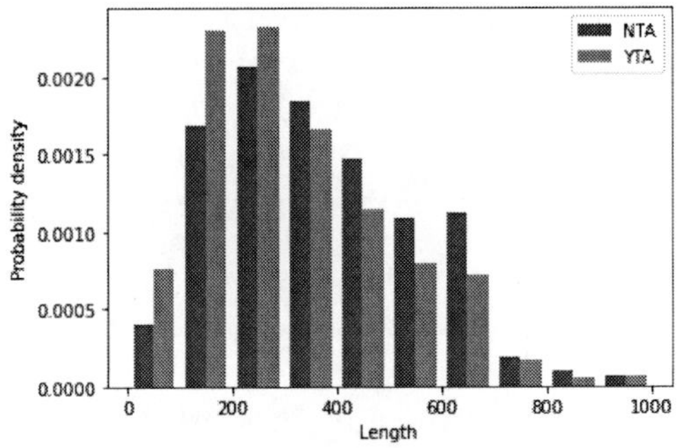

Figure 3: Normalized histogram of word length distributions across verdicts. The few posts with lengths > 1000 tokens are omitted for clarity. The distributions were found to be significantly different by the t-test, Z-test, and Kolmogorov-Smirnov test ($p < 0.005$).

For an ablation study, we have four feature sets, with the corresponding number of features in brackets:

- Length [1]: word count of the post, since NTA posts average more words than YTA posts
- Length+Passive [7]: counts of passive and 1P passive subjects, and rate of 1P passive subjects.
- Length+SRL [8]: unique `ARG0` (i.e., agent), `VERB`, and `ARG1` (i.e., patient) token counts (where # `ARG1` tokens per frame ≤ 2), count of sentences including `ARG0` and/or `ARG1` tokens, average number of `VERB`s per sentence as identified by the tagger, and 1P agent and patient token counts.
- Length+Passive+SRL [14]: features of both Length+Passive and Length+SRL.

Figure 2 provides an example of features extracted for a real post.

We assess these feature sets against 43,110 lexical-based features from a TF-IDF transform of lowercased unigrams and bigrams with 0.1% minimum document frequency.

The configurations for the linear and non-linear models are described below. The AITA data is split 60/20/20 for the train/val/test sets, after random shuffling. Both models are trained on this same split of data.

Linear Model We opt for a simple model to begin with to avoid overfitting on the dataset and for purposes of interpretability. For a linear model, we use the scikit-learn logistic regression model (LR) (Pedregosa et al., 2011). Hyperparameters for the logistic regression model include setting random state to 0, choosing "liblinear" as the solver, and setting the class weights to "balanced" to account for the label imbalance.

Non-Linear Model We incorporate a non-linear model, as we observed that our feature count distributions were weakly bi-modal even after grouping instances under the NTA/YTA labels (see Figure 3). We use the scikit-learn random forest model (RF) (Pedregosa et al., 2011). Hyperparameters for the random forest model include setting class weights to "balanced", "sqrt" for the maximum features, and 100 for number of estimators. Through tuning over the range [5,15], we found that setting the maximum depth to 7 prevented overfitting on the training data.

6 Task Results

To give the imbalanced labels equal importance, we evaluated macro-average scores. Weighted average scores were usually around 1% higher than the macro-average scores. Overall, the non-linear model achieves higher F1 scores for each of our feature sets, though the linear model does better with TF-IDF features (see Tables 5 and 6).

6.1 Linear Model Results

Compared to the random forest, the linear model achieves better performance with TF-IDF features (0.58 vs. 0.62 F1 score). Length+SRL has the best performance of our feature sets, with 0.56 precision and recall and 0.54 F1 score (see Table 5). The distinction in performance across feature sets is less clear than with the non-linear model, suggesting that the logistic regression model is not able to learn as well from these particular features.

From the ROC curves, we see that Length+SRL shows a little improvement over Length alone at higher thresholds, but does around equally at lower thresholds (see Figure 4a). The performance gap between TF-IDF features and our features is greater with the linear model.

We also see from the confusion matrix in Figure 4a that the best model version tends to predict YTA. Depending on desired use case — and recalling that we are not necessarily promoting judgment prediction as a deployed application — it may be better to err on the side of predicting one side or the other. If the priority is to catch all possible occurrences of the author being judged to be in the

	Prec	Rec	F1	AUC
Majority	0.30	0.50	0.37	—
TF-IDF	0.62	0.62	0.62	0.667
Length	0.55	0.55	0.53	0.576
+Passive	0.55	0.55	0.53	0.574
+SRL	**0.56**	**0.56**	**0.54**	**0.587**
+Passive+SRL	0.55	0.55	0.54	0.585

Table 5: Macro-average results of verdict prediction task with the LR model. Best scores among the feature sets are bolded.

	Prec	Rec	F1	AUC
Majority	0.30	0.50	0.37	—
TF-IDF	0.59	0.59	0.58	0.620
Length	0.55	0.55	0.55	0.568
+Passive	0.55	0.55	0.54	0.565
+SRL	**0.56**	**0.56**	**0.56**	**0.586**
+Passive+SRL	**0.56**	**0.56**	**0.56**	0.585

Table 6: Macro-average results of verdict prediction task with the RF model. Best scores among the feature sets are bolded.

wrong, this model would be better suited than the non-linear model. However, this model would also yield more false accusations, which could be more undesirable.

6.2 Non-Linear Model Results

Like the linear model, Length+SRL does best overall, with 0.56 for precision, recall, and F1 score (see Table 6). Length+Passive+SRL performs similarly.

From the ROC curves, we see that Length+SRL shows some improvement over Length alone (see Figure 4b). With these feature sets, we achieve performance close to that of a model trained with TF-IDF, with much fewer features: 43,110 vs. a mere 8. In addition, TF-IDF may overfit to topics (e.g., weddings), whereas our features are easier to transfer across domains.

From the confusion matrix in Figure 4b, we notice that even with balanced class labels, the best model still slightly favors predicting NTA.

7 Discussion

Despite noting the significant difference in first-person passive voice usage between verdicts, the feature set of Length+Passive yields slightly lower performance than the Length baseline for both models. This could be due to not having enough instances of passive voice, as each post has on average 1.39 counts of passive voice, of which 30.5% are first-person. Regex searches confirmed that the dependency-parser did not simply have poor recall, though the methods for passive voice extraction are not exact. Thus, the passive features may be acting as noise.

Length+SRL builds off of more SRL instances per post, so these features provide less noisy information. This feature set's performance beats that of the Length baseline for both models, suggesting that SRL features do play a role in making moral judgments. The SRL features do not store lexical information, which helps remove the influence of the content of the posts. Length+Passive+SRL performance likely suffers from the additional passive features' noise.

A notable difference is the non-linear model's tendency to favor NTA and the linear model's preference for YTA. A possible explanation for this is that the features corresponding to YTA situations are more linearly separable than those corresponding to NTA situations.

Comparing scores for the Length baseline, we see that the random forest has a 3.8% improvement in F1 score over logistic regression. This may suggest that post length is not a linear feature, which would account for nuances such as long YTA and short NTA posts (see Figure 1b for an example of a short NTA post).

Caveats We are certainly not saying that blameworthiness can be reduced to use of first-person descriptors. There are a multitude of features and factors at play, and there may be alternative parameters to consider for the task.

Even if we restrict attention to linguistic signals, there are quite a few confounds to point out. As just one example: it is possible that authors purposefully manipulate their use of first-person pronouns to appear less guilty. Another possibility to consider: there may be correlations between whether an author *believes* they are guilty and how they describe a situation, so that commenters are not picking up on the actual culpability in the described scenario so much as the author's self-blame.

Also, we can look beyond linguistic factors. For example, when deciding whether to "upvote" a particular judgment comment, voters may be affected by the (apparent) identity of the commenter (or, for that matter, the original post author) and the content of other comments. We have not accounted for such factors in our study.

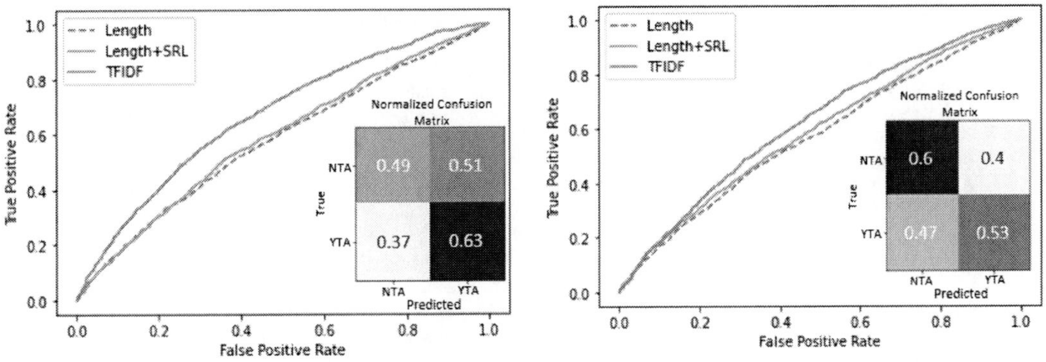

(a) LR model.

(b) RF model.

Figure 4: The ROC curves for verdict prediction task, for the feature sets described in the key, and the confusion matrices for the verdict prediction task results of the Length+SRL feature set.

We must also keep in mind that users of the forum constitute a particular sample of people that is likely not representative of many populations of interest.

8 Conclusion and Future Work

We introduce findings from moral cognitive science and psychology and assess their application to a forum of user-generated ethical situations. Statistical tests confirm that there are significant differences in usage of first-person passive voice along with first-person agents and patients among situations of different verdicts. Incorporating these differences as features in a verdict prediction task confirms the linkage between first-person agents and patients with assigned blame, though passive voice features appear too sparse to yield meaningful results.

From this study, we conclude that the manner in which a situation is described does appear to influence how blame is assigned. In the forum we work with, people seem to be judged by the way they present themselves, not just by their content, which aligns with previous cognitive science studies. Future endeavors in ethical AI could incorporate such theories to promote interpretability of models that produce moral decisions.

There are several areas of this project that could be refined and pursued further. We can repeat these experiments with the other verdicts, incorporating situations where all parties or no parties are blamed. We can use stricter length control than the sentence-level comparison, since the average sentence length still differs between posts of different verdicts. We should also incorporate validation that the SRL methodology effectively extracts the moral agents and patients we are trying to analyze. Another direction we would like to pursue, and one also mentioned by a reviewer, is to group situations by topic to try to control for other confounds in the moral situations. Finally, we hope to be able to incorporate the range of votes from the comments accompanying each post to allow for more nuanced verdict prediction, as done with SCRUPLES in Lourie et al. (2021).

Acknowledgements

We thank the anonymous reviewers, Yoav Artzi, and Rishi Advani for their generous feedback and suggestions. This work was supported in part by ARO MURI grant ARO W911NF-19-0217.

References

Gerd Bohner. 2002. Writing about rape: Use of the passive voice and other distancing text features as an expression of perceived responsibility of the victim. *British Journal of Social Psychology*, 40:515–529.

Nicholas Botzer, Shawn Gu, and Tim Weninger. 2021. Analysis of moral judgement on Reddit. https://arxiv.org/abs/2101.07664.

Denis Emelin, Ronan Le Bras, Jena D. Hwang, Maxwell Forbes, and Yejin Choi. 2020. Moral stories: Situated reasoning about norms, intents, actions, and their consequences. *CoRR*, abs/2012.15738.

Matt Gardner, Joel Grus, Mark Neumann, Oyvind Tafjord, Pradeep Dasigi, Nelson F. Liu, Matthew Peters, Michael Schmitz, and Luke S. Zettlemoyer. 2017. AllenNLP: A deep semantic natural language processing platform.

Kurt Gray and Daniel M. Wegner. 2009. Moral typecasting: divergent perceptions of moral agents and moral patients. *Journal of Personality and social Psychology*, 96 3:505–20.

Kurt Gray and Daniel M. Wegner. 2011. To escape blame, don't be a hero—Be a victim. *Journal of Experimental Social Psychology*, 47(2):516–519.

Daniel Jurafsky and James H. Martin. 2019. *Speech and Language Processing*, 3 edition. Prentice Hall.

Nicholas Lourie, Ronan Le Bras, and Yejin Choi. 2021. Scruples: A corpus of community ethical judgments on 32,000 real-life anecdotes. In *AAAI*.

Laura Niemi and Liane Young. 2016. When and why we see victims as responsible: The impact of ideology on attitudes toward victims. *Personality and Social Psychology Bulletin*, 42.

F. Pedregosa, G. Varoquaux, A. Gramfort, V. Michel, B. Thirion, O. Grisel, M. Blondel, P. Prettenhofer, R. Weiss, V. Dubourg, J. Vanderplas, A. Passos, D. Cournapeau, M. Brucher, M. Perrot, and E. Duchesnay. 2011. Scikit-learn: Machine learning in Python. *Journal of Machine Learning Research*, 12:2825–2830.

Chelsea Schein, Amelia Goranson, and Kurt Gray. 2015. The uncensored truth about morality. *The Psychologist*, 28(12):982–985.

Peng Shi and Jimmy Lin. 2019. Simple BERT models for relation extraction and semantic role labeling. https://arxiv.org/abs/1904.05255.

A Additional Examples

Warning: Some content in these examples may be offensive or upsetting.

Figure 5 shows an example where there was relative disagreement about the guilty party. Figure 6 shows an example where there was general consensus about the verdict.

Title: AITA For not caring about gay pride?

Situation: I had thought I recently met two lovely people who happen to be homosexual. However, as I got to know them I soon began to dislike them. It seemed like they had to make it painfully obvious that they were gay. I felt like every other sentence they tried to squeeze in "Being a gay woman." and various other things such as that. it made me very uncomfortable, I don't have an issue with gay people but I wouldn't go as far as to say as I support them. We're all human, if you're gay then you're gay. Just keep me out of it, is all I ask. After this continued for awhile I decided to try and subtly hint at them that they were mentioning they were gay far too frequently.

When that didn't work, I resorted to telling them my beliefs on the subject and I was quickly resented, being called homophobic and unaccepting of them. (Even though I /clearly/ said I do accept them for their sexuality. I would just appreciate it if they didn't annoyingly mention it ever few minutes! Am I the asshole for this?

Top verdict: YTA. Start paying attention to how often hetero people talk about their dating, mating, and flirtations. Spoiler: ALL the time, but no one ever thinks they're "flaunting their heterosexuality".

Additional comment: [NTA], it's annoying when people make sexuality... Or any singular trait as the sole defining characteristic they have.

Figure 5: A situation where there was noticeable disagreement among comments. Depicted is the top-rated comment and one additional, contrary opinion.

Title: AITA for disagreeing with my husband in front of my son?
Situation: We (husband 30s, me 20s, and my son 8) were sitting on the couch talking about how technology has changed the world. My husband says, "Technology is really bad." I say, "It's not that bad, as long as you don't overuse it." That's literally all I said. After the kids went to bed, my husband blew up at me. He told me not to demean him in front on the kids. He called me names, threatened divorce, and told me he's a saint for staying married to me. His blow up was, in my eyes, completely unwarranted. He did apologize, but said if I hadn't voiced my disagreement in front of my son, he wouldn't have blown up. I've been profusely apologizing for disagreeing with him in front of the kids. He's convinced me that I was in the wrong. I should have watched my mouth. If I had, he wouldn't have gotten mad at me.

Top verdict: NTA - That's called a normal conversation. If you husband thinks you can't have your own opinions there is a problem. Your son should see that there are different perspectives and that his dad isn't the be all end all.
Additional comment: NTA. Your husband sounds nuts. Does he keep his mouth shut when he disagrees with you in front of the kids? It's normal to have healthy disagreements in front of kids and it's good to model that for them. If your husband has a pattern of this kind of behavior, he sounds emotionally abusive. If this is an isolated incident, watch closely to see if it repeats itself. This is not normal. And he isn't really going to divorce you over that. He wants you to be scared to disobey his rule again.

Figure 6: A situation wherein other comments in general agreement with the final verdict (i.e., that of the top-rated comment). We show only one additional comment due to space constraints.

Evaluating Deception Detection Model Robustness To Linguistic Variation

Maria Glenski, Ellyn Ayton, Robin Cosbey, Dustin Arendt, and Svitlana Volkova
Pacific Northwest National Laboratory
Richland, WA, USA
first.last@pnnl.gov

Abstract

With the increasing use of machine-learning driven algorithmic judgements, it is critical to develop models that are robust to evolving or manipulated inputs. We propose an extensive analysis of model robustness against linguistic variation in the setting of *deceptive news detection*, an important task in the context of misinformation spread online. We consider two prediction tasks and compare three state-of-the-art embeddings to highlight consistent trends in model performance, high confidence misclassifications, and high impact failures. By measuring the effectiveness of adversarial defense strategies and evaluating model susceptibility to adversarial attacks using character- and word-perturbed text, we find that character or mixed ensemble models are the most effective defenses and that character perturbation-based attack tactics are more successful.

1 Introduction

Over two-thirds of US adults get their news from social media, but over half (57%) "expect the news they see on social media to be largely inaccurate" (Shearer and Matsa, 2018). A 2020 Reuters Institute global news survey found a similar trend with 56% of respondents concerned with misinformation in online news (Newman et al., 2020). There are online and offline impacts from the spread of misinformation or deceptive news stories within online communities. However, the rate at which new content is submitted to social media platforms is a significant obstacle for approaches that require manual identification, annotation, or intervention. In recent efforts, evaluation has focused on aggregate performance metrics on test sets often collected from social media platforms like Twitter, Facebook, or Reddit (Rubin et al., 2016; Mitra et al., 2017; Wang, 2017) but these platforms are not representative in regards to user demographics or topics of discussion. Further, aggregate performance metrics are not sufficient to provide insight on generalizable performance.

When we consider the identification of deceptive news online — where humans often disagree on or challenge the judgements of others (Karduni et al., 2018, 2019; Ott et al., 2011) — we need more rigorous evaluations of model decisions, with a focus on expected performance across varied or manipulated inputs. Our work examining reliability of performance when faced with linguistic variations is a step towards comprehensively understanding model robustness that may highlight inequalities in cases of failure. Although machine learning models are often leveraged for their ability to tackle rapid response at scale, it is critical to understand nuanced model biases and the significant downstream consequences of model decisions on users.

A known gap exists in our understanding of underlying machine learning decision-making processes, particularly with deep learning "black-box" models. The use of traditional, aggregate metrics for model performance, such as accuracy or F1 score, are not sufficient in pursuit of this understanding. We argue that evaluations need to explicitly measure the extent to which model performance is affected by data with a varied topic distribution. Evaluations highlighting when models are correct, which examples can provide explanations, and clarification or reasoning for why a user should trust a given model are well-aligned with recent themes in research on machine learning interpretability, trust, fairness, accountability, and reliability (Lipton, 2018; Doshi-Velez and Kim, 2017; Hohman et al., 2018).

In this paper, we perform an adversarial model evaluation across two multimodal deception prediction tasks to identify which defensive strategies are most successful across a variety of attacks. Our main contribution is a framework of analysis for model robustness across variations in linguistic sig-

Proceedings of the Ninth International Workshop on Natural Language Processing for Social Media, pages 70–80
Online Workshop, June 10, 2021.

nals and representations that may be encountered in real-world applications of digital deception models (*e.g.,* natural linguistic differences, evolving tactics from deceptive adversaries to evade detection). In particular, we present evaluations on the susceptibility of widely used text embeddings to naive adversarial attacks, which types of text perturbations lead to the most high-confident errors, and to what extent our findings are task specific. The perturbed text emulates real examples of linguistic variations, e.g. non-native speakers, spelling mistakes, or shortened online speech. Our evaluations reveal how models react to perturbed text which we argue is a likely occurrence when deployed in a real-world setting.

2 Related Work

With the increasing concern for the impact of misinformation and deceptive news content online, many studies have explored or developed models that detect such news. Recent efforts focus on identifying a spectrum of deception: from binary classification of content as suspicious and trustworthy (Volkova et al., 2017) to a more fine-grained separation within deceptive classes (*e.g.,* propaganda, hoax, satire) (Rashkin et al., 2017). Additional work has explored the behavior of malicious users and bots (Glenski and Weninger, 2018; Kumar et al., 2017, 2018) and spread patterns of misinformation or rumors (Kwon et al., 2017; Vosoughi et al., 2018) to aid in classification tasks. Strong evidence suggests that enriched features such as images, temporal and structural attributes, and linguistic features boost model performance over dependence on textual characteristics alone (Wang, 2017; Qazvinian et al., 2011; Kwon et al., 2013). The need for effective, trustworthy, and interpretable detection models is a vital concern and must be an essential requirement for models where decisions or recommendations can significantly affect end users.

A variety of deep learning architectures applied to deception detection tasks include convolutional neural networks (CNNs) (Ajao et al., 2018; Wang, 2017; Volkova et al., 2017), long short-term memory (LSTM) models (Chen et al., 2018; Rath et al., 2017; Zubiaga et al., 2018; Zhang et al., 2019) , and LSTM variants with attention mechanisms (Guo et al., 2018; Li et al., 2019). Architecture and other aspects of neural network design typically depend on the classification task and require specialized hyperparameter tuning. In order to provide a fair comparison of model evaluations across tasks and for the purpose of consistency across experiments, we implement a multimodal LSTM model similar to recent work. Our approach allows for more accurate comparisons of factors related to adversarial susceptibility across classification tasks. Developing novel state-of-the-art models for deception detection or comparing multiple architectures is beyond the scope of this paper.

Although popularly used across many domains, deep learning systems can be extremely brittle when evaluated on examples outside of the training data distribution (Goodfellow et al., 2014; Moosavi-Dezfooli et al., 2017; Fawzi et al., 2018). Nguyen *et al* (2015) have shown that small perturbations in input data can cause highly probable misclassifications. Further research demonstrates additional attacks that make neural networks more susceptible to adversaries such as locally trained DNNs to crafted adversarial inputs (Papernot et al., 2016c,a) and gradient-based attacks (Biggio et al., 2013). To counteract these offensive strategies, proposed methods of defense include augmented training data with adversarial examples (Tramèr et al., 2018), training a separate model to distinguish genuine data from malicious data (Metzen et al., 2017), and implementing a defensive distillation mechanism to increase a model's resiliency to data poisoning (Papernot et al., 2016b). However, as defense strategies are created, new attacks are continually developed to circumvent them (Carlini and Wagner, 2017). While there is a focus on image perturbations and related attacks, textual data is similarly vulnerable to such strategies (Gao et al., 2018; Samanta and Mehta, 2017; Liang et al., 2018)). The susceptibility of deception detection models to text-based adversarial attacks as well as the effectiveness of defense strategies have not been extensively evaluated.

3 Methodology

In this section, we introduce our detection tasks, models, and evaluation methods. We randomly perturb words or characters with their nearest neighbors to mimic a low-effort adversarial attack (*e.g.,* replacing words with synonyms) as opposed to methods that assume an adversary has technical expertise or require sophisticated augmentations (*e.g.,* gradient-based algorithms). We argue that robustness against these low-effort attacks is a necessary first step towards trustworthy models; these attacks are reflective of natural or unintentional variations (*e.g.*, misspellings, non-native speaker discussions) as well as sophisticated strategies.

3.1 Deception Detection Tasks

We apply a comprehensive evaluation of model robustness and susceptibility to two classification tasks[1]: 3-way (trustworthy, propaganda, disinformation) and 4-way (clickbait, hoax, satire, conspiracy). Including both allows us to compare defense and attack strategies across models at varied levels of deception and evaluate method generalizability.

The 3-way task includes two extreme deceptive classes, propaganda and disinformation, and seeks to differentiate them from "trustworthy" sources (Derakhshan and Wardle, 2017). Due to the stronger intent to deceive of these classes, we expect a model to distinguish trustworthy news more easily and expect more confusion when classifying news as either propaganda or disinformation. Misclassifications of these as trustworthy will have a greater negative impact. To better identify high-impact errors, we collapse disinformation and propaganda into a single class as part of a binary sub-task separating trustworthy from deceptive.

The 4-way task centers lesser deceptive content, the classes included have a lower intent to deceive and are more difficult to distinguish from one another. For instance, satirical news sites produce humorous content or social commentary rather than deliberately false information and have a low intent to deceive audiences (Fletcher and Nielsen, 2017). Because of this inherent difference from the other deceptive news types, we include a binary sub-task separating satire from the remaining classes.

3.2 Data Collection and Annotation

Models were trained and tested on Twitter API data. Our corpus comprises English retweets with images from official news media Twitter accounts. Class labels are based on "verified" news sources and a public list of sources annotated along the spectrum of deceptive content (Volkova et al., 2017)[2] from 2016. Thus, we limit our corpus to that 12 month period of activity. The 3-way and 4-way task data consist of 54.5k and 2.5k tweets. Although there are limits to source-level annotations (*e.g.,* tweets of different deceptive classes shared from a single source), we advocate for focus on news sources rather than individual stories, similar to previous work (Vosoughi et al., 2018; Lazer et al., 2018). We posit the definitive element of deception to be the intent and tactics of the source.

3.3 Multimodal Deception Detection Models

We clean the tweet text by lowercasing and removing punctuation, mentions, hashtags, and URLs. We encode biased and subjective language as frequency vectors constructed from LIWC (Pennebaker et al., 2001) and several lexical dictionaries such as hedges and factives (Recasens et al., 2013) which are often used for text classification (Rashkin et al., 2017; Shu et al., 2019).

We implement a two-branch architecture[3] that leverages text, lexical features, and images. The text branch consists of a pre-trained text embedding layer, an LSTM layer, and a fully connected layer. The output is concatenated to the lexical feature vector before being passed to another fully connected layer. In the second branch, we pass the image vector through a fully connected, two layer network. The combined text embeddings and lexical features are concatenated with the processed image representation which is then fed to a fully connected network for classification. Our chosen architecture resembles current systems in deployment and allows us to complete complex analyses.

3.4 Model Evaluation Methods

We perform a comprehensive evaluation for both tasks over *embeddings*, *defenses*, and *attacks*. This section describes our text perturbation methods and our defense and attack frameworks.

3.4.1 Varying Text Representations

We consider three embedding techniques that have shown state-of-the-art performance on several NLP tasks: GLoVe (Pennington et al., 2014), ELMo (Peters et al., 2018), and BERT (Devlin et al., 2019). We recognize that each embedding method was trained on separate data[4], under different conditions, and produces various sized vectors. Thus, we fine-tune the embedding layer during training.

[1]Although we chose to use these two tasks, our framework is task-agnostic and can be applied to any classification task.

[2]`www.cs.jhu.edu/~svitlana/data/SuspiciousNewsAccountList.tsv`; `www.cs.jhu.edu/~svitlana/data/VerifiedNewsAccountList.tsv`

[3]Parameters selected by a random search: Adam optimizer, 10^{-6} learning rate, 0.2 drop out, and 10 training epochs.

[4]We use GloVe (Twitter 27B), ELMo (`tfhub.dev/google/elmo/2`), and BERT (`github.com/huggingface/transformers`)

Original Text	rt heres a list of foods banned in other countries but not america
Character Perturbed	rt heres a list of foods banned in other countries but not america
Glove Perturbed	rt heres a list of foods banned in other nations though not america

Figure 1: Examples of adversarial perturbations.

3.4.2 Linguistic Variation

We examine how changes to text input affect model performance using character and word perturbations and focus on the impact of naive linguistic variations in text. For character-level perturbations, we randomly replace 25% of characters in each tweet with a Unicode character that is indistinguishable from the original to a human (as shown in Figure 1). This approach, known in computer security as a homograph attack or script spoofing, has been investigated to identify phishing or spam (Fu et al., 2006b,a; Liu and Stamm, 2007) but has not been applied in the NLP domain to our knowledge. For word-level perturbations we randomly replace 25% of words with a nearest neighbor in the each embedding space using Annoy[5].

3.4.3 Defense Viewpoint

To evaluate the efficacy of common defenses to guard against adversarial attacks – augmenting the training data – we perturb our training set (Tr) to varying degrees using each linguistic variation strategy. We compare the following defenses:

- Tr: train with original examples;
- $Tr^{50\%}$: train with half of the examples perturbed;
- Tr': train with all examples perturbed;
- Ensemble (E): majority vote of ensemble of models trained on Tr, $Tr^{50\%}$, and Tr'.

Each defense has been perturbed for each embedding type. For example, we train our models using four variations of $Tr^{50\%}$: $Tr_C^{50\%}$ (50% of examples perturbed using the character-level attack), and three $Tr_W^{50\%}$ defenses with 50% of the examples perturbed using the word-level attack ($Tr_{BERT}^{50\%}$, $Tr_{ELMo}^{50\%}$, $Tr_{GLoVe}^{50\%}$).

We use three sets of ensembles: (1) E_C, an ensemble of models trained with Tr, $Tr_C^{50\%}$, and Tr'_C, (2) E_W, an ensemble of models trained with Tr, $Tr_W^{50\%}$, and Tr'_W, and (3) E_{C+W}, an ensemble of five models trained on Tr, $Tr_C^{50\%}$, Tr'_C, $Tr_W^{50\%}$, and Tr'_W. Higher confidence predictions are used in the case of ties.

We test the performance of models trained using each defense on fully perturbed (Te') and the original, unperturbed test data (Te). Ideally, we want models to perform well on both so we also consider three $Mixed$ test sets (Te + Te'_C + Te'_W), one for each Te'_W ($Mixed_{BERT}$, $Mixed_{ELMo}$, and $Mixed_{GLoVe}$).

3.4.4 Attack Viewpoint

We also evaluate the impact of the linguistic perturbations as adversarial attack strategies. The attack test sets were perturbed similarly to the train sets:

- Te: original examples (no attack);
- Te'_C: all examples perturbed (char-level);
- Te'_W: all examples perturbed (word-level).

As with the defense viewpoint, we have four sets of the Te' test data used to evaluate each attack condition: Te'_C, Te'_{BERT}, Te'_{ELMo}, Te'_{GLoVe}.

3.4.5 High Confidence And High Impact

For researchers and end-users to establish trust in the models they develop or use, it is essential to understand the circumstances in which a model would make a highly confident misclassification. Inherently, model confidence measures the certainty of a prediction and quantifies the expertise and stability of a model. We closely examine instances in which our models have incorrectly predicted the class of a tweet with high confidence (greater than 90%) to identify potential weaknesses of the models.

Traditional performance metrics (F1 score, precision, recall) treat misclassifications with high confidence and low confidence alike. While overall error is an important measure, a model with a slightly higher overall failure rate but lower confidence may result in a better "worst case" outcome if appropriately incorporated in a semi-automated or human-in-the-loop deployment strategy that considers the uncertainty of predictions or recommendations via the model confidence before taking action.

We also examine high impact errors using the binary sub-tasks for each classification task as described above. In this analysis, we identify how often models make significant errors. For example, mistaking a post labeled as disinformation for trustworthy (an opposite class) rather than propaganda (a similar class).

4 Experimental Results

In this section, we detail our results when evaluating different combinations of adversarial defenses

[5] https://github.com/spotify/annoy

3-way	Character ($\Delta Te'_C$)			Word ($\Delta Te'_W$)		
Defense	*BERT*	*ELMo*	*GloVe*	*BERT*	*ELMo*	*GloVe*
Tr	+36%	+34%	+33%	+37%	+37%	+38%
$Tr^{50\%}$	+2%	-2%	-2%	-1%	-3%	-3%
Tr'	+1%	-1%	-1%	-6%	-21%	-5%
E_C	+2%	+4%	+7%	-5%	-8%	-0%
E_W	+14%	+12%	+15%	+11%	+21%	+17%
E_{C+W}	+10%	+7%	+7%	+7%	+9%	+3%
4-way	**Character** ($\Delta Te'_C$)			**Word** ($\Delta Te'_W$)		
Defense	*BERT*	*ELMo*	*GloVe*	*BERT*	*ELMo*	*GloVe*
Tr	+14%	+52%	+0%	+5%	+53%	+6%
$Tr^{50\%}$	+32%	+31%	+36%	+16%	+10%	+16%
Tr'	+30%	+30%	+32%	-7%	-3%	-5%
E_C	+11%	+15%	+2%	+13%	+17%	+10%
E_W	+28%	+48%	+21%	+8%	+25%	+6%
E_{C+W}	+17%	+21%	+22%	+17%	+9%	+15%

Fewer errors on Te' More errors on Te'

Table 1: Relative difference in error rate for each task's perturbed test data (Te') compared to original Te.

and attacks. In order to produce a holistic evaluation of model susceptibility, we examine defenses and attacks separately. Although we consider the same model behavior, each position can highly impact the interpretation of the findings and key takeaways. We also want to understand model misclassifications, including those with high model confidence and those that can have a greater negative effect in practice which we accomplish with our high confidence and high impact analyses.

4.1 Defense Viewpoint

We compare results from the models trained on data with varying degrees of perturbation to understand which models provide the most effective defenses. We define success in the defender case as the lowest error rate across a variety of test data including original (Te), perturbed (Te'), and combinations of original and perturbed samples ($Mixed$). We start by presenting the *relative difference* in error rates which is the percentage increase or decrease in the error rate of the perturbed ($\hat{Te}'$) and original ($\hat{T}e$) test data. Relative difference is defined as:

$$\Delta Te'_x = \frac{\hat{Te}'_x - \hat{T}e}{\hat{T}e} \tag{1}$$

where x represents perturbation type (char or word). Relative difference results are shown in Table 1.

With the 3-way task, defenses across embeddings and test data appear effective and achieve low relative percent differences with the exception of models trained with the original examples (Tr). The Tr defense is ineffective against both the character- and word-perturbed text (Te'_C and Te'_W). Intuitively, this could be seen as an "out of domain" data attack where the perturbed test set has significantly changed the original distribution such that a model not trained on perturbed data is more susceptible to errors. The E_C models have a lower relative difference in errors on Te'_W than on Te'_C across all three embeddings used for text representations. Thus, an ensemble of models overcomes the setback of out of domain data.

On Te'_C data, we observe similar relative errors between the three embeddings for all defense types; however, the performance on Te'_W is much more varied with the largest change seen from the ELMo embeddings, -1% relative difference from the Tr' model on Te'_C and -21% relative difference from the same defense on Te'_W. We only see consistent behavior with the $Tr^{50\%}$ defense when tested on Te and Te' across embedding strategies and attack perturbations. A model trained on data containing 50% clean and 50% perturbed samples performs almost equally on the clean and perturbed test sets and exhibits less than a 5% difference in errors between the test sets for all embeddings.

Dissimilarly, the 4-way task defenses display higher relative differences in errors on Te'_C and Te'_W with the exception of the Tr' defense. Under the Te'_W attack, Tr' is the only defense to achieve fewer errors on the perturbed test set. We also see more variation in the relative errors across embeddings for the same defenses. For instance, with BERT, the Tr model defending against the Te'_C attack has a 14% relative error difference while the equivalent ELMo and GloVe models have 52% and 0% relative error differences, respectively. This trend appears across defenses and in some cases highlights the ineffectiveness of these defenses.

With both tasks, there are fewer errors on Te'_W using Tr' as the defense, regardless of embedding type, specifically 21% fewer errors on the 3-way task and 3% fewer errors on the 4-way task with ELMo embeddings. Although the results on the tasks look dissimilar in terms of "best generalizability" (*i.e.,* show good performance on both Te and Te'), we see that character-based ensemble models exhibit the most consistent defense across tasks. The ability to have a single model (E_C) perform uniformly well across tasks outweighs the slight performance increase with individualized models per task. The ensemble defenses that leverage character-based defenses (E_C or E_{C+W})

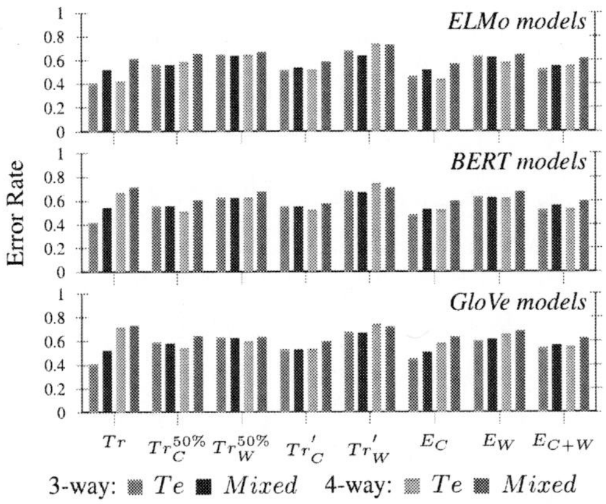

Figure 2: Defense effectiveness illustrated by error rate as a function of defense strategy for each model when tested on Te or $Mixed$ (Te + Te'_C + Te'_W) data.

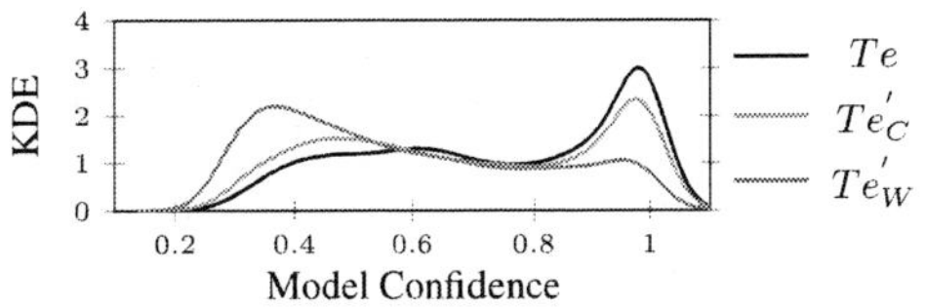

Figure 3: Kernel density estimation (KDE) plots illustrating distribution of model confidences.

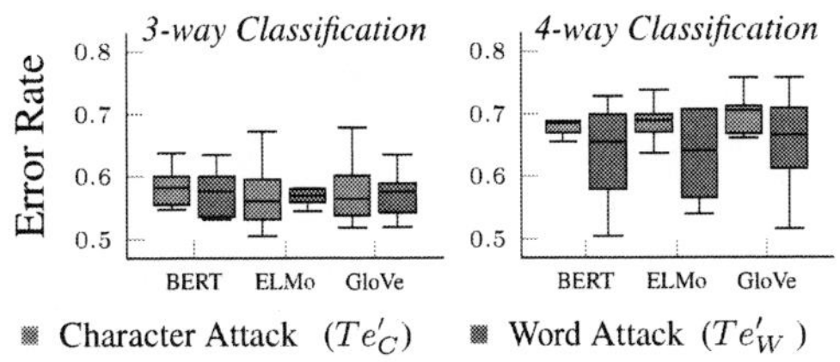

Figure 4: Box plots showing the effectiveness of the character and word perturbation attack tactics via error rates across BERT-, ELMo-, and GloVe-based models.

are more generalizable to novel test data which is beneficial when considering real-world data.

Performance on a variety of test data alone does not indicate the best defense. If a given defense performs similarly across datasets, it may simply perform equally poorly. Pairing additional analysis shown in Figure 2 with generalizability results highlighted in Table 1, we can better investigate effective defenses. In Figure 2, we plot the error rates of each defense when paired with clean (Te) or a mixed combination of clean and poisoned (Te + Te'_C + Te'_W) examples. While the ELMo Tr models in Table 1 had the highest relative differences in error, these models outperform the same BERT and GloVe models. The best defenses (*i.e.*, with the lowest error rates) are the same models that were most consistently generalizable across attack types – E_C and E_{C+W}. *These results indicate that defenses that include character-perturbed training data (E_C and E_{C+W}) are the most effective against character- and word-based attacks.*

4.2 Attack Viewpoint

Next, we examine susceptibility to adversarial attacks from the view of the attacker. We consider the impact on model confidence, and we analyze how a given attack impacts the uncertainty of classifications overall. For example, in a human-machine teaming scenario, a deception detection model would be used to flag content for a human fact-checker who may rely on the model's confidence when choosing whether to trust the classification.

In Figure 3, KDE plots illustrate model confidence distributions across examples from three test sets. We find that Te'_W peaks at lower model confidences and flattens out as model confidence increases. By contrast, Te and Te'_C peak at a model confidence close to 1. This shows that there is more confusion for predictions made on word-perturbed test data. If an analyst or end user relies on model confidence when choosing to accept a prediction, a significant difference in uncertainty of model classification can affect that decision. For example, when testing on clean examples (Te), the shift to a lower overall confidence may be enough to degrade the efficacy of the recommendation, even if the model has correctly classified the example.

Having examined the impact of attacks on model confidence, we next compare the effectiveness of each attack tactic when success is defined by the number of misclassifications. In Figure 4, box plots show the number of misclassifications as error rates. Te'_C and Te'_W attacks achieve similar median error rates in the 3-way task, and the maximum error rates are greater for the character than the word attacks. Although the 4-way task shows more discrepancies across attacks, again we see the character attacks display larger rates of error. *With both tasks, we see the largest number of misclassifications typically result from character-based attacks.*

Of note, the impact on the 3-way task is consistent across embedding types and attacks (the median error rates range from 56% to 59%). We see the widest range and largest maximum error rate with ELMo- and GloVe-based models when attacked with character-perturbed text. Contrastly, the 4-way task displays similar trends across em-

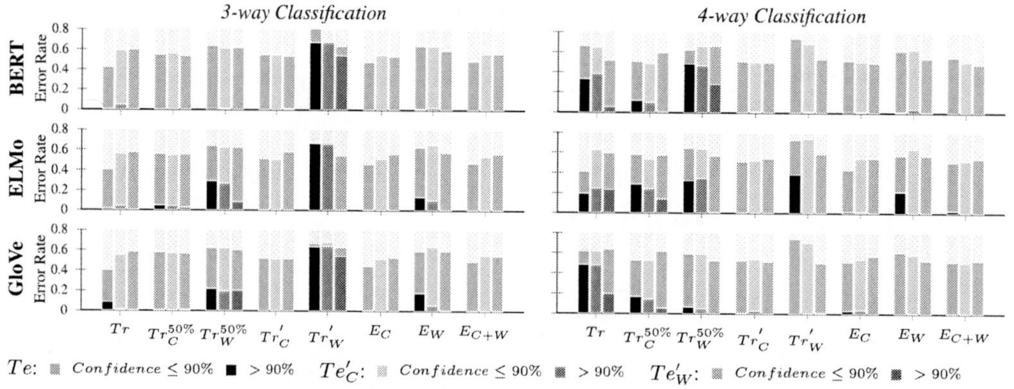

Figure 5: Error rates highlighting the prevalence of *high confidence* ($> 90\%$) errors when tested on each dataset.

beddings but not across attack types. Although we see a greater range of error rates with the word attacks, the character attacks achieve a larger median and mean error rates than either Te or Te'_W.

4.3 High Confidence Misclassifications

Next, we examine high confidence misclassifications which are integral to understanding model behavior and the limitations faced by deceptive news detection approaches. Figure 5 highlights error rates across test data distinguishing high confidence ($> 90\%$) from lower confidence ($\leq 90\%$).

With the 3-way task, we observe that high confidence misclassifications account for a majority of all errors from the Tr'_W models (85.7% of errors with the Te'_W attack are considered high confidence). This is larger than the errors from any of the other models. We also notice one exception to this finding: the Tr'_W ELMo model makes very few (less than 0.5%) high confident incorrect predictions for the Te'_W test set. With the 4-way task, we do not see the same frequency of high confidence errors although $Tr_W^{50\%}$ displays high rates of high confidence misclassifications on BERT and ELMo models when tested with Te and Te'_C.

Previously, we detailed stronger performance from the E_C and E_{C+W} defenses. As shown in Figure 5, both ensemble defenses display the lowest (or second lowest) error rates across attacks. Moreover, these models exhibit sparse high confidence misclassifications when reviewing averaged confidence scores across ensembled models. This is advantageous model behavior in a real-world setting when predicted model confidences must act as a proxy for uncertainty, and, in instances when ground truth labels are unknown, as a means to calibrate users' trust in model classifications.

4.4 High Impact Misclassifications

Finally, we contrast model performance for each task and our devised binary sub-tasks (trustworthy versus deceptive for the 3-way task and satire versus not satire for the 4-way task). Figure 6 demonstrates model tendencies towards high impact misclassifications across defenses, embeddings, and test sets. A higher binary F1 score indicates fewer high impact misclassifications – *i.e.,* more errors due to misclassifications among similar classes as compared to more errors due to misclassifications among significantly different classes. All models exhibit higher F1 scores on the binary sub-task than the multiclass task, as would be expected since the binary task presents an "easier" problem with an increased random chance for correct classification.

We examine consistent trends for each test set (indicated by color) or embedding type (indicated by mark size) across defenses. Values plotted in the same color cluster more consistently than those plotted in the same size. Two defenses show the most consistency in performance across configurations. $Tr_W^{50\%}$ displays low performance on both the binary and multiclass formulations of the 3-way task and Tr'_C displays high performance (relative to each task) across formulations for both the 3-way and 4-way tasks, with more consistency and higher performance on the 4-way task. Similar to Tr'_C, $Tr_C^{50\%}$ displays high performance across both tasks, although this defense is more consistent on the 3-way task. Although the Tr model is the best configuration when testing on Te, the Tr model shows much lower efficacy when tested against both attacks. *Overall, configurations using*

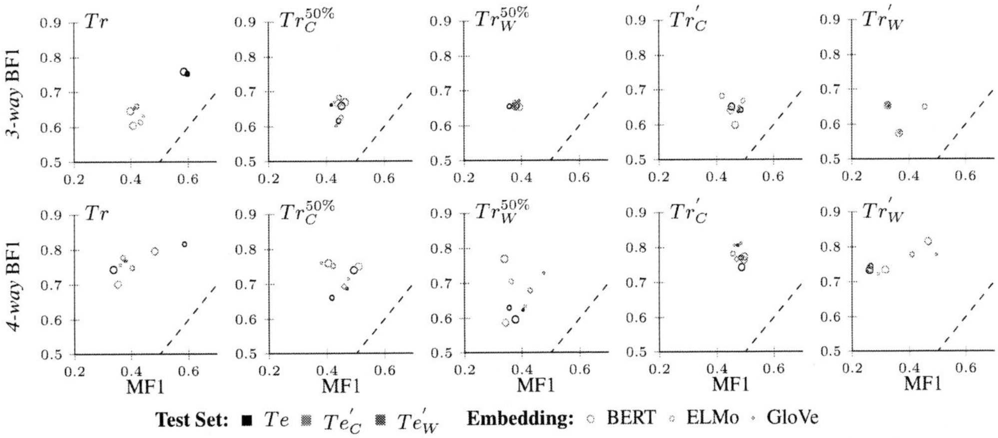

Figure 6: Binary F1 (BF1) as a function of multiclass F1 (MF1). Dashed lines indicate equal performance.

the character-based defenses result in the fewest overall high impact misclassifications.

Interestingly, we see that defenses are more effective at the binary sub-task for the 4-way classification (satire versus not satire) than the binary sub-task for the 3-way classification (trustworthy versus deceptive). Both trustworthy and deceptive news media attempt to present the information and news they share as factual, truthful content. In contrast, satire is distinct from other types of deceptive news as well as distinct from trustworthy news sources because it does not intend to present content as factual or accurate. This distinction between the classes considered in the binary sub-tasks can explain the observed difference in performance.

5 Discussion and Future Work

Linguistic variation in text (adversarial or otherwise) is frequently encountered in real-world settings. As such, we have presented extensive evaluations concerning the robustness of deception detection models to perturbed inputs. To the best of our knowledge, we are the first to evaluate model susceptibility in regards to adversarial linguistic attacks, investigate model behavior behind high confident or high impact failures, and present effective defensive strategies to these types of attacks. Our comprehensive set of perturbation experiments identify key findings from not only the defender perspective (the most effective strategy of defense across multiple or combined attacks) but also the attacker perspective (the most effective method of attack) – a focus of analysis not previously studied. In regard to the defense viewpoint, we show that ensemble-based approaches leveraging perturbed (adversarial) and non-perturbed (original) training examples perform consistently well. With the attack viewpoint, character-based attacks hinder performance regardless or model, defense, or task.

Our adversarial analyses have also illustrated the danger of relying on single performance metrics. Models that achieve optimal performance on a specific task or adversarial situation may significantly under-perform with slight alterations in scope or context. For example, although the E_C and E_{C+W} models saw second best performance on either classification task, they outperformed the "best models" when considering all possible attacks. The models with the highest overall performance were also not consistently found to have the lowest high confidence or high impact misclassifications – an important consideration if a model is being considered for use on live platforms where decisions can significantly impact users.

The results highlighted in this work provide justification for enhanced development and analysis of deception detection models. Although we rely on a consistent model architecture in order to make equitable comparisons across tasks and datasets, the evaluation framework we present can be replicated with additional models, complex architectures, and variants in test data. This work relies on uniform perturbation attacks as opposed to strategic perturbation strategies that target specific substrings – such as pseudonymous terms, phrases, or monikers. Subsequent experiments will investigate more complex strategic attacks and their ability to evade or confuse deception detection models.

Acknowledgements

This research was supported by the Laboratory Directed Research and Development Program at Pacific Northwest National Laboratory, a multi-program national laboratory operated by Battelle for the U.S. Department of Energy.

References

Oluwaseun Ajao, Deepayan Bhowmik, and Shahrzad Zargari. 2018. Fake news identification on twitter with hybrid cnn and rnn models. In *Proceedings of the 9th International Conference on Social Media and Society*. ACM.

Battista Biggio, Igino Corona, Davide Maiorca, Blaine Nelson, Nedim Šrndić, Pavel Laskov, Giorgio Giacinto, and Fabio Roli. 2013. Evasion attacks against machine learning at test time. In *Joint European conference on machine learning and knowledge discovery in databases*, pages 387–402. Springer.

Nicholas Carlini and David Wagner. 2017. Towards evaluating the robustness of neural networks. In *2017 IEEE Symposium on Security and Privacy (SP)*, pages 39–57. IEEE.

Weiling Chen, Yan Zhang, Chai Kiat Yeo, Chiew Tong Lau, and Bu Sung Lee. 2018. Unsupervised rumor detection based on users' behaviors using neural networks. *Pattern Recognition Letters*, 105:226–233.

Hossein Derakhshan and Claire Wardle. 2017. Information disorder: definitions. *AA. VV., Understanding and addressing the disinformation ecosystem*, pages 5–12.

Jacob Devlin, Ming-Wei Chang, Kenton Lee, and Kristina Toutanova. 2019. BERT: Pre-training of deep bidirectional transformers for language understanding. In *Proceedings of NAACL-HLT*.

Finale Doshi-Velez and Been Kim. 2017. Towards a rigorous science of interpretable machine learning. *arXiv preprint arXiv:1702.08608*.

Alhussein Fawzi, Omar Fawzi, and Pascal Frossard. 2018. Analysis of classifiers' robustness to adversarial perturbations. *Machine Learning*, 107(3):481–508.

Richard Fletcher and Rasmus Kleis Nielsen. 2017. People dont trust news media–and this is key to the global misinformation debate. *AA. VV., Understanding and Addressing the Disinformation Ecosystem*, pages 13–17.

Anthony Y Fu, Xiaotie Deng, Liu Wenyin, and Greg Little. 2006a. The methodology and an application to fight against unicode attacks. In *Proceedings of the second symposium on Usable privacy and security*, pages 91–101. ACM.

Anthony Y Fu, Wan Zhang, Xiaotie Deng, and Liu Wenyin. 2006b. Safeguard against unicode attacks: generation and applications of uc-simlist. In *Proceedings of WWW*.

Ji Gao, Jack Lanchantin, Mary Lou Soffa, and Yanjun Qi. 2018. Black-box generation of adversarial text sequences to evade deep learning classifiers. In *2018 IEEE Security and Privacy Workshops (SPW)*, pages 50–56. IEEE.

Maria Glenski and Tim Weninger. 2018. How humans versus bots react to deceptive and trusted news sources: A case study of active users. In *Proceedings of ASONAM*. IEEE/ACM.

Ian J Goodfellow, Jonathon Shlens, and Christian Szegedy. 2014. Explaining and harnessing adversarial examples. *arXiv preprint arXiv:1412.6572*.

Han Guo, Juan Cao, Yazi Zhang, Junbo Guo, and Jintao Li. 2018. Rumor detection with hierarchical social attention network. In *Proceedings of the 27th ACM International Conference on Information and Knowledge Management*. ACM.

Fred Matthew Hohman, Minsuk Kahng, Robert Pienta, and Duen Horng Chau. 2018. Visual analytics in deep learning: An interrogative survey for the next frontiers. *IEEE transactions on visualization and computer graphics*.

Alireza Karduni, Isaac Cho, Ryan Wesslen, Sashank Santhanam, Svitlana Volkova, Dustin L Arendt, Samira Shaikh, and Wenwen Dou. 2019. Vulnerable to misinformation?: Verifi! In *Proceedings of IUI*. ACM.

Alireza Karduni, Ryan Wesslen, Sashank Santhanam, Isaac Cho, Svitlana Volkova, Dustin Arendt, Samira Shaikh, and Wenwen Dou. 2018. Can you verifi this? studying uncertainty and decision-making about misinformation using visual analytics. In *Proceedings of ICWSM*.

Srijan Kumar, Justin Cheng, Jure Leskovec, and VS Subrahmanian. 2017. An army of me: Sockpuppets in online discussion communities. In *Proceedings of WWW*, pages 857–866.

Srijan Kumar, Bryan Hooi, Disha Makhija, Mohit Kumar, Christos Faloutsos, and VS Subrahmanian. 2018. Rev2: Fraudulent user prediction in rating platforms. In *Proceedings of ACM WSDM*. ACM.

Sejeong Kwon, Meeyoung Cha, and Kyomin Jung. 2017. Rumor detection over varying time windows. *PloS One*, 12(1):e0168344.

Sejeong Kwon, Meeyoung Cha, Kyomin Jung, Wei Chen, and Yajun Wang. 2013. Prominent features of rumor propagation in online social media. In *Proceedings of the 13th International Conference on Data Mining*, pages 1103–1108. IEEE.

David MJ Lazer, Matthew A Baum, Yochai Benkler, Adam J Berinsky, Kelly M Greenhill, Filippo Menczer, Miriam J Metzger, Brendan Nyhan, Gordon Pennycook, David Rothschild, et al. 2018. The science of fake news. *Science*, 359(6380):1094–1096.

Quanzhi Li, Qiong Zhang, and Luo Si. 2019. Rumor detection by exploiting user credibility information, attention and multi-task learning. In *Proceedings of the 57th Annual Meeting of the Association for Computational Linguistics*, pages 1173–1179.

Bin Liang, Hongcheng Li, Miaoqiang Su, Pan Bian, Xirong Li, and Wenchang Shi. 2018. Deep text classification can be fooled. In *Proceedings of IJCAI.*

Zachary C Lipton. 2018. The mythos of model interpretability. *Queue*, 16(3):31–57.

Changwei Liu and Sid Stamm. 2007. Fighting unicode-obfuscated spam. In *Proceedings of the anti-phishing working groups 2nd annual eCrime researchers summit*, pages 45–59. ACM.

Jan Hendrik Metzen, Tim Genewein, Volker Fischer, and Bastian Bischoff. 2017. On detecting adversarial perturbations. *arXiv preprint arXiv:1702.04267.*

Tanushree Mitra, Graham P Wright, and Eric Gilbert. 2017. A parsimonious language model of social media credibility across disparate events. ACM CSCW.

Seyed-Mohsen Moosavi-Dezfooli, Alhussein Fawzi, Omar Fawzi, and Pascal Frossard. 2017. Universal adversarial perturbations. In *Proceedings of IEEE CVPR*, pages 1765–1773.

Nic Newman, Richard Fletcher, Anne Schulz, Simge Andı, and Rasmus Kleis Nielsen. 2020. Reuters institute digital news report 2020. *Reuters Institute.*

Anh Nguyen, Jason Yosinski, and Jeff Clune. 2015. Deep neural networks are easily fooled: High confidence predictions for unrecognizable images. In *Proceedings of IEEE CVPR*, pages 427–436.

Myle Ott, Yejin Choi, Claire Cardie, and Jeffrey T Hancock. 2011. Finding deceptive opinion spam by any stretch of the imagination. In *Proceedings of ACL*, pages 309–319. ACL.

Nicolas Papernot, Patrick McDaniel, Somesh Jha, Matt Fredrikson, Z Berkay Celik, and Ananthram Swami. 2016a. The limitations of deep learning in adversarial settings. pages 372–387. IEEE.

Nicolas Papernot, Patrick McDaniel, Xi Wu, Somesh Jha, and Ananthram Swami. 2016b. Distillation as a defense to adversarial perturbations against deep neural networks. In *2016 IEEE Symposium on Security and Privacy (SP)*, pages 582–597. IEEE.

Nicolas Papernot, Patrick D. McDaniel, Ian J. Goodfellow, Somesh Jha, Z. Berkay Celik, and Ananthram Swami. 2016c. Practical black-box attacks against deep learning systems using adversarial examples. *CoRR.*

James Pennebaker, Martha Francis, and Roger Booth. 2001. Linguistic inquiry and word count: Liwc 2001. *Mahway: Lawrence Erlbaum Associates*, 71.

Jeffrey Pennington, Richard Socher, and Christopher Manning. 2014. Glove: Global vectors for word representation. In *Proceedings of EMNLP*. ACL.

Matthew Peters, Mark Neumann, Mohit Iyyer, Matt Gardner, Christopher Clark, Kenton Lee, and Luke Zettlemoyer. 2018. Deep contextualized word representations. In *Proceedings of NAACL-HLT.*

Vahed Qazvinian, Emily Rosengren, Dragomir R Radev, and Qiaozhu Mei. 2011. Rumor has it: Identifying misinformation in microblogs. In *Proceedings of EMNLP*, pages 1589–1599.

Hannah Rashkin, Eunsol Choi, Jin Yea Jang, Svitlana Volkova, and Yejin Choi. 2017. Truth of varying shades: Analyzing language in fake news and political fact-checking. In *Proceedings of EMNLP.*

Bhavtosh Rath, Wei Gao, Jing Ma, and Jaideep Srivastava. 2017. From retweet to believability: Utilizing trust to identify rumor spreaders on twitter. In *Proceedings of ASONAM.*

Marta Recasens, Cristian Danescu-Niculescu-Mizil, and Dan Jurafsky. 2013. Linguistic models for analyzing and detecting biased language. In *Proceedings of ACL*, pages 1650–1659.

Victoria L Rubin, Niall J Conroy, Yimin Chen, and Sarah Cornwell. 2016. Fake news or truth? Using satirical cues to detect potentially misleading news. In *Proceedings of NAACL-HLT.*

Suranjana Samanta and Sameep Mehta. 2017. Towards crafting text adversarial samples. *arXiv preprint arXiv:1707.02812.*

Elisa Shearer and Katerina Eva Matsa. 2018. News use across social media platforms 2018.

Kai Shu, Suhang Wang, and Huan Liu. 2019. Beyond news contents: The role of social context for fake news detection. In *Proceedings of WSDM*, pages 312–320. ACM.

Florian Tramèr, Alexey Kurakin, Nicolas Papernot, Ian Goodfellow, Dan Boneh, and Patrick McDaniel. 2018. Ensemble adversarial training: Attacks and defenses. In *ICLR.*

Svitlana Volkova, Kyle Shaffer, Jin Yea Jang, and Nathan Hodas. 2017. Separating facts from fiction: Linguistic models to classify suspicious and trusted news posts on twitter. In *Proceedings of ACL*, volume 2, pages 647–653.

Soroush Vosoughi, Deb Roy, and Sinan Aral. 2018. The spread of true and false news online. *Science*, 359(6380).

William Yang Wang. 2017. "liar, liar pants on fire": A new benchmark dataset for fake news detection. In *Proceedings of ACL*, pages 422–426.

Qiang Zhang, Aldo Lipani, Shangsong Liang, and Emine Yilmaz. 2019. Reply-aided detection of misinformation via bayesian deep learning. In *Proceedings of WWW*, pages 2333–2343. ACM.

Arkaitz Zubiaga, Elena Kochkina, Maria Liakata, Rob Procter, Michal Lukasik, Kalina Bontcheva, Trevor Cohn, and Isabelle Augenstein. 2018. Discourse-aware rumour stance classification in social media using sequential classifiers. *Information Processing & Management*, 54(2):273–290.

Reconsidering Annotator Disagreement about Racist Language: Noise or Signal?

Savannah Larimore
Washington University in St. Louis

Ian Kennedy
University of Washington

Breon Haskett
University of Washington

Alina Arseniev-Koehler
University of California - Los Angeles

Abstract

An abundance of methodological work aims to detect hateful and racist language in text. However, these tools are hampered by problems like low annotator agreement and remain largely disconnected from theoretical work on race and racism in the social sciences. Using annotations of 5188 tweets from 291 annotators, we investigate how annotator perceptions of racism in tweets vary by annotator racial identity and two text features of the tweets: relevant keywords and latent topics identified through structural topic modeling. We provide a descriptive summary of our data and estimate a series of linear models to determine if annotator racial identity and our 12 topics, alone or in combination, explain the way racial sentiment was annotated, net of relevant annotator characteristics and tweet features. Our results show that White and non-White annotators exhibit significant differences in ratings when reading tweets with high prevalence of certain racially-charged topics. We conclude by suggesting how future methodological work can draw on our results and further incorporate social science theory into analyses.

1 Introduction

Hateful and racist language is abundant on social media platforms like Twitter and a growing body of work aims to develop tools to detect such language in these spaces. Such a tool would offer opportunities to intervene, like providing automatic trigger warnings, and would provide a powerful barometer to measure racism. However, these efforts are hampered by low interrater agreement, low modeling performance, and a lack of consensus on what counts as racist language (e.g., Kwok and Wang, 2013; Burnap and Williams, 2016; Waseem, 2016; Schmidt and Wiegand, 2017). These efforts are also largely disconnected from rich understandings of race and racism in the social sciences (but, see Waseem, 2016). Indeed, social scientists have long acknowledged the difficulties of measuring racism, even when using traditional social science methods (e.g., interviews and surveys), due to social desirability biases and the increasingly covert nature of racism (Bonilla-Silva, 2006).

In this paper, we reconsider efforts to annotate for racism in light of sociological work on race and racism. Instead of generalizing our detection of racism, we narrow our scope to focus on anti-Black racism. In other words, we focus on racialized language directed at or centering on Black Americans. Using human annotations[1] for the racial sentiment (positive or negative) of 5188 Tweets, we describe how ratings vary by annotators' own racial identity. Our findings suggest that White raters respond differently to particular types of racialized language on Twitter, as identified by structural topic modeling (STM), than non-White raters. Failing to account for this systematic difference could lead researchers to consider tweets which non-White annotators identify as including negative sentiment as innocuous because more numerous White annotators rate those same tweets as positive or neutral. We conclude by suggesting several ways in which future work can account for the variability in annotations that comes from annotators' own racial identities.

1.1 Annotating for Racism

Collecting annotations is a key step to developing a tool to detect racial sentiment in text data. At the same time, the challenges of this task have been well-documented as ratings depend upon the ability of human annotators to consistently identify the racial sentiment of words and phrases (Zou and Schiebinger, 2018). Empirical work often finds large amounts of disagreement in these annotations, even with carefully designed annotations

[1]We use the terms rating/annotation and rater/annotator interchangeably throughout.

Proceedings of the Ninth International Workshop on Natural Language Processing for Social Media, pages 81–90
Online Workshop, June 10, 2021.

schemes (e.g., Bartlett et al., 2014; Schmidt and Wiegand, 2017).

As these efforts have shown, perceptions of racial sentiment are contextual and subjective, making the prevalence of racism in text sources inherently difficult to detect. Recent social scientific work (Bonilla-Silva, 2006; Carter and Murphy, 2015; Krysan and Moberg, 2016; Tynes and Markoe, 2010) has taken that difficulty as its subject, and sought to capture and understand the variation in perceptions of racism or racial sentiment, by showing how individuals' perceptions of racism vary systematically based on the their *own* racial identity. These findings suggest that annotator disagreement is not merely noise to smooth over. Rather, annotator disagreement for racism includes important variation that should be disaggregated and accounted for.

1.2 Varying Perceptions of Racism

Differential attitudes about and perceptions of racism based on an individuals' own racial identity are well-documented. White Americans tend to hold more overtly racist beliefs, are less likely to believe racial discrimination is prevalent in modern society, and are less likely to recognize racial microaggressions than Black Americans (Bonilla-Silva, 2006; Carter and Murphy, 2015; Krysan and Moberg, 2016; Tynes and Markoe, 2010). In addition, Krysan and Moberg (2016) note that White Americans increasingly disregard racial topics on questionnaires, signaling that they have "no interest" in issues of racial inequality. Likewise, fewer White Americans agree that racial inequality is due to overt discrimination, arguing instead that racial discrimination is a thing of the past and that in contemporary society, everyone has equally fair life chances (Bonilla-Silva, 2006). As Carter and Murphy (2015) note, White and Black Americans may differ in their views of racial inequality because White Americans compare contemporary racial inequalities to the past, referencing slavery and Jim Crow and naturally concluding that conditions have improved, while Black Americans compare the present to an imagined future, in which an ideal state of racial equality has been achieved.

These differences also extend to how we perceive racism in online platforms. Williams et al. (2016) find that while White students were equally as likely as students of color to perceive racially-themed internet memes as offensive, students of color tended to rate these same memes as more offensive than White students. That is, while White students could identify that a meme was racist, they rated the level of offensiveness lower than students of color. In addition, Tynes and Markoe (2010) find that European American college students were less likely than African American college students to react negatively to racially-themed party images on social media. Furthermore, European American students reported higher levels of color-blind racial attitudes and students with lower levels of color-blind attitudes were more likely to react as "bothered" by the images, implying that both race and racial attitudes influence perceptions of racism online. Similarly, Daniels (2009) finds that critical race literacy matters more than internet literacy in identifying racially biased or "cloaked" websites (i.e., websites that appear to promote racial justice but are actually maintained by White supremacist organizations). This finding suggests that students who lack a critical race consciousness may be less likely to identify racist materials online and that White students may be particularly susceptible.

The subtlety of racism that pervades social media sites like Twitter may also influence perceptions of racism. As Carter and Murphy (2015) note, Whites tend to focus only on blatant, overt forms of racism (e.g., racial slurs, mentions of racial violence) but are less attuned to microaggressions and other, subtler forms of racism. As such, scholars have also advocated for a methodological move away from "bag of words" approaches to the evaluation of racism on social media (Watanabe et al., 2018) because these approaches reinforce a focus on blatant, overt forms of racism, and neglect more subtle, or contextually racist tweets (Chaudhry, 2015).

Similarly, Kwok and Wang (2013), noting the subtlety of racism pervading social media posts, argue that to get evaluations of tweets that accurately assesses meaning, features of tweets other than the text must be included. Tweet features set the rules of engagement by offering markers of credibility, sarcasm, and persuasiveness (Sharma and Brooker, 2016; Hamshaw et al., 2018). Tweet features such as links, hashtags, and number of comments have been shown to illuminate the context of the tweet's message (Burnap and Williams, 2016). The inclusion of these features in evaluation offers deeper context and more realistic evaluation of tweets allowing for greater attention to the differential evaluations of people in racially marginalized groups engaging with the social media platform.

Here, we expand on previous research by investigating how annotator racial identity and tweet features interact to influence perceptions of racism on Twitter. Our analysis builds on previous research that uses racist speech as a stimulus (Leets, 2001; Cowan and Hodge, 1996; Tynes and Markoe, 2010), either in print or digital media, and calls for renewed attention to variations based on annotator racial identity and how these variations ultimately influence instruments to measure racial sentiment. We extend this body of work by including potentially racist speech sourced randomly from Twitter, rather than developed by researchers, and by including tweet features as well as annotator racial identity in our analyses.

2 Hypotheses

Based on previous work in annotation and a sociologically informed understanding of race and racism, we propose three hypotheses:

$\mathbf{H_1}$**:** Annotations will vary, on average, based on the racial identity of the annotator: White raters will rate tweets as having a more positive racial sentiment on average compared to non-White raters.

$\mathbf{H_2}$**:** Annotations of racial sentiment will vary by the racially charged keywords in the tweet and the latent topics in the tweet. Tweets with racialized keywords (e.g., N****r) will be rated as more negative than those without.

$\mathbf{H_3}$**:** Annotations will vary based on the interaction of text features (racially charged keywords and latent topics) and the racial identity of the annotator: Compared to non-White raters, White raters will interpret particular topics as having a more positive racial sentiment, and interpret other topics as having a more negative racial sentiment.

3 Methods

3.1 Data

We combine data from two separate research projects, producing a final sample of 291 human raters applied to 5188 unique tweets. The first project collected 1348 tweets from Twitter's Streaming API from June 2018 to September 2019. The second project collected 3840 tweets from the Digital Online Life and You Project (DOLLY; a repository all geotagged tweets since December 2011) (Morcos et al.). For both projects, tweets were restricted to those that were sent from the contiguous United States, were written in English, and contained at least one keyword relevant to the analysis. To limit our sample to tweets that concerned Black Americans, we used common hate speech terms, the term "black girl magic", and the same keywords to identify tweets about Black Americans as Flores (2017).

For the second project, tweets were also restricted to a 10% sample of all tweets sent from 19 metropolitan statistical areas between January 2012 and December 2016. While both data collection processes yielded millions of unique tweets, both projects sampled several thousand tweets for annotation based on available funding to compensate annotators or access to undergraduate classrooms (for a similar methodology, see Burnap and Williams, 2016). We then collected human annotations using Amazon Mechanical Turks and college students from two separate classrooms at the same university, for a total on 291 annotators. All annotators were instructed to use the same annotation tool, were provided with brief training, and we applied a coding structure such that each unique tweet was rated by at least 5 annotators.

Annotators also reported their race and gender identities. Race was reported using the following categories: White/Caucasian/European, Black/African American, Asian/Pacific Islander, Latino/Hispanic/Spanish, and Other. Annotators were allowed to select more than one race. For the current analyses and due to sample size restrictions, we collapsed the annotator race into two categories: 1) Non-Hispanic White/Caucasian/European alone (henceforth, "White") and 2) All other racial classifications (henceforth, "non-White"). Gender was reported as woman, man, or other gender.

A total of 52.23% of our 291 raters identified as White, and 46.05% identified as non-White and 1.72% were missing race, respectively. A total of 38.49% of our raters identified as women, 58.73% identified as men, and 1.37% were missing gender. On average, our raters were 27.45 years. Given these characteristics, our raters are similar to Twitter users in regard to age and gender, but are perhaps more likely to identify as White (Perrin and Anderson, 2019).

3.2 Variables

Our outcome variable is a continuous measure for racial sentiment, which we operationalize as how "positively" or "negatively" a tweet was rated. Raters used a 7-point Likert scale to describe the sentiment of the tweet, ranging from "very negative" (i.e., -3) to "very positive" (i.e., +3), with a "neutral" rating at the center of the scale (i.e., 0).

Our key independent variables are two text features of tweets (relevant keywords and latent topics) and the racial identity of annotators. Relevant keywords were inductively identified by the research team from a close reading of the tweets. Keywords of theoretical significance (e.g., mentions of racialized violence; animal epithets) were also considered. This process yielded 8 groups of keywords: 1) keywords with allusions to sex or sexuality (e.g., "sex") 2) keywords about people (e.g., "ppl") 3) animal epithets 4) spelling variations of N***a 5) spelling variations of N***er 6) derogatory words towards women (e.g,. "B***h") 7) spelling variations of F**k 8) keywords about racialized violence (e.g., lyn**). Each of these 8 groups of keywords were treated as a binary variable (1 = any keyword in the group is present in the tweet).

Latent topics were identified using the STM package in R and we used STM's built-in methods to select a model with 12 topics (Roberts et al., 2019). We labeled each topic by 1) examining the words with the highest probability of being generated by the topic 2) examining the top words for the topic based on STM's "FR-EX" measure that uses word frequency and exclusivity within a topic (Roberts et al., 2014), and 3) reading the 20 tweets which have the highest loading onto the topic. Topics were treated as continuous (i.e., the "amount" of a topic in a given tweet). Racial identity was measured as White or non-White, as described previously.

We include several covariates in our models. First, we control for annotator gender identity (woman/man/other) and age (years). Second, we include binary indicators for the following tweet features: if a URL link is present and if there is a mention included, indicating a conversation between users. Third, we control for the length of the tweet, measured in characters.

3.3 Analysis

Our analysis proceeds in three steps. First, we provide descriptive summaries of our data. We summarize our STM results, and provide Krippendorf's alpha coefficients (Krippendorff, 1980) to assess inter-rater reliability for all raters, for White raters, and for non-White raters.

Second, we estimate three linear models, each respectively testing our three hypotheses. Model 1, the "Annotator Race" model, regresses racial sentiment on a binary indicator for annotator racial identity (1 = White). Model 2, the "Text Features" model, regreses racial sentiment on binary indicators for relevant keywords and continuous measures for topics (described in Variables). Model 3, the "Interaction" model, regresses racial sentiment on three interaction terms: one for each statistically significant, theoretically-informed topics identified in Model 1 (i.e., topics 2, 5, and 9), interacted with annotator racial identity. As such, Model 3 treats annotator racial identity as an effect modification variable in the analysis because we expect that annotator racial identity will modify ratings of tweets based on salient topics.

For Models 2 and 3, we include all covariates (described in our Variables section). For Model 3, we additionally control for all keywords and topics included in Model 1. Using the results from Model 3, we also compute predicted racial sentiment ratings based on the amount of a topic in a given tweet and the racial identity of an annotator. We visualize regression coefficients and 95% confidence intervals in Figure 1 for all three models, and we visualize selected results on predicted sentiment ratings by amount of topic in Figures 2-4. Analyses were performed in R (R Core Team, 2017) using α= 0.05 for statistical significance.

Third, we qualitatively describe annotated tweets that illustrate the results of our interaction models based on proportion of a given topic and a high degree of inter-rater disagreement between White and non-White raters.[2]

[2]Specifically, for a given topic, we first selected the tweet with the most amount of a topic by percentile x > 90%. Second, narrowed this candidate list of tweets to the 20 with most disagreement between White and Non-White raters. Finally, among this short list of 20 tweets, we selected the tweet best reflected the differences shown numerically in Figures 2, 3, and 4.

4 Results

4.1 Descriptive Analysis

Table 1 provides a summary of our 12 topics. This summary includes topic labels, the seven most representative words (by "FR-EX" as described earlier), and the tweet which loads most highly onto each topic. As might be expected from our corpus, many of the 12 topics are relevant to race, such as a topic we label "Racial Arguments" and a topic we label "Police Brutality." To be clear, these topics may be mentioned in positive, neutral, or negative lights. For example, a tweet containing the topic "Police Brutality" might be reporting on successful efforts to minimize police brutality. We refer to the topic by the numeric ID it was assigned by STM and the title we assigned the topic.

Overall agreement on racial sentiment was low among raters (Krippendorf alpha = 0.39), but higher within White raters (Krippendorf alpha = 0.44). Among non-White raters, agreement was also low (Krippendorf alpha = 0.34). This low agreement echoes prior work on the challenges of annotating racially charged language (e.g., Bartlett et al., 2014; Schmidt and Wiegand, 2017), as described earlier. Importantly, the goal of this study was *not* to arrive at annotations with high agreement (i.e., for training a predictive model); instead our goal was to examine patterns of agreement and disagreement in annotations.

4.2 Regression Analysis

The results of our regression analysis are shown in Figure 1. We present the results for each consecutive model, showing the main effects for annotator racial identity and text features in Models 1 and 2, respectively, before turning to the interaction terms in Model 3. We do so to highlight changes across models as predictors are introduced and to confirm effect moderation but note that constitutive terms for the interactions in Model 3 should not be interpreted as unconditional marginal effects (Brambor et al., 2006).

In H_1, we expected a difference in average racial sentiment rating between White and non-White raters. Using Model 1, we find that the association between annotator racial identity (as White) and sentiment is positive and statistically significant, but small (β=.071, p<.001).[3] This suggests that while, on average, White raters tend to rate racial sentiment of tweets as higher than do non-White raters, this difference may not influence our annotations in a substantial way. Thus, we conclude that we find limited support for this hypothesis.

In H_2, we expected that text features of the tweet would significantly influence sentiment ratings. Using Model 2, we find strong support for this hypothesis: all of our topics and keyword features are significantly associated with sentiment rating (see Figure 1). This result confirms the intuition that raters are responding to a variety of racially coded language as they make their annotations. Notably, we also observe that the effect of these text features on raters' sentiment is far greater than the main effect of racial identity.

In H_3, we expected that the difference between White and non-White raters' ratings depends on how much of a topic was present in a tweet. We tested this using Model 3, where we interacted topics and rater racial identity. We find that the interaction terms for seven of our topics are significantly associated with racial sentiment (see figure 1), providing strong support for H_3.

We illustrate several of these interaction effects more directly in Figures 2-4 for three of the topics (Topic 2: Police Brutality, Topic 5: Empowering History, and Topic 9: Antiracist Politics). These figures show the *expected* racial sentiment rating of a tweet in our model against how much the tweet loads onto a given topic, among White and non-White raters.[4] The x-axis of each plot ranges from the 1st percentile of topic values in our data to the 100th percentile. These figures show that for the topics with significant interactions, substantial differences by annotator race arise when certain topics are very prevalent in the tweet. Thus, while Model 1 suggests that White and non-White raters have small differences in rating across *all* tweets, Model 3 shows that for tweets about *certain* topics, White and non-White raters in fact rate tweets quite differently. We examine examples of this di-

[3]We note that similar conclusions may be reached with Model 2, where the coefficient for annotator racial identity is also significant but small (β=.042, p<.01).

[4]Because the vector of topics in an STM sum to one, increasing one topic implies decreasing others, which are also included in our models and therefore will also influence the estimated rating. Moreover, the topics are often correlated, so just decreasing the other topics evenly would produce a potentially misleading result. For these plots, as we increased our focal topic–Topic 2 in Figure 2–we adjusted the other topics based on their average in our data for that value of Topic 2. That means that the plots reflect the estimated tweet rating for White and non-White raters for various values of Topic 2 and the average values of other topics at those values of Topic 2, with other covariates held at their means.

Table 1. Topic Titles and Top Words (by "FR-EX")

Topic Title	*Top Words*	*Example Tweet*
Topic 1: Breaking Stereotypes	chick, til, retail, wut, firework, camp, gramma	People salty cause they never seen a black guy work at PacSun before
Topic 2: Police Brutality	man, teacher, fool, nicki, pride, doctor, histor	Lorenzo Clerkley, a 14 year old black kid who was with friends playing with a BB gun in broad daylight was shot 4 times by an officer after being given 0.6 second warnings
Topic 3: Racial Arguments	shit, use, word, poor, stupid, respect, mexican	I'm sorry to intrude on this but that's kind of a screwed up concept to say that white people are inherently racist? Races and ethnicities of all kinds have conquered and enslaved others throughout mankind but only one group gets it all pinned onto them?
Topic 4: Black Women and Girls	get, let, twitter, amaz, els, seem, bro	In 1968, Shirley Chisolm (1924-2005) was the 1st Af-Am woman elected to Congress (D-NY). In 1972, she was the 1st woman to seek the Democratic nomination for POTUS. A staunch women's rights activist, she delivered this speech in support of the ERA in 1970.
Topic 5: Empowering History	girl, king, magic, martin, luther, celebr, sell	Pioneers : African American surgeon, Daniel Hale Williams, opened the first interracial Hospital in Chicago in 1891 and performed the first documented open-heart surgery in 1893.
Topic 6: Monkey	atwitterhandl, your, aint, shes, season, theyr	atwitterhandle atwitterhandle some of his stuff is alright I guess but overall I cant stand that cheeto dread monkey
Topic 7: Empowering Information	african, american, definit, murder, dog, student, leader	#FridayFeeling new #exhibit open at #DunnMuseum features local #AfricanAmerican history of Booker T. Washington Progressive Club. Open January 11 - February 24.
Topic 8: Irreverent Interactions	fuck, back, big, turn, damn, wtf, light	Driving on the highway past the big black dude who was grinding up weed while driving the kids bouncy house truckgtgtgtgt you do you dawg
Topic 9: Antiracist Politics	like, look, color, start, lot, run, everyth	Associates with white nationalists and open bigots. He's the architect of the Muslim ban and cruel policies that separate children from families at the border. If it looks like a duck, walks like a duck, quacks like a duck - it's a duck.
Topic 10: Black the Color	awebsit, shop, doesnt, widow, coffe, disgrac, hot	Drinking a Catskill Mountain Black IPA by Gilded Otter Gilded Otter Brewing Company awebsite photo
Topic 11: Debates about Race and Racism	mentionplacehold, minor, bait, control, societi, kkk, negro	[50 mentions] And that's a bullshit statement you know I really don't know why you white leftist hate your own race so much ... what you just said is no different than saying black people can't be racist
Topic 12: Honest Opinions	world, next, month, learn, post, honest, number	I'm a 41 year old African American born in Minneapolis and have lived close to Seattle my entire life. Everytime I hear this manufactured crisis by the media I change the channel. If the media fails us again/2016 this country will never recover,?media will never be trusted again.

vergence in our qualitative analysis.

4.3 Qualitative Analysis

To provide qualitative examples of our findings, we identify exemplary tweets in Table 2 from each of the three topics displayed in Figures 2-4. For topic 2: Police Brutality, we find that White raters considered this tweet "moderately positive", with an average racial sentiment rating of 2.0. In contrast, non-White raters considered this tweet closer to neutral, with an average racial sentiment rating of 0.4. This difference is particularly striking, as this tweet makes reference to wrongful detention, something that sociological and computational research would suggest White raters would also consider negative. While this tweet suggests an attempt to make amends within the news story presented in the tweet, the perception of the racial sentiment is quite different across raters.

For Topic 5: Empowering History, we find White raters consider this exemplary tweet "moderately positive", while non-White raters consider this tweet "neutral", on average. This tweet quotes Dr. Martin Luther King Jr. and suggests that references to historical figures may signal different things for White and non-White raters. Further, the connection to a specific Christian observance of Lent signals little racialized content for some. For Topic 9: Anti-racist politics, we find that White raters consider this exemplary tweet "neutral" while non-White raters consider it "moderately positive". This implies that the White raters who viewed this tweet may not have considered anti-racist work to have a positive racial sentiment.

Figure 1: Regression Coefficients and 95% Confidence Intervals For Three Regression Models

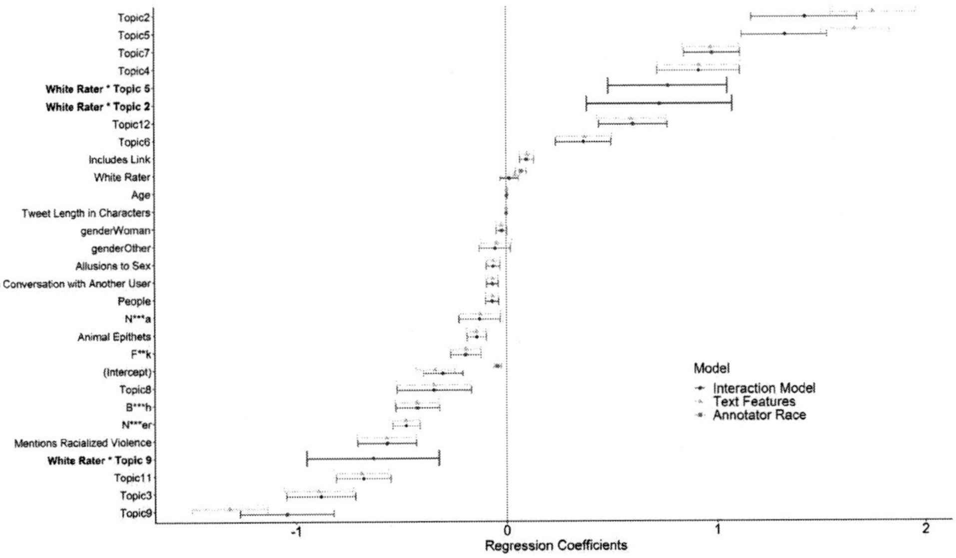

Note: The "Annotator Race" model regresses racial sentiment on annotator racial identity. The "Text Features" model regresses racial sentiment on annotator racial identity, racially charged keywords, latent topics and covariates. The "Interaction" model regresses racial sentiment on all terms in Model 2 as well as interaction terms between selected topics and annotator racial identity.

Figure 2: Topic 2 Estimated Tweet Rating Including Annotator Race Interaction

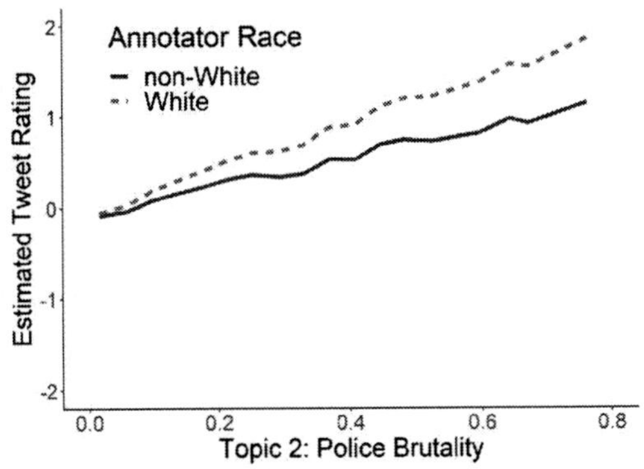

Figure 3: Topic 5 Estimated Tweet Rating Including Annotator Race Interaction

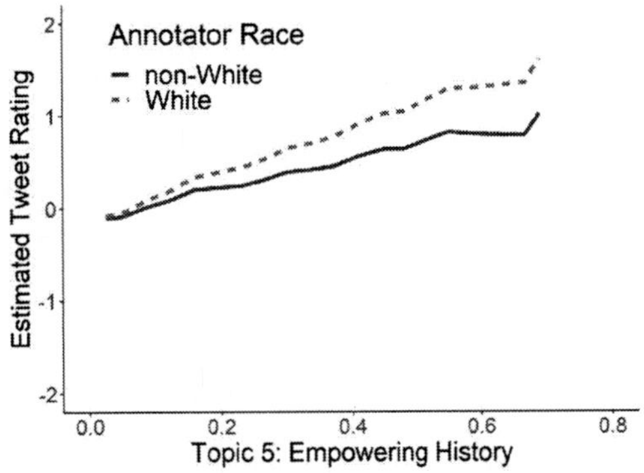

In contrast to our results from H_1, which show that the average difference in sentiment rating by annotator race is small, these qualitative results add further evidence to support H_3: that raters of different racial identities interpret topics differently. These qualitative examples illustrate that differences between raters are not just statistically significant but also practically meaningful.

5 Conclusions

The goal of our analysis was to determine if and how annotator racial identity influenced perceptions of the racial sentiment of a tweet regarding Black Americans. When we examine the mean difference between White and non-White annotators (Model 1), we find a small but significant difference in sentiment ratings. When we consider White and non-White raters responses to different amounts of topics in the tweets (Model 3) we find strong evidence that annotator racial identity *does* inform perceptions of sentiment towards Black people for seven of our twelve topics. Our results suggest that White and non-White raters interpret these seven topics differently and as these

Table 2. Exemplary Tweets of Interaction Model, by Latent Topic

Topic Title	*White Raters*	*Non-White Raters*	*Exemplary Tweet*
Topic 2: Police Brutality	2.0	0.4	The meeting is in response to a incident earlier this month in which an African American man was detained shortly by police while cleaning outside his home in Boulder.
Topic 5: Empowering History	2	0	Forgiveness is not an occasional act it is a permanent attitude Dr Martin Luther King JrHow about this for Lent
Topic 9: Antiracist Politics	0	2	Sounds like good is locked in battle with perfect. I am a white person trying to fight white supremacy, and I will never not be flawed. I don't need your cookie, but it would be nice not to take friendly fire.

Figure 4: Topic 9 Estimated Tweet Rating Including Annotator Race Interaction

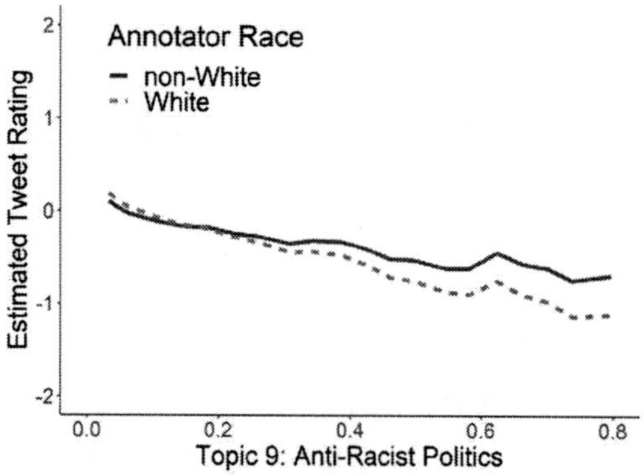

topics increase in tweets (Figures 2-4), this gap in interpretation widens.

Notably, the topics we identify as most divisive are some of the very topics which social scientists may be most interested in analyzing: references to police brutality, references to historical figures or events, and discussions of anti-racist politics. Our descriptive qualitative analysis suggests that White annotators may not be as attuned to the nuances of these topics in tweets. Future work might expand on these results to investigate raters' rationale for their ratings.

Given that perceptions of racism vary by annotator's own race, it is crucial that future work considers whose interpretations are reflected in annotations for racism. Indeed, annotators' interpretations end up being a gold standard from which models learn to detect what counts as racist or not. While we focus on the role of annotators' racial identities, many other dimensions of annotators' identities likely also influence their responses on annotation tasks more generally. This issue extends beyond annotation tasks: across the disciplines, there is growing recognition that much of the social scientific knowledge produced to-date is specific to the population from which we most often draw participants (Henrich et al., 2010).

We suggest several takeaways for future research. First, researchers should use purposeful sampling (Palinkas et al., 2015) to gather annotations from diverse populations of annotators. This may be challenging given that platforms for collecting annotations may include a particular demographic of workers. In particular, young, white, and well-educated workers are over-represented on MTurk (Hitlin, 2016). Second, research using human annotation might collect (and report) annotator demographics, in order to be explicit about whose interpretations the annotations do (or do not) reflect. Third, given the many possible identities, researchers might consider several possible strategies to focus on a particular demographic of annotators. Researchers might focus on the populations for whom the gold standard is most important, or might be most divisive. We suggest that the gold standards for racist language should reflect the interpretations of who is impacted most the standard. For example, annotations for anti-Black racism should ideally reflect how Black individuals interpret the data. Perhaps annotations could be weighted when training classifiers to detect racist language, so that annotators whose identities are most affected by the gold standard have stronger influences on the gold standard.

Human annotation lies at the crux of many advances and tools in computer science. Our work also fits into a broader, growing body of scholarship which reconsiders how researchers' choices and assumptions around human annotation shapes the tools and information that annotation is used to produce (e.g., Sap et al., 2019; Al Kuwatly et al., 2020; Wich et al., 2020; Blodgett et al., 2020). Annotations for racist and hate speech must be reflexively collected and used to avoid contributing to other forms of biases along the way.

Acknowledgements

This work benefited from support from the Summer Institute for Computational Social Science (SICSS) for initial annotator funding, a Graduate Student Research Funding Award from the Sociology Department at the University of Washington and the National Science Foundation Graduate Research Fellowship Program under Grant No. DGE-1650604. We also extend our gratitude to Matthew Zook and Ate Poorthuis, for maintaining and sharing the DOLLY data for this project, and the 291 annotators for providing ratings.

Ethical Considerations

This study was approved by the University of Washington Institutional Review Board. We only collected public tweets, and the annotation tools that we used did not display the profile IDs of the Twitter user who authored the tweet. We also reviewed tweets to make sure that authors were not members of groups at an elevated risk of harassment or doxing (e.g., transgender persons). Prior to beginning the annotation task, annotators were informed that the task may involve reading offensive content and were required to provide consent. In addition, we did not collect any identifying information from annotators and only report demographics in the aggregate. Finally, annotators were given the opportunity to exit the task at any time and allowed to write a debriefing response at the end of the task.

References

Hala Al Kuwatly, Maximilian Wich, and Georg Groh. 2020. Identifying and measuring annotator bias based on annotators' demographic characteristics. In *Proceedings of the Fourth Workshop on Online Abuse and Harms*, pages 184–190.

Jamie Bartlett, Jeremy Reffin, Noelle Rumball, and Sarah Williamson. 2014. Anti-social media. *Demos*, (2014):1–51.

Su Lin Blodgett, Solon Barocas, Hal Daumé III, and Hanna Wallach. 2020. Language (technology) is power: A critical survey of "bias" in NLP. In *Proceedings of the 58th Annual Meeting of the Association for Computational Linguistics*, pages 5454–5476, Online. Association for Computational Linguistics.

Eduardo Bonilla-Silva. 2006. *Racism without racists: Color-blind racism and the persistence of racial inequality in the United States*. Rowman & Littlefield Publishers, Oxford, UK.

Thomas Brambor, William Roberts Clark, and Matt Golder. 2006. Understanding interaction models: Improving empirical analyses. *Political analysis*, pages 63–82.

Pete Burnap and Matthew L Williams. 2016. Us and them: identifying cyber hate on twitter across multiple protected characteristics. *EPJ Data science*, 5(11):1–15.

Evelyn R Carter and Mary C Murphy. 2015. Group-based differences in perceptions of racism: What counts, to whom, and why? *Social and Personality Psychology Compass*, 9(6):269–280.

Irfan Chaudhry. 2015. # hashtagging hate: Using twitter to track racism online. *First Monday*, 20.

Gloria Cowan and Cyndi Hodge. 1996. Judgments of hate speech: The effects of target group, publicness, and behavioral responses of the target. *Journal of Applied Social Psychology*, 26(4):355–374.

Jessie Daniels. 2009. *Cyber racism: White supremacy online and the new attack on civil rights*. Rowman & Littlefield Publishers, Plymouth, UK.

René D Flores. 2017. Do anti-immigrant laws shape public sentiment? a study of arizona's sb 1070 using twitter data. *American Journal of Sociology*, 123(2):333–384.

Richard JT Hamshaw, Julie Barnett, and Jane S Lucas. 2018. Tweeting and eating: The effect of links and likes on food-hypersensitive consumers' perceptions of tweets. *Frontiers in public health*, 6:1–12.

Joseph Henrich, Steven J Heine, and Ara Norenzayan. 2010. The weirdest people in the world? *Behavioral and brain sciences*, 33(2-3):61–83.

Paul Hitlin. 2016. Research in the crowdsourcing age, a case study' pew research center. Technical report, Pew Research Center.

Klaus Krippendorff. 1980. *Content Analysis: An Introduction to its Methodology*. Sage Publications, Los Angeles, CA.

Maria Krysan and Sarah Moberg. 2016. A portrait of african american and white racial attitudes. *University of Illinois, Institute of Government and Public Affairs*.

Irene Kwok and Yuzhou Wang. 2013. Locate the hate: Detecting tweets against blacks. In *Proceedings of the twenty-seventh AAAI conference on artificial intelligence*, pages 1621–1622.

Laura Leets. 2001. Explaining perceptions of racist speech. *Communication Research*, 28(5):676–706.

Mark Morcos, Ate Poorthuis, and Matthew Zook. The dolly project (digital online life and you). Technical report, Floating.Sheep.

Lawrence A Palinkas, Sarah M Horwitz, Carla A Green, Jennifer P Wisdom, Naihua Duan, and Kimberly Hoagwood. 2015. Purposeful sampling for qualitative data collection and analysis in mixed method implementation research. *Administration and policy in mental health and mental health services research*, 42(5):533–544.

Andrew Perrin and Monica Anderson. 2019. Share of u.s. adults using social media, including facebook, is mostly unchanged since 2018. Technical report, Pew Research Center.

R Core Team. 2017. *R: A Language and Environment for Statistical Computing*. R Foundation for Statistical Computing, Vienna, Austria.

Margaret E. Roberts, Brandon M. Stewart, and Dustin Tingley. 2019. stm: An R package for structural topic models. *Journal of Statistical Software*, 91(2):1–40.

Margaret E Roberts, Brandon M Stewart, Dustin Tingley, Christopher Lucas, Jetson Leder-Luis, Shana Kushner Gadarian, Bethany Albertson, and David G Rand. 2014. Structural topic models for open-ended survey responses. *American Journal of Political Science*, 58(4):1064–1082.

Maarten Sap, Dallas Card, Saadia Gabriel, Yejin Choi, and Noah A Smith. 2019. The risk of racial bias in hate speech detection. In *Proceedings of the 57th Annual Meeting of the Association for Computational Linguistics*, pages 1668–1678.

Anna Schmidt and Michael Wiegand. 2017. A survey on hate speech detection using natural language processing. In *Proceedings of the Fifth International workshop on natural language processing for social media*, pages 1–10.

Sanjay Sharma and Phillip Brooker. 2016. #notracist: Exploring racism denial talk on twitter. In *Digital sociologies*, pages 463–485. Policy Press.

Brendesha M Tynes and Suzanne L Markoe. 2010. The role of color-blind racial attitudes in reactions to racial discrimination on social network sites. *Journal of Diversity in Higher Education*, 3(1):1–13.

Zeerak Waseem. 2016. Are you a racist or am i seeing things? annotator influence on hate speech detection on twitter. In *Proceedings of the first workshop on NLP and computational social science*, pages 138–142.

Hajime Watanabe, Mondher Bouazizi, and Tomoaki Ohtsuki. 2018. Hate speech on twitter: A pragmatic approach to collect hateful and offensive expressions and perform hate speech detection. *IEEE access*, 6:13825–13835.

Maximilian Wich, Hala Al Kuwatly, and Georg Groh. 2020. Investigating annotator bias with a graph-based approach. In *Proceedings of the Fourth Workshop on Online Abuse and Harms*, pages 191–199.

Amanda Williams, Clio Oliver, Katherine Aumer, and Chanel Meyers. 2016. Racial microaggressions and perceptions of internet memes. *Computers in Human Behavior*, 63:424–432.

James Zou and Londa Schiebinger. 2018. Ai can be sexist and racist—it's time to make it fair. *Nature Publishing Group*, 559:324–326.

Understanding and Interpreting the Impact of User Context in Hate Speech Detection

Edoardo Mosca
TU Munich,
Department of Informatics,
Germany
edoardo.mosca@tum.de

Maximilian Wich
TU Munich,
Department of Informatics,
Germany
maximilian.wich@tum.de

Georg Groh
TU Munich,
Department of Informatics,
Germany
grohg@in.tum.de

Abstract

As hate speech spreads on social media and online communities, research continues to work on its automatic detection. Recently, recognition performance has been increasing thanks to advances in deep learning and the integration of user features. This work investigates the effects that such features can have on a detection model. Unlike previous research, we show that simple performance comparison does not expose the full impact of including contextual- and user information. By leveraging explainability techniques, we show (1) that user features play a role in the model's decision and (2) how they affect the feature space learned by the model. Besides revealing that—and also illustrating *why*—user features are the reason for performance gains, we show how such techniques can be combined to better understand the model and to detect unintended bias.

1 Introduction

Communication and information exchange between people is taking place on online platforms at a continuously increasing rate. While these means allow everyone to express themselves freely at any time, they are massively contributing to the spread of negative phenomenons such as online harassment and abusive behavior. Among those, which are all to discourage, online hate speech has attracted the attention of many researchers due to its deleterious effects (Munro, 2011; Williams et al., 2020; Duggan, 2017).

The extremely large volume of online content and the high speed at which new one is generated exclude immediately the chance of content moderation being done manually. This realization has naturally captured the attention of the *Machine Learning* (ML) field, seeking to craft automatic and scalable solutions (MacAvaney et al., 2019; Waseem et al., 2017; Davidson et al., 2017).

Methods for detecting hate speech and similar abusive behavior have been thus on the rise, consistently improving in terms of performance and generalization (Schmidt and Wiegand, 2017; Mishra et al., 2019b). However, even the current state of the art still faces limitations in accuracy and is yet not ready to be deployed in practice. Hate speech recognition remains an extremely difficult task (Waseem et al., 2017), in particular when the expression of hate is implicit and hidden behind figures of speech and sarcasm.

Alongside language features, recent works have considered utilizing user features as an additional source of knowledge to provide detection models with context information (Fehn Unsvåg and Gambäck, 2018; Ribeiro et al., 2018). As a general trend, models incorporating context exhibit improved performance compared to their pure text-based counterparts (Mishra et al., 2018, 2019a). Nevertheless, the effect, which these additional features have on the model, has not been interpreted or understood yet. So far, models have mostly been compared only in terms of performance metrics. The goal of this work is to shed light on the impact generated by including user features—or more in general context—into hate speech detection methods. Our methodology heavily relies on a combination of modern techniques coming from the field of *eXplainable Artificial Intelligence* (XAI).

We show that adding user and social context to models is the reason for performance gains. We also explore the model's learned features space to understand how such features are leveraged for detection. At the same time, we discover that models incorporating user features suffer less from bias in the text. Unfortunately, those same models contain a new type of bias that originates from adding user information.

Proceedings of the Ninth International Workshop on Natural Language Processing for Social Media, pages 91–102
Online Workshop, June 10, 2021. ©2021 Association for Computational Linguistics

2 Related Work

2.1 Explainability for Recognition Models

A limited amount of research has focused on applying XAI techniques to the hate speech recognition case. For instance, Wang (2018) adapts a number of explainability techniques from the computer vision and applies them to a hate speech classifier trained on Davidson et al. (2017). Feature occlusion was used to highlight the most relevant words for the final classifier prediction and activation maximization selected the terms that the classifier captured and judged as relevant at a dataset-level. Vijayaraghavan et al. (2019) constructs an interpretable multi-modal detector that uses text alongside social and cultural context features. The authors leverage attention scores to quantify the relevance of different input features. Wich et al. (2020) applies post-hoc explainability on a custom dataset in German to expose and estimate the impact of political bias on hate speech classifiers. More in detail, left- and right-wing political bias within the training data is visualized via DeepSHAP-based explanations (Lundberg and Lee, 2017).

MacAvaney et al. (2019) combines together multiple simple classifiers to assemble a transparent model. Risch et al. (2020) reviews and compares several explainability techniques applied to hate speech classifiers. Their experimentation includes popular post-hoc approaches such as LIME (Ribeiro et al., 2016) and LRP (Bach et al., 2015) as well as self-explanatory detectors (Risch et al., 2020).

For our use case, we apply *post-hoc explainability* approaches (Lipton, 2018). We use external techniques to explain models that would otherwise be black-boxes (Arrieta et al., 2020). In contrast, *transparent models* are interpretable thanks to their intuitive and simple design.

2.2 Context Features for Hate Speech Detection

Models have been continuously improving since the first documented step towards automatic hate speech detection Spertus (1997). The evolution of recognition approaches has been favored by advances in *Natural Language Processing* (NLP) research (Mishra et al., 2019b). For instance, s.o.t.a detectors like Mozafari et al. (2020) exploit high-performing language models such as BERT (Devlin et al., 2019).

A different research branch took an alternative path and explored the inclusion of social context alongside text. These additional features are usually referred to with the terms *user features*, *context features*, or *social features*. Some tried incorporating the gender (Waseem, 2016) and the profile's geolocation and language (Galán-García et al., 2016). Others instead utilized the user's number of followers or friends (Fehn Unsvåg and Gambäck, 2018).

Modeling users' social and conversational interactions via their corresponding graph was also shown to be rewarding (Mishra et al., 2019b; Cecillon et al., 2019). Ribeiro et al. (2018) creates additional features by measuring properties like betweenness and eigenvector centrality. Mishra et al. (2018) and Mishra et al. (2019a) instead fed the graph directly to the model either embedded as matrix or via using graph convolutional neural network (Hamilton et al., 2017).

While previous work explored the usage of a wide range of context features (Fehn Unsvåg and Gambäck, 2018), detection models have only been compared in terms of performance metrics. Besides accuracy, researchers have not focused on other changes that such features could have on the model. Our work shows that indeed this addition entails a large impact on the recognition algorithm's behavior and substantially changes its characteristics.

3 Experimental Setup

In this section, we describe in detail the different datasets and detection models that we include in our interpretability-driven analysis.

3.1 Data and Preprocessing

Previous research has produced several datasets to support further developments in the hate speech detection area (Founta et al., 2018; Warner and Hirschberg, 2012). Some became relatively popular to benchmark and test new ideas and improvements in recognition techniques. For our experimentation, we pick the DAVIDSON (Davidson et al., 2017) and the WASEEM (Waseem and Hovy, 2016) datasets. The choice was motivated by their variety of speech classes and popularity as detection benchmarks.

Both benchmarks consist of a collection of tweets coupled with classification tasks with three possible classes. DAVIDSON contains $\sim 25,000$ tweets of which $1,430$ are labeled as *hate*, $19,190$ as *offensive*, and $4,163$ as *neither* (Davidson et al., 2017). As classification outcomes in WASEEM instead, we have *racism*, *sexism*, and *neither*. The three classes contain $3,378$, $1,970$, and $11,501$ tweets respectively (Waseem and Hovy, 2016). We were not able to retrieve the remaining 65 of the original $16,914$ samples.

We follow the same preprocessing steps for both datasets. First, terms belonging to categories like *url, email, percent, number, user,* and *time* are annotated via a category token. For instance, *"341"* is replaced by "*<number>*". After that, we apply word segmentation and spell correction based on Twitter word statistics. Both methods and statistics were provided by the *ekphrasis* [1] text preprocessing tool (Baziotis et al., 2017).

In addition to the tweets that represent the text (or content) component of our input features, we also retrieve information about the tweet's authors and their relationships. In a similar fashion as done in Mishra et al. (2018), we construct a *community graph* $G = (V, E)$ where each node represents a user and two nodes are connected if at least one of the two users follows the other one. We were able to retrieve $|V| = 6,725$ users and $|E| = 19,597$ relationships for DAVIDSON, while for WASEEM we have $|V| = 2,024$ and $|E| = 9,955$.

The respective average node degrees are $2,914$ and $4,918$ and the overall graphs' densities:

$$D = \frac{2 \cdot |E|}{|V|(|V| - 1)}$$

are 0.00087 and 0.00486 respectively.

We immediately notice that both graphs are very sparse. In particular, we have $3,393$ users not connected to anyone in DAVIDSON and 927 in WASEEM. For reference, Mishra et al. (2018) achieves a graph density of 0.0075 on WASEEM, with only ~ 400 authors being solitary, i.e. with no connections. We assume the difference is reasonable as data availability considerably decreases over time.

3.2 Detection Models

Our experimentation and findings are based on the comparison of two detection models, one that solely relies on text features and one that instead incorporates context features. To better capture their behavioral differences, we build them to be relatively simple and also to not differ in the text-processing part.

[1]https://github.com/cbaziotis/ekphrasis

The first model, shown in figure 1, computes the three classification probabilities only based on the tweets' content. The input text is fed to the model as *Bag of Words* (BoW), which is then processed by two fully connected layers. We refer to this model as *text model*.

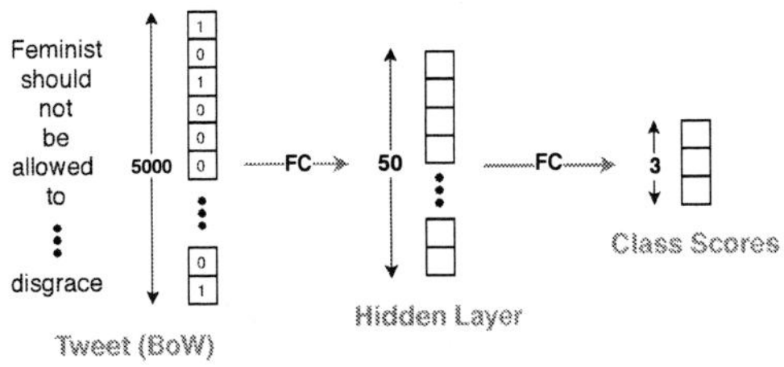

Figure 1: Architecture of the text model.

The second model instead leverages the information coming from three input sources: the tweet's text, the user's vocabulary, and the follower network. The first input is identical to what is fed to the text model. The second is constructed from all the tweets of the author in the dataset and aims to model their overall writing style. Concretely, we merge the tweets' BoW representations, i.e. we apply a logical-OR to their corresponding vectors. The third is the author's follower network and describes their online surrounding community. On a more technical note, this can be extracted as a row from the adjacency matrix of our community graph described in section 3.1. Note that s.o.t.a hate speech detector used similar context features (Mishra et al., 2018, 2019a). We refer to this model as *social model*.

As sketched in figure 2, the different input sources are initially processed separately in the model's architecture. After the first layer, the intermediate representations from the different branches are concatenated together and fed to two more layers to compute the final output. Note that the text- and social models have the same dimensions for their final hidden layer and can be seen as equivalent networks working on different inputs.

4 Proposed Analysis

We now describe our methodology in detail. Recall that our models differ precisely on the usage of user features. As we will see shortly, their comparison beyond accuracy measurements sheds light on the different model properties and hence on the potential impact of incorporating context features.

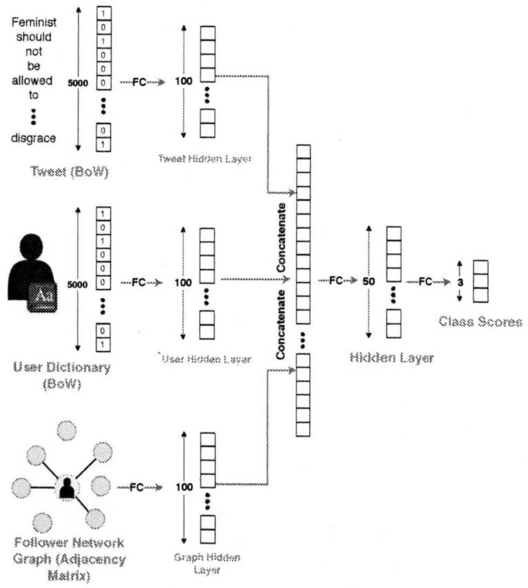

Figure 2: Architecture of the social model.

4.1 Training and Performance

We apply the same training and testing procedure to all models and datasets. We keep the 60% of the data for training while splitting the remaining equally between validation and test set, i.e. 20% each.

Tables 1 and 2 report our results in terms of F1 scores for WASEEM (Waseem and Hovy, 2016) and DAVIDSON (Davidson et al., 2017) respectively. To increase our confidence in their validity, we average the performance over five runs with randomly picked train/validation/test sets. We observe different trends for the two datasets.

Speech Class	Text Model	Social Model
Racism	0.711	0.735
Sexism	0.703	0.832
Neither	0.881	0.907
Overall	0.829	0.872

Table 1: F1 Scores on Waseem and Hovy (2016).

On WASEEM, the social model considerably outperforms (by 4.3%) our text model. The performance gain is general and not restricted to any single class. Quite surprisingly, our text model performs better on racist tweets than sexist ones, although the sexism class is almost twice as big. This suggests that sexism is, at least in this case, somewhat harder to detect by just looking at the tweet content. On the contrary, our social model shows an impressive improvement in the sexism class (almost 13%), suggesting the presence of detectable patterns in sexist users and their social interactions.

Speech Class	Text Model	Social Model
Hate	0.154	0.347
Offensive	0.939	0.939
Neither	0.809	0.815
Overall	0.876	0.886

Table 2: F1 Scores on Davidson et al. (2017).

On DAVIDSON, we only observe a contained improvement (1%). Moreover, the jump in performance is restricted to the hate class, containing a tiny amount of samples. We believe the difference between the two datasets should be expected due to the lower amount of user data available for DAVIDSON. Considering these results, we focus on applying our technique on the WASEEM dataset in the remainder of this paper. Nevertheless, the respective results on DAVIDSON can be found in the appendix A. While on both datasets we do not outperform the current s.o.t.a—Mishra et al. (2019a) on WASEEM and Mozafari et al. (2020) on DAVIDSON—our results are comparable and thus satisfactory for our purposes.

4.2 Shapley Values Estimation

We now apply a first post-hoc explainability method. For each feature we calculate its corresponding *Shapley value* (Shapley, 1953; Lundberg and Lee, 2017). That is, we quantify the relevance that each feature has for the prediction of a specific output. Shapley values have been shown—both theoretically and empirically—to be an ideal estimator for feature relevance (Lundberg and Lee, 2017).

As exact Shapley values are exponentially complex to determine, we use accurate approximation methods as done in (Lundberg and Lee, 2017; Štrumbelj and Kononenko, 2014). Figure 3 shows concrete examples in which Shapley values are calculated for both models on two test tweets from WASEEM.

For our social model, we consider the user vocabulary and the follower network as single features for simplicity. Notably, the context is used by the social model and can play a significant role in its prediction. Hence, we can confirm the context features to be the reason for the performance gains. We can empirically exclude that the differences between the text- and the social model architectures justify the jump in performance.

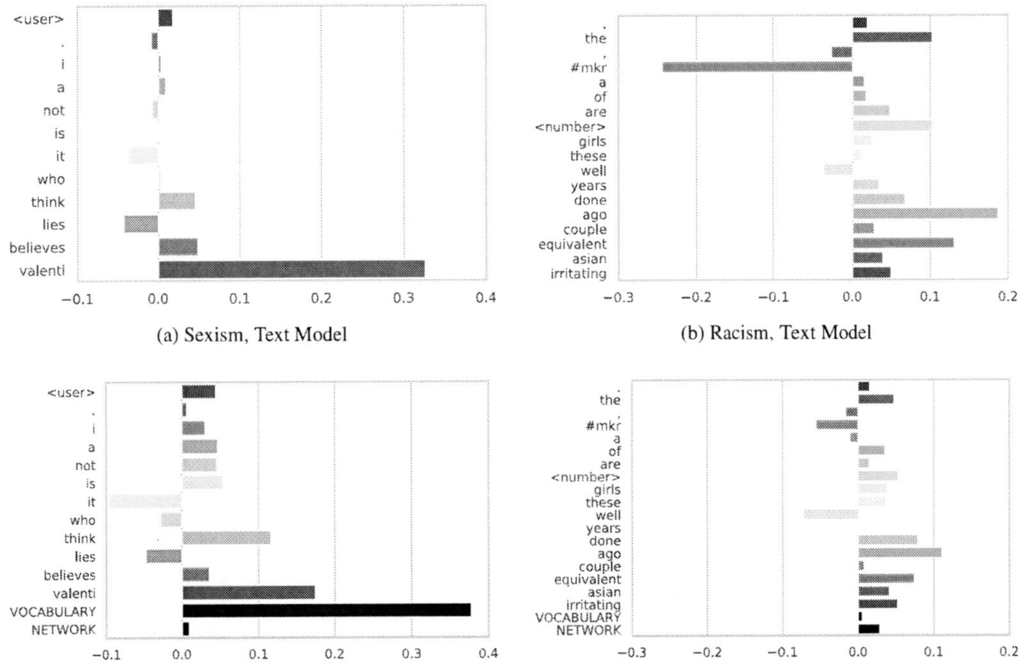

(a) Sexism, Text Model

(b) Racism, Text Model

(c) Sexism, Social Model

(d) Racism, Social Model

Figure 3: Example of features contribution, computed via Shapley value approximation, for our text and social models. In (a) and (c) we use as input the tweet "*<user> I think Arquette is a dummy who believes it. Not a Valenti who knowingly lies.*". The sexist tweet refers to the actress Patricia Arquette, who spoke in favour of gender equality, and the feminist writer Jessica Valenti. Some words are missing in the plot as our BoW dimension is limited during preprocessing. In (b) and (d), we use the racist tweet "*These girls are the equivalent of the irritating Asian girls a couple of years ago. Well done, 7. #MKR*". The hashtag refers to the Australian cooking show "*My Kitchen Rules*".

4.3 Feature Space Exploration

We have seen that detection models can benefit from the inclusion of context features. We now focus on understanding *why* this is the case. Shapley values and more in general feature attribution methods can quantify *how much* single features contribute to the prediction. Yet, alone, they do not give us any intuition to answer our why-question.

We look at the feature space learned by our models, which can be considered a global explainability technique. For our text model, we remove the last layer and feed the tweets to the remaining architecture. The output is a 50-dimensional embedding for each tweet. We employ the *t-Distributed Stochastic Neighbor Embedding* (t-SNE) (Van der Maaten and Hinton, 2008) to reduce the embeddings to two dimensions for visualization purposes.

The resulting plot, in figure 4d, shows all the tweets in a single cluster. Racist tweets look more concentrated in one area than sexist ones, suggesting that sexism is somewhat harder to detect for the model. This result is coherent with our per-class performance scores.

We apply the same procedure to the social model. In this case, we visualize the hidden layer of each separate branch as well as the final hidden layer analogous to the text model. Not surprisingly, the tweet branch (figure 4a) looks very similar to the feature space learned by our text model. The user's vocabulary branch (figure 4b) instead shows the samples distributed in well-separated clusters. Notably, racist tweets have been restricted to one cluster and we can also observe pure-sexist and pure-neither clusters. The follower network branch (figure 4c) looks similar though cluster separation is not as strong. Once more, we notice racism more concentrated than sexism, which is considerably more mixed with regular tweets. To some extent, this result is in line with the notion of *homophily* among racist users (Mathew et al., 2019).

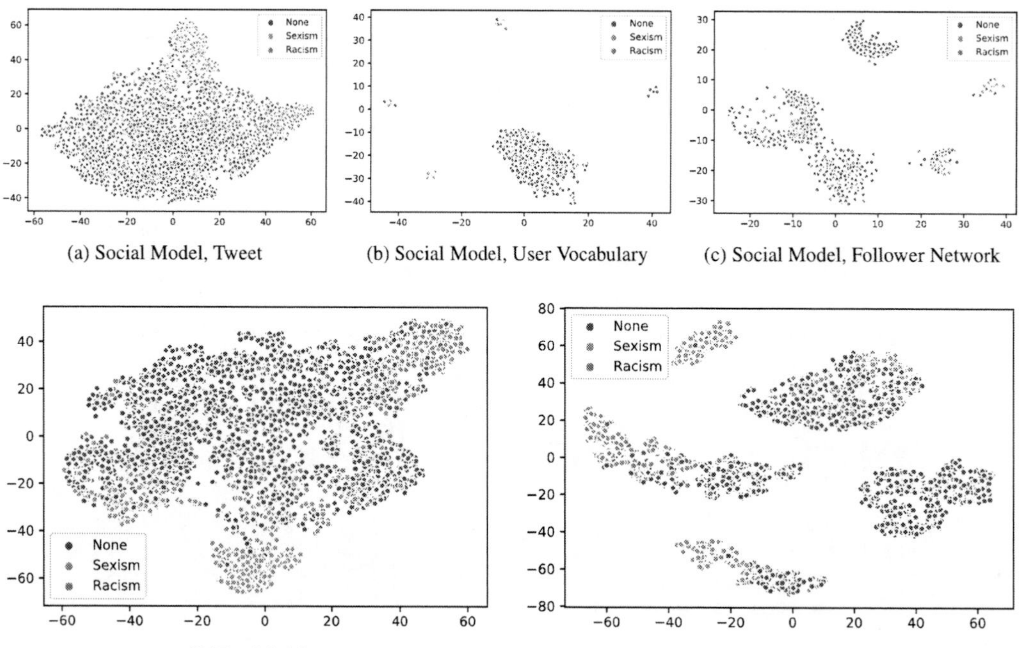

(a) Social Model, Tweet (b) Social Model, User Vocabulary (c) Social Model, Follower Network

(d) Text Model (e) Social Model

Figure 4: WASEEM tweets, colored by label, in the features space learned by our text model (d) and social model (a,b,c for the independent branches, e combined).

Intuitively, being able to divide users into different clusters based on their behavior should be helpful for classification at later layers. This is confirmed by the combined feature space plot (figure 4e). Indeed, tweets are now structured in multiple clusters instead of a single one as for our text model. Also in this case, we observe several pure or almost-pure groups.

The corresponding visualizations and results for DAVIDSON can be found in appendix A.

4.4 Targeted Behavioral Analysis: Explaining a Novel Tweet

We have seen how different explainability techniques convey different types of information on the examined model. Computing Shapley values and visualizing the learned feature space can also be used in combination as they complement each other. If used together, they can both quantify the relevance of each feature as well as show how certain types of features are leveraged by the model to better distinguish between classes.

So far, our explanations are relative to the datasets used for model training and testing. However, to better understand a classifier it should also be tested beyond its test set. This can be simply done by feeding the model with a novel tweet. Via artificially crafting tweets, we can check the model's behavior in specific cases. For instance, we can inspect how it reacts to specific sub-types of hate.

Let us consider the anti-Islamic tweet "*muslims are the worst, together with their god*". If fed to our model, it is classified as racist with a 75% confidence following our expectations. Figures 5a and 5c show explanations for the tweet. We can see that the word "*muslim*" plays a big role by looking at its corresponding Shapley value. At the same time, the projection of the novel tweet onto the feature space shows how the sample is collocated together with the other racist tweets by the text model.

If we now change our hypothetical tweet to be anti-black—"*black people are the worst, together with their slang*"—we observe a different model behavior (figures 5b and 5d). In fact, now the tweet is not classified as racist. No word has a substantial impact on the prediction. We can also notice a slight shift of the sample in the features space, away from the racism cluster. If changing the target of the hate changes the prediction, then the model/dataset probably contains bias against that target. Model interpretability further reveals how

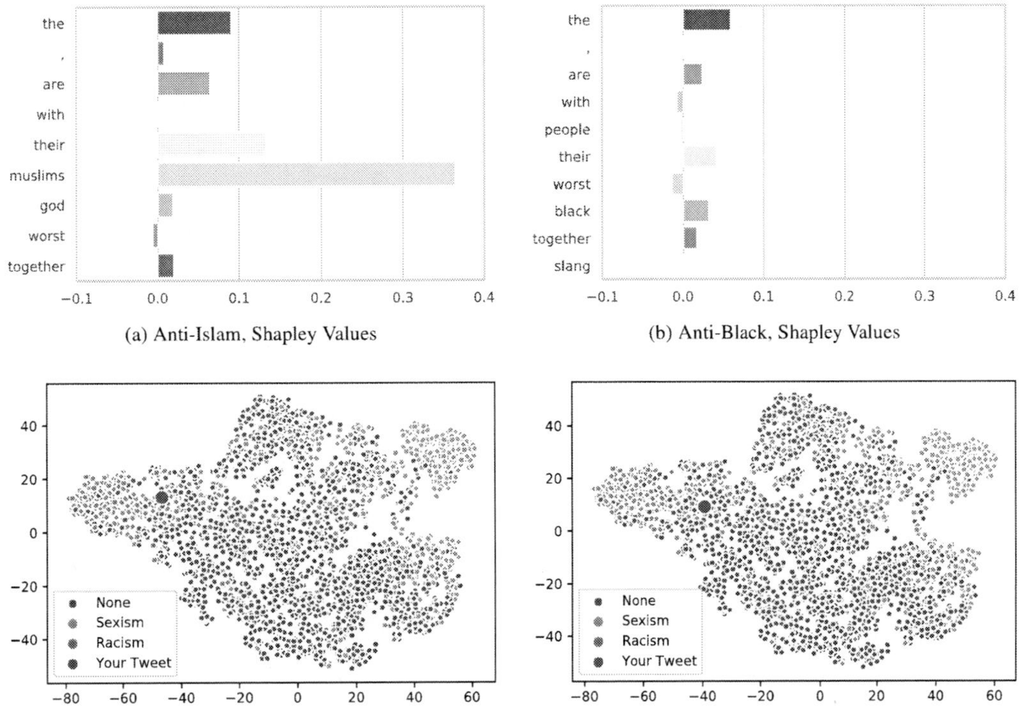

(a) Anti-Islam, Shapley Values

(b) Anti-Black, Shapley Values

(c) Anti-Islam, Embedding in Latent Space

(d) Anti-Black, Embedding in Latent Space

Figure 5: Features contribution (Shapley values w.r.t. the racism class) and embedding in the text model's latent space of an islamophobic and a anti-black racist tweets. The two sentences had, according to our text model, the 75% and 24% probability of being racist respectively.

its behavior reacts to different targets.

We run the same experiment with our social model. This time, it correctly classifies the anti-black tweet as racist (55% confidence). This suggests that text bias could be mitigated by using models that do not only rely on the text input. However, the social model is much more sensitive to changes in the user-derived features. To test this, we feed the model the same tweet and only change the author that generated it. For a fair comparison, we pick one random user with other racist tweets, one random user with other sexist tweets, and one random user with no hateful tweets in the dataset. We refer to these users as racist, sexist, and regular users respectively.

Our crafted tweet is classified as racist when coming from a racist user (64%). However, it is instead judged non-hateful in both the other cases (12% and 19% for a sexist and user with no hate background respectively). Evidently, racist tweets also need some contribution from the social features to be judged as racist.

A very informative explanation comes again from both the Shapley values and the feature space exploration (figure 6). On the left side, we can see the Shapley value for the racist and regular users. Results relative to the sexist user are analogous to the regular user and reported in the supplementary material (A.3). All the words have a similar contribution to the racism class in all cases. However, the difference in the authors plays a substantial role in the decision. Only the racist user positively contributes to the racism class. On the right side of 6, we can see the embedding in the latent space for each case. Different input authors cause the tweet to be embedded in different clusters. Only in the first one the model actually considers the possibility of the tweet being racist.

Hence, while adding user-derived features might mitigate the effects of bias in the text, it generates a new form of bias that could discriminate users based on their previous behavior and hinder the model from classifying correctly hateful content.

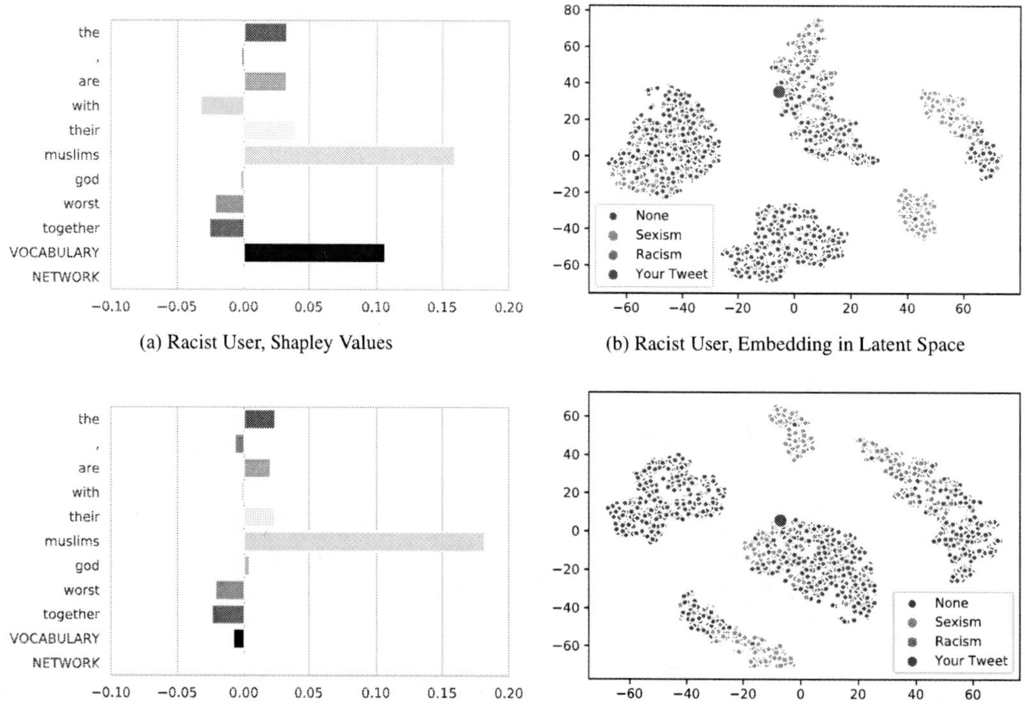

(a) Racist User, Shapley Values

(b) Racist User, Embedding in Latent Space

(c) Regular User, Shapley Values

(d) Regular User, Embedding in Latent Space

Figure 6: Features contribution (w.r.t. racism class) and embeddings of the islamophobic tweet in the social model's latent space. The two pairs of plots are w.r.t. two predictions done with different users as input: a racist one (a,b, 64%), and a regular one (c,d, 19%).

5 Conclusion and Future Work

In our work, we investigated the effects of user features in hate speech detection. In previous studies, this was done by comparing models based on performance metric. We have shown that post-hoc explainability techniques provide a much deeper understanding of the models' behavior. In our case, when applied to two models that differ specifically on the usage of context features, the in-depth comparison reveals the impact that such additional features can have.

The two utilized techniques—*Shapley values estimation* and *learned feature space exploration*—convey different kinds of information. The first one quantifies how each feature plays a role but does not tell us what is happening in the background. The second one illustrates the model's perception of the tweets but does not provide any quantitative information for the prediction. Furthermore, we have seen that artificially crafting and modifying a tweet can be useful to examine the models' behavior in particular scenarios. In concrete examples, the two approaches worked as bias detectors present in the text as well as in the user features.

We believe that analyzing detection models is vital for understanding how certain features shape the way data is processed. Accuracy alone is by no means a sufficient metric to decide which model to prefer. Our work shows that even models that perform significantly better can potentially lead to new types of bias. We urge researchers in the field to compare recognition approaches beyond accuracy to avoid potential harm to affected users.

Data scarcity is still a main issue faced by current researchers, especially when it comes to context features. We believe that larger and more complete datasets will improve our understanding of how certain features interact and will help future research in advancing both in accuracy and bias mitigation.

Acknowledgments

This paper is based on a joined work in the context of Edoardo Mosca's master's thesis (Mosca, 2020).

References

Alejandro Barredo Arrieta, Natalia Díaz-Rodríguez, Javier Del Ser, Adrien Bennetot, Siham Tabik, Alberto Barbado, Salvador García, Sergio Gil-López, Daniel Molina, Richard Benjamins, et al. 2020. Explainable Artificial Intelligence (XAI): Concepts, taxonomies, opportunities and challenges toward responsible AI. *Information Fusion*, 58:82–115.

Sebastian Bach, Alexander Binder, Grégoire Montavon, Frederick Klauschen, Klaus-Robert Müller, and Wojciech Samek. 2015. On pixel-wise explanations for non-linear classifier decisions by layer-wise relevance propagation. *PloS one*, 10(7).

Christos Baziotis, Nikos Pelekis, and Christos Doulkeridis. 2017. Datastories at semeval-2017 task 4: Deep lstm with attention for message-level and topic-based sentiment analysis. In *Proceedings of the 11th International Workshop on Semantic Evaluation (SemEval-2017)*, pages 747–754.

Noé Cecillon, Vincent Labatut, Richard Dufour, and Georges Linarès. 2019. Abusive language detection in online conversations by combining content- and graph-based features. In *ICWSM International Workshop on Modeling and Mining Social-Media-Driven Complex Networks*, volume 2, page 8. Frontiers.

Thomas Davidson, Dana Warmsley, Michael Macy, and Ingmar Weber. 2017. Automated hate speech detection and the problem of offensive language. In *Proceedings of the International AAAI Conference on Web and Social Media*, volume 11.

Jacob Devlin, Ming-Wei Chang, Kenton Lee, and Kristina Toutanova. 2019. BERT: Pre-training of deep bidirectional transformers for language understanding. In *Proceedings of the 2019 Conference of the North American Chapter of the Association for Computational Linguistics: Human Language Technologies, Volume 1 (Long and Short Papers)*, pages 4171–4186, Minneapolis, Minnesota. Association for Computational Linguistics.

Maeve Duggan. 2017. *Online harassment 2017*. Pew Research Center.

Elise Fehn Unsvåg and Björn Gambäck. 2018. The Effects of User Features on Twitter Hate Speech Detection. In *Proc. 2nd Workshop on Abusive Language Online*, pages 75–85.

Antigoni-Maria Founta, Constantinos Djouvas, Despoina Chatzakou, Ilias Leontiadis, Jeremy Blackburn, Gianluca Stringhini, Athena Vakali, Michael Sirivianos, and Nicolas Kourtellis. 2018. Large scale crowdsourcing and characterization of twitter abusive behavior. In *Proc. 11th ICWSM*, pages 491–500.

Patxi Galán-García, José Gaviria de la Puerta, Carlos Laorden Gómez, Igor Santos, and Pablo García Bringas. 2016. Supervised machine learning for the detection of troll profiles in twitter social network: Application to a real case of cyberbullying. *Logic Journal of the IGPL*, 24(1):42–53.

Will Hamilton, Zhitao Ying, and Jure Leskovec. 2017. Inductive representation learning on large graphs. In *Advances in Neural Information Processing Systems*, volume 30. Curran Associates, Inc.

Zachary C Lipton. 2018. The mythos of model interpretability. *Queue*, 16(3):31–57.

Scott M Lundberg and Su-In Lee. 2017. A unified approach to interpreting model predictions. In *Advances in neural information processing systems*, pages 4765–4774.

Laurens Van der Maaten and Geoffrey Hinton. 2008. Visualizing data using t-sne. *Journal of machine learning research*, 9(11).

Sean MacAvaney, Hao-Ren Yao, Eugene Yang, Katina Russell, Nazli Goharian, and Ophir Frieder. 2019. Hate speech detection: Challenges and solutions. *PloS one*, 14(8).

Binny Mathew, Ritam Dutt, Pawan Goyal, and Animesh Mukherjee. 2019. Spread of hate speech in online social media. In *Proceedings of the 10th ACM conference on web science*, pages 173–182.

Pushkar Mishra, Marco Del Tredici, Helen Yannakoudakis, and Ekaterina Shutova. 2018. Author profiling for abuse detection. In *Proceedings of the 27th International Conference on Computational Linguistics*, pages 1088–1098.

Pushkar Mishra, Marco Del Tredici, Helen Yannakoudakis, and Ekaterina Shutova. 2019a. Abusive language detection with graph convolutional networks. In *Proceedings of the 2019 Conference of the North American Chapter of the Association for Computational Linguistics: Human Language Technologies, NAACL-HLT 2019*, pages 2145–2150.

Pushkar Mishra, Helen Yannakoudakis, and Ekaterina Shutova. 2019b. Tackling online abuse: A survey of automated abuse detection methods. *arXiv preprint arXiv:1908.06024*.

Edoardo Mosca. 2020. Explainability of hate speech detection models. Master's thesis, Technical University of Munich. Advised and supervised by Maximilian Wich and Georg Groh.

Marzieh Mozafari, Reza Farahbakhsh, and Noël Crespi. 2020. A BERT-Based Transfer Learning Approach for Hate Speech Detection in Online Social Media. *Studies in Computational Intelligence*, 881 SCI:928–940.

Emily R Munro. 2011. The protection of children online: a brief scoping review to identify vulnerable groups. *Childhood Wellbeing Research Centre*.

Manoel Horta Ribeiro, Pedro H Calais, Yuri A Santos, Virgílio AF Almeida, and Wagner Meira Jr. 2018. Characterizing and detecting hateful users on twitter. In *Twelfth international AAAI conference on web and social media*.

Marco Tulio Ribeiro, Sameer Singh, and Carlos Guestrin. 2016. "Why should I trust you?" Explaining the predictions of any classifier. In *Proc. 22nd ACM SIGKDD Intl. Conf. Knowledge Discovery and Data Mining*, pages 1135–1144.

Julian Risch, Robin Ruff, and Ralf Krestel. 2020. Offensive language detection explained. In *Proceedings of the Second Workshop on Trolling, Aggression and Cyberbullying*, pages 137–143.

Anna Schmidt and Michael Wiegand. 2017. A survey on hate speech detection using natural language processing. In *Proc. 5th Intl. Workshop on Natural Language Processing for Social Media*, pages 1–10.

Lloyd S Shapley. 1953. A value for n-person games. *Contributions to the Theory of Games*, 2(28):307–317.

Ellen Spertus. 1997. Smokey: Automatic recognition of hostile messages. In *Proceedings of Innovative Applications of Artificial Intelligence (IAAI)*, pages 1058–1065.

Erik Štrumbelj and Igor Kononenko. 2014. Explaining prediction models and individual predictions with feature contributions. *Knowledge and information systems*, 41(3):647–665.

Prashanth Vijayaraghavan, Hugo Larochelle, and Deb Roy. 2019. Interpretable Multi-Modal Hate Speech Detection. In *Intl. Conf. Machine Learning AI for Social Good Workshop*.

Cindy Wang. 2018. Interpreting neural network hate speech classifiers. In *Proc. 2nd Workshop on Abusive Language Online*, pages 86–92.

William Warner and Julia Hirschberg. 2012. Detecting hate speech on the world wide web. In *Proceedings of the second workshop on language in social media*, pages 19–26.

Zeerak Waseem. 2016. Are You a Racist or Am I Seeing Things? Annotator Influence on Hate Speech Detection on Twitter. In *Proc. First Workshop on NLP and Computational Social Science*, pages 138–142.

Zeerak Waseem, Thomas Davidson, Dana Warmsley, and Ingmar Weber. 2017. Understanding abuse: A typology of abusive language detection subtasks. *arXiv preprint arXiv:1705.09899*.

Zeerak Waseem and Dirk Hovy. 2016. Hateful symbols or hateful people? predictive features for hate speech detection on twitter. In *Proceedings of the NAACL student research workshop*, pages 88–93.

Maximilian Wich, Jan Bauer, and Georg Groh. 2020. Impact of politically biased data on hate speech classification. In *Proceedings of the Fourth Workshop on Online Abuse and Harms*, pages 54–64.

Matthew L Williams, Pete Burnap, Amir Javed, Han Liu, and Sefa Ozalp. 2020. Hate in the machine: Anti-black and anti-muslim social media posts as predictors of offline racially and religiously aggravated crime. *The British Journal of Criminology*, 60(1):93–117.

A Results on the Davidson Dataset

A.1 Feature Space learned by the Text Model

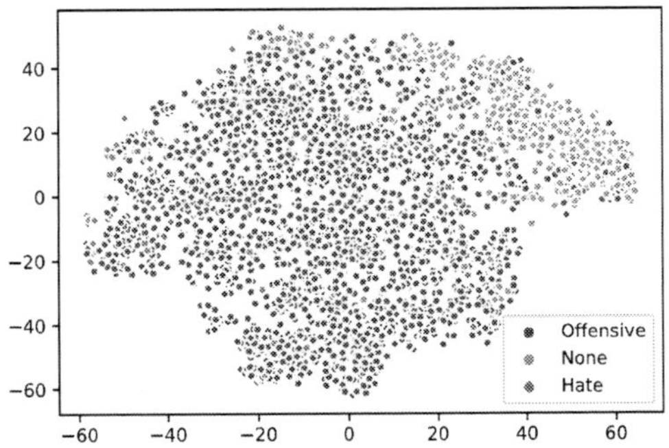

Figure 7: DAVIDSON tweets, colored by label, in the feature space learned by the text model.

Figure 7 shows the feature space learned by our text model on DAVIDSON. Overall, the distribution looks similar as the one of WASEEM visualized in figure 4d. We can notice that hate tweets are extremely sparse and mixed with the offensive ones. This is reflected by the poor model performance on the hate class, possibly caused by the conceptual overlap that these two classes have. On the other hand, non-harmful tweets are mostly concentrated in one area of the plot, confirming the satisfactory F1 scored achieved.

A.2 Feature Space learned by the Social Model

Figure 8 shows the feature space learned by our social model on DAVIDSON. As done for WASEEM, we report the plots both for the single branches as well as for their combination. The tweet branch (figure 8a) has a similar structure to figure 7. However, hateful tweets are also concentrated in a small portion of the space. This reflects the improved performance that the social model had on the hate class. This suggests that the information coming from the other input sources reinforces the signal backpropagated to the tweet branch, resulting in a less chaotic mixture of hateful and offensive tweets. The user vocabulary (figure 8b) and the follower network branch (figure 8c) do not present the same characteristics as seen on WASEEM. In this case, we do not have the data points separated into multiple clusters. The same goes for the overall learned feature space (figure 8d), where all the tweets are contained in one single cloud. This is consistent with what we observed in terms of F1 Scores. In contrast to what occurred on WASEEM, user features did not cause a substantial impact on the feature space on DAVIDSON and thus did not produce a large leap in performance.

A.3 Complement to Figure 6

Figure 6 compares the model's behavior on the same tweet but with different authors, one racist and one regular. For completeness, figure 9 shows the corresponding plots—Shapley values and embedding onto the features space—for the same tweet when generated by a sexist user. The result is analogous to the one obtained with the regular user. Also in this case the tweet is not classified as racist (12% confidence). The estimated Shapley values show a substantial impact of the user vocabulary against the racism class. The embedding onto the latent space shows once more that changing the author caused the tweet to embed in a different cluster, hence excluding the possibility of the content being classified correctly.

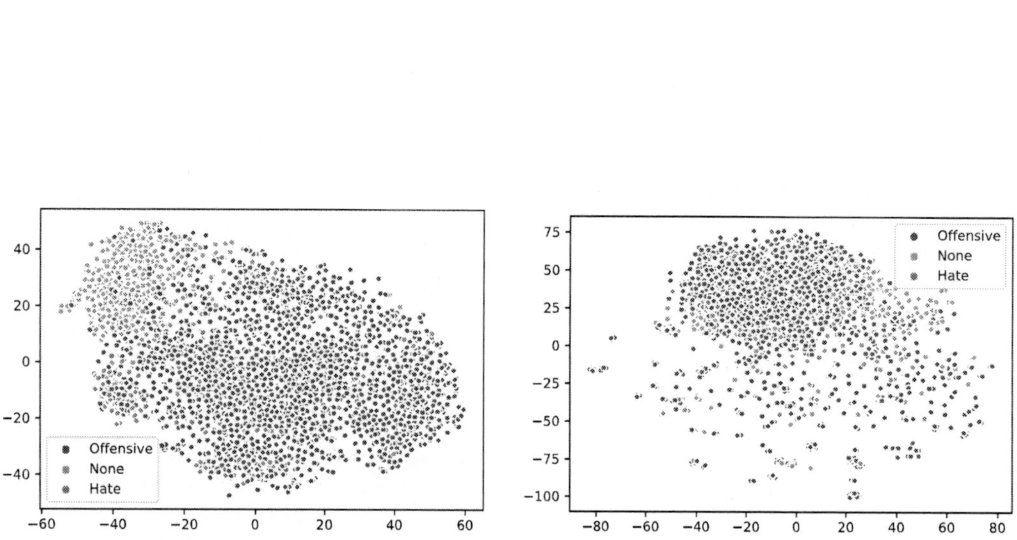

(a) Tweet Branch

(b) User Vocabulary Branch

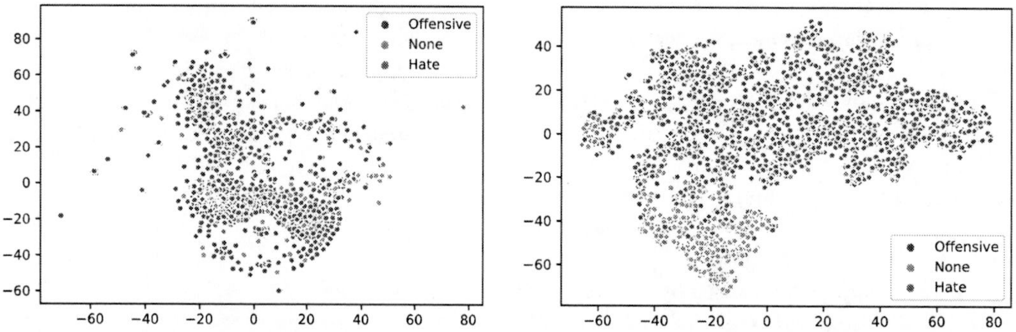

(c) Follower Network Branch

(d) Last Hidden Layer

Figure 8: Latent space visualization of our social model on DAVIDSON, colored by label. The features are extracted from the single branches before the concatenation: tweet (a), user's vocabulary (b), follower network (c). The last plot (d) shows instead the final learned features space, after all branches are combined and processed together.

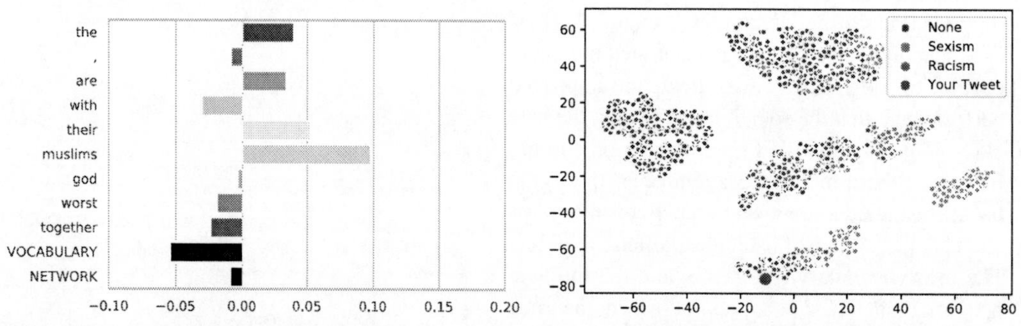

(a) Sexist User, Shapley Values

(b) Sexist User, Embedding in Latent Space

Figure 9: Features contribution (w.r.t. racism class) and embeddings of the islamophobic tweet in the social model's latent space. The pair of plots are w.r.t. the prediction done with sexist author.

Self-Contextualized Attention for Abusive Language Identification

Horacio Jarquín-Vásquez and **Hugo Jair Escalante** and **Manuel Montes-y-Gómez**
Instituto Nacional de Astrofísica, Óptica y Electrónica (INAOE)
Luis Enrique Erro #1, Sta María Tonanzintla, 72840 San Andrés Cholula, Pue.
{horacio.jarquin, hugojair, mmontesg}@inaoep.mx

Abstract

The use of attention mechanisms in deep learning approaches has become popular in natural language processing due to its outstanding performance. The use of these mechanisms allows one managing the importance of the elements of a sequence in accordance to their context, however, this importance has been observed independently between the pairs of elements of a sequence (self-attention) and between the application domain of a sequence (contextual attention), leading to the loss of relevant information and limiting the representation of the sequences. To tackle these particular issues we propose the self-contextualized attention mechanism, which trades off the previous limitations, by considering the internal and contextual relationships between the elements of a sequence. The proposed mechanism was evaluated in four standard collections for the abusive language identification task achieving encouraging results. It outperformed the current attention mechanisms and showed a competitive performance with respect to state-of-the-art approaches.

1 Introduction

The integration of social media platforms into the everyday lives of billions of users has increased the number of online social interactions, promoting the exchange of different opinions and points of view that would otherwise be ignored by traditional media. The use of these social media platforms has revolutionized the way people communicate and share information. Unfortunately, not all of these interactions are constructive, as the presence of Abusive Language (AL) has spread to these media.

AL is characterized by the presence of insults, teasing, criticism and intimidation (Cecillon et al., 2019). Mainly, it includes epithets directed at an individual's characteristic, which are personally offensive, degrading and insulting. Because of its negative social impact (Kumar et al., 2018), the automatic identification of AL has stimulated the interest of social media companies and governments (Hinduja and Patchin, 2010). Derived from this, multiple efforts have been made to combat the proliferation of AL, starting from the codes of conduct, norms and regulations in the content publication on social media[1], to the use of Natural Language Processing (NLP) for the computational analysis of language (Schmidt and Wiegand, 2017).

Concerning the several efforts and approximations made by the NLP community, one of the most relevant issues in the AL identification task is to distinguish between the use of profane words and vulgarities in offensive and non-offensive texts. This indicates that the importance and interpretation of each word is highly context dependent, and, accordingly, this particular issue evidences one of the reasons why traditional bag-of-words methods tend to generate many false positives in their predictions. Few works related to this task have explored the importance of words according to their context; particularly, the use of Deep Learning (DL) approaches with the addition of the Attention Mechanism (AM) has been explored as an alternative to solve this issue (Pavlopoulos et al., 2017; Chakrabarty et al., 2019; Jarquín-Vásquez et al., 2020).

The idea behind the use of the AM is to provide the classification model with the ability to focus on a subset of inputs (or features), handling in this way the importance of words in accordance to their context. Due to their outstanding performance in many NLP tasks, several AM have been proposed in recent years (Chaudhari et al., 2020), which can be divided into two main approaches: Self-Attention (SA) (Vaswani et al., 2017) and Contextual Attention (CA) (Yang et al., 2016) mechanisms. Specifically, SA takes the relationships among words within the same sentence, whereas,

[1] http://ec.europa.eu/justice/fundamental-rights/files/hate_speech_code_of_conduct_en.pdf

Proceedings of the Ninth International Workshop on Natural Language Processing for Social Media, pages 103–112
Online Workshop, June 10, 2021.

CA selectively focuses on words with respect to some external query vector, which adjusts according to the training task. The more important the word is in determining the answer to that query, the more focus it is given.

Despite their outstanding performance, both approaches have their own limitations. On one hand, CA ignores the internal relationships between the words of a sequence, correspondingly, SA does not consider the global relationships within the words of different sequences, which causes the loss of relevant information in the application domain (training task). Clearly, the limitations of these AM are complimentary and a hybrid AM could overcome the individual issues. In this work we extend the use of the AM by proposing the Self-Contextualized Attention (SCA) mechanism, an AM that trades off the previous limitations, by taking advantage of both SA and CA mechanisms. The proposed SCA mechanism is designed to be applied to any sequence of word encoding features, nevertheless, due to the high context-dependency of words that this specific task has, in this work we exclusively focus on the AL identification task.

The main contributions in this paper are: After identifying a Deep Neural Network (DNN) architecture that is rather stable and well-performing, we propose and integrate the SCA mechanism into the DL architecture, subsequently we conduct a quantitative and qualitative study of the effectiveness of our proposed AM against the use of SA, CA and some other novel approaches to the AL identification task. To the best of our knowledge this is the first effort in combining both AM variants.

This paper is organized as follows: In Section 2, we present some previous works related to the AL identification task, along with other hybrid AM approaches. In Section 3, we describe our proposed SCA mechanism, as well as the employed classification framework; in Section 4, we present the datasets used to evaluate our SCA mechanism, their implementation details, as well as the external resources fed to the classification framework. Section 5 reports and discusses our quantitative and qualitative results. Finally, Section 6 summarizes our findings and discusses future work.

2 Related work

Considering the well-acknowledged increase of AL on social media platforms, several datasets (Zeerak and Dirk, 2016; Davidson et al., 2017; Marcos et al., 2019) and evaluation campaigns (Fersini et al., 2018; Kumar et al., 2018; Aragón et al., 2020), have been proposed in order to mitigate the impact of such a kind of messages.

The detection of AL has been mainly addressed from a supervised perspective, considering a great variety of features. Initial works used a combination of hand-crafted features such as bag-of-words representations, considering word and character n-grams (Burnap and Williams, 2016), as well as, syntactical and linguistical features (Nobata et al., 2016). Aiming to improve the generalization of the classifiers, some other works have explored the use of DL by taking word or character sequences from texts to learn abusive patterns without the need for explicit feature engineering; the use of word embeddings as features predominates in these works (Zhang et al., 2018; Saksesi et al., 2018; Amrutha and Bindu, 2019). More recently, there has been a trend within the NLP community regarding the use of Transformers for the improvement of text representations. In particular, for the identification of AL, transfer learning has been applied considering different pre-trained models, such as ELMO, GPT-2 and BERT (Liu et al., 2019; Nikolov and Radivchev, 2019).

Regarding the classification stage, a vast range of approaches and techniques have also been proposed. These approaches could be divided into two main categories; the first category relies on traditional classification algorithms such as Naive Bayes, Support Vector Machines (SVM), Logistic Regression and Random Forest (Burnap and Williams, 2016; Nobata et al., 2016; Davidson et al., 2017; Schmidt and Wiegand, 2017). On the other hand, the second category includes DL approaches, which rely on the use of Convolutional Neural Networks (CNN) and Recurrent Neural Networks (RNN), to accomplish the tasks of feature extraction (Badjatiya et al., 2017; Gambäck and Sikdar, 2017) and dependency learning (Badjatiya et al., 2017; Saksesi et al., 2018). In addition to this, the combination of both types of Neural Networks have been used for the development of powerful structures that capture order information between the extracted features (Zhang et al., 2018; Amrutha and Bindu, 2019).

Finally, most recent works in abusive AL identification have considered DL architectures with the addition of an AM. One of the first works introducing attention into the task used the SA mechanism to detect abuse in portal news and Wikipedia (Pavlopoulos et al., 2017). Subsequently, (Chakrabarty et al., 2019) showed that the use of CA introduced by (Yang et al., 2016) improved the results of SA in this task. Later in (Jarquín-Vásquez et al., 2020) the use of the CA is extended at a word n-grams level, showing the advantages in the usage of word sequences when identifying AL. Regarding other tasks outside the AL identification, some hybrid AMs have been proposed for the combination and representation of different instances and modalities (Khullar and Arora, 2020; Zhang et al., 2020), unlike these hybrid approaches, the proposed SCA mechanism combines the features of the SA and CA mechanisms at an instance level. Motivated by these previous works and with the goal of creating an AM that handles both, the internal and external relationships between words, in this paper we propose the SCA mechanism.

3 Self-contextualized attention

This section is divided into two subsections. First we introduce our proposed SCA mechanism, which is designed to be applied to any sequence of encoding features. Subsequently, we present the DNN architecture used as our classification framework. For more details related to the AMs, we refer the reader to the following work: (Chaudhari et al., 2020).

3.1 Self-contextualized attention mechanism

Given a sequence of encoding features $H = \{h_1, h_2, ..., h_n\}$, where $H \in \mathbb{R}^{k \times n}$, k is the number of the encoding features and h_i refers to the $i\text{-}th$ element of H, the purpose of our proposed SCA mechanism is to generate a global context-aware representation G, that considers both the internal and external relationships between the encoding features of H. Figure 1 shows the general architecture of our proposed SCA mechanism. This architecture is divided into three major stages, each of them is illustrated by the 3 rectangles, corresponding to the SA, CA and SCA stages. Below, we present in detail the aforementioned stages.

SA stage: as in (Pavlopoulos et al., 2017) the main purpose of SA is the building of connections within the elements of the same sequence, but at different positions. The use of SA allows the modeling of both long-range and local dependencies, this is captured by the attention filter $\alpha_s \in \mathbb{R}^{n \times n}$ defined in the Equation 1. This attention filter is calculated with the dot product similarity between all the pairs of elements of H, later these values are smoothed with the use of a softmax function. Finally, the context-aware representation $S \in \mathbb{R}^{k \times n}$ shown in the Equation 2, is calculated with the matrix multiplication of H and α_s^T, where α_s is used to highlight and filter out the most and less relevant encoding features, respectively.

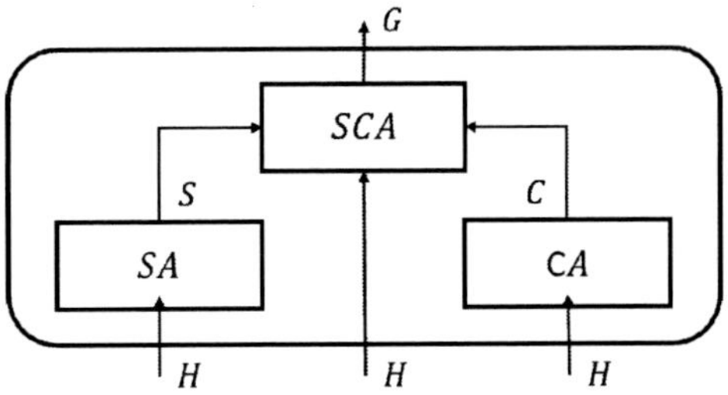

Figure 1: Proposed self-contextualized attention mechanism.

$$\alpha_s = softmax(H^T \cdot H) \tag{1}$$

$$S = H\alpha_s^T \tag{2}$$

CA stage: unlike the previous stage, the CA mechanism uses a context vector $u_h \in \mathbb{R}^k$, which is randomly initialized and jointly learned during the training process, this vector is used as a query vector in order to obtain the attention values $\alpha_c \in \mathbb{R}^n$ by measuring the similarity between the elements of the sequence H and the application domain represented by u_h. This similarity is calculated in the Equation 3 by calculating the scalar dot product of u_h^T and H; the resulting values are smoothed with the use of a softmax function. Contrasting the CA mechanism proposed by (Yang et al., 2016), instead of using a weighted sum between each attention value and its corresponding encoding features for the final sequence representation, our context-aware representation $C \in \mathbb{R}^{k \times n}$ shown in Equation 4, takes all the information of the attention values, by doing an element-wise multiplication $\odot$, within each scalar of α_c and its corresponding encoding features h_i.

$$\alpha_c = softmax(u_h^T \cdot H) \tag{3}$$

$$C = \alpha_c \odot H \tag{4}$$

SCA stage: since the previous stages generate two different context-aware representations S and

C, respectively. The purpose of this stage is to merge these representations in order to create a global context-aware representation $G \in \mathbb{R}^{k \times n}$ that integrates both, the internal and external relationships. These relationships are captured with the global attention filter $\alpha_g \in \mathbb{R}^{n \times n}$, which is calculated by the smoothed dot product similarity between S and C, as shown in Equation 5. This attention filter can be seen as a high level attention representation, since it is calculated based on the local dependencies and the application domain. Finally, the global context-aware representation G is calculated in Equation 6 with the matrix multiplication of H and α_g^T.

$$\alpha_g = softmax(S^T \cdot C) \quad (5)$$

$$G = H\alpha_g^T \quad (6)$$

The proposed SCA mechanism can be applied to any sequence of encoding features H. For the purposes of this work, each element of the sequence is represented by the word encoding features h_i.

3.2 Classification framework

In order to integrate our proposed SCA mechanism into the AL identification task, we adapt a modular and well-performing DNN architecture, as our classification framework. This architecture was presented in (Yang et al., 2016; Chakrabarty et al., 2019) and its designed to modularly manage different AM. The adapted architecture is shown in Figure 2; it consists of four main stages, which are described below.

The first and second stages correspond to the input and encoding stages, respectively. The *input stage* is integrated by the embedding matrix $X \in \mathbb{R}^{d \times n}$, which is represented by a sequence of n d-dimensional word vectors x_i. Subsequently, the embedding matrix X passes as input to the *encoding stage*, which is conformed by a Bidirectional Gated Recurrent Unit (Bi-GRU) layer. The Bi-GRU layer accomplish the sequence encoding task by summarizing the information of the whole sequence X centered around each word annotation; the producing encoding stage generates a sequence of encoding features $H \in \mathbb{R}^{k \times n}$.

Since not all words contribute equally for the meaning and representation of a sequence, the *third stage* corresponds to the attention stage, including the SCA mechanism and the average pooling layer. Specifically, the sequence encoded features H are passed as input to the SCA mechanism, which generates a global context-aware representation G; since the next stage uses a vector for the classification layers, the matrix G is reduced with the average pooling layer, generating a high level representation vector $g \in \mathbb{R}^k$, which summarizes the most relevant information from G. Finally, the *Fourth stage* uses the representation vector g as input for the classification layers; two layers handle the final classification, a dense layer with a Rectified Linear Unit (ReLU) activation function, and a fully-connected softmax layer to obtain the class probabilities and get the final classification. The implementation details and the hyperparameter settings are presented in Section 4.2.

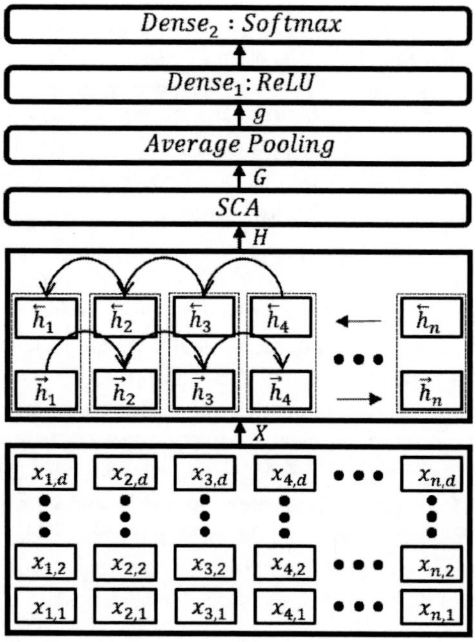

Figure 2: Adapted classification framework, based on a DNN architecture.

4 Experimental settings

This section presents the experimental settings. First, we introduce the four evaluation datasets, which correspond to Twitter collections. Then, with the purpose of facilitating the replicability of our results, we present our method's implementation details, starting from the text preprocessing phase, up to the configuration of the classification framework.

4.1 Datasets for AL identification

AL can be of different types, its main divisions are distinguished by the target and severity of the insults. Accordingly, different collections and evaluation campaigns have considered different kinds of AL for its study. Below we present a brief description of the four English datasets we used in our experiments. From now on we will refer to them as DS1, DS2, DS3, and DS4.

DS1 (Davidson et al., 2017) and DS2 (Zeerak and Dirk, 2016) were some of the first large-scale datasets for abusive tweet detection; DS1 focuses on the identification of racist and sexist tweets, whereas DS2 focuses on identifying tweets with abusive language and hate speech. On the other hand, DS3 (Marcos et al., 2019) and DS4 (Fersini et al., 2018) were used in the *SemEval-2019 Task 6*, and in the *Evalita 2018* Task on Automatic Misogyny Identification (AMI) respectively. DS3 focuses on identifying offensive tweets, whereas DS4 focuses on identifying misogyny in tweets. Both shared tasks provide a fine-grained evaluation through different sub-tasks; in this work, we focus on the sub-task A (binary classification of offenses and misogyny, respectively).

Figure 3 resumes the information about the classes distribution of the four collections.

4.2 Implementation details

Different text preprocessing operations were applied: user mentions and links were replaced by the default tokens *<user>* and *<url>*; in order to enrich the vocabulary, all hashtags were segmented by words (*e.g.* #BuildTheWall - build the wall) with the use of the ekphrasis library, proposed in (Baziotis et al., 2017); in addition to this, all emojis were converted into words (*e.g.* ☺ - smiley face) using the demoji[2] library; stop words were removed, with the exception of personal pronouns; all text was lowercased and non-alphabetical characters as well as consecutive repeated words were removed. For word representation we used pre-trained fastText embeddings (Mikolov et al., 2018), trained with subword information on Common Crawl, which have been recognized as useful for this task according to the study presented in (Corazza et al., 2020).

Table 1 presents the hyperparameter settings of the adapted DNN. The network was trained for a total of 15 epochs, with a learning rate of 1e–4, using the Adam optimizer (Kingma and Ba, 2015) and a Dropout rate of 15%. In order to compare the robustness of our proposal, we consider four baseline architectures: the first architecture is based on a simple Bi-GRU network, which receives words as input but does not use any attention layers; the second and third architectures employ the same Bi-GRU network with the addition of a SA and CA layer, respectively; finally, in order to compare the performance of our proposed SCA mechanism against a novel AL identification approach, the fourth baseline is based on a fine-tuned BERT[3] base model (12 layers, 768 hidden size, 12 attention heads per layer), built with the addition of the task-specific inputs and the end-to-end fine-tuning of all parameters. As described in (Devlin et al., 2019), we take the last layer encoding of the classification token <CLS> and use it as input for the softmax classification layer. These four baselines architectures and our classification framework are referred in the experiments as: $Bi-GRU$, $Bi-GRU_{SA}$, $Bi-GRU_{CA}$, $BERT_{BASE}$, and $Bi-GRU_{SCA}$, respectively. It is important to mention that the first three baseline architectures used the same hyperparameter settings.

Vectors and Variables		Size
n		50
d		300
k, u_h		128
Layer	**Input size**	**Output size**
Embedding	50	50x300
Bi-GRU	50x300	50x128
SCA	50x128	50x128
Avg Pooling	50x128	128
Dense_1	128	64
Dense_2	64	#Classes

Table 1: DNN architecture hyperparameters.

5 Experimental results

This section is organized in three subsections. Sections 5.1 and 5.2 present the quantitative results of the experimentation, corresponding to the comparison of our proposed SCA mechanism against the baselines and state-of-the-art results. Finally, Section 5.3 presents some qualitative results of the SCA mechanism, through the analysis and visualization of the attention values.

[2] https://pypi.org/project/demoji/

[3] https://tfhub.dev/tensorflow/small_bert/bert_en_uncased_L-12_H-768_A-12/1

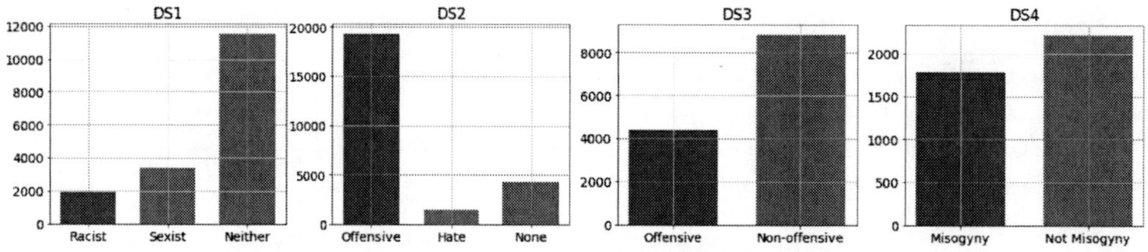

Figure 3: The classes distribution of the four used datasets.

5.1 Quantitative effectiveness of the SCA mechanism

Table 2 shows the results of the mean and standard deviation corresponding to the 10-fold cross validation evaluation applied to our classification framework DNN architecture ($Bi-GRU_{SCA}$), as well as the four baselines simplified architectures $Bi-GRU$, $Bi-GRU_{SA}$, $Bi-GRU_{CA}$ and $BERT_{BASE}$. For sake of comparison, we evaluate all the collections using the macro-average F_1 score, which is commonly used in the AL identification task.

Centering the analysis of results on the first three baselines and on our classification framework (columns 2 - 5), the results indicate that the use of AM outperformed the base Bi-GRU network (column 2 vs columns 3 - 5) by at least a margin of 1.1%. In addition, the use of the CA outperformed the use of SA (column 4 vs column 3) by at least a margin of 1.2%, which is consistent according to the results obtained in (Chakrabarty et al., 2019). Finally, comparing the use of our proposed SCA mechanism against the use of SA and CA (column 5 vs columns 3 and 4), better results are obtained in the four evaluation datasets, improving the results by at least a margin of 1.1%. Since the use CA baseline outperforms the SA based one, we compared $Bi-GRU_{SCA}$ vs $Bi-GRU_{CA}$ with the Chi Squared Test, obtaining statistically significant values with $p \leq 0.001$.

Table 2 also compares the results from our proposed SCA mechanism with respect to the $BERT_{BASE}$ baseline (column 5 vs column 6). It is shown that the $Bi-GRU_{SCA}$ DNN obtained better results in 3 out of 4 datasets. In addition to the outstanding results, the use of our $Bi-GRU_{SCA}$ DNN has a considerably lower number of parameters compared to the $BERT_{BASE}$ model (110M vs 7M), which greatly reduces the computing power necessary to run our DNN. Finally, compared to some novel approaches for the AL identification task (Alshaalan and Al-Khalifa, 2020), our DNN improves the model interpretability, through the SCA mechanism.

5.2 Comparison with the state-of-the-art

In this subsection we compare our proposed DNN architecture ($Bi-GRU_{SCA}$) with state-of-the-art approaches. Since the datasets DS1 and DS2 are presented as a single dataset, in order to have a fair comparison with other works, these were partitioned into 80% for training, 10% for validation and 10% for testing, in addition, the weighted-average F_1 score was used as an evaluation measure for these datasets. In the case of DS3 and DS4 datasets, the partitions corresponding to the training and testing were considered for the evaluation; since these datasets come from shared tasks, the evaluation measures were adjusted to each of them, specifically, DS3 and DS4 were evaluated using the macro-average F_1 score and the accuracy, respectively.

Table 3 presents the results of our proposed $Bi-GRU_{SCA}$ DNN architecture in comparison with state-of-the-art results. It shows that the $Bi-GRU_{SCA}$ DNN obtained better results in 2 out of 4 datasets. It is important to note that the state-of-the-art results from the DS2 and DS3 datasets only improved our results by margin of 1% and 0.03%, respectively. Specifically, in (Mozafari et al., 2019), which corresponds to the DS1 and DS2 state-of-the-art results, the use of a BERT-based CNN is implemented for the feature extraction of the transformer encoders, generating a hierarchical encoded vector, used for the AL classification.

Regarding the state-of-the-art results from the DS3 and DS4 datasets, the best performance teams corresponding to each shared task were considered, on the one hand, *NULI* the best performance team in the DS3 shared task (Liu et al., 2019), used a BERT-base-uncased model with default-parameters, using a max sentence length of 64 and a variety of text pre-processing techniques, on the

Dataset	$Bi-GRU$	$Bi-GRU_{SA}$	$Bi-GRU_{CA}$	$Bi-GRU_{SCA}$	$BERT_{BASE}$
DS1	0.7614 ±0.0083	0.8162 ±0.0079	0.8271 ±0.0069	**0.8378 ±0.0082**	0.8291 ±0.0076
DS2	0.7438 ±0.0072	0.7721 ±0.0081	0.7874 ±0.0074	0.7984 ±0.0078	**0.8052 ±0.0083**
DS3	0.7698 ±0.0081	0.8052 ±0.0078	0.8247 ±0.0085	**0.8423 ±0.0064**	0.8398 ±0.0081
DS4	0.6541 ±0.0096	0.6654 ±0.0073	0.6782 ±0.0067	**0.6937 ±0.0086**	0.6906 ±0.0076

Table 2: Comparison results from the four baselines architectures and our classification framework in four datasets for AL identification (*all the collections were evaluated with the macro-average* F_1).

Dataset	$Bi-GRU_{SCA}$	*state-of-the-art*	*Reference*
DS1	**0.89**	0.88	(Mozafari et al., 2019)
DS2	0.91	**0.92**	(Mozafari et al., 2019)
DS3	0.826	**0.829**	(Liu et al., 2019)
DS4	**0.738**	0.704	(Saha et al., 2018)

Table 3: Comparison results from our classification framework and state-of-the-art approaches in four datasets for AL identification (*DS1 and DS2 were evaluated with the weighted-average* F_1, *DS3 and DS4 were evaluated using the macro-average* F_1 *and the accuracy, respectively*).

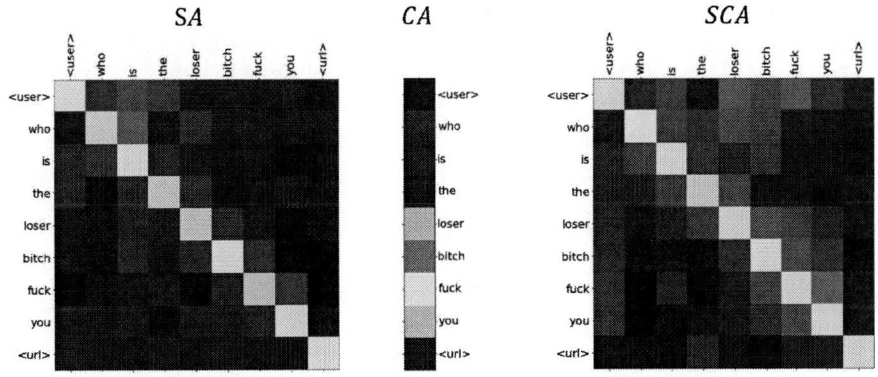

Figure 4: Attention heatmaps visualization, corresponding to the α_s, α_c, and α_g attention filter values. The Example shown in the attention heatmaps was taken from the DS3 dataset.

other hand, *hateminers* achieved the highest performance on the DS4 shared task (Saha et al., 2018), with a run based on a vector representation that concatenates sentence embedding, TF-IDF and average word embeddings coupled with a Logistic Regression model. Unlike the reported state-of-the-art approaches, the use of our SCA mechanism on a simple and well-performed DNN, obtains competitive results, without the use of complex DNN (Mozafari et al., 2019), or large amounts of resources and features (Saha et al., 2018).

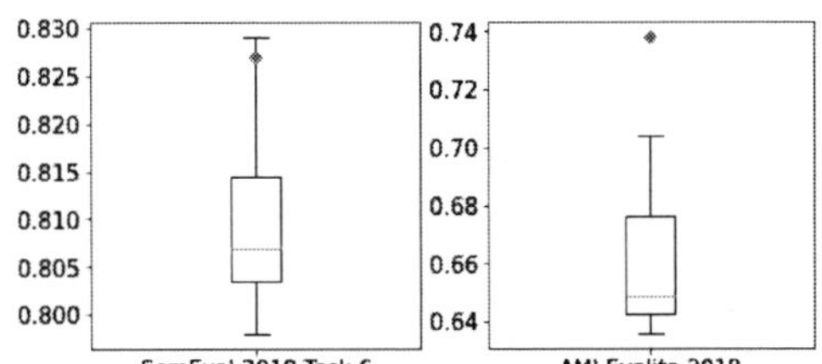

Figure 5: Comparative Boxplot graphs from our results (red rhombus) vs. the top-10 results of the shared tasks.

The boxplot graphs shown in Figure 5, compares our $Bi-GRU_{SCA}$ performance results (red rhombus) against the top-10 results corresponding to the shared tasks *SemEval 2019 Task 6* and *AMI Evalita 2018*, respectively. As shown in the graphs, our results are competitive with respect to the top-10 results obtained by the best participating teams in each sub-task A. In both boxplot graphs our results remain above the third quartile, specifically, in the *AMI Evalita 2018* shared task an outstanding performance is obtained with the use of our proposed SCA mechanism in the classification framework.

5.3 Qualitative effectiveness of the SCA mechanism

NOTE: This subsection contains examples of language that may be offensive to some readers, these do not represent the perspectives of the authors.

In order to understand the effectiveness of our proposed SCA mechanism in the improvement of the sequences representation, this subsection presents the qualitative results of the analysis and visualization of the attention values. Since the SCA mechanism integrates both, the SA and CA mechanisms, the attention values were considered at these three different levels, with the analysis of the α_s, α_c and α_g attention filters, which correspond to the SA, CA and SCA mechanisms.

Figure 4 shows the visualization of the attention heatmaps corresponding to the three attention filters values integrated by the SCA mechanism. The example shown in the figure *"<user> who is the loser bitch fuck you <url>"* corresponds to an offensive instance taken from the DS3 dataset. As shown in the figure, the values of the attention filter α_s, corresponding to the SA, tend to be more relevant with respect to their own elements and their closest neighbors, for example, in the case of the most relevant words to *"who"*, the same word *"who"* is found, followed by the word *"is"*, likewise, in the case of the most relevant words to *"fuck"*, the words *"fuck"*, *"you"* and *"bitch"* are found. On the other hand, the values of the attention filter α_c, corresponding to the CA, indicate the most relevant words for the AL identification; as can be seen in the central heatmap from the Figure 4, the most relevant words are: *"loser"*, *"bitch"* and *"fuck"*, which indeed correspond to words potentially used in offensive contexts.

Finally, the values of the attention filter α_g, corresponding to the SCA, are shown in the right heatmap from Figure 4. The attention filter α_g shows the combination of both AM, which improves the representation of an instance. For example, in the produced visualization from the most relevant words to *"<user>"*, a closer relationship to offensive words is now presented, highlighting the words: *"loser"*, *"bitch"* and *"fuck"*, which are often used to offend, something similar is presented with the words *"who"* and *"is"*. On the other hand, the words *"fuck"*, *"you"* and *"bitch"*, in addition to having a better relationship with other offensive words as *"loser"*, are also related to the target of the offense: *"<user>"*.

6 Conclusions and future work

One of the main problems in the use of current AMs is the loss of contextual or internal information between the elements of a sequence. To tackle this issue we proposed the SCA mechanism, which integrates the SA and CA mechanisms for the construction of a representation that considers both, the internal and contextual relationships between the elements of a sequence. Due to the highly context-dependent interpretation of words in the AL identification, in this work we explore the use of the proposed SCA mechanism in the AL identification. The results obtained in four collections, considering different kinds of AL, were encouraging; they improved state-of-the-art approaches in 2 out of 4 datasets. In addition to this, the SA and CA mechanisms were evaluated against the SCA mechanism, the results show a quantitative and qualitative improvement in the use of the SCA mechanism, which allowed concluding that the use of the SCA mechanism is useful for discriminating between offensive and non-offensive contexts.

Since the most recent approaches are based on Transformers, as future work we plan to explore the use of our proposed SCA mechanism in the design of a multi-head SCA architecture. Additionally, we consider exploring new ways of combining the SA and CA mechanisms, as well as some novel approaches in the building of the SCA mechanism without the need of computing the SA and CA mechanisms individually. Finally, we consider the application of the proposed SCA mechanism in other related tasks where the interpretation of words is highly context dependent such as the detection of deception or the detection of depressed social media users.

Acknowledgements

We thank CONACyT-Mexico for partially supporting this work under project grant CB-2015-01-257383 and scholarship 925996.

References

Raghad Alshaalan and Hend Al-Khalifa. 2020. Hate speech detection in saudi twittersphere: A deep learning approach. In *Proceedings of the Fifth Arabic Natural Language Processing Workshop*, pages 12–23, Barcelona, Spain (Online). Association for Computational Linguistics.

B. R. Amrutha and K. R. Bindu. 2019. Detecting hate speech in tweets using different deep neural network architectures. In *2019 International Conference on Intelligent Computing and Control Systems (ICCS)*, pages 923–926.

Mario Ezra Aragón, Horacio Jesús Jarquín-Vásquez, Manuel Montes-y-Gómez, Hugo Jair Escalante, Luis Villaseñor Pineda, Helena Gómez-Adorno, Juan Pablo Posadas-Durán, and Gemma Bel-Enguix. 2020. Overview of MEX-A3T at iberlef 2020: Fake news and aggressiveness analysis in mexican spanish. In *Proceedings of the Iberian Languages Evaluation Forum (IberLEF 2020) co-located with 36th Conference of the Spanish Society for Natural Language Processing (SEPLN 2020), Málaga, Spain, September 23th, 2020*, volume 2664 of *CEUR Workshop Proceedings*, pages 222–235. CEUR-WS.org.

Pinkesh Badjatiya, Shashank Gupta, Manish Gupta, and Vasudeva Varma. 2017. Deep learning for hate speech detection in tweets. In *Proceedings of the 26th International Conference on World Wide Web Companion*, Republic and Canton of Geneva, CHE. International World Wide Web Conferences Steering Committee.

Christos Baziotis, Nikos Pelekis, and Christos Doulkeridis. 2017. Datastories at semeval-2017 task 4: Deep lstm with attention for message-level and topic-based sentiment analysis. In *Proceedings of the 11th International Workshop on Semantic Evaluation (SemEval-2017)*, pages 747–754, Vancouver, Canada. Association for Computational Linguistics.

Pete Burnap and Matthew L. Williams. 2016. Us and them: identifying cyber hate on twitter across multiple protected characteristics. *EPJ Data Sci.*, 5:11.

Noé Cecillon, Vincent Labatut, Richard Dufour, and G. Linarès. 2019. Abusive language detection in online conversations by combining content- and graph-based features. *Frontiers in Big Data*, 2.

Tuhin Chakrabarty, Kilol Gupta, and Smaranda Muresan. 2019. Pay "attention" to your context when classifying abusive language. In *Proceedings of the Third Workshop on Abusive Language Online*, pages 70–79. Association for Computational Linguistics.

Sneha Chaudhari, Gungor Polatkan, R. Ramanath, and Varun Mithal. 2020. An attentive survey of attention models. *Association for Computing Machinery*, 37.

Michele Corazza, Stefano Menini, Elena Cabrio, Sara Tonelli, and Serena Villata. 2020. A multilingual evaluation for online hate speech detection. *ACM Transactions on Internet Technology*, 20(2).

Thomas Davidson, Dana Warmsley, Michael W. Macy, and Ingmar Weber. 2017. Automated hate speech detection and the problem of offensive language. In *Proceedings of the Eleventh International Conference on Web and Social Media, ICWSM 2017, Montréal, Québec, Canada, May 15-18, 2017*, pages 512–515. AAAI Press.

Jacob Devlin, Ming-Wei Chang, Kenton Lee, and Kristina Toutanova. 2019. BERT: Pre-training of deep bidirectional transformers for language understanding. In *Proceedings of the 2019 Conference of the North American Chapter of the Association for Computational Linguistics: Human Language Technologies, Volume 1 (Long and Short Papers)*, pages 4171–4186. Association for Computational Linguistics.

Elisabetta Fersini, Debora Nozza, and Paolo Rosso. 2018. Overview of the evalita 2018 task on automatic misogyny identification (AMI). In *Proceedings of the Sixth Evaluation Campaign of Natural Language Processing and Speech Tools for Italian. Final Workshop (EVALITA 2018) co-located with the Fifth Italian Conference on Computational Linguistics (CLiC-it)*, volume 2263 of *CEUR Workshop Proceedings*. CEUR-WS.org.

Björn Gambäck and Utpal Kumar Sikdar. 2017. Using convolutional neural networks to classify hate-speech. In *Proceedings of the First Workshop on Abusive Language Online*, pages 85–90. Association for Computational Linguistics.

Sameer Hinduja and Justin W. Patchin. 2010. Bullying, cyberbullying, and suicide. *Archives of Suicide Research*, 14(3):206–221.

Horacio Jesús Jarquín-Vásquez, Manuel Montes-y Gómez, and Luis Villaseñor-Pineda. 2020. Not all swear words are used equal: Attention over word n-grams for abusive language identification. In *Pattern Recognition*, pages 282–292, Cham. Springer International Publishing.

Aman Khullar and Udit Arora. 2020. MAST: Multimodal abstractive summarization with trimodal hierarchical attention. In *Proceedings of the First International Workshop on Natural Language Processing Beyond Text*, pages 60–69. Association for Computational Linguistics.

Diederik P. Kingma and Jimmy Ba. 2015. Adam: A method for stochastic optimization. In *3rd International Conference on Learning Representations, ICLR 2015, San Diego, CA, USA, May 7-9, 2015, Conference Track Proceedings*.

Ritesh Kumar, Aishwarya N. Reganti, Akshit Bhatia, and Tushar Maheshwari. 2018. Aggression-annotated corpus of Hindi-English code-mixed data. In *Proceedings of the Eleventh International Conference on Language Resources and Evaluation (LREC 2018)*, Miyazaki, Japan. European Language Resources Association (ELRA).

Ping Liu, Wen Li, and Liang Zou. 2019. NULI at SemEval-2019 task 6: Transfer learning for offensive language detection using bidirectional transformers. In *Proceedings of the 13th International Workshop on Semantic Evaluation*, pages 87–91. Association for Computational Linguistics.

Zampieri Marcos, Malmasi Shervin, Nakov Preslav, Rosenthal Sara, Noura Farra, and Ritesh Kumar. 2019. Semeval-2019 task 6: Identifying and categorizing offensive language in social media (offenseval). In *Proceedings of the 13th International Workshop on Semantic Evaluation*, pages 75–86. Association for Computational Linguistics.

Tomas Mikolov, Edouard Grave, Piotr Bojanowski, Christian Puhrsch, and Armand Joulin. 2018. Advances in pre-training distributed word representations. In *Proceedings of the Eleventh International Conference on Language Resources and Evaluation (LREC 2018)*. European Language Resources Association (ELRA).

Marzieh Mozafari, Reza Farahbakhsh, and Noël Crespi. 2019. A bert-based transfer learning approach for hate speech detection in online social media. In *Complex Networks and Their Applications VIII - Volume 1 Proceedings of the Eighth International Conference on Complex Networks and Their Applications COMPLEX NETWORKS 2019, Lisbon, Portugal, December 10-12, 2019*, volume 881 of *Studies in Computational Intelligence*, pages 928–940. Springer.

Alex Nikolov and Victor Radivchev. 2019. Nikolov-radivchev at SemEval-2019 task 6: Offensive tweet classification with BERT and ensembles. In *Proceedings of the 13th International Workshop on Semantic Evaluation*, pages 691–695, Minneapolis, Minnesota, USA. Association for Computational Linguistics.

Chikashi Nobata, Joel Tetreault, Achint Thomas, Yashar Mehdad, and Yi Chang. 2016. Abusive language detection in online user content. In *Proceedings of the 25th International Conference on World Wide Web*, page 145–153. International World Wide Web Conferences Steering Committee.

John Pavlopoulos, Prodromos Malakasiotis, and Ion Androutsopoulos. 2017. Deeper attention to abusive user content moderation. In *Proceedings of the 2017 Conference on Empirical Methods in Natural Language Processing*, pages 1125–1135, Copenhagen, Denmark. Association for Computational Linguistics.

Punyajoy Saha, Binny Mathew, Pawan Goyal, and Animesh Mukherjee. 2018. Hateminers : Detecting hate speech against women. *CoRR*, abs/1812.06700.

Arum Sucia Saksesi, M. Nasrun, and C. Setianingsih. 2018. Analysis text of hate speech detection using recurrent neural network. In *2018 International Conference on Control, Electronics, Renewable Energy and Communications (ICCEREC)*, pages 242–248.

Anna Schmidt and Michael Wiegand. 2017. A survey on hate speech detection using natural language processing. In *Proceedings of the Fifth International Workshop on Natural Language Processing for Social Media*, pages 1–10, Valencia, Spain. Association for Computational Linguistics.

Ashish Vaswani, Noam Shazeer, Niki Parmar, Jakob Uszkoreit, Llion Jones, Aidan N Gomez, Ł ukasz Kaiser, and Illia Polosukhin. 2017. Attention is all you need. In *Advances in Neural Information Processing Systems*, volume 30. Curran Associates, Inc.

Zichao Yang, Diyi Yang, Chris Dyer, Xiaodong He, Alex Smola, and Eduard Hovy. 2016. Hierarchical attention networks for document classification. In *Proceedings of the 2016 Conference of the North American Chapter of the Association for Computational Linguistics: Human Language Technologies*, pages 1480–1489. Association for Computational Linguistics.

Waseem Zeerak and Hovy Dirk. 2016. Hateful symbols or hateful people? predictive features for hate speech detection on twitter. In *Proceedings of the NAACL Student Research Workshop*, pages 88–93. Association for Computational Linguistics.

Dongxiang Zhang, Yuyang Nie, Sai Wu, Yanyan Shen, and Kian-Lee Tan. 2020. Multi-context attention for entity matching. In *Proceedings of The Web Conference 2020*, WWW '20, page 2634–2640. Association for Computing Machinery.

Ziqi Zhang, David Robinson, and Jonathan Tepper. 2018. Detecting hate speech on twitter using a convolution-gru based deep neural network. In *The Semantic Web*, pages 745–760, Cham. Springer International Publishing.

Unsupervised Domain Adaptation in Cross-corpora Abusive Language Detection

Tulika Bose, Irina Illina, Dominique Fohr
Universite de Lorraine, CNRS, Inria, LORIA, F-54000 Nancy, France
tulika.bose, illina, dominique.fohr@loria.fr

Abstract

The state-of-the-art abusive language detection models report great in-corpus performance, but underperform when evaluated on abusive comments that differ from the training scenario. As human annotation involves substantial time and effort, models that can adapt to newly collected comments can prove to be useful. In this paper, we investigate the effectiveness of several Unsupervised Domain Adaptation (UDA) approaches for the task of cross-corpora abusive language detection. In comparison, we adapt a variant of the BERT model, trained on large-scale abusive comments, using Masked Language Model (MLM) fine-tuning. Our evaluation shows that the UDA approaches result in sub-optimal performance, while the MLM fine-tuning does better in the cross-corpora setting. Detailed analysis reveals the limitations of the UDA approaches and emphasizes the need to build efficient adaptation methods for this task.

1 Introduction

Social networking platforms have been used as a medium for expressing opinions, ideas, and feelings. This has resulted in a serious concern of *abusive* language, which is commonly described as hurtful, obscene, or toxic towards an individual or a group sharing common societal characteristics such as race, religion, gender, etc. The huge amount of comments generated every day on these platforms make it increasingly infeasible for manual moderators to review every comment for its abusive content. As such, automated abuse detection mechanisms are employed to assist moderators. We consider the variations of online abuse, toxicity, hate speech, and offensive language as abusive language and this work addresses the detection of abusive versus non-abusive comments.

Supervised classification approaches for abuse detection require a large amount of expensive annotated data (Lee et al., 2018). Moreover, models already trained on the available annotated corpus report degraded performance on new content (Yin and Zubiaga, 2021; Swamy et al., 2019; Wiegand et al., 2019). This is due to phenomena like change of topics discussed in social media, and differences across corpora, such as varying sampling strategies, targets of abuse, abusive language forms, etc. These call for approaches that can adapt to newly seen content out of the original training corpus. Annotating such content is non-trivial and may require substantial time and effort (Poletto et al., 2019; Ombui et al., 2019). Thus, Unsupervised Domain Adaptation (UDA) methods that can adapt without the target domain labels (Ramponi and Plank, 2020), turn out to be attractive in this task. Given an automatic text classification or tagging task, such as abusive language detection, a corpus with coherence can be considered a domain (Ramponi and Plank, 2020; Plank, 2011). Under this condition, domain adaptation approaches can be applied in cross-corpora evaluation setups. This motivates us to explore UDA for cross-corpora abusive language detection.

A task related to abuse detection is sentiment classification (Bauwelinck and Lefever, 2019; Rajamanickam et al., 2020), and it involves an extensive body of work on domain adaptation. In this work, we analyze if the problem of cross-corpora abusive language detection can be addressed by the existing advancements in domain adaptation. Alongside different UDA approaches, we also evaluate the effectiveness of recently proposed HateBERT model (Caselli et al., 2021) that has fine-tuned BERT (Devlin et al., 2019) on a large corpus of abusive language from Reddit using the Masked Language Model (MLM) objective. Furthermore, we perform the MLM fine-tuning of HateBERT on target corpus, which can be considered a form of unsupervised adaptation. Our contribution is summarised below:

- We investigate some of the best perform-

Proceedings of the Ninth International Workshop on Natural Language Processing for Social Media, pages 113–122
Online Workshop, June 10, 2021.

ing UDA approaches, originally proposed for cross-domain sentiment classification, and analyze their performance on the task of cross-corpora abusive language detection. We provide some insights on the sub-optimal performance of these approaches. To the best of our knowledge, this is the first work that analyzes UDA approaches for cross-corpora abuse detection.

- We analyze the performance of HateBERT in our cross-corpora evaluation set-up. In particular, we use the Masked Language Model (MLM) objective to further fine-tune HateBERT over the unlabeled target corpus, and subsequently perform supervised fine-tuning over the source corpus.

The remaining of this paper is structured as follows: Section 2 discusses the shifts across different abusive corpora. Section 3 surveys some recently proposed UDA models for sentiment classification and discusses the main differences in the approaches. Section 4 presents the experimental settings used in our evaluation. The results of our evaluation and a discussion on performances of different approaches are present in Section 5. Finally, Section 6 concludes the paper and highlights some future work.

2 Shifts in Abusive Language Corpora

Saha and Sindhwani (2012) have detailed the problem of changing topics in social media with time. Hence, temporal or contextual shifts are commonly witnessed across different abusive corpora. For example, the datasets by Waseem and Hovy (2016); Basile et al. (2019) were collected in or before 2016, and during 2018, respectively, and also involve different contexts of discussion.

Moreover, sampling strategies across datasets also introduce bias in the data (Wiegand et al., 2019), and could be a cause for differences across datasets. For instance, Davidson et al. (2017) sample tweets containing keywords from a hate speech lexicon, which has resulted in the corpus having a major proportion (83%) of abusive content. As mentioned by Waseem et al. (2018), tweets in Davidson et al. (2017) originate from the United States, whereas Waseem and Hovy (2016) sample them without such a demographic constraint.

Apart from sampling differences, the targets and types of abuse may vary across datasets. For instance, even though women are targeted both in Waseem and Hovy (2016) and Davidson et al. (2017), the former involves more subtle and implicit forms of abuse, while the the latter involves explicit abuse involving profane words. Besides, religious minorities are the other targeted groups in Waseem and Hovy (2016), while African Americans are targeted in Davidson et al. (2017). Owing to these differences across corpora, abusive language detection in a cross-corpora setting remains a challenge. This has been empirically validated by Wiegand et al. (2019); Arango et al. (2019); Swamy et al. (2019); Karan and Šnajder (2018) with performance degradation across the cross-corpora evaluation settings. Thus, it can be concluded that the different collection time frames, sampling strategies, and targets of abuse would induce a shift in the data.

3 Unsupervised Domain Adaptation

As discussed by Ramponi and Plank (2020); Plank (2011), a coherent type of corpus can typically be considered a domain for tasks such as automatic text classification. We, therefore, decide to apply domain adaptation methods for our task of cross-corpora abuse detection. Besides, UDA methods aim to adapt a classifier learned on the source domain D_S to the target domain D_T, where only the unlabeled target domain samples X_T and the labeled source domain samples X_S are assumed to be available. We denote the source labels by Y_S. In this work, we use the unlabeled samples X_T for adaptation and evaluate the performance over the remaining unseen target samples from D_T.

3.1 Survey of UDA Approaches

There is a vast body of research on UDA for the related task of cross-domain sentiment classification. Amongst them, the feature-centric approaches typically construct an aligned feature space either using pivot features (Blitzer et al., 2006) or using Autoencoders (Glorot et al., 2011; Chen et al., 2012). Besides these, domain adversarial training is used widely as a loss-centric approach to maximize the confusion in domain identification and align the source and target representations (Ganin et al., 2016; Ganin and Lempitsky, 2015). Owing to their success in cross-domain sentiment classification, we decide to apply the following pivot-based and domain-adversarial UDA approaches to the task of cross-corpora abusive language detection.

Pivot-based approaches: Following Blitzer et al. (2006), pivot-based approaches extract a set of common shared features, called pivots, across domains that are (i) frequent in X_S and X_T; and (ii) highly correlated with Y_S. *Pivot Based Language Modeling* (**PBLM**) (Ziser and Reichart, 2018) has outperformed the Autoencoder based pivot prediction (Ziser and Reichart, 2017). It performs representation learning by employing a Long Short-Term Memory (LSTM) based language model to predict the pivots using other non-pivots features in the input samples from both X_S and X_T. Convolutional Neural Networks (CNN) and LSTM based classifiers are subsequently employed for the final supervised training with X_S and Y_S. *Pivot-based Encoder Representation of Language* (**PERL**) (Ben-David et al., 2020), a recently proposed UDA model, integrates BERT (Devlin et al., 2019) with pivot-based fine-tuning using the MLM objective. It involves prediction of the masked unigram/ bigram pivots from the non-pivots of the input samples from both X_S and X_T. This is followed by supervised task training with a convolution, average pooling and a linear layer over the encoded representations of the input samples from X_S. During the supervised task training, the encoder weights are kept frozen. Both PBLM and PERL use unigrams and bi-grams as pivots, although higher order n-grams can also be used.

Domain adversarial approaches: *Hierarchical Attention Transfer Network* (**HATN**) (Li et al., 2017, 2018) employs the domain classification based adversarial training using X_S and X_T, along with an attention mechanism using X_S and Y_S to automate the pivot construction. The Gradient Reversal Layer (GRL) (Ganin and Lempitsky, 2015) is used in the adversarial training to ensure that the learned pivots are domain-shared, and the attention mechanism ensures that they are useful for the end task. During training, the pivots are predicted using the non-pivots while jointly performing the domain adversarial training, and the supervised end-task training. Recently BERT-based approaches for UDA are proposed by Du et al. (2020); Ryu and Lee (2020) that also apply the domain adversarial training. *Adversarial Adaptation with Distillation* (**AAD**) (Ryu and Lee, 2020) is such a domain adversarial approach that is applied over BERT. Unlike HATN, in AAD, the domain adversarial training is done with the framework of the Adversarial Discriminative Domain Adaptation (ADDA) (Tzeng et al., 2017), using X_S and X_T. This aims to make the source and target representations similar. Moreover, it leverages knowledge distillation (Hinton et al., 2015) as an additional loss function during adaptation.

3.2 Adaptation through Masked Language Model Fine-tuning with HateBERT

Rietzler et al. (2020); Xu et al. (2019) show that the language model fine-tuning of BERT (using the MLM and the Next Sentence Prediction task) results in incorporating domain-specific knowledge into the model and is useful for cross-domain adaptation. This step does not require task-specific labels. The recently proposed HateBERT model (Caselli et al., 2021) extends the pre-trained BERT model using the MLM objective over a large corpus of unlabeled abusive comments from Reddit. This is expected to shift the pre-trained BERT model towards abusive language. It is shown by Caselli et al. (2021) that HateBERT is more portable across abusive language datasets, as compared to BERT. We, thus, decide to perform further analysis over HateBERT for our task.

In particular, we begin with the HateBERT model and perform MLM fine-tuning incorporating the unlabeled train set from the target corpus. We hypothesize that performing this step should incorporate the variations in the abusive language present in the target corpus into the model. For the classification task, supervised fine-tuning is performed over the MLM fine-tuned model obtained from the previous step, using X_S and Y_S.

4 Experimental Setup

4.1 Data Description and Pre-processing

Datasets	Number of comments		Average comment length	Abuse %
	Train	Test		
Davidson	19817	2477	14.1	83.2
Waseem	8720	1090	14.7	26.8
HatEval	9000	3000	21.3	42.1

Table 1: Statistics of the datasets used (average comment length is reported in terms of word numbers).

We present experiments over three different publicly available abusive language corpora from Twitter as they cover different forms of abuse, namely

Davidson (Davidson et al., 2017),*Waseem* (Waseem and Hovy, 2016) and *HatEval* (Basile et al., 2019). Following the precedent of other works on cross-corpora abuse detection (Wiegand et al., 2019; Swamy et al., 2019; Karan and Šnajder, 2018), we target a binary classification task with classes: *abusive* and *non-abusive*. We randomly split *Davidson* and *Waseem* into train (80%), development (10%), and test (10%), whereas in the case of *HatEval*, we use the standard partition of the shared task. Statistics of the train-test splits of these datasets are listed in Table 1.

During pre-processing, we remove the URLs and retain the frequently occurring Twitter handles (user names) present in the datasets, as they could provide important information.[1] The words contained in hashtags are split using the tool CrazyTokenizer[2] and the words are converted into lowercase.

4.2 Evaluation Setup

Given the three corpora listed above, we experiment with all the six pairs of X_S and X_T for our cross-corpora analysis. The UDA approaches leverage the respective unlabeled train sets in D_T for adaptation, along with the train sets in D_S. The abusive language classifier is subsequently trained on the labeled train set in D_S and evaluated on the test set in D_T. In the "no adaptation" case, the HateBERT model is fine-tuned in a supervised manner on the labeled source corpus train set, and evaluated on the target test set. Unsupervised adaptation using HateBERT involves training of the HateBERT model on the target corpus train set using the MLM objective. This is followed by a supervised fine-tuning on the source corpus train set.

We use the original implementations of the UDA models[3] and the pre-trained HateBERT[4] model for our experiments. We select the best model checkpoints by performing early-stopping of the training while evaluating the performance on the respective development sets in D_S. FastText[5] word vectors, pre-trained over Wikipedia, are used for word embedding initialization for both HATN and PBLM. PERL and AAD are initialized with the BERT base-uncased model.[6] In PBLM, we employ the LSTM based classifier.[7] For both PERL and PBLM, words with the highest mutual information with respect to the source labels and occurring at least 10 times in both the source and target corpora are considered as pivots (Ziser and Reichart, 2018).

5 Results and Analysis

Dataset	Macro F1	Frequent words in abusive comments
Davidson	93.8±0.1	b*tch, h*e, f*ck, p*ssy, n*gga, ass, f*ck, shit
Waseem	85.5±0.4	#notsexist, #mkr, female, girl, kat, men, woman, feminist
HatEval	51.9±1.7	woman, refugee, immigrant, trump, #buildthatwall, illegal, b*tch, f*ck

Table 2: F1 macro-average (mean ± std-dev) for in-corpus classification using supervised fine-tuning of HateBERT.

Our evaluation reports the mean and standard deviation of macro averaged F1 scores, obtained by an approach, over five runs with different random initializations. We first present the in-corpus performance of the HateBERT model in Table 2, obtained after supervised fine-tuning on the respective datasets, along with the frequent abuse-related words. As shown in Table 2, the in-corpus performance is high for *Davidson* and *Waseem*, but not for *HatEval*. *HatEval* shared task presents a challenging test set and similar performance have been reported in prior work (Caselli et al., 2021). Cross-corpora performance of HateBERT and the UDA models discussed in Section 3.1, is presented in Table 3. Comparing Table 2 and Table 3, substantial degradation of performance is observed across the datasets in the cross-corpora setting. This highlights the challenge of cross-corpora performance in abusive language detection.

Cross-corpora evaluation in Table 3 shows that all the UDA methods experience drop in average performance when compared to the no-adaptation

[1] Eg., the Twitter handle @realDonaldTrump.

[2] https://redditscore.readthedocs.io/en/master/tokenizing.html

[3] PBLM: https://github.com/yftah89/PBLM-Domain-Adaptation, HATN: https://github.com/hsqmlzno1/HATN, PERL: https://github.com/eyalbd2/PERL, AAD: https://github.com/bzantium/bert-AAD

[4] https://osf.io/tbd58/

[5] https://fasttext.cc/

[6] https://github.com/huggingface/transformers

[7] CNN classifier obtained similar performance.

Source →Target	No-adaptation	Unsupervised Domain Adaptation				
	HateBERT supervised fine-tune only	HateBERT MLM fine-tune on Target	PBLM	PERL-BERT	HATN	AAD-BERT
Hat →Was	66.4±1.1	**68.0**±1.0	57.5±3.4	57.1±1.8	57.3±1.7	60.4±7.8
Was →Hat	**57.8**±0.6	56.5±1.1	51.0±5.2	55.3±0.7	53.5±0.4	55.7±1.3
Dav →Was	**67.5**±0.5	66.7±0.8	57.2±4.8	67.4±1.0	57.5±6.7	41.5±2.8
Was →Dav	60.1±4.4	**67.1**±2.9	46.5±1.3	48.3±1.5	28.0±2.3	35.6±3.7
Hat →Dav	63.8±2.3	**67.8**±1.6	61.8±5.7	62.6±3.8	61.5±5.8	55.2±0.7
Dav →Hat	51.3±0.2	**51.4**±0.4	49.9±0.2	50.3±0.9	50.3±0.5	50.4±3.0
Average	61.2	**62.9**	54.0	56.8	51.4	49.8

Table 3: Macro average F1 scores (mean±std-dev) on different source and target pairs for cross-corpora abuse detection (Hat : HatEval, Was : Waseem, Dav : Davidson). The best in each row is marked in bold.

case of supervised fine-tuning of HateBERT. However, the additional step of MLM fine-tuning of HateBERT on the unlabeled train set from target corpus results in an improved performance in most of the cases. In the following sub-sections, we perform a detailed analysis to get further insights into the sub-optimal performance of the UDA approaches for our task.

5.1 Pivot Characteristics in Pivot-based Approaches

To understand the performance of the pivot-based models, we probe the characteristics of the pivots used by these models as they control the transfer of information across source and target corpora. As mentioned in Section 3.1, one of the criteria for pivot selection is their affinity to the available labels. Accordingly, if the adaptation results in better performance, a higher proportion of pivots would have more affinity to one of the two classes. In the following, we aim to study this particular characteristic across the source train set and the target test set. To compute class affinities, we obtain a ratio of the class membership of every pivot p_i:

$$r_i = \frac{\text{\#abusive comments with } p_i}{\text{\#non-abusive comments with } p_i} \quad (1)$$

The ratios obtained for the train set of the source and the test set of the target, for the pivot p_i, are denoted as ${r_i}^s$ and ${r_i}^t$, respectively. A pivot p_i with similar class affinities in both the source train and target test should satisfy:

$$({r_i}^s, {r_i}^t) < 1 - th \text{ or } ({r_i}^s, {r_i}^t) > 1 + th \quad (2)$$

Here, th denotes the threshold. Ratios less than $(1 - th)$ indicate affinity towards non-abusive class, while those greater than $(1 + th)$ indicate affinity towards the abusive class. For every source →target pair, we select the pivots that satisfy Equation (2) with threshold th = 0.3, and calculate the percentage of the selected pivots as:

$$\text{perc}_{s \to t} = \frac{\text{\#pivots satisfying Equation (2)}}{\text{\#Total pivots}} \times 100 \quad (3)$$

This indicates the percentage of pivots having similar affinity towards one of the two classes. We now analyze this percentage in the best and the worst case scenarios of PBLM.[8]

Worst cases: For the worst case of *Waseem →Davidson*, Equation (3) yields a low $\text{perc}_{s \to t}$ of 18.8%. This indicates that the percentage of pivots having similar class affinities, across the source and the target, remains low in the worst performing pair.

Best case: The best case in PBLM corresponds to *HatEval →Davidson*. In this case, Equation (3) yields a relatively higher $\text{perc}_{s \to t}$ of 51.4%. This is because the pivots extracted in this case involve a lot of profane words. Since in *Davidson*, the majority of abusive content involves the use of profane words (as also reflected in Table 2), the pivots extracted by PBLM can represent the target corpus well in this case.

[8]Pivot extraction criteria are same for PBLM and PERL and similar percentages are expected with PERL.

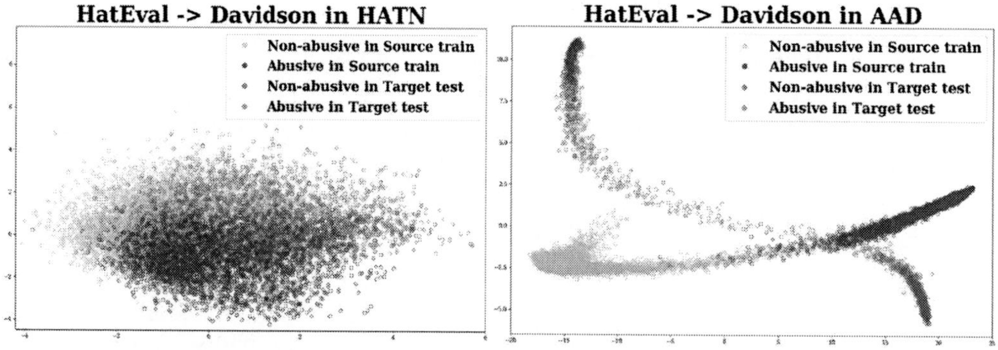

(a) (b)

Figure 1: (Best viewed in color) PCA based visualization of *HatEval →Davidson* in the adversarial approaches.

5.2 Domain Adversarial Approaches

On an average, the adversarial approach of HATN performs slightly better than AAD. In order to analyze the difference, we investigate the representation spaces of the two approaches for the best case of HATN i.e. *HatEval →Davidson*. To this end, we apply the Principal Component Analysis (PCA) to obtain the two-dimensional visualization of the feature spaces from the train set of the source corpus *HatEval* and the test set of the target corpus *Davidson*. The PCA plots are shown in Figure 1. Adversarial training in both the HATN and AAD models tends to bring the representation regions of the source and target corpora close to each other. At the same time, separation of abusive and non-abusive classes in source train set seems to be happening in both the models. However, in the representation space of AAD, samples corresponding to abusive and non-abusive classes in the target test set do not follow the class separation seen in the source train set. But in the representation space of HATN, samples in the target test set appear to follow the class separation exhibited by its source train set. Considering the abusive class as positive, this is reflected in the higher number of *True Positives* in HATN as compared to that of AAD for this pair (#TP for HATN: 1393, #TP for AAD: 1105), while the *True Negatives* remain almost the same (#TN for HATN: 370, #TN for AAD: 373).

One of the limitations of these domain adversarial approaches is the class-agnostic alignment of the common source-target representation space. As discussed in Saito et al. (2018), methods that do not consider the class boundary information while aligning the source and target distributions, often result in having ambiguous and non-discriminative target domain features near class boundaries. Besides, such an alignment can be achieved without having access to the target domain class labels (Saito et al., 2018). As such, an effective alignment should also attempt to minimize the intra-class, and maximize the inter-class domain discrepancy (Kang et al., 2019).

5.3 MLM Fine-tuning of HateBERT

It is evident from Table 3 that the MLM fine-tuning of HateBERT, before the subsequent supervised fine-tuning over the source corpus, results in improved performance in majority of the cases. We investigated the MLM fine-tuning over different combinations of the source and target corpora, in order to identify the best configuration. These include: a combination of the train sets from all the three corpora, combining the source and target train sets, and using only the target train set. Table 4 shows that MLM fine-tuning over only the unlabeled target corpus results in the best overall performance. This is in agreement to Rietzler et al. (2020) who observe a better capture of domain-specific knowledge with fine-tuning only on the target domain.

5.4 Bridging the Gap between PERL and HateBERT MLM Fine-tuning

Since PERL originally incorporates BERT, Table 3 reports the performance of PERL initialized with the pre-trained BERT model. As discussed in Section 3.1, PERL applies MLM fine-tuning over the pre-trained BERT model, where only the pivots are predicted rather than all the masked tokens. Following Ben-David et al. (2020), after the encoder weights are learned during the MLM fine-tuning

Source →Target	HBERT MLM on all 3 corpora	HBERT MLM on Source + Target	HBERT MLM on Target
Hat →Was	**69.7**±0.8	68.9±0.6	68.0±1.0
Was →Hat	**57.2**±1.4	56.8±1.1	56.5±1.1
Dav →Was	60.2±0.7	58.8±0.8	**66.7**±0.8
Was →Dav	63.4±3.9	63.4±3.9	**67.1**±2.9
Hat →Dav	66.6±1.1	66.7±2.1	**67.8**±1.6
Dav →Hat	51.4±0.2	**51.5**±0.1	51.4±0.4
Average	61.4	61.0	**62.9**

Table 4: Macro average F1 scores (mean ± std-dev) for Masked Language Model fine-tuning of HateBERT (HBERT MLM) over different corpora combinations, before supervised fine-tuning on source; Hat : HatEval, Was : Waseem, Dav : Davidson. The best in each row is marked in bold.

Source →Target	PERL-BERT (frozen encoder layers)	PERL-HBERT (frozen encoder layers)	PERL-HBERT (with layer updates)
Hat →Was	57.1±1.8	63.2±1.7	**68.3**±0.8
Was →Hat	55.3±0.7	55.0±0.9	**57.8**±0.8
Dav →Was	**67.4**±1.0	65.9±1.3	57.3±3.1
Was →Dav	48.3±1.5	48.1±3.7	**64.4**±2.1
Hat →Dav	62.6±3.8	63.6±0.9	**66.1**±1.8
Dav →Hat	50.3±0.9	50.4±0.6	**51.1**±0.3
Average	56.8	57.7	**60.8**

Table 5: Macro average F1 scores (mean ± std-dev) of PERL initialized with BERT and HateBERT (HBERT) with frozen encoder layers, and PERL initialized with HateBERT with updates across all layers, for all the pairs (Hat : HatEval, Was : Waseem, Dav : Davidson). The best in each row is marked in bold.

step of PERL, they are kept frozen during supervised training for the classification task. As an additional verification, we try to leverage the HateBERT model for initializing PERL in the same way as BERT is used in the original PERL model, with frozen encoder layers. As shown in Table 5, this does not result in substantial performance gains over PERL-BERT on average. As a further extension, we update all the layers in PERL during the supervised training step and use the same hyperparameters as those used for HateBERT (Caselli et al., 2021).[9] This results in improved performance from PERL. However, it stills remains behind the best performing HateBERT model with MLM fine-tuning on target.

5.5 Source Corpora Specific Behaviour

In general, when models are trained over *HatEval*, they are found to be more robust towards addressing the shifts across corpora. One of the primary reasons is that *HatEval* captures wider forms of abuse directed towards both immigrants and women. The most frequent words in Table 2 also highlight the same. The corpus involves a mix of implicit as well as explicit abusive language.

On the contrary, models trained over *Waseem* are generally unable to adapt well in cross-corpora settings. Since only tweet IDs were made available in *Waseem*, we observe that our crawled comments in this dataset rarely involve abuse directed towards target groups other than women (99.3% of the abusive comments are sexist and 0.6% racist). This is because majority of these comments have been removed before crawling. Besides, *Waseem* mostly involves subtle and implicit abuse, and less use of profane words.

6 Conclusion and Future Work

This work analyzed the efficacy of some successful Unsupervised Domain Adaptation approaches of cross-domain sentiment classification in cross-corpora abuse detection. Our experiments highlighted some of the problems with these approaches that render them sub-optimal in the cross-corpora abuse detection task. While the extraction of pivots, in the pivot-based models, is not optimal enough to capture the shared space across domains, the domain adversarial methods underperform substantially. The analysis of the Masked Language Model fine-tuning of HateBERT on the target corpus displayed improvements in general as compared to only fine-tuning HateBERT over the source corpus, suggesting that it helps in adapting the model towards target-specific language variations. The overall performance of all the approaches, however, indicates that building robust and portable abuse detection models is a challenging problem, far from being solved.

Future work along the lines of domain adversarial training should explore methods which learn

[9]Note that the ablation study in Ben-David et al. (2020) discusses the effect of the number of unfrozen encoder layers only in the MLM fine-tuning step, but not in the supervised training step for the end task.

class boundaries that generalize well to the target corpora while performing alignment of the source and target representation spaces. Such an alignment can be performed without target class labels by minimizing the intra-class domain discrepancy (Kang et al., 2019). Pivot-based approaches should explore pivot extraction methods that account for higher-level semantics of abusive language across source and target corpora.

Acknowledgements

This work was supported partly by the french PIA project "Lorraine Université d'Excellence", reference ANR-15-IDEX-04-LUE.

References

Aymé Arango, Jorge Pérez, and Barbara Poblete. 2019. Hate speech detection is not as easy as you may think: A closer look at model validation. In *Proceedings of the 42nd International ACM SIGIR Conference on Research and Development in Information Retrieval*, SIGIR'19, page 45–54, New York, NY, USA. Association for Computing Machinery.

Valerio Basile, Cristina Bosco, Elisabetta Fersini, Debora Nozza, Viviana Patti, Francisco Manuel Rangel Pardo, Paolo Rosso, and Manuela Sanguinetti. 2019. SemEval-2019 task 5: Multilingual detection of hate speech against immigrants and women in twitter. In *Proceedings of the 13th International Workshop on Semantic Evaluation*, pages 54–63, Minneapolis, Minnesota, USA. Association for Computational Linguistics.

Nina Bauwelinck and Els Lefever. 2019. Measuring the impact of sentiment for hate speech detection on twitter. In *Proceedings of HUSO 2019, The fifth international conference on human and social analytics*, pages 17–22. IARIA, International Academy, Research, and Industry Association.

Eyal Ben-David, Carmel Rabinovitz, and Roi Reichart. 2020. Perl: Pivot-based domain adaptation for pre-trained deep contextualized embedding models. *Transactions of the Association for Computational Linguistics*, 8:504–5221.

John Blitzer, Ryan McDonald, and Fernando Pereira. 2006. Domain adaptation with structural correspondence learning. In *Proceedings of the 2006 Conference on Empirical Methods in Natural Language Processing*, pages 120–128, Sydney, Australia. Association for Computational Linguistics.

Tommaso Caselli, Valerio Basile, Jelena Mitrović, and Michael Granitzer. 2021. Hatebert: Retraining bert for abusive language detection in english. *arXiv preprint arXiv:2010.12472*.

Minmin Chen, Zhixiang Xu, Kilian Q. Weinberger, and Fei Sha. 2012. Marginalized denoising autoencoders for domain adaptation. In *Proceedings of the 29th International Conference on Machine Learning*, ICML'12, page 1627–1634, Madison, WI, USA. Omnipress.

Thomas Davidson, Dana Warmsley, Michael Macy, and Ingmar Weber. 2017. Automated hate speech detection and the problem of offensive language. In *Proceedings of the 11th International AAAI Conference on Web and Social Media*, ICWSM '17, pages 512–515.

Jacob Devlin, Ming-Wei Chang, Kenton Lee, and Kristina Toutanova. 2019. BERT: Pre-training of deep bidirectional transformers for language understanding. In *Proceedings of the 2019 Conference of the North American Chapter of the Association for Computational Linguistics: Human Language Technologies, Volume 1 (Long and Short Papers)*, pages 4171–4186, Minneapolis, Minnesota. Association for Computational Linguistics.

Chunning Du, Haifeng Sun, Jingyu Wang, Qi Qi, and Jianxin Liao. 2020. Adversarial and domain-aware BERT for cross-domain sentiment analysis. In *Proceedings of the 58th Annual Meeting of the Association for Computational Linguistics*, pages 4019–4028, Online. Association for Computational Linguistics.

Yaroslav Ganin and Victor Lempitsky. 2015. Unsupervised domain adaptation by backpropagation. In *Proceedings of the 32nd International Conference on Machine Learning*, volume 37 of *Proceedings of Machine Learning Research*, pages 1180–1189, Lille, France. PMLR.

Yaroslav Ganin, Evgeniya Ustinova, Hana Ajakan, Pascal Germain, Hugo Larochelle, François Laviolette, Mario Marchand, and Victor Lempitsky. 2016. Domain-adversarial training of neural networks. *J. Mach. Learn. Res.*, 17(1):2096–2030.

Xavier Glorot, Antoine Bordes, and Yoshua Bengio. 2011. Domain adaptation for large-scale sentiment classification: A deep learning approach. In *Proceedings of the 28th International Conference on Machine Learning*, ICML'11, page 513–520, Madison, WI, USA. Omnipress.

Geoffrey Hinton, Oriol Vinyals, and Jeffrey Dean. 2015. Distilling the knowledge in a neural network. In *NIPS Deep Learning and Representation Learning Workshop*.

Guoliang Kang, Lu Jiang, Yi Yang, and Alexander G Hauptmann. 2019. Contrastive adaptation network for unsupervised domain adaptation. In *Proceedings of the IEEE/CVF Conference on Computer Vision and Pattern Recognition*, pages 4893–4902.

Mladen Karan and Jan Šnajder. 2018. Cross-domain detection of abusive language online. In *Proceed-*

ings of the 2nd Workshop on Abusive Language Online (ALW2), pages 132–137, Brussels, Belgium. Association for Computational Linguistics.

Younghun Lee, Seunghyun Yoon, and Kyomin Jung. 2018. Comparative studies of detecting abusive language on twitter. In *Proceedings of the 2nd Workshop on Abusive Language Online (ALW2)*, pages 101–106, Brussels, Belgium. Association for Computational Linguistics.

Zheng Li, Ying Wei, Yu Zhang, and Qiang Yang. 2018. Hierarchical attention transfer network for cross-domain sentiment classification. In *AAAI Conference on Artificial Intelligence*.

Zheng Li, Yu Zhang, Ying Wei, Yuxiang Wu, and Qiang Yang. 2017. End-to-end adversarial memory network for cross-domain sentiment classification. In *Proceedings of the International Joint Conference on Artificial Intelligence (IJCAI 2017)*.

Edward Ombui, Moses Karani, and Lawrence Muchemi. 2019. Annotation framework for hate speech identification in tweets: Case study of tweets during kenyan elections. *2019 IST-Africa Week Conference (IST-Africa)*, pages 1–9.

Barbara Plank. 2011. *Domain adaptation for parsing*. Ph.D. thesis, University of Groningen.

Fabio Poletto, Valerio Basile, Cristina Bosco, Viviana Patti, and Marco Stranisci. 2019. Annotating hate speech: Three schemes at comparison. In *Proceedings of the Sixth Italian Conference on Computational Linguistics, Bari, Italy, November 13-15, 2019*, volume 2481 of *CEUR Workshop Proceedings*. CEUR-WS.org.

Santhosh Rajamanickam, Pushkar Mishra, Helen Yannakoudakis, and Ekaterina Shutova. 2020. Joint modelling of emotion and abusive language detection. In *Proceedings of the 58th Annual Meeting of the Association for Computational Linguistics*, pages 4270–4279, Online. Association for Computational Linguistics.

Alan Ramponi and Barbara Plank. 2020. Neural unsupervised domain adaptation in NLP—A survey. In *Proceedings of the 28th International Conference on Computational Linguistics*, pages 6838–6855, Barcelona, Spain (Online). International Committee on Computational Linguistics.

Alexander Rietzler, Sebastian Stabinger, Paul Opitz, and Stefan Engl. 2020. Adapt or get left behind: Domain adaptation through BERT language model finetuning for aspect-target sentiment classification. In *Proceedings of the 12th Language Resources and Evaluation Conference*, pages 4933–4941, Marseille, France. European Language Resources Association.

Minho Ryu and Kichun Lee. 2020. Knowledge distillation for bert unsupervised domain adaptation. *arXiv preprint arXiv:2010.11478*.

Ankan Saha and Vikas Sindhwani. 2012. Learning evolving and emerging topics in social media: A dynamic nmf approach with temporal regularization. In *Proceedings of the Fifth ACM International Conference on Web Search and Data Mining*, WSDM '12, page 693–702, New York, NY, USA. Association for Computing Machinery.

Kuniaki Saito, Kohei Watanabe, Yoshitaka Ushiku, and Tatsuya Harada. 2018. Maximum classifier discrepancy for unsupervised domain adaptation. In *Proceedings of the IEEE conference on computer vision and pattern recognition*, pages 3723–3732.

Steve Durairaj Swamy, Anupam Jamatia, and Björn Gambäck. 2019. Studying generalisability across abusive language detection datasets. In *Proceedings of the 23rd Conference on Computational Natural Language Learning (CoNLL)*, pages 940–950, Hong Kong, China. Association for Computational Linguistics.

E. Tzeng, J. Hoffman, K. Saenko, and T. Darrell. 2017. Adversarial discriminative domain adaptation. In *2017 IEEE Conference on Computer Vision and Pattern Recognition (CVPR)*, pages 2962–2971.

Zeerak Waseem and Dirk Hovy. 2016. Hateful symbols or hateful people? predictive features for hate speech detection on Twitter. In *Proceedings of the NAACL Student Research Workshop*, pages 88–93, San Diego, California. Association for Computational Linguistics.

Zeerak Waseem, James Thorne, and Joachim Bingel. 2018. Bridging the gaps: Multi task learning for domain transfer of hate speech detection. In *Golbeck J. (eds) Online Harassment. Human–Computer Interaction Series*, pages 29–55, Cham. Springer International Publishing.

Michael Wiegand, Josef Ruppenhofer, and Thomas Kleinbauer. 2019. Detection of Abusive Language: the Problem of Biased Datasets. In *Proceedings of the 2019 Conference of the North American Chapter of the Association for Computational Linguistics: Human Language Technologies, Volume 1 (Long and Short Papers)*, pages 602–608, Minneapolis, Minnesota. Association for Computational Linguistics.

Hu Xu, Bing Liu, Lei Shu, and Philip Yu. 2019. BERT post-training for review reading comprehension and aspect-based sentiment analysis. In *Proceedings of the 2019 Conference of the North American Chapter of the Association for Computational Linguistics: Human Language Technologies, Volume 1 (Long and Short Papers)*, pages 2324–2335, Minneapolis, Minnesota. Association for Computational Linguistics.

Wenjie Yin and Arkaitz Zubiaga. 2021. Towards generalisable hate speech detection: a review on obstacles and solutions. *arXiv preprint arXiv:2102.08886*.

Yftah Ziser and Roi Reichart. 2017. Neural structural correspondence learning for domain adaptation. In *Proceedings of the 21st Conference on Computational Natural Language Learning (CoNLL 2017)*, pages 400–410, Vancouver, Canada. Association for Computational Linguistics.

Yftah Ziser and Roi Reichart. 2018. Pivot based language modeling for improved neural domain adaptation. In *Proceedings of the 2018 Conference of the North American Chapter of the Association for Computational Linguistics: Human Language Technologies, Volume 1 (Long Papers)*, pages 1241–1251, New Orleans, Louisiana. Association for Computational Linguistics.

Using Noisy Self-Reports to Predict Twitter User Demographics

Zach Wood-Doughty*, **Paiheng Xu***, **Xiao Liu**, **Mark Dredze**
Department of Computer Science
John Hopkins University, Baltimore, MD 21218
zach@cs.jhu.edu,paiheng@jhu.edu,xliu119@jhu.edu,mdredze@cs.jhu.edu

Abstract

Computational social science studies often contextualize content analysis within standard demographics. Since demographics are unavailable on many social media platforms (e.g. Twitter), numerous studies have inferred demographics automatically. Despite many studies presenting proof-of-concept inference of race and ethnicity, training of practical systems remains elusive since there are few annotated datasets. Existing datasets are small, inaccurate, or fail to cover the four most common racial and ethnic groups in the United States. We present a method to identify self-reports of race and ethnicity from Twitter profile descriptions. Despite the noise of automated supervision, our self-report datasets enable improvements in classification performance on gold standard self-report survey data. The result is a reproducible method for creating large-scale training resources for race and ethnicity.

1 Introduction

Contextualization of population studies with demographics forms a central analysis method within the social sciences. In domains such as political science or public health, standard demographic panels in telephone surveys enable better analyses of opinions and trends. Demographics such as age, gender, race, and location are often proxies for important socio-cultural groups. As the social sciences increasingly rely on computational analyses of online text data, the unavailability of demographic attributes hinders comparison of these studies to traditional methods (Al Baghal et al., 2020; Amir et al., 2019; Jiang and Vosoughi, 2020).

Computational social science increasingly utilizes methods for the automatic inference of demographic attributes from social media, such as Twitter (Burger et al., 2011; Chen et al., 2015; Ardehaly and Culotta, 2017; Jung et al., 2018; Huang and Paul, 2019). Demographics factor into social media studies across domains such as health, politics, and linguistics (O'Connor et al., 2010; Eisenstein et al., 2014). Off-the-shelf software packages support the inference of gender and location (Knowles et al., 2016; Dredze et al., 2013; Wang et al., 2019).

Unlike age or geolocation, race and ethnicity are sociocultural categories with competing definitions and measurement approaches (Comstock et al., 2004; Vargas and Stainback, 2016; Culley, 2006; Andrus et al., 2021). Despite this complexity, understanding race and ethnicity is crucial for public health research (Coldman et al., 1988; Dressler et al., 2005; Fiscella and Fremont, 2006; Elliott et al., 2008, 2009). Analyses that explore mental health on Twitter (Loveys et al., 2018) should consider racial disparities in healthcare (Satcher, 2001; Amir et al., 2019) or online interactions (Delisle et al., 2019; Burnap and Williams, 2016). Despite the importance of race and ethnicity in these studies, and multiple proof-of-concept classification studies, there are no readily-available systems that can infer demographics for the most common United States racial/ethnic groups. This gap arises from major limitations for all publicly-available data resources.

A high-quality dataset for this task has several desiderata. First, it should cover enough categories to match standard demographics panels. Second, the dataset must be sufficiently large to support training

* Equal contribution

Proceedings of the Ninth International Workshop on Natural Language Processing for Social Media, pages 123–137
Online Workshop, June 10, 2021.

Citation	Annotation	% Missing	# Users	% W	% B	% H/L	% A
Preoţiuc-Pietro et al. (2015)	Survey	4.7	3572	80.8	9.5	6.1	3.6
Culotta et al. (2015)	Crowdsourced	60.0	308	50.0	19.5	30.5	0
Volkova and Bachrach (2015)	Crowdsourced	36.5	3174	48.0	35.8	8.9	3.0
Total Matching Users	Self-report	-	2.50M	26.8	53.8	11.3	8.1
Query-Bigram	Self-report	8.1	112k	51.2	40.8	1.4	6.6
Heuristic-Filter	Self-report	40.6	135k	42.2	45.9	5.6	6.4
Balanced-Group-Person	Self-report	0.0	31k	25.0	25.0	25.0	25.0

Table 1: Previously-published Twitter datasets annotated for race/ethnicity and datasets collected in this work. "% Missing" shows the percent of users that could not be scraped in 2019. "# Users" shows the number users that are currently available. The abbreviations W, B, H/L, and A corresponds to White, Black, Hispanic/Latinx, Asian respectively, which we use for the rest of the paper. Per-group percentages are from non-missing data.

accurate systems. Third, the dataset should be reproducible; Twitter datasets shrink as users delete or restrict accounts, and models become less useful due to domain drift (Huang and Paul, 2018).

We present a method for automatically constructing a large Twitter dataset for race and ethnicity. Keyword-matching produces a large, high-recall corpus of Twitter users who potentially self-identify as a racial or ethnic group, building on past work that considered self-reports (Mohammady and Culotta, 2014; Beller et al., 2014; Coppersmith et al., 2014). We then learn a set of filters to improve precision by removing users who match keywords but do not self-report their demographics. Our approach can be automatically repeated in the future to update the dataset. While our automatic supervision contains noise – self-descriptions are hard to identify and potentially unreliable – our large dataset demonstrates benefits when compared to or combined with previous crowdsourced datasets. We validate this comparison on a gold-standard survey dataset of self-reported labels (Preoţiuc-Pietro and Ungar, 2018). We release our code publicly[1]. We also release our collected datasets and trained models to researchers with approval from an IRB or similar ethics board, contingent on compliance with our data usage agreement[2].

2 Ethical Considerations

Complexities of racial identity raise ethical considerations, requiring discussion of the benefits and harms of this work (Benton et al., 2017). The benefits are clear in settings such as public health; many studies use social media data to research health behaviors or support health-based interventions (Paul and Dredze, 2011; Sinnenberg et al., 2017). These methods have transformed areas of public health which otherwise lack accessible data (Ayers et al., 2014). Aligning social media analyses with traditional data sources requires demographic information.

The concerns and potential harms of this work are more complex. Ongoing discussions in the literature concern the need for informed consent from social media users (Fiesler and Proferes, 2018; Marwick and boyd, 2011; Olteanu et al., 2019). Twitter's privacy policy states that the company "make[s] public data on Twitter available to the world," but many users may not be aware of the scope or nature of research conducted using their data (Mikal et al., 2016). Participant consent must be *informed*, and we should study users' comprehension of terms of service when conducting sensitive research. IRBs have applied established human subjects research regulations in ruling that passive monitoring of social media data falls under public data exemptions.

While our data usage agreement prohibits such behavior, a malicious actor could attempt to use predicted user demographics to track or harass minority groups. Despite the severity of such a worst-case scenario, there are two arguments why the benefits may outweigh the harms. First, if open-source methods and models were used for such malicious behavior, platform moderators could simply

[1] https://bitbucket.org/mdredze/demographer

[2] http://www.cs.jhu.edu/~mdredze/demographics-training-data/

incorporate those tools into combatting any automated harassment. Second, harassment against historically disenfranchised groups is already extremely widespread. Open-source tools would provide more good than harm in the hands of researchers or platform moderators (Jiang and Vosoughi, 2020). Recent work has show that women on Twitter, especially journalists and politicians, receive disproportionate amounts of abuse (Delisle et al., 2019). On Facebook, advertisers have used the platform's knowledge of users' racial identities to illegally discriminate when posting job or housing ads (Benner et al., 2019; Angwin and Parris Jr, 2016). To protect against misuse of our work, we follow Twitter's developer terms which prohibit efforts to "target, segment, or profile individuals" based on several sensitive categories, including racial or ethnic origin, detailed in our data use agreement. Predictions should not be analyzed to profile individual users but rather must only be used for aggregated analyses.

Another concern of any predictive model for sensitive traits is that a descriptive model could be interpreted as a prescriptive assessment (Ho et al., 2015; Crawford, 2017). Individual language usage may also differ from population-level demographics patterns (Bamman et al., 2014). Additionally, our datasets and models do not cover smaller racial minorities (e.g. Pacific Islander) or the fine-grained complexities of mixed-race identities. More fine-grained methods are needed for many analyses, but current methods cannot support them.

Finally, we distinguish between biased models and biased applications. Our models are imperfect; if we only analyze a small sample of users and our models have high error rates, a difference that appears significant may be an artifact of misclassifications. Any downstream application must account for this uncertainty.

On the whole, we believe demographic tools provide significant benefits that justify the potential risks in their development. We make our data available to other researchers, but with limitations. We require that researchers comply with a data use agreement and obtain approval by an IRB or similar ethics committee. Our agreement restricts these tools to population-level analyses[3] and **not** the analysis of individual users. We exclude certain applications, such as targeting of individuals based on race or ethnicity. Any future research that makes demographically-contextualized conclusions from classifier predictions must explicitly consider ethical trade-offs specific to its application. Finally, our analysis of social media for public health research has been IRB reviewed and deemed exempt (45 CFR 46.101(b)(4)).

3 Datasets for Race and Ethnicity

Our tools and analysis focus on the United States, where recognized racial categories have varied over time (Hirschman et al., 2000; Lee and Tafoya, 2006). Current US census – and many surveys – record self-reported racial categories as White, Black, American Indian, Asian, and Pacific Islander. Surveys often frame ethnicity as Hispanic/Latinx origin or not; however, there is not necessarily a clear distinction between race and ethnicity (Gonzalez-Barrera and Lopez, 2015; Campbell and Rogalin, 2006; Cornell and Hartmann, 2006). Individuals may identify as both a race and an ethnicity, and 2% of Americans identify as multi-racial (Jones and Smith, 2001). Because of the limited data availability, we only consider the four largest race/ethnicity groups, which we model as mutually exclusive: White, Black, Asian, and Hispanic/Latinx. Our methodology could be extended to be more comprehensive, but we do not yet have the means to validate more fine-grained or intersectional approaches.

Table 1 lists three published datasets for race/ethnicity. Since only user ids can be shared, user account deletions over time cause substantial missing data. Past work has taken varied approaches to annotate racial demographics. Culotta et al. (2015) and Volkova and Bachrach (2015) relied on manual annotation, noting inter-annotator agreement estimated at 80% and Cohen's κ of 0.71, respectively. Crowdsourced annotation

[3]Twitter's API "restricted use cases" explicitly permit aggregated analyses.

	Raw	Color	Plural	Bigram	Quote	All
Precision	76.7	78.6	76.7	82.5	78.6	**86.8**
Removed by filter	-	314k	212k	281k	4k	784k

Table 2: Applying our HF filters (§ 4) individually and together. Precision is on dev set from Appendix B, after thresholding on self-report score.

assumes that racial identity can be accurately perceived by others, an assumption that has serious flaws for gender and age (Flekova et al., 2016; Preoţiuc-Pietro et al., 2017). Rule-based or statistical systems for data collection can be effective (Burger et al., 2011; Chang et al., 2010), but raise concerns about selection bias: if we only label users who take a certain action, a model trained on those users may not generalize to users who do not take that action (Wood-Doughty et al., 2017).

Gold-standard labels for sensitive traits requires individual survey responses, but this yields small or skewed datasets due to the expense (Preoţiuc-Pietro and Ungar, 2018). Our approach instead relies on automated supervision from racial self-identification and minimal manual annotation to refine our dataset labels. We are not the first to use users' self-identification to label Twitter users' demographics, but past work has relied heavily either on restrictive regular expressions or manual annotation (Pennacchiotti and Popescu, 2011; Mohammady and Culotta, 2014). Such work has also been limited to datasets of under 10,000 users. We expand on previous work to construct a much larger dataset and evaluate it via trained model performance on ground-truth survey data.

4 Data Collection of Self-Reports

We construct a regular expression for terms associated with racial identity. We select tweets from Twitter's 1% sample from July 2011 to July 2019 in which the user's profile description contains one of the following racial keywords in English: `black`, `african-american`, `white`, `caucasian`, `asian`, `hispanic`, `latin`, `latina`, `latino`, `latinx`. While there are other terms that signify racial identity, these match common survey panels (Hirschman et al., 2000) and our empirical evaluation is limited because our survey dataset only covers four classes. We omit self-reports that indicate a country of origin (e.g. "Colombian" or "Chinese-American"), smaller racial minorities (e.g. "Native American" or "two or more races"), or more ambiguous terms, leaving such groups for future work. If a user appears multiple times, we use their latest description.

We select users whose profile descriptions contain a query keyword, which heavily skews towards color terms ("white", "black"). This produces 2.67M users, 2.50M of which match exactly one racial/ethnic class (Table 1, "Total Matching Users"). While this is several orders of magnitude larger than existing datasets, many user descriptions that match racial keywords are not racial self-reports. We next consider approaches to filter these users' profile descriptions to obtain three self-report datasets of different sizes and precisions.

For all three datasets, we use a model that assigns a "self-report" score based on the likelihood that a profile contains a self-report. We then use a binary cutoff to only include users with a high enough self-report score. We obtain this score by leveraging lexical co-occurrence, an important cue for word associations (Spence and Owens, 1990; Church and Hanks, 1989). We combine relative frequencies of co-occurring words within a fixed window, weighed by distance between query and co-occurring self-report words. For example, if "farmer" is a self-report word, then "Black farmer" should score higher than "Black beans farmer" since the query and self-report word are closer. We choose the window size and threshold for this score function on a manually-labeled tuning set, after which our scoring function achieves 72.4% accuracy on a manually-labeled test set. Details on preprocessing and our self-report score are in Appendices A and B.

Our first dataset selects users with a bigram containing a racial keyword followed by a "person keyword." Our person keywords are: `man`, `woman`, `person`, `individual`, `guy`, `gal`, `boy`, and `girl` so this method matches users with descriptions containing bigrams such as

"Black woman" or "Asian guy." We expect this method to have high precision, but it has extreme label imbalance; 91% of the users are labeled as either white or black. From the Twitter 1% sample, this dataset contains 122k users, but only 112k users could be re-scraped in 2019. We refer to this dataset as **Query-Bigram (QB)**.

As **QB** contains only 112k users, we consider a less restrictive approach. Our second dataset uses four heuristic filters to remove false positives from the original 2.67M users. Many descriptions spuriously match "black" and "white" in addition to other colors, so we filtered out all words from a color-list (Berlin and Kay, 1991). Second, we filter out racial keywords followed by plural nouns (e.g. "white people"), using NLTK `TweetTokenizer` (Bird et al., 2009) to obtain part-of-speech tags. We curate a list of 286 Google bigrams that frequently contain a query but are unlikely to be self-reports (e.g. "black sheep,") (Michel et al., 2011). Finally, we ignore query words that appear inside quotation marks. Table 2 shows how precision and dataset size change as we apply these filters. Applying all four gives a total of 1.72M users; after thresholding on self-report score we are left with 228k users. 135k such users could be scraped in 2019, producing our **Heuristic-Filtered (HF)** dataset.

As **QB** and **HF** are quite imbalanced, we design a third dataset to equally represent all four classes. Across both our **QB** and **HF** datasets we have only 7,756 Hispanic/Latinx users that we could scrape in 2019, making it our smallest demographic class. We thus use our self-report scores to select the highest-scoring 7,756 users from each of other classes, producing our **Class-Balanced (CB)** dataset of 31k users.

5 Experimental Evaluation

We now conduct an empirical evaluation of our noisy self-report datasets. Showing that our datasets produce accurate classifiers demonstrates the value of our noisy self-report method for dataset construction. We train supervised classifiers on both our and existing datasets, comparing classifier performance in two evaluation settings.

We divide the six datasets described in Table 1 into training, dev, and test sets. We use the gold-standard self-report survey data from Preoţiuc-Pietro et al. (2015) as our held-out test set for evaluating all models. We combine the crowdsourced data from Volkova and Bachrach (2015) and Culotta et al. (2015) into a single dataset containing 3.5k users, which we then split 60%/40% to create a training and development set. The training set is our baseline comparison, referred to as **Crowd** in our results tables. We also create class-balanced versions of the dev and test sets with 156 and 452 users, respectively. Finally, we use each of our three collected datasets (**QB, HF, CB**) as training sets, and use a combination of each with the **Crowd** training set. Thus in total, we have seven training datasets, which make up the bottom seven rows of our results in Table 3, below. These results show our three models evaluated on the imbalanced and balanced test sets.

The balanced and imbalanced dev sets are used for all model and training set combinations in Table 3, which controls for the effect of model hyper-parameter selection. Cross-validation could be used in practical low-resource settings, but we use a single held-out dev set, which we subsample in the balanced case.

5.1 Demographic Prediction Models

We consider three demographic inference models which we train on each training set. The first follows Wood-Doughty et al. (2018) and uses a single tweet per user. A character-level CNN maps the user's name to an embedding which is combined with features from the profile metadata, such as user verification and follower count. These are passed through a two fully-connected layers to produce classifications. This model is referred to as "Names" in Table 3. The second model from Volkova and Bachrach (2015) uses a bag-of-words representation of the words in the user's recent tweets as the input to a sparse logistic regression classifier. The vocabulary is the 77k non-stopwords that occur at least twice in the dev set. We download up to the 200 most recent tweets for each user from the Twitter API. This model is referred to as "Unigrams" in Table 3. The third model

	Imbalanced prediction						Balanced prediction					
	Names		Unigrams		BERT		Names		Unigrams		BERT	
Dataset/Baseline	F1	Acc%	F1	Acc%	F1	Acc%	F1	Acc%	F1	Acc%	F1	Acc%
Random	.250	25.0	.250	25.0	.250	25.0	.250	25.0	.250	25.0	.250	25.0
Majority	.224	**80.8**	.224	80.8	.224	**80.8**	.100	25.0	.100	25.0	.100	25.0
Crowd	.268	74.9	.432	**83.2**	**.402**	74.8	.213	.322	.343	40.9	.402	43.7
QB	**.335**	71.7	.394	71.4	.371	61.0	.316	.377	.406	46.5	.461	48.3
Crowd+QB	.331	74.3	**.460**	78.4	.383	62.4	.276	.344	.453	47.6	.484	50.1
HF	.324	64.4	.401	72.4	.346	62.3	.308	.377	.418	47.3	.408	44.1
Crowd+HF	.198	54.0	.449	76.9	.360	62.1	.149	.233	**.466**	**50.9**	.441	47.4
CB	.299	49.4	.300	43.3	.285	39.0	.379	.381	.463	48.9	.474	49.0
Crowd+CB	.249	35.9	.449	74.6	.349	52.0	**.386**	**.390**	.465	48.9	**.514**	**52.6**

Table 3: Experimental results for baseline methods, models trained on the crowdsourced datasets, and models trained on our self-report datasets. The best result in each column is in bold. Dataset abbreviations are defined in § 4. "+" indicates a combined dataset of crowdsourced data plus our self-report data. Section 5 and Appendix C contain the training and evaluation details.

	Imbalanced			
Method	W	B	H/L	A
Random	25.0	25.0	25.0	25.0
Majority	100.	-	-	-
Crowd	95.1	49.8	0.9	19.1
QB	77.7	74.0	5.4	30.1
Crowd+QB	86.5	66.5	13.7	29.2
HF	78.9	74.3	7.4	25.6
Crowd+HF	84.2	72.1	14.7	24.8
CB	41.1	77.1	16.7	51.3
Crowd+CB	81.1	68.7	20.1	30.1
	Balanced			
Method	W	B	H/L	A
Random	25.0	25.0	25.0	25.0
Majority	100.	-	-	-
Crowd	95.6	51.3	15.0	1.8
QB	75.2	75.2	5.3	30.1
Crowd+QB	76.1	67.3	25.6	21.2
HF	77.9	77.0	8.9	25.6
Crowd+HF	87.6	73.5	15.9	26.5
CB	41.6	82.3	20.4	51.3
Crowd+CB	72.6	72.6	19.5	31.0

Table 4: Class-specific accuracy for Unigram models. Dashes indicate 0% accuracy. In general, the more class-imbalanced a dataset is, the worse it does on the smaller classes. In the imbalanced setting, the Unigram model trained on the Crowd dataset achieves the best accuracy solely due to its 95.1% accuracy on the users labeled as White.

uses DistilBERT (Sanh et al., 2019) to embed those same 200 tweets into a fixed-length representation, which is then passed through logistic regression with L2 regularization to

	W	B	H/L	A
White	12.7	4.0	3.6	4.9
Black	3.3	16.9	1.8	3.1
Hispanic/Latinx	7.6	4.0	6.5	6.7
Asian	6.2	2.2	1.8	14.7

Table 5: Balanced confusion matrix for BERT on Crowd+CB. Rows show true labels and columns predictions. Each cell shows test set percentage.

produce a classification. This model is referred to as "BERT" in Table 3. For all models we tune hyperparameters using the crowdsourced dev set. Training details for all models are in Appendix C and released in our code.

5.2 Evaluation and Baselines

We consider multiple evaluation setups to explore the extreme class imbalance of the survey and crowdsourced datasets (Table 1). First, we evaluate both total accuracy and macro-averaged F1 score, which penalizes poor performance on less-frequent classes. Second, we separately evaluate tuning and testing our models on either imbalanced or balanced dev and test sets, to see how it affects per-class classifier accuracy. Finally, we train our unigram and BERT models to reweigh examples with the inverse probability of the class label in the training data.

We also show the performance of two naïve strategies: randomly guessing across the four demographic categories, and deterministically guessing the majority category. These

	# Users	LD	CPT	TTR	HPT	Formality	Politeness	Top SAGE Keywords
A	9442	.751	.075	.533	.155*	-1.770	.4595	liked, visit, hahaha, art, youtube
B	70838	.747	.067	.532	.096†	-1.750	.4584	avrillavigne, ni**as, black, ni**a, wit
H/L	8349	.731	.051	.563	.145*	-1.802	.4609	justinbieber, justin, online, follow
W	57724	.759	.085	.510	.081†	-1.697	.4614	bc, realdonaldtrump, snapchat, dog, holy

Table 6: Comparison of the mean values for each numerical feature between groups. The last column has the top keywords per group as differentiated according to the SAGE model. Methods are described in § 7. Abbreviations: LD, Lexical Diversity; CPT, Contractions/tweet; TTR, Type-Token Ratio; HPT, Hashtags/tweet. Almost all differences are significant; only those numbers that share superscript symbols are **not** significantly different at a 0.05 confidence level when using a Mann-Whitney U test.

baselines highlight the trade-offs between accuracy and F1. Because the imbalanced test set is so imbalanced, the "Majority" baseline strategy can achieve high overall accuracy, but very low F1. The Random baseline has low overall accuracy but slightly better F1 than the Majority strategy. These two baselines provide the first two rows of Table 3.

We stress these evaluation details because the class-imbalance may have serious implications for downstream applications. Models trained to do well on the majority class at the expense of minority classes could bias downstream analyses by under-representing minority groups. In public health applications with disparities between groups (LaVeist, 2005), not accounting for imbalances between the training and test datasets could exacerbate rather than ameliorate inequalities.

6 Experimental Results and Discussion

Table 3 shows several trends. The BERT and Unigram models, using 200 tweets per user, generally outperform the single-tweet Names models. In the imbalanced evaluations, we see a large trade-off between accuracy and F1, with models achieving higher overall accuracy when they ignore the smaller Asian and Hispanic/Latinx classes. Even the trivial "Majority" baseline is competitive due to the extreme class-imbalance. While models trained only on **Crowd** achieve significantly higher accuracy on the imbalanced test set than models trained on our datasets, this is only because of their excellent performance on White users. Table 4 shows the class-specific accuracy of Unigram models; the model trained only on the imbalanced **Crowd** dataset achives 95.1% accuracy on White users, but lower than 50%, 1%, and 20% accuracy on Black, Hispanic/Latinx, and Asian users. While more sophisticated approaches to addressing the extreme class imbalance could close the gap between training on **Crowd** alone and using our noisy datasets, we can see the benefits of our data in the balanced evaluation.

Across all balanced evaluations, all but one of the models trained with our collected datasets outperform models trained only on **Crowd** in both accuracy and F1. Several models improve by more than .10 F1 over models trained only on **Crowd**. The BERT models achieve the best performance in the balanced evaluation, while performing relatively poorly on imbalanced data. This occurs because the BERT models achieve high accuracy on the Black and Asian classes, which are underrepresented in our imbalanced test set. We show a confusion matrix for our best balanced model in Table 5.

These models are quite simple, and more complex models could improve performance independent of the dataset. However, by limiting ourselves to simpler models, we can demonstrate that for learning a classifier that performs well on four-class classification of race and ethnicity, our noisy datasets are clearly beneficial. While the self-reports are noisy, we collect enough data to support better classifiers on held-out, gold-standard labels. Despite this experimental improvement, real-world applications may require more accurate classifiers or may need to prioritize classifiers with high precision or recall for a particular group. Such research requires a careful contextualization of what conclusions can be drawn from the available data and models; classifier error may exaggerate

	Asian	Black	Hispanic/Latinx	White	Random
% users in dataset	6.71	49.44	5.83	38.02	–
% users with 1+ tweets from Android	38.95*†	38.33*	39.41†	25.46	–
% users with 1+ tweets from iPhone	60.28	58.21	54.89	75.37	–
% users with 1+ tweets from Desktop	43.34	30.59	44.87	31.04	–
% users with profile URL	34.09*	29.71	34.75*	24.78	20.8
% users with custom profile image	98.83	99.29*†	99.24*‡	99.33†‡	95.4
% users with geotagging enabled	48.65*	53.27	49.54*	56.04	33.1
% users with 1+ geotagged tweet	8.35*	6.46	7.81*	5.43	7.9
Average statuses count	11974	18709	12449	14177	–
Average tweets per month	177.83	255.41	182.13	200.85	739
(m) % tweets that mention a user	59.73	58.71	60.44*	61.77*	22.3
(m) % tweets that include an image	20.44*	17.20	18.39	19.17*	33.9
(m) % tweets that include a URL	20.99	21.64	24.01	17.22	–

Table 7: Profile Behavioral Features. The first four columns show our **HF** users, the fifth shows a random sample of 1M users reported in (Wood-Doughty et al., 2017), when available. (m) indicates micro-averaging; all others are macro-averaged across users. Almost all differences between **HF** groups are statistically significant according to a Mann-Whitney U Test. However, if two entries in the same row share a superscript, they are not significantly different at a 0.05 confidence level. We cannot test significance against the random sample.

differences between groups.

7 Twitter Behaviors across Groups

Our experiments show that our datasets enable better predictive models, but say nothing about *how* self-reporting users use Twitter. Do different groups in our dataset differ in other behaviors? We explore this using a variety of quantitative analyses of Twitter user behavior, following similarly-motivated public health research (Coppersmith et al., 2014; Homan et al., 2014; Gkotsis et al., 2016). Two interpretations are possible for these group-level differences: either user behavior correlates with demographic categories (Wood-Doughty et al., 2017), or the *choice to self-report* correlates with these behaviors. These can both be true, and our current methods cannot distinguish between them. While our empirical evaluation shows that our data is still useful for training classifiers to predict gold-standard labels, possible selection bias may influence real-world applications.

Lexical features are widely used to study Twitter (Pennacchiotti and Popescu, 2011; Blodgett et al., 2016). For each user in our dataset, we follow §3.1 of Inuwa-Dutse et al. (2018) and calculate Type-Token Ratio[4], Lexical Diversity[5] (Tweedie and Baayen, 1998), and the number of hashtags and English contractions they use per tweet. We then use existing trained models for analyzing formality and politeness (Pavlick and Tetreault, 2016; Danescu-Niculescu-Mizil et al., 2013) of online text. The formality score is estimated with a regression model over lexical and syntactic features including n-grams, dependency parse, and word embeddings. The politeness classifier uses unigram features and lexicons for gratitude and sentiment. We use the published implementations.[6,7] For both trained models, we macro-average over users' scores to obtain a value for each demographic group. We also use a SAGE (Eisenstein et al., 2011) lexical variation implementation to find the words that most distinguish each group. The means of the six quantitative features and the top five SAGE keywords for each group is shown in Table 6.

We then consider a few basic measures of Twitter usage, computed from the profile information of each user. Table 7 contains the mean value of these features, describing the broad range of basic user behaviors on the Twitter platform. Almost all differences

[4]The number of unique tokens in a tweet divided by the total number of tokens in the tweet.

[5]The total number of tokens in a tweet without URLs, user mentions and stopwords divided by the total number of tokens in the tweet.

[6]https://github.com/YahooArchive/formality-classifier

[7]https://github.com/sudhof/politeness

in these behavioral features are significant across groups. Device usage shows the biggest difference; White users are much more likely to have used an iPhone than an Android to tweet. In past work, Pavalanathan and Eisenstein (2015) demonstrated that the use of Twitter geotagging was more prevalent in metropolitan areas and among younger users. Table 7 follows Wood-Doughty et al. (2017) which calculated these features for a sample of 1M Twitter users. Users in our datasets comparatively more often customize their profile image or URL or enable geotagging. More bots or spam in the random sample may partially account for these differences (Morstatter et al., 2013). Table 8 in Appendix D also compares lists of the most common common emojis, emoticons, and part-of-speech tags within each group.

These analyses show substantial differences between the groups labeled by our self-report methods, suggesting our noisy self-reports correlate with actual Twitter usage behavior. However, it cannot reveal whether these differences primarily correlate with racial/ethnic groups or whether these differences appear from how users decide whether to self-report a race/ethnicity keyword. Researchers working on downstream public health applications (e.g. Gkotsis et al. (2016)) may want to account for these empirical differences between groups in our training datasets when drawing conclusions about users in other datasets.

8 Limitations and Future Work

We have presented a reproducible method for automatically identifying self-reports of race and ethnicity to construct an annotated dataset for training demographic inference models. While our automated annotations are imperfect, we show that our data can replace or supplement manually-annotated data. Our data collection methodology does not rely on large-scale crowd-sourcing, making it more reproducible and easier to keep datasets up-to-date. These contributions enable the development and distribution of tools to facilitate demographic contextualization in computational social science research.

There are several important extensions to consider. First, our analysis focuses on the United States and English-language racial keywords; most countries have a unique cultural conceptualizations of race/ethnicity and unique demographic composition, and may require a country-specific focus. We only cover four categories of race/ethnicity, ignoring smaller populations and multi-racial categories (Jones and Smith, 2001). We use a limited set of query terms, which ignores the diversity of how people may choose to self-report their identities. While our methods scale easily to additional categories and/or racial keywords, our evaluation method requires a gold-standard test set that covers those groups. For specific applications, a domain expert might prioritize precision or recall for a specific demographic class. This may involve fine-tuning a classifier on a dataset constructed with a particular class-imbalance; the details of that imbalance should be contextualized with the general class distribution of the population on Twitter. Our analyses could be compared against human perceptions of users' racial identity, though past work has suggested such perceptions have underlying biases (Preoţiuc-Pietro et al., 2017). Finally, past work has highlighted various biases in demographic inference (Pavalanathan and Eisenstein, 2015; Wood-Doughty et al., 2017), and our analyses cannot fully rule out the presence of such biases in our data or models. In future work, we strongly encourage the study of racial self-identities and social cultural issues as supported by computational analyses. These issues should be viewed from a global perspective, especially with regards to biases in our collection methods (Landeiro and Culotta, 2016).

We release our code in the `Demographer` package to enable training new models and constructing future updated datasets. We also release our trained models and annotated Twitter user ids for academic researchers that agree to the data use agreement and obtain approval from an ethics board.

References

Tarek Al Baghal, Luke Sloan, Curtis Jessop, Matthew L Williams, and Pete Burnap. 2020. Linking twitter and survey data: The impact of survey mode and demographics on consent rates across three uk studies. *Social Science Computer Review*, 38(5):517–532.

Silvio Amir, Mark Dredze, and John W. Ayers. 2019. Population level mental health surveillance over social media with digital cohorts. In *CLPsych*.

McKane Andrus, Elena Spitzer, Jeffrey Brown, and Alice Xiang. 2021. What we can't measure, we can't understand: Challenges to demographic data procurement in the pursuit of fairness. In *Proceedings of the 2021 ACM Conference on Fairness, Accountability, and Transparency*, FAccT '21, page 249–260, New York, NY, USA. Association for Computing Machinery.

Julia Angwin and Terry Parris Jr. 2016. Facebook lets advertisers exclude users by race. *ProPublica blog*, 28.

Ehsan Mohammady Ardehaly and Aron Culotta. 2017. Co-training for demographic classification using deep learning from label proportions. In *2017 IEEE International Conference on Data Mining Workshops (ICDMW)*, pages 1017–1024. IEEE.

John W Ayers, Benjamin M Althouse, and Mark Dredze. 2014. Could behavioral medicine lead the web data revolution? *Jama*, 311(14):1399–1400.

David Bamman, Jacob Eisenstein, and Tyler Schnoebelen. 2014. Gender identity and lexical variation in social media. *Journal of Sociolinguistics*, 18(2):135–160.

Charley Beller, Rebecca Knowles, Craig Harman, Shane Bergsma, Margaret Mitchell, and Benjamin Van Durme. 2014. I'm a belieber: Social roles via self-identification and conceptual attributes. In *ACL*.

Emily M. Bender and Batya Friedman. 2018. Data statements for natural language processing: Toward mitigating system bias and enabling better science. *Transactions of the Association for Computational Linguistics*, 6:587–604.

Katie Benner, Glenn Thrush, and Mike Isaac. 2019. Facebook engages in housing discrimination with its ad practices, us says. *The New York Times*, 28:2019.

Adrian Benton, Glen Coppersmith, and Mark Dredze. 2017. Ethical research protocols for social media health research. In *Proceedings of the First ACL Workshop on Ethics in Natural Language Processing*, pages 94–102, Valencia, Spain. Association for Computational Linguistics.

Brent Berlin and Paul Kay. 1991. *Basic color terms: Their universality and evolution*. Univ of California Press.

Steven Bird, Ewan Klein, and Edward Loper. 2009. *Natural language processing with Python: analyzing text with the natural language toolkit*. "O'Reilly Media, Inc.".

Su Lin Blodgett, Lisa Green, and Brendan O'Connor. 2016. Demographic dialectal variation in social media: A case study of African-American English. In *Proceedings of the 2016 Conference on Empirical Methods in Natural Language Processing*, pages 1119–1130, Austin, Texas. Association for Computational Linguistics.

John D Burger, John Henderson, George Kim, and Guido Zarrella. 2011. Discriminating gender on twitter. In *EMNLP*.

Pete Burnap and Matthew L Williams. 2016. Us and them: identifying cyber hate on twitter across multiple protected characteristics. *EPJ Data Science*, 5(1):11.

Mary E Campbell and Christabel L Rogalin. 2006. Categorical imperatives: The interaction of latino and racial identification. *Social Science Quarterly*, 87(5):1030–1052.

Jonathan Chang, Itamar Rosenn, Lars Backstrom, and Cameron Marlow. 2010. epluribus: Ethnicity on social networks. In *ICWSM*.

Xin Chen, Yu Wang, Eugene Agichtein, and Fusheng Wang. 2015. A comparative study of demographic attribute inference in twitter. *ICWSM*, 15:590–593.

Kenneth Ward Church and Patrick Hanks. 1989. Word association norms, mutual information, and lexicography. In *27th Annual Meeting of the Association for Computational Linguistics*, pages 76–83, Vancouver, British Columbia, Canada. Association for Computational Linguistics.

Andrew J Coldman, Terry Braun, and Richard P Gallagher. 1988. The classification of ethnic status using name information. *Journal of Epidemiology & Community Health*, 42(4):390–395.

R Dawn Comstock, Edward M Castillo, and Suzanne P Lindsay. 2004. Four-year review of the use of race and ethnicity in epidemiologic and public health research. *American journal of epidemiology*, 159(6):611–619.

Glen Coppersmith, Mark Dredze, and Craig Harman. 2014. Quantifying mental health signals in twitter. In *CLPsych*.

Stephen Cornell and Douglas Hartmann. 2006. *Ethnicity and race: Making identities in a changing world*. Sage Publications.

Kate Crawford. 2017. The trouble with bias. In *Conference on Neural Information Processing Systems, invited speaker*.

Lorraine Culley. 2006. Transcending transculturalism? race, ethnicity and health-care. *Nursing Inquiry*, 13(2):144–153.

Aron Culotta, Nirmal Kumar, and Jennifer Cutler. 2015. Predicting the demographics of twitter users from website traffic data. In *Proceedings of the AAAI Conference on Artificial Intelligence*, volume 29.

Cristian Danescu-Niculescu-Mizil, Moritz Sudhof, Dan Jurafsky, Jure Leskovec, and Christopher Potts. 2013. A computational approach to politeness with application to social factors. In *Proceedings of the 51st Annual Meeting of the Association for Computational Linguistics (Volume 1: Long Papers)*, pages 250–259, Sofia, Bulgaria. Association for Computational Linguistics.

Laure Delisle, Alfredo Kalaitzis, Krzysztof Majewski, Archy de Berker, Milena Marin, and Julien Cornebise. 2019. A large-scale crowdsourced analysis of abuse against women journalists and politicians on twitter. *CoRR*, abs/1902.03093.

Mark Dredze, Michael J Paul, Shane Bergsma, and Hieu Tran. 2013. Carmen: A twitter geolocation system with applications to public health. In *AAAI workshop on expanding the boundaries of health informatics using AI (HIAI)*, volume 23, page 45. Citeseer.

William W Dressler, Kathryn S Oths, and Clarence C Gravlee. 2005. Race and ethnicity in public health research: models to explain health disparities. *Annu. Rev. Anthropol.*, 34:231–252.

Jacob Eisenstein, Amr Ahmed, and Eric P. Xing. 2011. Sparse additive generative models of text. In *Proceedings of the 28th International Conference on Machine Learning, ICML 2011, Bellevue, Washington, USA, June 28 - July 2, 2011*, pages 1041–1048. Omnipress.

Jacob Eisenstein, Brendan O'Connor, Noah A Smith, and Eric P Xing. 2014. Diffusion of lexical change in social media. *PloS one*, 9(11):e113114.

Marc N Elliott, Allen Fremont, Peter A Morrison, Philip Pantoja, and Nicole Lurie. 2008. A new method for estimating race/ethnicity and associated disparities where administrative records lack self-reported race/ethnicity. *Health services research*, 43(5p1):1722–1736.

Marc N Elliott, Peter A Morrison, Allen Fremont, Daniel F McCaffrey, Philip Pantoja, and Nicole Lurie. 2009. Using the census bureau's surname list to improve estimates of race/ethnicity and associated disparities. *Health Services and Outcomes Research Methodology*, 9(2):69–83.

Casey Fiesler and Nicholas Proferes. 2018. 'participant' perceptions of twitter research ethics. *Social Media+ Society*, 4(1):2056305118763366.

Kevin Fiscella and Allen M Fremont. 2006. Use of geocoding and surname analysis to estimate race and ethnicity. *Health services research*, 41(4p1):1482–1500.

Lucie Flekova, Jordan Carpenter, Salvatore Giorgi, Lyle Ungar, and Daniel Preoţiuc-Pietro. 2016. Analyzing biases in human perception of user age and gender from text. In *Proceedings of the 54th Annual Meeting of the Association for Computational Linguistics (Volume 1: Long Papers)*, pages 843–854, Berlin, Germany. Association for Computational Linguistics.

George Gkotsis, Anika Oellrich, Tim Hubbard, Richard Dobson, Maria Liakata, Sumithra Velupillai, and Rina Dutta. 2016. The language of mental health problems in social media. In *Proceedings of the Third Workshop on Computational Linguistics and Clinical Psychology*, pages 63–73, San Diego, CA, USA. Association for Computational Linguistics.

A Gonzalez-Barrera and MH Lopez. 2015. Is being hispanic a matter of race, ethnicity or both? *Pew Research Center*.

Charles Hirschman, Richard Alba, and Reynolds Farley. 2000. The meaning and measurement of race in the US census: Glimpses into the future. *Demography*, 37(3).

Arnold K Ho, Steven O Roberts, and Susan A Gelman. 2015. Essentialism and racial bias jointly contribute to the categorization of multiracial individuals. *Psychological Science*, 26(10):1639–1645.

Christopher Homan, Ravdeep Johar, Tong Liu, Megan Lytle, Vincent Silenzio, and Cecilia Ovesdotter Alm. 2014. Toward macro-insights for suicide prevention: Analyzing fine-grained distress at scale. In *Proceedings of the Workshop on Computational Linguistics and Clinical Psychology: From Linguistic Signal to Clinical Reality*, pages 107–117, Baltimore, Maryland, USA. Association for Computational Linguistics.

Xiaolei Huang and Michael J. Paul. 2018. Examining temporality in document classification. In *Proceedings of the 56th Annual Meeting of the Association for Computational Linguistics (Volume 2: Short Papers)*, pages 694–699, Melbourne, Australia. Association for Computational Linguistics.

Xiaolei Huang and Michael J. Paul. 2019. Neural user factor adaptation for text classification: Learning to generalize across author demographics. In *Proceedings of the Eighth Joint Conference on Lexical and Computational Semantics (*SEM 2019)*, pages 136–146, Minneapolis, Minnesota. Association for Computational Linguistics.

Isa Inuwa-Dutse, Bello Shehu Bello, and Ioannis Korkontzelos. 2018. Lexical analysis of automated accounts on twitter. *arXiv:1812.07947*.

Jiachen Jiang and Soroush Vosoughi. 2020. Not judging a user by their cover: Understanding harm in multi-modal processing within social media research. In *Proceedings of the 2nd International Workshop on Fairness, Accountability, Transparency and Ethics in Multimedia*, pages 6–12.

Nicholas A Jones and Amy Symens Smith. 2001. *The two or more races population, 2000*, volume 8. US Department of Commerce, Economics and Statistics Administration, US.

Soon-Gyo Jung, Jisun An, Haewoon Kwak, Joni Salminen, and Bernard Jansen. 2018. Assessing the accuracy of four popular face recognition tools for inferring gender, age, and race. In *Proceedings of the International AAAI Conference on Web and Social Media*, volume 12.

Rebecca Knowles, Josh Carroll, and Mark Dredze. 2016. Demographer: Extremely simple name demographics. In *Proceedings of the First Workshop on NLP and Computational Social Science*, pages 108–113.

Virgile Landeiro and Aron Culotta. 2016. Robust text classification in the presence of confounding bias. In *Proceedings of the AAAI Conference on Artificial Intelligence*, volume 30.

Thomas A LaVeist. 2005. *Minority populations and health: An introduction to health disparities in the United States*, volume 4. John Wiley & Sons.

Sharon M Lee and Sonya M Tafoya. 2006. Rethinking us census racial and ethnic categories for the 21st century. *Journal of Economic and Social Measurement*, 31(3-4):233–252.

Kate Loveys, Jonathan Torrez, Alex Fine, Glen Moriarty, and Glen Coppersmith. 2018. Cross-cultural differences in language markers of depression online. In *Proceedings of the Fifth Workshop on Computational Linguistics and Clinical Psychology: From Keyboard to Clinic*, pages 78–87.

Alice E Marwick and danah boyd. 2011. I tweet honestly, i tweet passionately: Twitter users, context collapse, and the imagined audience. *New media & society*, 13(1):114–133.

Jean-Baptiste Michel, Yuan Kui Shen, Aviva Presser Aiden, Adrian Veres, Matthew K Gray, Joseph P Pickett, Dale Hoiberg, Dan Clancy, Peter Norvig, Jon Orwant, et al. 2011. Quantitative analysis of culture using millions of digitized books. *science*, 331(6014):176–182.

Jude Mikal, Samantha Hurst, and Mike Conway. 2016. Ethical issues in using twitter for population-level depression monitoring: a qualitative study. *BMC medical ethics*, 17(1):22.

Ehsan Mohammady and Aron Culotta. 2014. Using county demographics to infer attributes of Twitter users. In *Proceedings of the Joint Workshop on Social Dynamics and Personal Attributes in Social Media*, pages 7–16, Baltimore, Maryland. Association for Computational Linguistics.

Fred Morstatter, Jürgen Pfeffer, Huan Liu, and Kathleen M Carley. 2013. Is the sample good enough? comparing data from twitter's streaming api with twitter's firehose. In *ICWSM*.

Brendan O'Connor, Ramnath Balasubramanyan, Bryan R Routledge, and Noah A Smith. 2010. From tweets to polls: Linking text sentiment to public opinion time series. *ICWSM*, 11(122-129):1–2.

Alexandra Olteanu, Carlos Castillo, Fernando Diaz, and Emre Kiciman. 2019. Social data: Biases, methodological pitfalls, and ethical boundaries. *Frontiers in Big Data*, 2:13.

Michael Paul and Mark Dredze. 2011. You are what you tweet: Analyzing twitter for public health. In *Proceedings of the International AAAI Conference on Web and Social Media*, volume 5.

Umashanthi Pavalanathan and Jacob Eisenstein. 2015. Confounds and consequences in geotagged twitter data. *arXiv:1506.02275*.

Ellie Pavlick and Joel Tetreault. 2016. An empirical analysis of formality in online communication. *Transactions of the Association for Computational Linguistics*, 4:61–74.

Marco Pennacchiotti and Ana-Maria Popescu. 2011. A machine learning approach to twitter user classification. In *Proceedings of the International AAAI Conference on Web and Social Media*, volume 5.

Daniel Preoţiuc-Pietro, Sharath Chandra Guntuku, and Lyle Ungar. 2017. Controlling human perception of basic user traits. In *Proceedings of the 2017 Conference on Empirical Methods in Natural Language Processing*, pages 2335–2341, Copenhagen, Denmark. Association for Computational Linguistics.

Daniel Preoţiuc-Pietro and Lyle Ungar. 2018. User-level race and ethnicity predictors from Twitter text. In *Proceedings of the 27th International Conference on Computational Linguistics*, pages 1534–1545, Santa Fe, New Mexico, USA. Association for Computational Linguistics.

Daniel Preoţiuc-Pietro, Svitlana Volkova, Vasileios Lampos, Yoram Bachrach, and Nikolaos Aletras. 2015. Studying user income through language, behaviour and affect in social media. *PloS one*, 10(9):e0138717.

Victor Sanh, Lysandre Debut, Julien Chaumond, and Thomas Wolf. 2019. Distilbert, a distilled version of bert: smaller, faster, cheaper and lighter. *arXiv preprint arXiv:1910.01108v4*.

David Satcher. 2001. Mental health: Culture, race, and ethnicityîíñupplement to mental health: A report of the surgeon general.

Lauren Sinnenberg, Alison M Buttenheim, Kevin Padrez, Christina Mancheno, Lyle Ungar, and Raina M Merchant. 2017. Twitter as a tool for health research: a systematic review. *American journal of public health*, 107(1):e1–e8.

Donald P Spence and Kimberly C Owens. 1990. Lexical co-occurrence and association strength. *Journal of Psycholinguistic Research*, 19(5):317–330.

Fiona J Tweedie and R Harald Baayen. 1998. How variable may a constant be? measures of lexical richness in perspective. *Computers and the Humanities*, 32(5):323–352.

Nicholas Vargas and Kevin Stainback. 2016. Documenting contested racial identities among self-identified latina/os, asians, blacks, and whites. *American Behavioral Scientist*, 60(4):442–464.

Svitlana Volkova and Yoram Bachrach. 2015. On predicting sociodemographic traits and emotions from communications in social networks and their implications to online self-disclosure. *Cyberpsychology, Behavior, and Social Networking*, 18(12):726–736.

Zijian Wang, Scott A. Hale, David Ifeoluwa Adelani, Przemyslaw A. Grabowicz, Timo Hartmann, Fabian Flöck, and David Jurgens. 2019. Demographic inference and representative population estimates from multilingual social media data. In *The World Wide Web Conference, WWW 2019, San Francisco, CA, USA, May 13-17, 2019*, pages 2056–2067. ACM.

Zach Wood-Doughty, Praateek Mahajan, and Mark Dredze. 2018. Johns Hopkins or johnny-hopkins: Classifying individuals versus organizations on Twitter. In *Proceedings of the Second Workshop on Computational Modeling of People's Opinions, Personality, and Emotions in Social Media*, pages 56–61, New Orleans, Louisiana, USA. Association for Computational Linguistics.

Zach Wood-Doughty, Michael Smith, David Broniatowski, and Mark Dredze. 2017. How does Twitter user behavior vary across demographic groups? In *Proceedings of the Second Workshop on NLP and Computational Social Science*, pages 83–89, Vancouver, Canada. Association for Computational Linguistics.

A Preprocessing, Tokenizing, and Tagging

We lowercase all descriptions and use NLTK Tweet Tokenizer (Bird et al., 2009) to get the PoS tags. Our candidate self-report words are scraped from 177M Twitter descriptions using the regex and PoS pattern, `{I'/I a}m (+ RB)( + DT) (+ JJ) + NN`. We collect both adjectives and nouns from the pattern above, and refine the matches by keeping adjectives and nouns that match the majority tag in the Google N-gram corpus. We filter out plural words (e.g. "white **people**") using a PoS tag pattern, `JJ + NNPS/NNS`, and refer to our set of self-report words as S.

B Calculating the "Self-Report" Score

To calculate the score described in § 4, we first obtain simple co-occurrence weighting by counting the occurrences $O_s(w_s)$ of word w_s as a self-report word, and its overal occurrences $O(w_s)$. Then:

$$R = \sum_{w_s \in S^{win}} \frac{1}{D(w_s, q)} \cdot \frac{O_s(w_s)}{O(w_s)},$$

where S^{win} is the self-report words in the fixed window size, $D(w_s, q)$ denotes the distance between w_s and query word q.

We also consider a TF-IDF weighting as:

$$R_{\text{tfidf}} = \sum_{w_s \in S^{win}} \frac{1}{D(w_s, q)} \cdot \frac{O_s(w_s)}{O(w_s)} \cdot \log \frac{\sum_{w \in S} O_s(w)}{O_s(w_s)}$$

To fine-tune our self-report score, three authors manually labeled a tuning set of 400 descriptions as to whether the user was self-reporting a matching query word, using a three-label nominal scale of "yes," "no," and "unsure.' We discarded 6 that we classified as organizations (Wood-Doughty et al., 2018), and had an Krippendorff α 0.8058 on the remaining 394. We use majority voting strategy to get binary labels and select the self-report score's hyperparameters of window size and threshold, and whether to use the tf-idf weighting, based on the precision calculated on this tuning set.

To ensure that these chosen hyperparameters did not overfit to the tuning set, we sampled an additional 199 users from **HF**. Using a three-label nominal scale of "yes," "no," or "unsure," the three annotators achieved a Krippendorff's alpha of 0.625. After converting to binary "yes" and "no" by taking majority voting and discarding 7 users who were majority "unsure," our best model achieves 72.4% accuracy on the test set with simple weighting, window size 5, and threshold of 0.35.

C Model Training Details

Our name model uses a CNN implementation released in Wood-Doughty et al. (2018). We use a CNN with 256 filters of width 3. The user's name (not screen name) is truncated at 50 characters and embedded into a 256 dimensional character embedding. We fine-tuned the learning rate on our dev data, trained for 250 epochs, and used early-stopping on dev-set F1 to pick which model to evaluate on the test set.

Our unigram model follows Volkova and Bachrach (2015), using a simple sparse logistic regression. We use an implementation from Scikit-Learn, and tune the regularization parameter on the dev set. We introduce a hyperparameter to down-weight the contribution of our users compared to the baseline users; we also set that parameter on the dev set.

For BERT model, we first get embedding for every tweet by taking the vector with size 768 on special [CLS] token in the last hidden layer. The element-wise average of all tweet embeddings from one user is then passed through a logistic regression model with L2 regularization to make the classification. Similarly, the regularization parameter is tuned on the dev set. We fine-tuned DistilBERT model on tweets collected from training set split of the crowdsourced dataset. However, after observing limited performance improvement we just use pre-trained DistilBERT model.

Top k	Emojis 20	50	Hashtags 20	50	PoS bigrams 20	50
A v. B	-0.67	-0.26	-0.85	-0.87	0.29	0.19
A v. H/L	-0.10	-0.07	-0.84	-0.86	0.55	0.02
A v. W	-0.38	0.13	-0.83	-0.80	0.02	-0.02
B v. H/L	-0.65	-0.38	-0.83	-0.82	0.52	0.03
B v. W	-0.48	-0.16	-0.79	-0.72	0.04	0.24
H/L v. W	-0.40	-0.13	-0.91	-0.89	-0.17	-0.28

Table 8: Kendall's τ correlation coefficients for top items of different list features. For hashtags in particular we see large negative coefficients.

D Additional Analyses of Twitter Behavior across Groups

This appendix contains an additional analysis following § 7.

In addition to the SAGE keyword comparison, we explore topical differences between groups by compiling ranked lists of common emojis, emoticons, and part-of-speech tags within each group. Table 8 shows a comparison of Kendall τ rank correlation between these To compare across groups, we look at the top k items in each list and calculate Kendall τ rank correlation coefficients for each pair of demographic groups (Morstatter et al., 2013). Table 8 shows pairwise τ correlations. These coefficients vary between -1 and 1 for perfect negative and positive correlations. For emojis, all correlations are negative for $k = 20$, but increase at $k = 50$. For hashtags, however, correlations are strongly negative for all values of k, suggesting that groups labeled by our method substantially differ in the topics they discuss. While we use English keywords for data collection, topic difference may be confounded by users' native language(s).

E Data Statement

Following Bender and Friedman (2018), we highlight characteristics of our collected noisy self-report data that may be important for mitigating ethical and scientific missteps.

Curation rationale Examples of Twitter users who self-report their racial identity using English-language keywords.

Language variety While our dataset contains predominantly English (en-US), there is substantial diversity in language due to the international and due to the informal setting of Twitter. When we randomly sample 1000 users from our `Heuristic Filter` list and consider up to 100 tweets per user, we find that the Twitter-produced `lang` field indicates that 78.5% of the tweets are in English, with the next three most-common `lang` labels as Spanish (3.8%), Portuguese (3.7%), and Undetermined (3.3%).

Speaker demographics The speakers in our dataset are Twitter users. To be included in our initial dataset, users must use an English racial self-report keyword in their Twitter profile description, and must not be labeled as an organization by the classifier from Wood-Doughty et al. (2018). We then perform additional filtering of users, detailed in the paper, to improve the likelihood that a racial self-report keyword is actually self-reporting race.

Annotator demographics Our small manual annotation was conducted by three authors, Asian and White men, ages 20-30, with native languages of Chinese and English.

Speech situation Twitter user profiles and tweets.

Text characteristics Informal Twitter user descriptions and tweets. We make no restrictions on the content of the tweets.

PANDORA Talks: Personality and Demographics on Reddit

Matej Gjurković **Mladen Karan** **Iva Vukojević** **Mihaela Bošnjak** **Jan Šnajder**
Text Analysis and Knowledge Engineering Lab
Faculty of Electrical Engineering and Computing, University of Zagreb
Unska 3, 10000 Zagreb, Croatia
name.surname@fer.hr

Abstract

Personality and demographics are important variables in social sciences and computational sociolinguistics. However, datasets with both personality and demographic labels are scarce. To address this, we present PANDORA, the first dataset of Reddit comments of 10k users partially labeled with three personality models and demographics (age, gender, and location), including 1.6k users labeled with the well-established Big 5 personality model. We showcase the usefulness of this dataset on three experiments, where we leverage the more readily available data from other personality models to predict the Big 5 traits, analyze gender classification biases arising from psycho-demographic variables, and carry out a confirmatory and exploratory analysis based on psychological theories. Finally, we present benchmark prediction models for all personality and demographic variables.

1 Introduction

Personality and demographics describe differences between people at the individual and group level. This makes them important for much of social sciences research, where they may be used as either target or control variables. One field that can greatly benefit from textual datasets with personality and demographic data is computational sociolinguistics (Nguyen et al., 2016), which uses NLP methods to study language use in society.

Conversely, personality and demographic data can be useful in the development of NLP systems. Recent advances in machine learning have brought significant improvements in NLP systems' performance across many tasks, but these typically come at the cost of more complex and less interpretable models, often susceptible to biases (Chang et al., 2019). Biases are commonly caused by societal biases present in data, and eliminating them requires a thorough understanding of the data used to train the model. One way to do this is to consider demographic and personality variables, as language use and interpretation is affected by both. Incorporating these variables into the design and analysis of NLP models can help interpret model's decisions, avoid societal biases, and control for confounders.

The demographic variables of age, gender, and location have been widely used in computational sociolinguistics (Bamman et al., 2014; Peersman et al., 2011; Eisenstein et al., 2010), while in NLP there is ample work on predicting these variables or using them in other NLP tasks. In contrast, advances in text-based personality research are lagging behind. This can be traced to the fact that (1) personality-labeled datasets are scarce and (2) personality labels are much harder to infer from text than demographic variables such as age and gender. In addition, the few existing datasets have serious limitations: a small number of authors or comments, comments of limited length, non-anonymity, or topic bias. While most of these limitations have been addressed by the recently published MBTI9k Reddit dataset (Gjurković and Šnajder, 2018), this dataset still has two deficiencies. Firstly, it uses the Myers-Briggs Type Indicator (MBTI) model (Myers et al., 1990), which – while popular among the general public and in business – is discredited by most personality psychologists (Barbuto Jr, 1997). The alternative is the well-known Five Factor Model (or Big 5) (McCrae and John, 1992), which, however, is less popular, and thus labels for it are harder to obtain. Another deficiency of MBTI9k is the lack of demographics, limiting model interpretability and use in sociolinguistics.

Our work seeks to address these problems by introducing a new dataset – *Personality ANd Demographics Of Reddit Authors* (PANDORA) – the first dataset from Reddit labeled with personality and demographic data. PANDORA comprises over 17M comments written by more than 10k Reddit users, labeled with Big 5 and/or two other person-

Proceedings of the Ninth International Workshop on Natural Language Processing for Social Media, pages 138–152
Online Workshop, June 10, 2021. ©2021 Association for Computational Linguistics

ality models (MBTI, Enneagram), alongside age, gender, location, and language. In particular, Big 5 labels are available for more than 1.6k users, who jointly produced more than 3M comments.

PANDORA provides exciting opportunities for sociolinguistic research and development of NLP models. In this paper we showcase its usefulness through three experiments. In the first, inspired by work on domain adaptation and multitask learning, we show how the MBTI and Enneagram labels can be used to predict the labels from the well-established Big 5 model. We leverage the fact that more data is available for MBTI and Enneagram, and exploit the correlations between the traits of the different models and their manifestations in text. In the second experiment we demonstrate how the complete psycho-demographic profile can help in pinpointing biases in gender classification. We show that a gender classifier trained on a large Reddit dataset fails to predict gender for users with certain combinations of personality traits more often than for other users. Finally, the third experiment showcases the usefulness of PANDORA in social sciences: building on existing theories from psychology, we perform a confirmatory and exploratory analysis between propensity for philosophy and certain psycho-demographic variables.

We also report on baselines for personality and demographics prediction on PANDORA. We treat Big 5 and other personality and demographics variables as targets for supervised machine learning, and evaluate a number of benchmark models with different feature sets. We make PANDORA available[1] for the research community, in the hope this will stimulate further research.

2 Background and Related Work

Personality models and assessment. Myers-Briggs Type Indicator (MBTI; Myers et al., 1990) and Five Factor Model (FFM; McCrae and John, 1992) are two most commonly used personality models. Myers-Briggs Type Indicator (MBTI) categorizes people in 16 personality types defined by four dichotomies: Introversion/Extraversion (way of gaining energy), Sensing/iNtuition (way of gathering information), Thinking/Feeling (way of making decisions), and Judging/Perceiving (preferences in interacting with others). The main criticism of MBTI focuses on low validity (Bess and Harvey, 2002; McCrae and Costa, 1989).

Contrary to MBTI, FFM (McCrae and John, 1992) has a dimensional approach to personality and describes people as somewhere on the continuum of five personality traits (Big 5): Extraversion (outgoingness), Agreeableness (care for social harmony), Conscientiousness (orderliness and self-discipline), Neuroticism (tendency to experience distress), and Openness to Experience (appreciation for art and intellectual stimuli). Big 5 personality traits are generally assessed using inventories e.g., personality tests.[2] Moreover, personality has been shown to relate to some demographic variables, including gender (Schmitt et al., 2008), age (Soto et al., 2011), and location (Schmitt et al., 2007). Results show that females score higher than males in agreeableness, extraversion, conscientiousness, and neuroticism (Schmitt et al., 2008), and that expression of all five traits subtly changes during lifetime (Soto et al., 2011). There is also evidence of correlations between MBTI and FFM (Furnham, 1996; McCrae and Costa, 1989).

NLP and personality. Research on personality and language developed from early works on essays (Pennebaker and King, 1999; Argamon et al., 2005; Luyckx and Daelemans, 2008), emails (Oberlander and Gill, 2006), EAR devices (Mehl et al., 2001), and blogs (Iacobelli et al., 2011), followed by early research on social networks (Quercia et al., 2011; Golbeck et al., 2011). In recent years, most research is done on Facebook (Schwartz et al., 2013; Celli et al., 2013; Park et al., 2015; Tandera et al., 2017; Vivek Kulkarni, 2018; Xue et al., 2018), Twitter (Plank and Hovy, 2015; Verhoeven et al., 2016; Tighe and Cheng, 2018; Ramos et al., 2018; Celli and Lepri, 2018), and Reddit (Gjurković and Šnajder, 2018; Wu et al., 2020). Due to labeling cost and privacy concerns, it has become increasingly challenging to obtain personality datasets, especially large-scale dataset are virtually nonexistent . Wiegmann et al. (2019) provide an overview of the datasets, some of which are not publicly available.

After MyPersonality dataset (Kosinski et al., 2015) became unavailable to the research community, subsequent research had to rely on the few smaller datasets based on essays (Pennebaker and

[1] https://psy.takelab.fer.hr

[2] The usual inventories for assessing Big 5 are International Personality Item Pool (IPIP; Goldberg et al., 2006), Revised NEO Personality Inventory (NEO-PI-R; Costa et al., 1991), or Big 5 Inventory (BFI; John et al., 1991). Another common inventory is HEXACO (Lee and Ashton, 2018), which adds a sixth trait, Honesty-Humility.

King, 1999), personality forums,[3] Twitter (Plank and Hovy, 2015; Verhoeven et al., 2016), and a small portion of the MyPersonality dataset (Kosinski et al., 2013) used in PAN workshops (Celli et al., 2013, 2014; Rangel et al., 2015).

To the best of our knowledge, the only work that attempted to compare prediction models for both MBTI and Big 5 is that of Celli and Lepri (2018), carried out on Twitter data. However, they did not leverage the MBTI labels in the prediction of Big 5 traits, as their dataset contained no users labeled with both personality models.

As most recent personality predictions models are based on deep learning (Majumder et al., 2017; Xue et al., 2018; Rissola et al., 2019; Wu et al., 2020; Lynn et al., 2020; Vu et al., 2020; Mehta et al., 2020; Mehta et al., 2020), large-scale multi-labeled datasets such as PANDORA can be used to develop new architectures and minimize the risk of models overfitting to spurious correlations.

User Factor Adaption. Another important line of research that would benefit from datasets like PANDORA is debiasing based on demographic data (Liu et al., 2017; Zhang et al., 2018; Pryzant et al., 2018; Elazar and Goldberg, 2018; Huang and Paul, 2019). Current research is done on demographics, with the exception of the work of Lynn et al. (2017), who use personality traits, albeit predicted. Different social media sites attract different types of users, and we expect more research of this kind on Reddit, especially considering that Reddit is the source of data for many studies on mental health (De Choudhury et al., 2016; Yates et al., 2017; Sekulic et al., 2018; Cohan et al., 2018; Turcan and McKeown, 2019; Sekulic and Strube, 2019).

3 PANDORA Dataset

Reddit is one of the most popular websites worldwide. Its users, Redditors, spend most of their online time on site and have more page views than users of other websites. This, along with the fact that users are anonymous and that the website is organized in more than a million different topics (subreddits), makes Reddit suitable for various kinds of sociolinguistic studies. To compile their MBTI9k Reddit dataset, Gjurković and Šnajder (2018) used the Pushift Reddit dataset (Baumgartner et al., 2020) to retrieve the comments dating back to 2015. We adopt MBTI9k as the starting point for PANDORA.

Ethical Research Statement. We are following the ethics code for psychological research by which researchers may dispense with informed consent of each participant for archival research, for which disclosure of responses would not place participants at risk of criminal or civil liability, or damage their financial standing, employability, or reputation, and if confidentiality is protected. As per Reddit User Agreement, users agree not to disclose sensitive information of other users and they consent that their comments are publicly available and exposed through API to other services. The users may request to have their content removed, and we have taken this into account by removing such content; future requests will be treated in the same way and escalated to Reddit. Our study has been approved by an academic IRB.

3.1 MBTI and Enneagram Labels

Gjurković and Šnajder (2018) relied on *flairs* to extract the MBTI labels. Flairs are short descriptions with which users introduce themselves on various subreddits, and on MBTI-related subreddits they typically report on MBTI test results. Owing to the fact that MBTI labels are easily identifiable, they used regular expressions to obtain the labels from flairs (and occasionally from comments). We use their labels for PANDORA, but additionally manually label for Enneagram, which users also typically report in their flairs. In total, 9,084 users reported their MBTI type in the flair, and 793 additionally reported their Enneagram type. Table 1 shows the distribution of MBTI types and dimensions (we omit Enneagram due to space constraints).

3.2 Big 5 Labels

Obtaining Big 5 labels turned out to be more challenging. Unlike MBTI and Enneagram tests, Big 5 tests result in a score for each of the five traits. Moreover, the score format itself is not standardized, thus scores are reported in various formats and they are typically reported not in flairs but in comments replying to posts which mention a specific online test. Normalization of scores poses a series of challenges. Firstly, different web sites use different inventories (e.g., *HEXACO*, *NEO PI-R*, *Aspect-scale*), some of which are publicly available while others are proprietary. The different tests use different names for traits (e.g., emotional stability as the opposite of neuroticism) or use abbreviations

[3] http://www.kaggle.com/datasnaek/mbti-type

(e.g., *OCEAN*, where *O* stands for openness, etc.). Secondly, test scores may be reported as either raw scores, percentages, or percentiles. Percentiles may be calculated based on the distribution of users that took the test or on distribution of specific groups of offline test-takers (e.g., students), in the latter case commonly adjusted for age and gender. Moreover, scores can be either numeric or descriptive, the former being in different ranges (e.g., *-100–100*, *0–100*, *1–5*) and the latter being different for each test (e.g., descriptions *typical* and *average* may map to the same underlying score). On top of this, users may decide to copy-paste the results, describe them in their own words (e.g., *rock-bottom* for low score) – often misspelling the names of the traits – or combine both. Lastly, in some cases the results do not even come from inventory-based assessments but from text-based personality prediction services (e.g., *Apply Magic Sauce* and *Watson Personality*).

Extraction. The fact that Big 5 scores are reported in full-text comments rather than flairs and that their form is not standardized makes it difficult to extract the scores fully automatically. Instead, we opted for a semiautomatic approach as follows. First, we retrieved candidate comments containing three traits most likely to be spelled correctly (*agreeableness*, *openness*, and *extraversion*). For each comment, we retrieved the corresponding post and determined what test it refers to based on the link provided, if the link was present. We first discarded all comment referring to text-based prediction services, and then used a set of regular expressions specific to the report of each test to extract personality scores from the comment. Next, we manually verified all the extracted scores and the associated comments to ensure that the comments indeed refer to a Big 5 test report and that the scores have been extracted correctly. For about 80% of reports the scores were extracted correctly, while for the remaining 20% we extracted the scores manually. This resulted in Big 5 scores for 1027 users, reported from 12 different tests. Left out from this procedure were the comments for which the test is unknown, as they were replying to posts without a link to the test. To also extract scores from these reports, we trained a test identification classifier on the reports of the 1,008 users, using character n-grams as features, and reaching an F1-macro score of 81.4% on held-out test data. We use this classifier to identify the tests referred to in the remaining comments and repeat the previous score extraction procedure. This yielded scores for additional 600 users, for a total of 1,608 users.

Normalization. To normalize the extracted scores, we first heuristically mapped score descriptions of various tests to numeric values in the 0–100 range in increments of 10. As mentioned, scores may refer to either raw scores, percentiles, or descriptions. Both percentiles and raw scores are mostly reported on the same 0–100 scale, so we refer to the information on the test used to interpret the score correctly. Finally, we convert raw scores and percentages reported by Truity[4] and HEXACO[5] to percentiles based on score distribution parameters. HEXACO reports distribution parameters publicly, while Truity provided us with parameters of the distribution of their test-takers.

Finally, for all users labeled with Big 5 labels, we retrieved all their comments from the year 2015 onward, and add these to the MBTI dataset from §3.1. The resulting dataset consists of 17,640,062 comments written by 10,288 users. There are 393 users labeled with both Big 5 and MBTI.

3.3 Demographic Labels

To obtain age, gender, and location labels, we again turn to textual descriptions provided in flairs. For each of the 10,228 users, we collected all the distinct flairs from all their comments in the dataset, and then manually inspected these flairs for age, gender, and location information. For users who reported their age in two or more flairs at different time points, we consider the age from most recent one. Additionally, we extract comment-level self-reports of users' age (e.g., *I'm 18 years old*) and gender (e.g., *I'm female/male*). As for location, users report location at different levels, mostly countries, states, and cities, but also continents and regions. We normalize location names, and map countries to country codes, countries to continents, and states to regions. Most users are from English speaking countries, and regionally evenly distributed in US and Canada (cf. Appendix). Table 1 shows the average number per user. Lastly, Table 2 gives intersection counts between personality models and other demographic variables.

[4]https://www.truity.com/

[5]http://hexaco.org/hexaco-online

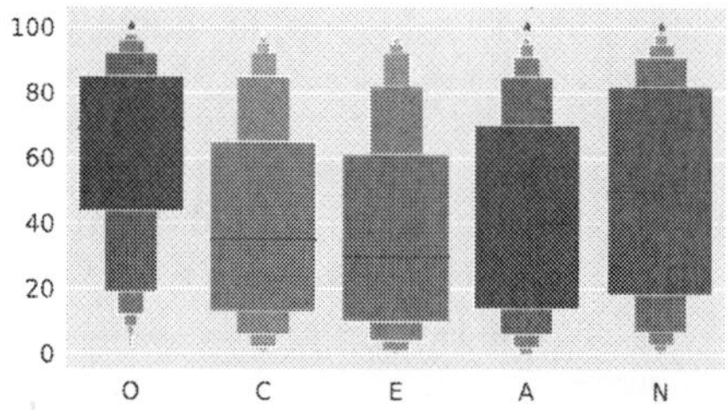

Figure 1: Distribution of Big 5 percentile scores

Big 5 Trait	All	Females	Males
Openness	62.5	62.9	64.3
Conscientiousness	40.2	43.3	41.6
Extraversion	37.4	39.7	37.6
Agreeableness	42.4	44.1	38.9
Neuroticism	49.8	51.6	46.9
Age	25.7	26.7	25.6
# Comments	1819	2004	3055
MBTI Dimension	# Users	MBTI Dimension	# Users
Introverted	7134	Extraverted	1920
Intuitive	8024	Sensing	1030
Thinking	5837	Feeling	3217
Perceiving	5302	Judging	3752

Table 1: Means of Big 5 percentile scores (n=1608), age (n=2324), number of comments per user (n=10,255) and distribution of MBTI traits (n=9054)

Variable	Big 5	MBTI	Enneagram	Unique
Gender	599	2695	345	3084
Female	232	1184	149	1331
Male	367	1511	196	1753
Age	638	1890	290	2324
Country	235	1984	182	2146
Region	74	800	65	852
Big 5	–	393	64	1608
MBTI	393	–	793	9084
Enneagram	64	793	–	794

Table 2: Intersection details for personality models and the total number of unique labels

MBTI / Big 5	O	C	E	A	N
Introverted	−.062	−.062	**−.748**	−.055	**.157**
Intuitive	**.434**	−.027	−.042	.030	.065
Thinking	−.027	**.138**	−.043	**−.554**	**−.341**
Perceiving	**.132**	**−.575**	**.145**	.055	.031
Enneagram 1	−.139	**.271**	−.012	.004	−.163
Enneagram 2	.038	**.299**	.042	**.278**	−.034
Enneagram 3	.188	.004	.143	−.069	−.097
Enneagram 4	.087	−.078	−.137	**.320**	**.342**
Enneagram 5	−.064	.006	**−.358**	−.157	−.040
Enneagram 6	−.026	.003	−.053	−.007	**.276**
Enneagram 7	.015	**−.347**	**.393**	−.119	**−.356**
Enneagram 8	−.127	.230	.234	**−.363**	−.179
Enneagram 9	−.003	−.155	−.028	.018	.090

Table 3: Correlations between gold MBTI, Enneagram, and Big 5. Significant correlations ($p<.05$) are bolded.

3.4 Analysis

Table 1 and Figure 1 show the distributions of Big 5 scores per trait.[6] We observe that the average user in our dataset is average on neuroticism, more open, and less extraverted, agreeable, and conscientious. Furthermore, males are on average younger, less agreeable, and neurotic than females. Similarly, Table 1 shows that MBTI users have a preference for introversion, intuition (i.e., openness), thinking (i.e., less agreeable), and perceiving (less conscientious). This is not surprising if we look at Table 3, which shows high correlation between particular MBTI dimensions or Enneagram types, and Big 5 traits. Correlations between Big 5 and MBTI follow the same pattern as correlations from existing psychological research (McCrae and Costa, 1989).

4 Experiments

Coupling linguistic data with psycho-demographic profiles sets the stage for many interesting research questions. We showcase this with three experiments on PANDORA.

4.1 Predicting Big 5 with MBTI/Enneagram

MBTI and Enneagram are considerably more popular than Big 5 among the social media users. This makes it relatively easy to obtain the MBTI and Enneagram labels (§3.1), and develop well-performing prediction models using supervised machine learning. On the other hand, validity of MBTI and Enneagram has been severely criticized (Barbuto Jr, 1997; Thyer, 2015), which is why they are virtually not used in psychological research. This experiment investigates whether we can combine the best of both worlds: leverage the more abundant MBTI/Enneagram labels in PANDORA to predict Big 5 traits from text. We hypothesize that the questionable psychological validity of MBTI/Enneagram labels can be compensated by their number. We base this on moderate to strong correlations observed between the personality models (Table 3) and the presence of a considerable number of users with multiple labels (Table 2).

We frame the experiment as a domain adapta-

[6]As noted by Gjurković and Šnajder (2018), due to various selection biases involved our dataset may not be representative of Reddit users, and it is certainly not representative of internet users or the general population.

tion task of transferring MBTI/Enneagram labels to Big 5 labels, using a simple domain adaptation approach from (Daumé III, 2007) (cf. Appendix for more details). We train four text-based MBTI classifiers on a subset of PANDORA users for which we have MBTI labels but no Big 5 labels. We then apply these classifiers on a subset of PANDORA users for which we have both MBTI and Big 5 labels, obtaining a type-level accuracy of MBTI prediction of 45%. Table 4 shows correlations between MBTI and Big 5 gold labels and predicted MBTI labels (cf. Appendix for Enneagram correlations). As expected, we observe lower overall correlations in comparison with correlations on gold labels (Table 3). The main observable difference is that extraversion is now moderately correlated with predicted MBTI intuitive dimension. As majority of Big 5 traits significantly correlate with more than one MBTI dimension, we use these scores as features for training five regression models, one for each Big 5 trait. Lastly, we apply both classifiers on the subset of PANDORA users for which we have Big 5 labels but no MBTI labels (serving as domain adaptation target set). We use MBTI classifiers to obtain scores for the four MBTI dimensions, and then feed these to Big 5 models to obtain predictions for the five traits. The resulting correlations (Table 5) clearly indicate that predictions based on MBTI help in predicting Big 5 traits. Furthermore, the results justify the use of regression models as predicted Big 5 traits are more correlated with gold Big 5 traits then predicted MBTI dimensions, with the exception of conscientiousness, which is significantly correlated with perceiving/judging MBTI dimension. For instance, predicted openness is a better predictor of openness than the intuitive dimension.

	Predicted			
Gold	I/E	N/S	T/F	P/J
O	−.094	**.251**	−.087	.088
C	−.003	.033	.085	**−.419**
E	**−.516**	**.118**	−.142	−.002
A	.064	.068	**−.406**	.003
N	.076	−.026	**−.234**	.007
I/E	**.513**	−.096	.023	−.066
N/S	.046	**.411**	−.043	.032
T/F	−.061	−.036	**.627**	**.141**
P/J	**−.108**	−.033	.083	**.587**

Table 4: Correlations between predicted MBTI, Enneagram and Big 5 with gold Big 5 traits on users that reported both MBTI and Big 5. Significant correlations (p<.05) are shown in bold.

Predicted	O	C	E	A	N
I/E	**−.082**	.039	**−.262**	−.003	−.002
N/S	**.127**	−.021	.049	**.060**	.001
T/F	−.001	.038	−.039	**−.259**	**−.172**
P/J	.018	**−0.41**	.007	.034	.039
O	**.147**	**−.082**	**.212**	**.145**	**.070**
C	−.007	**.237**	.013	**−.112**	**−.090**
E	.098	−.028	**.272**	.044	.022
A	.006	**−.079**	.023	**.264**	**.176**
N	−.048	−.025	−.042	**.231**	**.162**

Table 5: Correlations between predicted MBTI, Enneagram and Big 5 with gold Big 5 traits on users that reported only Big 5 traits. Significant correlations (p<.05) are shown in bold.

4.2 Gender Classification Bias

Gender classification from text is a fundamental task in author profiling, and in particular author profiling on social media has recently received a lot of attention from the NLP community (Bamman et al., 2014; Sap et al., 2014; Ciot et al., 2013). Additionally, gender is often in the spotlight of research of fairness and bias in NLP (Sun et al., 2019). Biases are often introduced by demographic and other imbalances in training data. Here we look at personality profile as a potential source of bias, and set out to investigate whether a simple gender classification model trained on Reddit exhibits biases that could be traced back to personality traits. This is an important issue, given that Reddit is often used as a source of data for training NLP models, e.g., (Zhang et al., 2017; Cheng et al., 2017; Henderson et al., 2019; Sekulic and Strube, 2019).

To build a gender classifier, we retrieve a separate Reddit dataset and label it automatically for gender. To this end, we again rely on flairs, using strings"/f/" and "/m/" as female and male gender indicators, respectively.[7] This method yields a 98.5% precision on PANDORA. From the 34k users that used these patterns in their flairs, we sampled a balanced dataset of 24,954 users and retrieved over 30M of their comments, removing quoted text and all comments shorter than five words. Next, we aggregate the comments per user, and divide the users in an 80%–20% train-test split. For classification, we use logistic regression with 500-dimensional SVD vectors derived from Tf-Idf word n-grams.

[7]Although the construct of gender is not binary, we limit our present analysis to users who reported binary gender to obtain a more balanced dataset for bias analysis.

	Female			Male		
Variable	✓	✗	Δ	✓	✗	Δ
Age	26.78	25.83	**0.95***	25.46	26.90	−1.44
I/E	0.78	0.72	0.06	0.76	0.82	−0.06
N/S	0.86	0.91	−0.05	0.92	0.93	−0.01
T/F	0.47	0.64	**−0.17*****	0.61	0.29	**0.32*****
P/J	0.39	0.56	**−0.17*****	0.53	0.39	**0.14*****
O	61.40	68.18	−6,78	64.11	67.20	−3.09
C	45.28	36.44	8.84	41.10	47.50	−6.40
E	40.67	36.44	4.23	36.68	49.60	**−12.92***
A	45.07	40.78	4.29	38.43	44.70	−6.27
N	50.95	53.72	−2.77	46.81	47.50	−0.69

Table 6: Differences in means of psycho-demographic variables per gender and classification outcome. Significant correlations (*p<.05, ***p<.001) are in bold.

The test accuracy of the classifier was 89.9%. The accuracy of the classifier on 3,084 users from PANDORA with known gender was 89.3%.

We now turn to bias analysis. On PANDORA, the classifier failed to predict the correct gender for 8.1% male (142/1743) and 14.4% female (192/1331) users. As this is a statistically significant difference (p<0.05 with two-proportion Z-Test), we conclude that the classifier is biased. To investigate this further, we divide male and female users into those for which the predictions were correct and those for which they were incorrect. We then test for statistically significant differences (using two-proportion Z-test for binary variables and Kruskal-Wallis H-test for continuous variables) of psycho-demographic variables between correctly and incorrectly classified cases for both groups. Results are shown in Table 6. Differences are statistically significant for thinking and perceiving MBTI dimensions for both females and males, for extraversion Big 5 trait for males, and for age in females. Thinking and perceiving preference for females makes them more likely to be misclassified for males, and the reverse holds for males. Furthermore, the gender of more extraverted males is more likely to be misclassified. When it comes to age, younger females are more often in misclassified group. These findings clearly indicate that a complete psycho-demographic profile is a useful tool for bias analysis of machine learning models trained on social media text.

4.3 Propensity for Philosophy

Our last experiment investigates the usefulness of PANDORA for research in social sciences. One obvious type of use cases are confirmatory studies which aim to replicate present theories and findings on a dataset that has been obtained in a manner different from typical datasets in the field. Another type of use cases are exploratory studies that seek to identify new relations between psycho-demographic variables manifested in online talk. Here we present a use case of both types. We focus on propensity for philosophy of Reddit users (manifested as propensity for philosophical topics in online discussions), and seek to confirm its hypothesized positive relationship with openness to experiences (Johnson, 2014; Dollinger et al., 1996), cognitive processing (e.g., insight), and readability index. We expect this to be confirmed since all four variables share proneness to higher intellectual engagement. For exploratory analysis, we extend our analysis to emotion variables.

We conducted the analysis using hierarchical regression analysis with propensity for philosophical topics as the criterion variable and demographics, personality, emotions, cognitive processing, and text readability as predictors. As a measure of propensity for philosophical topics, we compute the "philosophy" feature (frequency of philosophical words) from Empath (Fast et al., 2016) for each user's comments. Similarly, for the predictors we compute posemo, negemo, and insight features from LIWC (Pennebaker et al., 2015) and Flesh-Kincaid Grade Level (F-K GL) readability score (Kincaid et al., 1975).[8] Emotion variables are inserted for the exploratory analysis. In the hierarchical regression analysis, demographics were added as control variables in the first step, Big 5 traits were added in the second step, emotion variables in the third step, and finally insight feature as a cognitive inclination variable and F-K GL readability index were added in the last step. The sample comprises 430 Reddit users, 273 males and 157 females, with the mean age of 26.79 (SD=7.954), who all had gold labels of gender, age, and Big 5.

The analysis yields interesting results.[9] Firstly, as much as the 41% of variance in the "philosophy" feature is explained by the 11 predictors. Secondly, openness to experiences, readability index, and insight are, as expected, all significant and positive predictors of the "philosophy" feature. Agreeable-

[8] We counted the frequencies per comment, divided it by total number of words in a comment, multiplied with 100, and averaged for total comments.

[9] Multivariate normality and multicollinearity were satisfied, and homoscedasticity was satisfied after removing 14 outliers based on standardized residuals.

Predictors	Regression coefficients				
	Step 1	Step 2	Step 3	Step 4	Step 5
Gender	−.26**	−.24**	−.20**	−.19**	−.17**
Age	−.01	−.03	−.02	.00	.01
O	–	.20**	.19**	.15**	.10**
C	–	.01	.05	.08	.07
E	–	.02	.03	.04	.04
A	–	−.12*	−.05	−.05	−.06
N	–	−.04	−.03	.01	.02
posemo	–	–	.15**	.17**	.03
negemo	–	–	.29**	.27**	.29**
insight	–	–	–	.36**	.27**
F-K GL	–	–	–	–	.34**
R^2	.07	.12	.22	.34	.43
Adjusted R^2	.06	.11	.20	.32	.41
R^2 change	.07**	.06**	.10**	.12**	.09**

Table 7: Hierarchical regression of propensity for philosophical topics ("philosophy" feature from Empath) on gender, age, Big 5 personality traits, Flesh-Kincaid Grade Level readability scores, positive and negative emotions features, and insight feature as predictors (n=430). The table shows regression coefficients and the goodness of fit as measured by R^2, adjusted R^2, and R^2 change. Significant correlations: *p<.05, **p<.01, ***p<.001

ness was a negative significant predictor before adding the emotion variables. This is not surprising, as people low in agreeableness are less likely to pander to others, and agreeableness shows significant correlations with both positive (.20) and negative emotions (-.13). Thirdly, the results imply alluring associations with emotion variables. Negative emotions were clearly positive predictors of frequency of discussing philosophical topics. However, positive emotions were a significant predictor until the last step when F-K GL was added to the model. This was due to moderate correlation between posemo and F-K GL (-0.40). Lastly, males had higher frequency of words related to philosophy than females. To sum up, the hypothesis is confirmed and exploratory analysis yields interesting results which could motivate further research.

5 Prediction Models

In this section we describe baseline models for predicting personality and demographic variables from user comments in PANDORA.

We consider the following sets of features: (1) **N-grams:** Tf-Idf weighted 1–3 word ngrams and 2–5 character n-grams; (2) **Stylistic**: the counts of words, characters, and syllables, mono/polysyllable words, long words, unique words, as well as all readability metrics implemented in Textacy[10]; (3) **Dictionaries**: words mapped to Tf-Idf categories from LIWC (Pennebaker et al., 2015), Empath (Fast et al., 2016), and NRC Emotion Lexicon (Mohammad and Turney, 2013) dictionaries; (4) **Gender**: predictions of the gender classifier from §4.2; (5) **Subreddit distributions**: a matrix where each row is a distribution of post counts across all subreddits for a particular user, reduced using PCA to 50 features per user; (6) **Subreddit other**: counts of downs, score, gilded, ups, as well as the controversiality scores for a comment; (7) **Named entities**: the number of named entities per comment, as extracted using Spacy;[11] (8) **Part-of-speech**: counts for each part-of-speech; (9) **Predictions** (only for predicting Big 5 traits): MBTI/Enneagram predictions obtained by a classifier built on held-out data. Features (2), (4), and (6–9) are calculated at the level of individual comments and aggregated to min, max, mean, standard deviation, and median values for each user.

We build six regression models (age and Big 5 traits) and eight classification models (four MBTI dimensions, gender, region, Enneagram). We experiment with linear/logistic regression (LR) from sklearn (Pedregosa et al., 2011) and deep learning models (NN). We trained a separate NN model for each task. In each model, a single user is represented as a matrix, with rows representing the user's comments. The comments were encoded using 1024-dimensional vectors derived using BERT (Devlin et al., 2019). BERT comment vectors are fed into convolution layers, max pooling, and several fully connected layers. Hyperparameters and additional information can be found in the Appendix.

We evaluate the models using 5-fold cross-validation with a separate stratified split for each target. We use regression F-tests to select top-K features, and optimize model hyperparameters and K on held-out data for each fold separately.

Results are shown in Table 8. LR performs best when using only the n-gram features. An exception are Big 5 trait predictions, which benefit considerably from adding the MBTI/Enneagram predictions as features, building on Section 4.1 and Table 3. Also, using 1000 comments rather than last 100 (as in NN) increased scores up to 5 points.

[10]https://chartbeat-labs.github.io/textacy

[11]https://spacy.io/

	LR					
	NO	N	O	NOP	NP	NN
Classification (Macro-averaged F1 score)						
Introverted	.649	**.654**	.559	–	–	.546
Intuitive	.599	**.606**	.518	–	–	.528
Thinking	.730	**.739**	.678	–	–	.634
Perceiving	.626	**.642**	.586	–	–	.566
Enneagram	.155	**.251**	.145	–	–	.143
Gender	.889	**.904**	.825	–	–	.843
Region	.206	**.626**	.144	–	–	.478
Regression (Pearson correlation coefficient)						
Agreeableness	.181	.232	.085	.237	**.270**	.210
Openness	.235	**.265**	.180	.235	.250	.159
Conscientiousness	.194	.162	.093	.245	**.273**	.120
Neuroticism	.194	.244	.138	.266	**.283**	.149
Extraversion	.271	.327	.058	.286	**.387**	.167
Age	.704	**.750**	.469	–	–	.396

Table 8: Prediction results for the different traits for LR and NN models. For the LR model, we show the results for different feature combinations, including N-grams (N), MBTI/Enneagram predictions (P), and all other features (O). Best results are shown in bold.

6 Conclusion

PANDORA dataset comprises 17M comments, personality, and demographic labels for over 10k Reddit users, including 1.6k users with Big 5 labels. To our knowledge, this is the first Reddit dataset with Big 5 traits, and also the first covering multiple personality models (Big 5, MBTI, Enneagram). We showcased the usefulness of PANDORA with three experiments, showing (1) how more readily available MBTI/Enneagram labels can be used to estimate Big 5 traits, (2) that a gender classifier trained on Reddit exhibits bias on users of certain personality traits, and (3) that certain psycho-demographic variables are good predictors of propensity for philosophy of Reddit users. We also trained and evaluated benchmark prediction models for all psycho-demographic variables. The poor performance of deep learning baseline models, the rich set of labels, and the large number of comments per user in PANDORA suggest that further efforts should be directed toward efficient user representations and more advanced deep learning architectures.

Acknowledgements

We thank the reviewers for their remarks. This work has been fully supported by the Croatian Science Foundation under the project IP-2020-02-8671 PSYTXT ("Computational Models for Text-Based Personality Prediction and Analysis").

References

Shlomo Argamon, Sushant Dhawle, Moshe Koppel, and James Pennebaker. 2005. Lexical predictors of personality type. In *Proceedings of the Joint Annual Meeting of the Interface and the Classification Society*, pages 1–16.

David Bamman, Jacob Eisenstein, and Tyler Schnoebelen. 2014. Gender identity and lexical variation in social media. *Journal of Sociolinguistics*, 18(2):135–160.

John E. Barbuto Jr. 1997. A critique of the Myers-Briggs Type Indicator and its operationalization of Carl Jung's psychological types. *Psychological Reports*, 80(2):611–625.

Jason Baumgartner, Savvas Zannettou, Brian Keegan, Megan Squire, and Jeremy Blackburn. 2020. The pushshift reddit dataset. *Proceedings of the International AAAI Conference on Web and Social Media*, 14(1):830–839.

Tammy L. Bess and Robert J. Harvey. 2002. Bimodal score distributions and the myers–briggs type indicator: Fact or artifact? *Journal of Personality Assessment*, 78(1):176–186.

Fabio Celli and Bruno Lepri. 2018. Is big five better than mbti? A personality computing challenge using twitter data. In *Proceedings of the Fifth Italian Conference on Computational Linguistics (CLiC-it 2018), Torino, Italy, December 10-12, 2018*, volume 2253 of *CEUR Workshop Proceedings*. CEUR-WS.org.

Fabio Celli, Bruno Lepri, Joan-Isaac Biel, Daniel Gatica-Perez, Giuseppe Riccardi, and Fabio Pianesi. 2014. The workshop on computational personality recognition 2014. In *Proceedings of the 22nd ACM international conference on Multimedia*, pages 1245–1246. ACM.

Fabio Celli, Fabio Pianesi, David Stillwell, and Michal Kosinski. 2013. Workshop on computational personality recognition: Shared task. In *Proceedings of the AAAI Workshop on Computational Personality Recognition*, pages 2–5.

Kai-Wei Chang, Vinod Prabhakaran, and Vicente Ordonez. 2019. Bias and fairness in natural language processing. In *Proceedings of the 2019 Conference on Empirical Methods in Natural Language Processing and the 9th International Joint Conference on Natural Language Processing (EMNLP-IJCNLP): Tutorial Abstracts*.

Hao Cheng, Hao Fang, and Mari Ostendorf. 2017. A factored neural network model for characterizing online discussions in vector space. In *Proceedings of the 2017 Conference on Empirical Methods in Natural Language Processing*, pages 2296–2306, Copenhagen, Denmark. Association for Computational Linguistics.

Morgane Ciot, Morgan Sonderegger, and Derek Ruths. 2013. Gender inference of Twitter users in non-English contexts. In *Proceedings of the 2013 Conference on Empirical Methods in Natural Language Processing*, pages 1136–1145, Seattle, Washington, USA. Association for Computational Linguistics.

Arman Cohan, Bart Desmet, Andrew Yates, Luca Soldaini, Sean MacAvaney, and Nazli Goharian. 2018. SMHD: a large-scale resource for exploring online language usage for multiple mental health conditions. In *Proceedings of the 27th International Conference on Computational Linguistics*, pages 1485–1497, Santa Fe, New Mexico, USA. Association for Computational Linguistics.

Paul T. Costa, Robert R. McCrae, and David A. Dye. 1991. Facet scales for agreeableness and cpnscientiousness: A revision of the neo personality inventory. *Personality and Individual Differences*, 12(9):887–898.

Hal Daumé III. 2007. Frustratingly easy domain adaptation. In *Proceedings of the 45th Annual Meeting of the Association of Computational Linguistics*, pages 256–263, Prague, Czech Republic. Association for Computational Linguistics.

Munmun De Choudhury, Emre Kiciman, Mark Dredze, Glen Coppersmith, and Mrinal Kumar. 2016. Discovering shifts to suicidal ideation from mental health content in social media. In *Proceedings of the 2016 CHI conference on human factors in computing systems*, pages 2098–2110. ACM.

Jacob Devlin, Ming-Wei Chang, Kenton Lee, and Kristina Toutanova. 2019. BERT: Pre-training of deep bidirectional transformers for language understanding. In *Proceedings of the 2019 Conference of the North American Chapter of the Association for Computational Linguistics: Human Language Technologies, Volume 1 (Long and Short Papers)*, pages 4171–4186, Minneapolis, Minnesota. Association for Computational Linguistics.

Stephen J. Dollinger, Frederick T. Leong, and Shawna K. Ulicni. 1996. On traits and values: With special reference to openness to experience. *Journal of Research in Personality*, 30(1):23–41.

Jacob Eisenstein, Brendan O'Connor, Noah A Smith, and Eric P Xing. 2010. A latent variable model for geographic lexical variation. In *Proceedings of the 2010 conference on empirical methods in natural language processing*, pages 1277–1287. Association for Computational Linguistics.

Yanai Elazar and Yoav Goldberg. 2018. Adversarial removal of demographic attributes from text data. In *Proceedings of the 2018 Conference on Empirical Methods in Natural Language Processing*, pages 11–21, Brussels, Belgium. Association for Computational Linguistics.

Ethan Fast, Binbin Chen, and Michael S Bernstein. 2016. Empath: Understanding topic signals in large-scale text. In *Proceedings of the 2016 CHI Conference on Human Factors in Computing Systems*, pages 4647–4657. ACM.

Adrian Furnham. 1996. The big five versus the big four: the relationship between the Myers-Briggs Type Indicator (MBTI) and NEO-PI five factor model of personality. *Personality and Individual Differences*, 21(2):303–307.

Matej Gjurković and Jan Šnajder. 2018. Reddit: A gold mine for personality prediction. In *Proceedings of the Second Workshop on Computational Modeling of People's Opinions, Personality, and Emotions in Social Media*, pages 87–97, New Orleans, Louisiana, USA. Association for Computational Linguistics.

Jennifer Golbeck, Cristina Robles, Michon Edmondson, and Karen Turner. 2011. Predicting personality from Twitter. In *Proceedings of 2011 IEEE International Conference on Privacy, Security, Risk and Trust (PASSAT) and IEEE International Conference on Social Computing (SocialCom)*, pages 149–156.

Lewis R. Goldberg. 1992. The development of markers for the big-five factor structure. *Psychological Assessment*, 4(1):26—-42.

Lewis R. Goldberg, John A. Johnson, Herbert W. Eber, Robert Hogan, Mihael C. Ashton, C. Robert Cloninger, and Harrison G. Gough. 2006. The geographic distribution of big five personality traits: Patterns and profiles of human self-description across 56 nations. *Journal of Research in Personality*, 40(1):84–96.

Matthew Henderson, Paweł Budzianowski, Iñigo Casanueva, Sam Coope, Daniela Gerz, Girish Kumar, Nikola Mrkšić, Georgios Spithourakis, Pei-Hao Su, Ivan Vulić, and Tsung-Hsien Wen. 2019. A repository of conversational datasets. In *Proceedings of the First Workshop on NLP for Conversational AI*, pages 1–10, Florence, Italy. Association for Computational Linguistics.

Xiaolei Huang and Michael J. Paul. 2019. Neural user factor adaptation for text classification: Learning to generalize across author demographics. In *Proceedings of the Eighth Joint Conference on Lexical and Computational Semantics (*SEM 2019)*, pages 136–146, Minneapolis, Minnesota. Association for Computational Linguistics.

Francisco Iacobelli, Alastair J. Gill, Scott Nowson, and Jon Oberlander. 2011. Large scale personality classification of bloggers. In *Affective computing and intelligent interaction*, pages 568–577. Springer.

Oliver P. John, Eileen M. Donahue, and Robert L. Kentle. 1991. *The Big Five Inventory–Versions 4a and 54*. Berkeley, CA: University of California,Berkeley, Institute of Personality and Social Research.

John A. Johnson. 2014. Measuring thirty facets of the five factor model with a 120-item public domain inventory: Development of the ipip-neo-120. *Journal of Research in Personality*, 51:78–89.

J. Peter Kincaid, Robert P. Jr. Fishburne, Rogers Richard L., and Chissom Brad S. 1975. Derivation of New Readability Formulas (Automated Readability Index, Fog Count and Flesch Reading Ease Formula) for Navy Enlisted Personnel.

Michal Kosinski, Sandra C. Matz, Samuel D. Gosling, Vesselin Popov, and David Stillwell. 2015. Facebook as a research tool for the social sciences: Opportunities, challenges, ethical considerations, and practical guidelines. *American Psychologist*, 70(6):543.

Michal Kosinski, David Stillwell, and Thore Graepel. 2013. Private traits and attributes are predictable from digital records of human behavior. *Proceedings of the National Academy of Sciences*, 110(15):5802–5805.

Kibeom Lee and Michael C. Ashton. 2018. Psychometric properties of the hexaco-100. *Assessment*, 25(5):543–556.

Pengfei Liu, Xipeng Qiu, and Xuanjing Huang. 2017. Adversarial multi-task learning for text classification. *Proceedings of the 55th Annual Meeting of the Association for Computational Linguistics (Volume 1: Long Papers)*.

Kim Luyckx and Walter Daelemans. 2008. Personae: A corpus for author and personality prediction from text. In *Proceedings of the Sixth International Conference on Language Resources and Evaluation (LREC'08)*, pages 2981–2987.

Veronica Lynn, Niranjan Balasubramanian, and H. Andrew Schwartz. 2020. Hierarchical modeling for user personality prediction: The role of message-level attention. In *Proceedings of the 58th Annual Meeting of the Association for Computational Linguistics*, pages 5306–5316, Online. Association for Computational Linguistics.

Veronica Lynn, Youngseo Son, Vivek Kulkarni, Niranjan Balasubramanian, and H. Andrew Schwartz. 2017. Human centered NLP with user-factor adaptation. In *Proceedings of the 2017 Conference on Empirical Methods in Natural Language Processing*, pages 1146–1155, Copenhagen, Denmark. Association for Computational Linguistics.

N. Majumder, S. Poria, A. Gelbukh, and E. Cambria. 2017. Deep learning-based document modeling for personality detection from text. *IEEE Intelligent Systems*, 32(2):74–79.

Robert R. McCrae and Paul T. Costa. 1989. Reinterpreting the Myers-Briggs type indicator from the perspective of the five-factor model of personality. *Journal of personality*, 57(1):17–40.

Robert R. McCrae and Oliver P. John. 1992. An introduction to the five-factor model and its applications. *Journal of Personality*, 60(2):175–215.

Matthias R. Mehl, James W. Pennebaker, D. Michael Crow, James Dabbs, and John H. Price. 2001. The electronically activated recorder (EAR): A device for sampling naturalistic daily activities and conversations. *Behavior Research Methods, Instruments, & Computers*, 33(4):517–523.

Y. Mehta, S. Fatehi, A. Kazameini, C. Stachl, E. Cambria, and S. Eetemadi. 2020. Bottom-up and top-down: Predicting personality with psycholinguistic and language model features. In *2020 IEEE International Conference on Data Mining (ICDM)*, pages 1184–1189.

Yash Mehta, Navonil Majumder, Alexander Gelbukh, and Erik Cambria. 2020. Recent trends in deep learning based personality detection. *Artificial Intelligence Review*, 53:2313–2339.

Saif M Mohammad and Peter D Turney. 2013. Crowdsourcing a word–emotion association lexicon. *Computational Intelligence*, 29(3):436–465.

Isabel Briggs Myers, Mary H. McCaulley, and Allen L. Hammer. 1990. *Introduction to Type: A description of the theory and applications of the Myers-Briggs type indicator*. Consulting Psychologists Press.

Dong Nguyen, A. Seza Doğruöz, Carolyn P. Rosé, and Franciska de Jong. 2016. Survey: Computational sociolinguistics: A Survey. *Computational Linguistics*, 42(3):537–593.

Jon Oberlander and Alastair J. Gill. 2006. Language with character: A stratified corpus comparison of individual differences in e-mail communication. *Discourse Processes*, 42(3):239–270.

Gregory Park, H Andrew Schwartz, Johannes C Eichstaedt, Margaret L Kern, Michal Kosinski, David J. Stillwell, Lyle H. Ungar, and Martin E.P. Seligman. 2015. Automatic personality assessment through social media language. *Journal of personality and social psychology*, 108(6):934.

F. Pedregosa, G. Varoquaux, A. Gramfort, V. Michel, B. Thirion, O. Grisel, M. Blondel, P. Prettenhofer, R. Weiss, V. Dubourg, J. Vanderplas, A. Passos, D. Cournapeau, M. Brucher, M. Perrot, and E. Duchesnay. 2011. Scikit-learn: Machine learning in Python. *Journal of Machine Learning Research*, 12:2825–2830.

Claudia Peersman, Walter Daelemans, and Leona Van Vaerenbergh. 2011. Predicting age and gender in online social networks. In *Proceedings of the 3rd international workshop on Search and mining user-generated contents*, pages 37–44. ACM.

James W. Pennebaker, Ryan L. Boyd, Kayla Jordan, and Kate Blackburn. 2015. The development and psychometric properties of LIWC2015. Technical report.

James W. Pennebaker and Laura A. King. 1999. Linguistic styles: Language use as an individual difference. *Journal of personality and social psychology*, 77(6):1296.

Barbara Plank and Dirk Hovy. 2015. Personality traits on Twitter –or– how to get 1,500 personality tests in a week. In *Proceedings of the 6th Workshop on Computational Approaches to Subjectivity, Sentiment and Social Media Analysis (WASSA 2015)*, pages 92–98.

Reid Pryzant, Kelly Shen, Dan Jurafsky, and Stefan Wagner. 2018. Deconfounded lexicon induction for interpretable social science. In *Proceedings of the 2018 Conference of the North American Chapter of the Association for Computational Linguistics: Human Language Technologies, Volume 1 (Long Papers)*, pages 1615–1625, New Orleans, Louisiana. Association for Computational Linguistic.

Daniele Quercia, Michal Kosinski, David Stillwell, and Jon Crowcroft. 2011. Our Twitter profiles, our selves: Predicting personality with Twitter. In *Proceedings of 2011 IEEE International Conference on Privacy, Security, Risk and Trust (PASSAT) and IEEE International Conference on Social Computing (SocialCom)*, pages 180–185.

Ricelli Ramos, Georges Neto, Barbara Silva, Danielle Monteiro, Ivandré Paraboni, and Rafael Dias. 2018. Building a corpus for personality-dependent natural language understanding and generation. In *Proceedings of the Eleventh International Conference on Language Resources and Evaluation (LREC 2018)*, Miyazaki, Japan. European Language Resources Association (ELRA).

Francisco Rangel, Paolo Rosso, Martin Potthast, Benno Stein, and Walter Daelemans. 2015. Overview of the 3rd author profiling task at PAN 2015. In *CLEF 2015 labs and workshops, notebook papers, CEUR Workshop Proceedings*, volume 1391.

Esteban Andres Rissola, Seyed Ali Bahrainian, and Fabio Crestani. 2019. Personality recognition in conversations using capsule neural networks. In *IEEE/WIC/ACM International Conference on Web Intelligence*, WI '19, page 180–187, New York, NY, USA. Association for Computing Machinery.

Maarten Sap, Gregory Park, Johannes Eichstaedt, Margaret Kern, David Stillwell, Michal Kosinski, Lyle Ungar, and Hansen Andrew Schwartz. 2014. Developing age and gender predictive lexica over social media. In *Proceedings of the 2014 Conference on Empirical Methods in Natural Language Processing (EMNLP)*, pages 1146–1151, Doha, Qatar. Association for Computational Linguistics.

David P. Schmitt, Juri Allik, Robert R. McCrae, and Veronica Benet-Martinez. 2007. The geographic distribution of big five personality traits: Patterns and profiles of human self-description across 56 nations. *Journal of cross-cultural psychology*, 38(2):173–212.

David P. Schmitt, Anu Realo, Martin Voracek, and Juri Allik. 2008. Why can't a man be more like a woman? sex differences in big five personality traits across 55 cultures. *Journal of Personality and Social Psychology*, 94(1):168–182.

Andrew H. Schwartz, Johannes C. Eichstaedt, Margaret L. Kern, Lukasz Dziurzynski, Stephanie M. Ramones, Megha Agrawal, Achal Shah, Michal Kosinski, David Stillwell, Martin E.P. Seligman, et al. 2013. Personality, gender, and age in the language of social media: The open-vocabulary approach. *PloS one*, 8(9):e73791.

Ivan Sekulic, Matej Gjurković, and Jan Šnajder. 2018. Not just depressed: Bipolar disorder prediction on Reddit. In *Proceedings of the 9th Workshop on Computational Approaches to Subjectivity, Sentiment and Social Media Analysis*, pages 72–78, Brussels, Belgium. Association for Computational Linguistics.

Ivan Sekulic and Michael Strube. 2019. Adapting deep learning methods for mental health prediction on social media. In *Proceedings of the 5th Workshop on Noisy User-generated Text (W-NUT 2019)*, pages 322–327, Hong Kong, China. Association for Computational Linguistics.

Christopher J. Soto, Oliver P. John, Samuel D. Gosling, and Jeff Potter. 2011. Age differences in personality traits from 10 to 65: Big five domains and facets in a large cross-sectional sample. *Journal of Personality and Social Psychology*, 100(2):330–348.

Tony Sun, Andrew Gaut, Shirlyn Tang, Yuxin Huang, Mai ElSherief, Jieyu Zhao, Diba Mirza, Elizabeth Belding, Kai-Wei Chang, and William Yang Wang. 2019. Mitigating gender bias in natural language processing: Literature review. In *Proceedings of the 57th Annual Meeting of the Association for Computational Linguistics*, pages 1630–1640, Florence, Italy. Association for Computational Linguistics.

Tommy Tandera, Derwin Suhartono, Rini Wongso, Yen Lina Prasetio, et al. 2017. Personality prediction system from Facebook users. *Procedia computer science*, 116:604–611.

Monica Thyer, Dr Bruce A.; Pignotti. 2015. *Science and Pseudoscience in Social Work Practice*. Springer Publishing Company.

Edward Tighe and Charibeth Cheng. 2018. Modeling personality traits of Filipino twitter users. In *Proceedings of the Second Workshop on Computational Modeling of People's Opinions, Personality, and Emotions in Social Media*, pages 112–122, New Orleans, Louisiana, USA. Association for Computational Linguistics.

Elsbeth Turcan and Kathy McKeown. 2019. Dreaddit: A Reddit dataset for stress analysis in social media. In *Proceedings of the Tenth International Workshop on Health Text Mining and Information Analysis (LOUHI 2019)*, pages 97–107, Hong Kong. Association for Computational Linguistics.

Ben Verhoeven, Walter Daelemans, and Barbara Plank. 2016. TwiSty: A multilingual Twitter stylometry corpus for gender and personality profiling. In *Proceedings of the Tenth International Conference on Language Resources and Evaluation (LREC 2016)*, pages 1632–1637.

David Stillwell Michal Kosinski Sandra Matz Lyle Ungar Steven Skiena H. Andrew Schwartz Vivek Kulkarni, Margaret L. Kern. 2018. Latent human traits in the language of social media: An open-vocabulary approach. *Plos One*, 13(11).

Huy Vu, Suhaib Abdurahman, Sudeep Bhatia, and Lyle Ungar. 2020. Predicting responses to psychological questionnaires from participants' social media posts and question text embeddings. In *Findings of the Association for Computational Linguistics: EMNLP 2020*, pages 1512–1524, Online. Association for Computational Linguistics.

Matti Wiegmann, Benno Stein, and Martin Potthast. 2019. Celebrity profiling. In *Proceedings of the 57th Annual Meeting of the Association for Computational Linguistics*, pages 2611–2618, Florence, Italy. Association for Computational Linguistics.

Xiaodong Wu, Weizhe Lin, Zhilin Wang, and Elena Rastorgueva. 2020. Author2vec: A framework for generating user embedding. *arXiv preprint arXiv:2003.11627*.

Di Xue, Lifa Wu, Zheng Hong, Shize Guo, Liang Gao, Zhiyong Wu, Xiaofeng Zhong, and Jianshan Sun. 2018. Deep learning-based personality recognition from text posts of online social networks. *Applied Intelligence*, pages 1–15.

Andrew Yates, Arman Cohan, and Nazli Goharian. 2017. Depression and self-harm risk assessment in online forums. In *Proceedings of the 2017 Conference on Empirical Methods in Natural Language Processing*, pages 2968–2978, Copenhagen, Denmark. Association for Computational Linguistics.

Amy Zhang, Bryan Culbertson, and Praveen Paritosh. 2017. Characterizing online discussion using coarse discourse sequences. In *11th AAAI International Conference on Web and Social Media (ICWSM)*, Montreal, Canada. Association for the Advancement of Artificial Intelligence.

Brian Hu Zhang, Blake Lemoine, and Margaret Mitchell. 2018. Mitigating unwanted biases with adversarial learning. In *Proceedings of the 2018 AAAI/ACM Conference on AI, Ethics, and Society*, AIES '18, pages 335–340, New York, NY, USA. ACM.

A Demographics of PANDORA

Continent	# Users	Continent	# Users
North America	1299	Africa	4
Europe	580	South America	24
Asia	103	Oceania	85
Country	**# Users**	**Region**	**# Users**
US	1107	US West	208
Canada	180	US Midwest	153
UK	164	US Southeast	144
Australia	72	US Northeast	138
Germany	53	US Southwest	100
Netherlands	37	Canada West	50
Sweden	33	Canada East	44

Table 9: Geographical distribution of users per continent, country, and region (for US and Canada)

Language	# Comments
English	16637211
Spanish	87309
French	72651
Italian	64819
German	63492
Portuguese	32037
Dutch	30219
Esperanto	19501
Swedish	16880
Polish	15134

Table 10: Language distribution

Table 9 shows that most users are from English speaking countries, and regionally evenly distributed in US and Canada. For mapping states to regions, there are different regional divisions for the U.S. and Canada. We used five regions for US, and three for Canada (for one region there was no users).

Additionally, for each comment we ran fast text based language identification.[12] Table 10 shows the number of comments for top 10 languages.

B Additional Information on Personality Scores

Table 11 shows counts of all 16 MBTI types. Four MBTI types (*INTP, INTJ, INFP* and *INFJ*) account for 75 percent of all users. This indicates that there is a shift in personality distributions in contrast to the general public. Table 12 contains means and standard deviations for descriptions and percentiles of every Big 5 trait. Table 13 shows the distribution of tests and their inventories in PANDORA.

[12]https://fasttext.cc/docs/en/language-identification.html

MBTI Type	Users	MBTI Type	Users
INTP	2833	ISTJ	194
INTJ	1841	ENFJ	162
INFP	1071	ISFP	123
INFJ	1051	ISFJ	109
ENTP	627	ESTP	71
ENFJ	616	ESFP	51
ISTP	408	ESTJ	43
ENTJ	319	ESFJ	29

Table 11: MBTI types for 9,048 users

Trait	Descriptions	Percentiles
Agreeableness	50.10 ± 29.10	42.39 ± 30.89
Openness	67.37 ± 26.76	67.27 ± 26.87
Conscientiousness	41.29 ± 27.97	40.48 ± 30.22
Extraversion	38.70 ± 27.53	37.09 ± 31.16
Neuroticism	55.95 ± 31.11	52.82 ± 31.97

Table 12: Big 5 results distribution on different reported scales for 1,652 users

Online test	Based on inventory	# Users	# Pred
Truity	IPIP, NEO-PI-R, Goldberg's (1992) markers	378	362
Understand Myself	Big 5 Aspects	268	167
IPIP 120	IPIP-NEO-120	120	83
IPIP 300	IPIP-NEO-300	60	18
Personality Assesor	BFI	66	10
HEXACO	HEXACO-PI-R	49	1
Outofservice	BFI	38	11
Qualtrics	–	19	8
123test	IPIP-NEO, NEO-PI-R	16	6

Table 13: Big 5 personality test distribution in reports

Predicted	O	C	E	A	N
Enneagram 1	.002	.032	−.028	.047	.025
Enneagram 2	−.011	**.108**	.030	**.135**	**.046**
Enneagram 3	**.085**	.014	**.071**	−.064	**−.069**
Enneagram 4	−.041	−.017	−.033	**.166**	**.159**
Enneagram 5	**.067**	−.035	**−.060**	**−.121**	**−.076**
Enneagram 6	−.051	.004	−.035	.046	**.113**
Enneagram 7	−.043	−.019	**.078**	**−.085**	**−.088**
Enneagram 8	.022	−.044	**.063**	**−.129**	**−.075**
Enneagram 9	−.034	−.016	**−.102**	.041	−.005

Table 14: Correlations between Enneagram types and Big 5 traits. Significant correlations ($p<.05$) are shown in bold.

C Predicting Big 5 with MBTI/Enneagram

Here we describe in more details the setup for predicting Big 5 labels using MBTI/Enneagram labels.

We frame the experiment as a domain adaptation task of transferring MBTI/Enneagram labels to Big 5 labels, and use one of the simplest domain adaptation approaches where we use source classifier (MBTI) predictions as features and linearly interpolate them on development set containing both MBTI and Big 5 to make predictions on Big 5 target set (e.g., *PRED* and *LININT* baselines from (Daumé III, 2007)). We first partition PANDORA into three subsets: comments of users for which we have both MBTI and Big 5 labels (M+B+, n=382), comments of users for which we have the MBTI but no Big 5 labels (M+B-, n=8,691), and comments of users for which we have the Big 5 but no MBTI labels (M-B+, n=1,588). We then proceed in three steps. In the first step, we train on M+B- four text-based MBTI classifiers, one for each MBTI dimension (logistic regression, optimized with 5-fold CV, using 7000 filter-selected, Tf-Idf-weighed 1–5 word and character n-grams as features).

In the second step, we use text-based MBTI classifiers to obtain MBTI labels on M+B+ (serving as domain adaptation source set), observing a type-level accuracy of 45% (82.4% for one-off prediction). The classifiers output probabilities, which can be interpreted as a score of the corresponding MBTI dimension. As majority of Big 5 traits significantly correlate with more than one MBTI dimension, we use these scores as features for training five regression models, one for each Big 5 trait (Ridge regression optimized with 5-fold CV). Additionally, we preformed a correlation analysis between Enneagram types and Big 5 traits. Results are shown in Table 14.

In the third step, we apply both classifiers on M-B+ (serving as domain adaptation target set): we first use MBTI classifiers to obtain scores for the four MBTI dimensions, and then feed these to Big 5 regression models to obtain predictions for the five traits.

D Parameters of the DL Model

The models consist of three parts: a convolutional layer, a max-pooling layer, and several fully connected (FC) layers. Convolutional kernels are as wide as BERT's representation and slide vertically over the matrix to aggregate information from several comments. We tried different kernel sizes varying from 2 to 6, and different numbers of kernels M varying from 4 to 6. Outputs of the convolutional layer are first sliced into a fixed number of K slices and then subject to max pooling. This results in M vectors of length K per user, one for each kernel, which are passed to several FC layers with Leaky ReLU activations. Regularization (L2-norm and dropout) is applied only to FC layers.

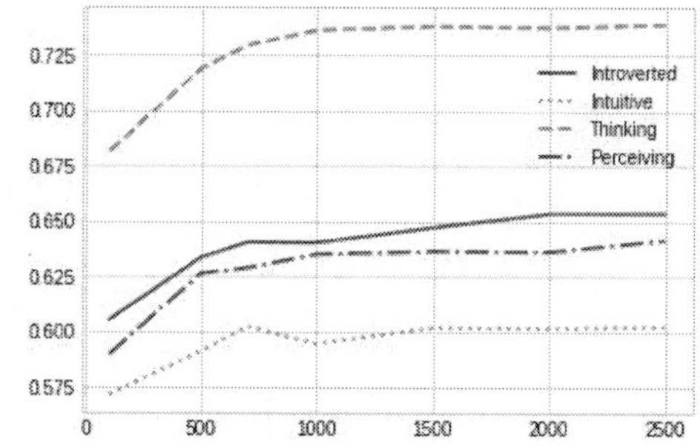

Figure 2: Learning curves of logistic regression for MBTI trait prediction

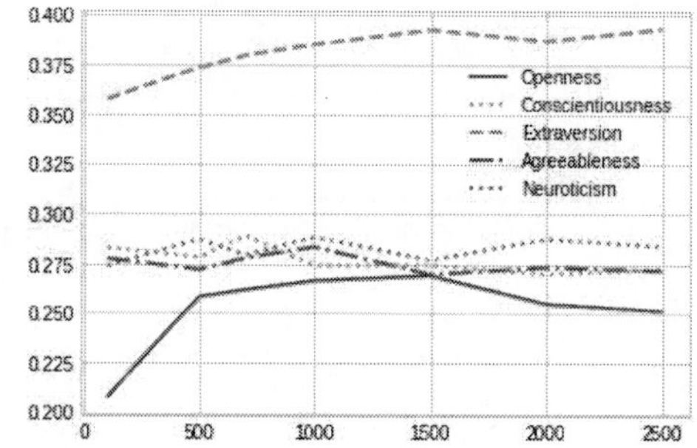

Figure 3: Learning curves of logistic regression for Big 5 trait prediction

E Learning Curves for the Logistic Regression Models

Figures 2 and 3 show the learning curves for logistic regression model with 1-gram features: x-axis is the number of comments and y-axis is model's F1-macro score. Performance plateaus at around 1000 comments, showing little significant changes when increasing the number of comments used for training beyond that amount.

Room to Grow: Understanding Personal Characteristics Behind Self Improvement Using Social Media

MeiXing Dong, Xueming Xu, Yiwei Zhang, Ian Stewart, Rada Mihalcea
University of Michigan, Ann Arbor, MI, USA
{meixingd,xueming,yiweizh,ianbstew,mihalcea}@umich.edu

Abstract

Many people aim for change, but not everyone succeeds. While there are a number of social psychology theories that propose motivation-related characteristics of those who persist with change, few computational studies have explored the motivational stage of personal change. In this paper, we investigate a new dataset consisting of the writings of people who manifest intention to change, some of whom persist while others do not. Using a variety of linguistic analysis techniques, we first examine the writing patterns that distinguish the two groups of people. Persistent people tend to reference more topics related to long-term self-improvement and use a more complicated writing style. Drawing on these consistent differences, we build a classifier that can reliably identify the people more likely to persist, based on their language. Our experiments provide new insights into the motivation-related behavior of people who persist with their intention to change.

1 Introduction

Many people aim for personal change at different points in their lives (Baranski et al., 2017). A glance at a list of top-selling books readily yields self-help manuals whose content ranges from implicitly motivating ("Seven Habits of Highly Effective People" (Covey and Covey, 2020)) to explicitly calling for action ("Lean In" (Sandberg, 2013)). However, simply wanting change is not sufficient to achieve change. Persistence through the process of pursuing personal change is important for actual change to happen, and changes rarely happen overnight. Often, research on behavior change focuses on understanding what makes people committed to regular or increased action, such as exercise (Marcus et al., 2000), or refraining from certain actions such as not overeating (Pappa et al., 2017) or not smoking (Kanner et al., 1999). An ever-growing number of technological tools, such as food diary apps and wearable activity trackers, have emerged to help monitor and motivate healthy behavior (Achananuparp et al., 2018; Chung et al., 2017). Regardless of the tools that they use, if someone is not ready for change yet, the intervention is likely to fail (Prochaska and Velicer, 1997).

Stage-based models of intentional behavior change posit that people progress through a sequence of two stages (Prochaska and Velicer, 1997; Schwarzer and Renner, 2000): *motivation* and *volition*. In the initial *motivation* stage, a person develops an intention or goal to act. A person's intention to adopt better behavior depends on factors such as: *risk perceptions*, or the belief that one is at risk of a negative outcome (e.g. "If I keep procrastinating, I'll fail all my classes."); *outcome expectancies*, or the belief that behavioral change would improve the outcome (e.g. "If I can have a more consistent daily routine, I will be more successful at work."); and *perceived self-efficacy*, or the belief that one is capable of doing the desired actions.

In this paper, we seek to understand the characteristics of people who are in the *motivation* stage of behavior change, and how they talk about behavior change. Traditional behavior change tactics focus on convincing people to take action without consideration for what happens during the lead up period (Prochaska and Velicer, 1997). Insight into how people act during these earlier stages can help us better understand their needs and inform interventions, such as recommending social media content that exemplify healthy approaches to self-improvement. They can also help predict later behavior and persistence using early signals.

1.1 Research Questions

We explore how we can computationally model change-seeking behavior and distinguish between those who maintain persistent interest in personal change during the *motivation* phase and those who do not. People often turn to social media to ex-

Proceedings of the Ninth International Workshop on Natural Language Processing for Social Media, pages 153–162
Online Workshop, June 10, 2021.

press their thoughts and emotions, which provides a rich data source for studying their perceptions and thoughts (Dong et al., 2019).

We address our research questions using a dataset consisting of the writings of 536 people from an online community focused on self-improvement (the Reddit community r/getdisciplined). In this dataset, we identify those who post frequently and those who post infrequently to identify persistent and non-persistent commitment to change. We analyze the discussed topics, linguistic style, and expressed emotions of the posts authored by the persistent and non-persistent groups of people. Specifically, in this paper, we address three main research questions:

1. What are the aspects of life that people want to improve?
2. What linguistic style do people use to signal their persistent interest in self-improvement?
3. How does persistent interest in self-improvement reflect in the emotions that authors express?

Using the features tested in the three separate analyses, we are able to classify persistently and non-persistently active authors with over 60% accuracy, even when using the posts that authors write prior to joining r/getdisciplined. Considering both the descriptive and predictive analyses, our findings indicate that persistent interest in change can be signalled by early changes in behavior in online discussions.

2 Related Work

Behavior Change. Personal and behavioral change have a long history in the field of psychology (Prochaska and Marcus, 1994). Improving health behaviors motivated much work in areas like smoking cessation and increasing physical activity. However, work on understanding how to encourage positive change has expanded to cover countless areas, like decreasing crime (Laub and Sampson, 2001), increasing environmentally friendly behavior (Semenza et al., 2008), and enhancing overall well-being (Bentley et al., 2013). This previous work has shown that many factors can influence an intervention's efficacy, a person's willingness to change, and which strategy to choose for a given person (DiClemente and Prochaska, 1998). Further, an intervention's efficacy may change based on where a person is in their process of change. Different stages in the process can be correlated with different levels of attitudes, such as risk perception or self-efficacy (Schwarzer, 2008). Such attitudes capture a person's estimate of their ability to perform and succeed in challenging situations and are often reflected in the actions that people choose to take or not to take later in later stages (Claro et al., 2016; Dweck, 2006; Velicer et al., 1990). Several theories of behavioral change delineate stages of change and advocate for interventions tailored to each stage (Prochaska and Velicer, 1997; Schwarzer, 2008).

Self-Improvement in Online Communities. In recent years, many have turned towards online communities and platforms, such as Reddit and Facebook, to help them make positive personal changes. The anonymity available in online discussions helps combat fears of stigma or lack of understanding (Ammari et al., 2019). This relative freedom of expression enables researchers to analyze how people seek help through online channels and what they seek (Jurgens et al., 2015). People join online communities to obtain support from those with similar experiences (Chung, 2014), to ask for guidance and resources (White and Dorman, 2001), and to seek accountability (Kummervold et al., 2002). Such support can lead to higher perceived self-efficacy (Turner et al., 1983).

However, as noted by prior work in behavior change, the type of help needed can be highly dependent on one's personal characteristics and situation. In our work, we seek to better understand this using Reddit. There has been considerable effort spent on learning about people's demographic attributes from social media posts (An and Weber, 2016). Work has also targeted internal attributes, such as personality and value, which can be more difficult to extract but can provide richer features for downstream tasks (Shen et al., 2019). However, few have studied general intentional personal change efforts based on social media posts. We tackle uncovering the underlying linguistic characteristics of those who maintain persistent interest in self-improvement.

3 Data

We focus on a Reddit community called r/getdisciplined, where people seek and give advice about how to achieve life goals and build better habits. This community boasts over 768,000 members as of March 2021 and is one of the largest self-improvement subreddits on Reddit. Whereas most self-improvement groups target specific behaviors or goals, such as exercising, losing weight, dieting, or improving mental health, this subreddit targets improving general mental habits. For instance, people ask questions such as "How do I relearn doing things just for fun?" and "How do I stop caring about people and craving their attention?" as opposed to questions that are more specific to activities like "Tips for increasing strength in arms?" or "How do I eat properly?"

Each submission, or original post that is not a comment, must designate the intent of the post using a set of specific tags. One can seek advice ([NeedAdvice], [Question]), give advice ([Advice], [Method]), facilitate discussion and accountability ([Discussion], [Plan]), or talk about r/getdisciplined overall ([Meta]). Most submissions seek advice from the community and tend to discuss fundamental issues such as procrastination, lack of motivation, and time management. A sample of submissions are shown in Table 1.

From the submissions, we can see clear distinctions between people who seek help. In the first submission, the author expresses that they think a negative trait, procrastination, is probably a set part of their personality and that they do not believe in themselves, resulting in expression of negative emotions ("mildly depressed"). On the other hand, the second submission seeking advice does not make any self-deprecating statements and asks only for productivity tips ("producing quality work"). This implies that they believe in their ability to change their habits with guidance. Across all submissions, it is clear that the writers have made concerted efforts to understand their own behavior.

We focus on people who join r/getdisciplined and then become active during a period of five months, from 2017/1 to 2017/5. These are people who had an initial intent to change which turned into continued engagement and persistent intent.[1] We categorize people as persistently active in the subreddit, or *persistent*, if they have posted at least four or more times in the given five months.[2] Only people who have posted in three unique months before and after the target period, respectively, are considered. This pre-processing ensures that there is sufficient data for analysis before, during, and after each person's participation in r/getdisciplined. We then randomly sample an equal number of *non-persistent* people, or people who have posted only once in the 5 months, with the same requirement for posts before and after. Table 2 shows the number of users and posts in our dataset. The total number of users, including both persistent users and a random sample of non-persistent users, is 536.

4 Characteristics of Persistent Interest in Change

We address the study's questions about persistence in personal change by analyzing the discussed topics, the linguistic style, and the expressed emotions in Reddit posts. We analyze both their general behavior on Reddit *prior* to joining r/getdisciplined as well as their *initial behavior* within r/getdisciplined. Investigating how people act before joining r/getdisciplined helps us learn about the mental or behavioral patterns that indicate a higher likelihood of their intent to change their behavior. As a complement to prior behavior, an individual's first post indicates how they are approaching behavior change.

4.1 What Are the Aspects of Life that People Want to Improve?

We uncover the particular areas of life that people seek to improve and their prevalence in discussion. We use topic modeling techniques to uncover the areas of interest that people discuss in their online posts, both within and outside of the context of personal change.

Participation in Subreddits. The subreddits, or Reddit communities, in which a person posts shows the general topics with which they engage. We therefore calculate how frequently each user posts in every subreddit, considering only the subreddits that receive 10 posts in aggregate by users that we observe. We consider only the posts made by the users before their first post in r/getdisciplined.

We show the top 50 subreddits for persistent and non-persistent users prior to joining r/getdisciplined in Table 3. We can see that persistent individuals are active in a number of topic-specific self-improvement subreddits, such as **Fitness**, **LifeProTips**, and **personalfinance**. Non-persistent individuals participate in many more gaming subreddits, i.e. related to leisure rather than self-improvement. Both groups post in popular subreddits like **AskMen**, **AskReddit**, and **funny**; the

[1] Data collected using `http://pushshift.io`

[2] This number of posts is the 90th percentile among people who posted during this time.

Post
I am a chronic procrastinator without any hope... do you know any drastic measures that might help me turn my life around? I have been procrastinating intensely for pretty much my whole life. It just seems to be a part of my personality at this point. I tried many things but I could never handle it. I have been mildly depressed for a long time now and have no belief in myself whatsoever.
How do you balance Parkinson's Law with producing quality work? I often find myself spending a lot of time on tasks, and I recently read about Parkinson's Law from Tim Ferriss' 4 Hour Workweek. The law states that a project or task will expand to fill the time you have allotted to it. It obviously takes a lot of time and hard work to produce something of quality, whether it be music, writing, etc. How do you stave off Parkinson's Law while still producing something of quality?

Table 1: Sample [NeedAdvice] posts from the r/getdisciplined subreddit.

Data Summary	
Total Number of Users	536
Posts from r/getdisciplined	6010
Posts from other subreddits	336455

Table 2: Summary statistics about the dataset, such as the number of users and posts.

prevalence of "ask-X" related subreddits suggests a level of open-mindedness to change that one would expect of people potentially committed to change.

Topics of General Discourse. To gain further insight into the topics that motivated people engage with, we turn to topic modeling. Latent topics can group concepts that overlap between subreddits and ones that differentiate posts in the same subreddit. We use the Latent Dirichlet Allocation (LDA) model (Blei et al., 2003) to discover topics in our dataset. LDA takes a set of documents, D, which each contain a sequence of words, and outputs a set of latent topics that make up the documents. We treat each post as a document d and consider all posts made by our target users in the six months prior to joining r/getdisciplined.

To choose the number of topics for the LDA model, we train models on the general posts made prior to r/getdisciplined with $k = 5, 10, 15, 20, 30$ and then manually inspect the resulting topics and their constituent words to evaluate intra-topic coherence and inter-topic separation. To do this, for each value of k we look for resulting topics whose words seemed to primarily be related to one topic, as well as having a lower number of overlapping words between topics. We intentionally keep to a smaller number of topics since we qualitatively found that increasing the number of topics past 30 led to much lower coherence. We choose the 30-topic LDA model for our analysis and later classification experiments. Using the resulting model, we examine the content of user posts pre-r/getdisciplined.

In Table 4, we show a subset of topics and label them through a manual inspection of the top words associated with the topic from the LDA model (e.g. "school", "college", and "classes" correspond to the topic labeled "Education"). We note the topics that differ significantly across posts made by persistent and non-persistent users before joining r/getdisciplined. We see that persistent users talk more about education, indicating pre-existing interest in a common area of self-improvement. On the other hand, non-persistent users discuss music, politics, and Reddit more, which are general or leisure interests that may be less related to one's personal life.

Topics of Interest in Self-improvement. The topics that people discuss in general on Reddit differ greatly from those that are discussed in a focused subreddit. To hone in on the content specific to r/getdisciplined, we train another 30-topic LDA model using all the posts made in r/getdisciplined between 2016/1 to 2020/2.

We represent each initial post with the distribution of topics that it contains, according to this LDA model. In Table 4, we again show a subset of topics and note those that differ significantly between the two groups of users. Persistent users discuss studying and academics more than non-persistent users, as well as time and time management, showing interest in longer-term shifts in how to go about their life. Non-persistent users engage in more words of encouragement and conversation, perhaps trying to establish connection with the community to increase the likelihood of helpful responses. They also speak about productivity more than persistent users, which is indicative of asking for straightforward productivity tips to solve immediate problems

User type	Top Subreddits
Persistent	Advice, DotA2, EliteDangerous, **Fitness**, GameStop, GlobalOffensiveTrade, **LifeProTips**, MakeupRehab, MarvelPuzzleQuest, RWBY, argentina, aww, conspiracy, cowboys, explainlikeimfive, fantasyfootball, hearthstone, me_irl, **personalfinance**, photography, relationships, summonerschool, wow
Non-persistent	BigBrother, CFB, CringeAnarchy, DeadBedrooms, HelloInternet, IAmA, NoMansSkyTheGame, NoStupidQuestions, OutreachHPG, Roadcam, SquaredCircle, SubredditDrama, WTF, Warframe, baseball, bjj, cars, casualiama, nottheonion, skyrimmods, skyrimrequiem, slatestarcodex, smashbros
Both	AdviceAnimals, AskMen, AskReddit, Jokes, MMA, Overwatch, Showerthoughts, The_Donald, funny, gaming, gifs, leagueoflegends, mildlyinteresting, movies, nba, news, nfl, pcmasterrace, pics, pokemon, pokemongo, politics, soccer, television, todayilearned, videos, worldnews

Table 3: Top 50 subreddits prior to joining r/getdisciplined for persistent and non-persistent users respectively, divided into those that correspond to only one group and both groups. Subreddits relevant to self-improvement are bolded.

Feature	P	NP	P-NP
1st post			
Studying	0.072	0.037	0.036*
Routines	0.114	0.085	0.028
Productivity	0.062	0.073	-0.011**
Mental Health	0.102	0.105	-0.002
Time	0.165	0.118	0.047*
Goals	0.086	0.071	0.015
Encouragement	0.021	0.049	-0.028*
Habits	0.129	0.083	0.046
Conversation	0.046	0.102	-0.056*
Work	0.130	0.125	0.005
Prior six months			
Music	0.092	0.093	-0.002**
Relationships	0.213	0.180	0.033
News	0.147	0.148	-0.001*
Finance	0.172	0.186	-0.014*
Politics	0.133	0.180	-0.047**
Gaming	0.164	0.188	-0.024
Education	0.228	0.189	0.039**
Reddit	0.102	0.122	-0.019**
Automobiles	0.112	0.133	-0.021*
Family	0.314	0.300	0.014

$* - p < 0.05, ** - p < 0.01, *** - p < 0.001$

Table 4: Mean distributions of topics among posts for persistent (P) and non-persistent (NP) users, as well as the differences between them (P-NP). Statistical significance is determined using a two-sided T-test, with the Benjamini-Hochberg Procedure applied to control for multiple hypotheses testing.

(e.g. "What apps can I use to help with work?"), rather than tackling longer-term change (e.g. "I really want to gain some discipline and self control. I would appreciate advice!").

4.2 What Linguistic Style Do People Use to Signal their Persistent Interest in Self-Improvement?

Patterns in how people express themselves through language can potentially tell us about how they think. Linguistic style has been shown to reflect numerous behavioral characteristics such as personality (Scherer, 1979), and intent (Pennebaker, 2011). We look at the length of each post, taking the number of words contained in the post as a feature. We also consider each post's readability as defined by its Flesch Reading Ease score (Kincaid et al., 1975): higher scores indicate longer average word length and sentence length, which implies more difficulty in reading. We compute these two scores for each post and use these two values as features in our predictive models. As before, we analyze the posts of persistent and non-persistent users both prior to posting in r/getdisciplined and in their first post in the subreddit.

General Linguistic Style. We show the average post lengths and Flesch Reading Ease scores for the prior posts of persistent and non-persistent users in Table 5. Persistent users tend to have longer posts than non-persistent users, which could indicate a more committed writing style (e.g., explaining all necessary details of a situation when posting). In contrast, the two groups' posts do not differ much in readability.

Feature	1st post P	NP	P-NP	Prior 6 mon. P	NP	P-NP
Linguistic Features						
Readability	-9.800	43.002	-52.802***	49.163	52.971	-3.807
Post Length	96.276	47.522	48.754***	40.572	34.548	6.024**
Emotions						
Anticipation	0.124	0.108	0.016	0.115	0.115	0.001
Disgust	0.031	0.024	0.007	0.044	0.044	-0.001
Sadness	0.045	0.042	0.003	0.067	0.066	0.002
Trust	0.109	0.090	0.019	0.135	0.133	0.003
Surprise	0.032	0.033	-0.000	0.054	0.054	-0.000
Anger	0.038	0.029	0.009	0.059	0.066	-0.007*
Negative	0.116	0.103	0.014	0.131	0.138	-0.007
Joy	0.060	0.062	-0.002	0.098	0.095	0.003
Fear	0.059	0.047	0.013	0.070	0.073	-0.003
Positive	0.210	0.199	0.011	0.226	0.216	0.010

$* - p < 0.05, ** - p < 0.01, *** - p < 0.001$

Table 5: Mean feature values of linguistic and emotion features in posts from persistent (P) and non-persistent (NP) users, as well as the differences between them (P-NP). Note that the differences for different measures are on different scales. Statistical significance is determined using a two-sided T-test, with the Benjamini-Hochberg Procedure applied to control for multiple hypotheses testing.

Self-Improvement Linguistic Style. Next, we look at the average post lengths and readability scores of initial posts in r/getdisciplined (Tab. 5). In contrast to the pre-joining posts, persistent users write significantly longer posts and lower readability, indicating more complex posts. Initial posts that ask for help without self-deprecation, such as the second post in Table 1 can include many details about the situation at hand so that others can offer pertinent advice.

4.3 How Does Persistent Interest in Self-improvement Reflect in the Emotions that Authors Express?

The third research question considers trends in emotional expression among people seeking motivation for change. Emotions can signal attitude towards one's intended behavior change. For instance, someone who believes that success is based on innate ability or who expects that they will fail at difficult tasks will probably shy away from goals that require large effort (Hutchinson et al., 2008). On the other hand, those who believe success results from hard work or believe in their own ability to tackle challenges may be more persistent in their efforts (Strecher et al., 1986).

To analyze such trends, we use the NRC Emotion Lexicon (Mohammad and Turney, 2013, 2010), which contains English words and their associations with positive and negative sentiment as well as eight basic and prototypical emotions (Plutchik, 1980): *anger, fear, anticipation, trust, surprise, sadness, joy, and disgust.* Complex emotions, such as *regret* or *gratitude*, can typically be viewed as combinations of these basic emotions. The lexicon contains 14,182 general domain words, each of which can be linked to multiple emotions.

Emotions in General Discourse. Building on our previous observation about the prevalence of emotional words, we now compare the rate of use among persistent and non-persistent people. We compute the total proportion of emotions expressed for each person by averaging the counts of emotion words used across the person's posts. Comparing the persistent and non-persistent people, we found that most of the emotions are equally found in posts by both groups. However, non-persistent users express more anger in general, which may indicate a tendency to be more easily discouraged when faced with difficulty in everyday situations.

Emotions of Self-improvement. We use the same emotion lexicon to extract the expressed emotions in each initial post to r/disciplined. The expressed emotions in first posts that do not differ significantly between persistent and non-persistent users (Table 5). However, we see that there is a general trend among everyone of expressing positive sentiment, anticipation, and trust, which signals that they are hopeful with respect to self-improvement and are open to discussing problems and solutions. There is also negative sentiment, which can indicate dissatisfaction towards their current situation and therefore desire to change.

5 Predicting Persistence in Change

Our analyses have identified that the people who persist in their self-improvement efforts exhibit consistent linguistic differences in topics, writing style, and emotional expression, versus those who do not persist. As a natural next step, we ask whether we can leverage these characteristics to automatically distinguish between these two groups. We set up a prediction task to determine whether a user is likely to become a persistent or non-persistent user on r/getdisciplined by considering: (1) their language use within six months prior to their initial post on r/getdisciplined; (2) their language use in their first post; and (3) their combined language use within the six months prior and their first post on r/getdisciplined.

To provide more fine-grained semantic representation of the post language, we also construct word embeddings (Mikolov et al., 2013) from the text of each post, using word2Vec embeddings pre-trained on news text.[3] Word embeddings are useful in capturing fine differences between words, such as differences in sentiment valence between similar words (e.g. "good" vs. "great"). For each initial post in r/disciplined, we average the word embeddings of each word in the post to generate a per-post embedding. To represent prior posts, we average the per-post embeddings for all posts of each user from the six months prior to joining r/getdisciplined. For readability, we also include an aggregate readability score based on a number of different readability metrics, in addition to the Flesch score used earlier.[4]

We compare the performance of classifiers that use different combinations of the linguistic features that we have shown to correlate with persistent behavior. Our task is the binary prediction of whether a user will continue to engage (persistent user) or leave after an initial post (non-persistent user). The experiments are performed using SVM classifiers (Cortes and Vapnik, 1995) and evaluated using 10-fold cross validation.[5] Since our dataset is balanced, both the random and majority class baselines correspond to an accuracy of 50%.

Features	Acc	Prec	Rec	F1
1st post				
Readability	0.61	0.59	0.72	0.65
Post Length	0.60	0.57	0.83	0.67
Emotionality	0.54	0.54	0.57	0.55
W2V	0.60	0.64	0.46	0.53
LDA	0.58	0.59	0.53	0.56
Combined	0.62	0.59	0.79	0.67
Prior six months				
Readability	0.53	0.52	0.63	0.57
Post Length	0.56	0.56	0.57	0.57
Emotionality	0.54	0.54	0.49	0.51
W2V	0.56	0.55	0.58	0.57
Subreddits	0.55	0.54	0.62	0.58
LDA	0.62	0.63	0.59	0.61
Combined	0.55	0.55	0.59	0.57
All	0.61	0.58	0.77	0.66

Table 6: Prediction results for binary classification of persistence in r/getdisciplined. Metrics: accuracy, precision, recall, and F1 score.

We present the results in Table 6, with classification performance shown for each feature set derived from a user's prior behavior, their first post in r/getdisciplined, and the combination of all features. Using all features, our models are able to achieve an average accuracy of over 60%. This shows that people who persist with change can be distinguished from those who do not, even before they commit to change by posting in r/getdisciplined. That said, the models that use only features from each user's initial post in r/getdisciplined yield the highest performance overall. This is in line with previous work showing that the initial posts that someone makes in a conversation can reliably predict future outcomes, such as whether a debate will derail (Zhang et al., 2018) or a user will remain loyal to a community (Hamilton et al., 2017). Moreover, someone's first post encapsulates how they approach self-improvement such as whether they think it is possible or is an insurmountable goal, which is reflected in their language use.

6 Discussion

The readability of a user's initial post appears highly indicative of their future engagement level. As shown previously in Section 4.2, persistent users tend to have lower readability in initial posts than non-persistent users. This could be because they come with the intention of engaging with the sub-

[3] `https://code.google.com/archive/p/word2vec/`

[4] `https://pypi.org/project/textstat/`

[5] We used the SVM classifier, with default parameters, as applied in Scikit-learn: `https://scikit-learn.org`

reddit, and therefore devote more time to their introductory post hoping for a similar reaction of engagement from the forum. Post length is also a strong signal for our models both when we're considering only each user's first post as well as their prior posts on Reddit. Similar to the readability feature, one possible explanation is the higher engagement with the community through longer posts. Users having longer posts prior to joining r/getdisciplined indicates a more consistently personal style of extensive writing and engagement, and therefore more willingness for self-disclosure.

The emotionality features provided some signal for the model, but were not as helpful as our other features. However, emotionality features derived from the 1st post resulted in higher recall than those derived from the prior six months, which could indicate that there is more expressed through emotion in the 1st post than in general text.

Prediction performance was consistently high when using word embeddings, which shows that the latent semantic information in embeddings is helpful. However, it is not significantly better than the other top features, indicating that there is room for improvement in representing more subtle linguistic information such as intent or attitude.

Topical content features derived through LDA were among the best performing features for activity from the prior 6 months, while a user's subreddit activity history was less predictive. The subreddits in which someone participates might be too coarse-grained for our task, whereas topic models can better capture the fine-grained behavior that relates to self-improvement and mindset.

Our results demonstrate how people with persistent interest in personal change act differently from those who do not maintain persistent interest. Our analyses showed that those with persistent change intent had higher prior engagement with topics that foster personal change, such as education. This kind of behavior represents a form of *gathering information* related to the intended form of change. Information gathering is an important aspect of a person's reflecting and considering their motivation for potential future change (Schwarzer, 2008). In addition to topics, we revealed differences in linguistic style between the two groups of people. Persistent users tended to have longer initial posts with lower readability.

Implications for Tailored Interventions We can use our findings and further work to tailor behavior change interventions towards people with different characteristics. Those characterized with lower persistence may be in an earlier behavior change stage, necessitating a different approach than those in later stages (DiClemente and Prochaska, 1998). For example, a social intervention could consist of a community moderator, or persistent community member, being paired with a likely non-persistent member (based on language use) to encourage them to stay committed to their goal (Vlahovic et al., 2014). Alternatively, a community-based intervention system could automatically recommend posts from persistent people, for the non-persistent people to read as a way to learn how to approach change in a healthier way (Cosley et al., 2007).

7 Conclusion

In this paper, we explored the behavior of users from an online community, r/getdisciplined, as a proxy for measuring persistent intent towards personal change. By analyzing user behavior prior to and immediately after joining the community, we showed quantitative differences between users who sustained intent towards general self-initiated change versus those who did not. Those who have persistent intent tended to engage more with change-oriented topics such as education even prior to expressing explicit intent to change.

We then leveraged these linguistic characteristics to build predictive models that were able to automatically distinguish people who continued engagement in r/getdisciplined and sustained their intent for self-improvement from those who did not continue, even before their first post.

Our results provide actionable insight for research areas that investigate behavior change. Understanding the underlying mechanisms associated with persistence in change can support the development of new approaches to help people change for the better.

Acknowledgments

This material is based in part upon work supported by the National Science Foundation (grant #1815291) and by the John Templeton Foundation (grant #61156). Any opinions, findings, and conclusions or recommendations expressed in this material are those of the authors and do not necessarily reflect the views of the National Science Foundation or the John Templeton Foundation.

References

Palakorn Achananuparp, Ee-Peng Lim, and Vibhanshu Abhishek. 2018. Does journaling encourage healthier choices? Analyzing healthy eating behaviors of food journalers. In *Proceedings of the 2018 International Conference on Digital Health*. 35–44.

Tawfiq Ammari, Sarita Schoenebeck, and Daniel Romero. 2019. Self-declared throwaway accounts on Reddit: How platform affordances and shared norms enable parenting disclosure and support. *Proceedings of the ACM on Human-Computer Interaction* 3, CSCW (2019), 1–30.

Jisun An and Ingmar Weber. 2016. # greysanatomy vs.# yankees: Demographics and Hashtag Use on Twitter. In *Tenth International AAAI Conference on Web and Social Media*.

Erica N Baranski, Patrick J Morse, and William L Dunlop. 2017. Lay conceptions of volitional personality change: From strategies pursued to stories told. *Journal of personality* 85, 3 (2017), 285–299.

Frank Bentley, Konrad Tollmar, Peter Stephenson, Laura Levy, Brian Jones, Scott Robertson, Ed Price, Richard Catrambone, and Jeff Wilson. 2013. Health Mashups: Presenting statistical patterns between wellbeing data and context in natural language to promote behavior change. *ACM Transactions on Computer-Human Interaction (TOCHI)* 20, 5 (2013), 1–27.

David M Blei, Andrew Y Ng, and Michael I Jordan. 2003. Latent dirichlet allocation. *Journal of machine Learning research* 3, Jan (2003), 993–1022.

Chia-Fang Chung, Elena Agapie, Jessica Schroeder, Sonali Mishra, James Fogarty, and Sean A Munson. 2017. When personal tracking becomes social: Examining the use of Instagram for healthy eating. In *Proceedings of the 2017 CHI Conference on Human Factors in Computing Systems*. 1674–1687.

Jae Eun Chung. 2014. Social networking in online support groups for health: how online social networking benefits patients. *Journal of health communication* 19, 6 (2014), 639–659.

Susana Claro, David Paunesku, and Carol S. Dweck. 2016. Growth mindset tempers the effects of poverty on academic achievement. *Proceedings of the National Academy of Sciences* 113, 31 (2016), 8664–8668. https://doi.org/10.1073/pnas.1608207113 arXiv:https://www.pnas.org/content/113/31/8664.full.pdf

Corinna Cortes and Vladimir Vapnik. 1995. Support-vector networks. *Machine learning* 20, 3 (1995), 273–297.

Dan Cosley, Dan Frankowski, Loren Terveen, and John Riedl. 2007. SuggestBot: using intelligent task routing to help people find work in wikipedia. In *Proceedings of the 12th international conference on Intelligent user interfaces*. 32–41.

Stephen R Covey and Sean Covey. 2020. *The 7 habits of highly effective people*. Simon & Schuster.

Carlo C DiClemente and James O Prochaska. 1998. Toward a comprehensive, transtheoretical model of change: Stages of change and addictive behaviors. (1998).

MeiXing Dong, David Jurgens, Carmen Banea, and Rada Mihalcea. 2019. Perceptions of Social Roles Across Cultures. In *International Conference on Social Informatics*. Springer, 157–172.

C.S. Dweck. 2006. *Mindset: The New Psychology of Success*. Random House Publishing Group. https://books.google.com/books?id=fdjqz0TPL2wC

William Hamilton, Justine Zhang, Cristian Danescu-Niculescu-Mizil, Dan Jurafsky, and Jure Leskovec. 2017. Loyalty in Online Communities. https://www.aaai.org/ocs/index.php/ICWSM/ICWSM17/paper/view/15710/14848

Jasmin C Hutchinson, Todd Sherman, Nevena Martinovic, and Gershon Tenenbaum. 2008. The effect of manipulated self-efficacy on perceived and sustained effort. *Journal of Applied Sport Psychology* 20, 4 (2008), 457–472.

David Jurgens, James McCorriston, and Derek Ruths. 2015. An analysis of exercising behavior in online populations. In *Ninth international aaai conference on web and social media*.

Richard E Kanner, John E Connett, David E Williams, A Sonia Buist, Lung Health Study Research Group, et al. 1999. Effects of randomized assignment to a smoking cessation intervention and changes in smoking habits on respiratory symptoms in smokers with early chronic obstructive pulmonary disease: the Lung Health Study. *The American journal of medicine* 106, 4 (1999), 410–416.

J Peter Kincaid, Robert P Fishburne Jr, Richard L Rogers, and Brad S Chissom. 1975. *Derivation of new readability formulas (automated readability index, fog count and flesch reading ease formula) for navy enlisted personnel*. Technical Report. Naval Technical Training Command Millington TN Research Branch.

Per E Kummervold, Deede Gammon, Svein Bergvik, Jan-Are K Johnsen, Toralf Hasvold, and Jan H Rosenvinge. 2002. Social support in a wired world: use of online mental health forums in Norway. *Nordic journal of psychiatry* 56, 1 (2002), 59–65.

John H Laub and Robert J Sampson. 2001. Understanding desistance from crime. *Crime and justice* 28 (2001), 1–69.

Bess H Marcus, LeighAnn H Forsyth, Elaine J Stone, Patricia M Dubbert, Thomas L McKenzie, Andrea L

Dunn, and Steven N Blair. 2000. Physical activity behavior change: issues in adoption and maintenance. *Health psychology* 19, 1S (2000), 32.

Tomas Mikolov, Ilya Sutskever, Kai Chen, Greg S Corrado, and Jeff Dean. 2013. Distributed representations of words and phrases and their compositionality. In *Advances in neural information processing systems*. 3111–3119.

Saif M Mohammad and Peter D Turney. 2010. Emotions evoked by common words and phrases: Using mechanical turk to create an emotion lexicon. In *Proceedings of the NAACL HLT 2010 workshop on computational approaches to analysis and generation of emotion in text*. Association for Computational Linguistics, 26–34.

Saif M. Mohammad and Peter D. Turney. 2013. Crowdsourcing a Word-Emotion Association Lexicon. 29, 3 (2013), 436–465.

Gisele Lobo Pappa, Tiago Oliveira Cunha, Paulo Viana Bicalho, Antonio Ribeiro, Ana Paula Couto Silva, Wagner Meira Jr, and Alline Maria Rezende Beleigoli. 2017. Factors associated with weight change in online weight management communities: a case study in the LoseIt Reddit community. *Journal of medical Internet research* 19, 1 (2017), e17.

James W Pennebaker. 2011. Using computer analyses to identify language style and aggressive intent: The secret life of function words. *Dynamics of Asymmetric Conflict* 4, 2 (2011), 92–102.

Robert Plutchik. 1980. A general psychoevolutionary theory of emotion. In *Theories of emotion*. Elsevier, 3–33.

James O Prochaska and Bess H Marcus. 1994. The transtheoretical model: Applications to exercise. (1994).

James O Prochaska and Wayne F Velicer. 1997. The transtheoretical model of health behavior change. *American journal of health promotion* 12, 1 (1997), 38–48.

Sheryl Sandberg. 2013. *Lean In: Women, Work and the Will to Lead*. Random House, Inc.

Klaus Rainer Scherer. 1979. *Personality markers in speech*. Cambridge University Press.

Ralf Schwarzer. 2008. Modeling health behavior change: How to predict and modify the adoption and maintenance of health behaviors. *Applied psychology* 57, 1 (2008), 1–29.

Ralf Schwarzer and Britta Renner. 2000. Social-cognitive predictors of health behavior: action self-efficacy and coping self-efficacy. *Health psychology* 19, 5 (2000), 487.

Jan C Semenza, David E Hall, Daniel J Wilson, Brian D Bontempo, David J Sailor, and Linda A George. 2008. Public perception of climate change: voluntary mitigation and barriers to behavior change. *American journal of preventive medicine* 35, 5 (2008), 479–487.

Yiting Shen, Steven R. Wilson, and Rada Mihalcea. 2019. Measuring Personal Values in Cross-Cultural User-Generated Content. In *Social Informatics*, Ingmar Weber, Kareem M. Darwish, Claudia Wagner, Emilio Zagheni, Laura Nelson, Samin Aref, and Fabian Flöck (Eds.). Springer International Publishing, Cham, 143–156.

Victor J Strecher, Brenda McEvoy DeVellis, Marshall H Becker, and Irwin M Rosenstock. 1986. The role of self-efficacy in achieving health behavior change. *Health education quarterly* 13, 1 (1986), 73–92.

R Jay Turner, B Gail Frankel, and Deborah M Levin. 1983. Social support: Conceptualization, measurement, and implications for mental health. *Research in community & mental health* (1983).

Wayne F Velicer, Carlo C Diclemente, Joseph S Rossi, and James O Prochaska. 1990. Relapse situations and self-efficacy: An integrative model. *Addictive behaviors* 15, 3 (1990), 271–283.

Tatiana A Vlahovic, Yi-Chia Wang, Robert E Kraut, and John M Levine. 2014. Support matching and satisfaction in an online breast cancer support community. In *Proceedings of the SIGCHI Conference on Human Factors in Computing Systems*. 1625–1634.

Marsha White and Steve M Dorman. 2001. Receiving social support online: implications for health education. *Health education research* 16, 6 (2001), 693–707.

Justine Zhang, Jonathan P Chang, Cristian Danescu-Niculescu-Mizil, Lucas Dixon, Yiqing Hua, Nithum Thain, and Dario Taraborelli. 2018. Conversations gone awry: Detecting early signs of conversational failure. *arXiv preprint arXiv:1805.05345* (2018).

Mitigating Temporal-Drift: A Simple Approach to Keep NER Models Crisp

Shuguang Chen [†], **Leonardo Neves** [‡] and **Thamar Solorio** [†]
University of Houston [†]
Snap Research [‡]
schen52@uh.edu, lneves@snap.com and tsolorio@uh.edu

Abstract

Performance of neural models for named entity recognition degrades over time, becoming stale. This degradation is due to temporal drift, the change in our target variables' statistical properties over time. This issue is especially problematic for social media data, where topics change rapidly. In order to mitigate the problem, data annotation and retraining of models is common. Despite its usefulness, this process is expensive and time-consuming, which motivates new research on efficient model updating. In this paper, we propose an intuitive approach to measure the potential trendiness of tweets and use this metric to select the most informative instances to use for training. We conduct experiments on three state-of-the-art models on the Temporal Twitter Dataset. Our approach shows larger increases in prediction accuracy with less training data than the alternatives, making it an attractive, practical solution. [1]

1 Introduction

Prediction performances of live machine learning systems degrade over time due to changes in the statistical properties of the data used for training them. This degradation, also known as temporal drift, happens in different ML tasks, including named entity recognition (NER). Due to the nature of the task, authors also call this language drift (Fromreide et al., 2014; Derczynski et al., 2015). Temporal drift effects are amplified in social media. Due to the ecosystem's very nature, topics reflect events and interests of a diverse user base and are continuously and rapidly evolving. To study the impact of language drift, we focus our analysis on the case of NER on Twitter data. Emerging and Trending topics are an essential part of Twitter. They change quite rapidly, reflecting diverse topics and world events of interest. Entities are a significant component of these changes, generating a diverse set of NE tokens. These ever-evolving topics pose a challenge as new entities frequently arise. The new entities are especially problematic as they might not exist in our previous vocabulary or can potentially transform the meaning of a previously observed term. Figure 1 shows tweets that include the emerging topic 'US'. After the release of the film, the topic 'US' became trending and aroused wide discussion. To mitigate the impact of temporal drift, we investigate how to effectively and efficiently adapt an already trained NER model to sustain prediction performance over time. We propose an intuitive approach to measure the trendiness of tweets and use this metric to select the most informative instances for retraining. We show that labeling instances based on this approach can yield better downstream performance than randomly sampling tweets for annotation.

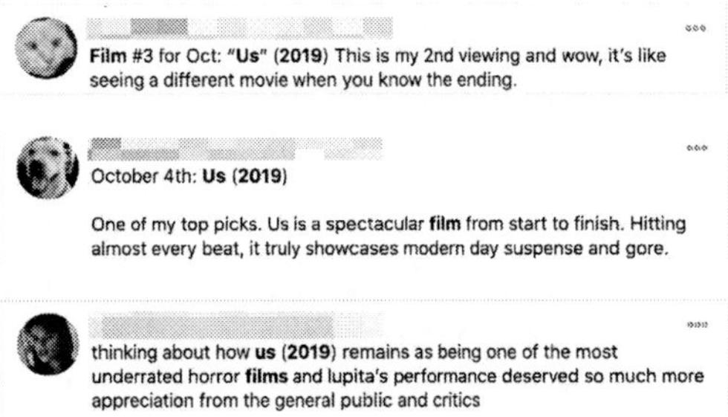

Figure 1: Examples of tweets that include the emerging topic '**US**', a horror movie released in 2019

Note that topics such as semantic shift (Hamilton et al., 2016; Rosenfeld and Erk, 2018) and active learning (Sinha et al., 2019; Kirsch et al., 2019) are related to the work we present here. In semantic shift, the core problem is how to trace temporal changes in lexical semantics, including linguistic drifts and cultural shifts. Unlike this task, our goal is to leverage the emergence of trends to guide an

[1] We release the code at https://github.com/RiTUAL-UH/trending_NER.

Proceedings of the Ninth International Workshop on Natural Language Processing for Social Media, pages 163–169
Online Workshop, June 10, 2021. ©2021 Association for Computational Linguistics

already trained model.

In active learning, researchers have focused on incremental annotation of instances by selecting the most informative ones. The goal is to achieve better results than random sampling. Multiple approaches exist to measure the informativeness of data points, but all of them are domain agnostic (Sinha et al., 2019; Kirsch et al., 2019). Our proposed solution is more straightforward than using uncertainty in ensembles or adversarial networks. However, it effectively increases model performance, and, similar to active learning approaches, it is more efficient than random sampling.

To summarize, we make the following contributions:

1. We propose an approach to measure the potential trendiness of tweets for selecting the most informative training samples.
2. We conduct extensive experiments and demonstrate the effectiveness of our approach for retraining a NER model.

2 Emerging Trend Detection

We want to exploit social media's inherent characteristics (Benhardus and Kalita, 2013; Mathioudakis and Koudas, 2010), with a focus on Twitter, to update model parameters efficiently. We assume that named entities associated with posts that are likely to become trends will be more informative and result in larger performance gains. Our emerging trend detection strategy is based on contrasting frequency of words in older data (training data) against frequency in newly collected data (recent data). More specifically, we formulate this task as detection of trending n-grams. We compute the trend scores for each n-gram, n, as follows:

$$score(n) = \frac{f_{n,R} - f_{n,P}}{f_{n,P} + k}$$

where $f_{n,R}$ and $f_{n,P}$ are the frequencies of n-gram n in the recent and past datasets, respectively. In practical applications, $f_{n,R}$ can refer to the frequency in newly collected data, while $f_{n,P}$ can refer to the frequency in older data. k is a normalization term used to mitigate the frequency of the highly-frequent n-grams in the recent datasets. When computing trend scores, we filter out stop words as they are usually the most common words but contain the least information. After we compute trend scores for all n-grams in newly collected data, we assign trend scores to the instances by summing over the scores of each n-gram in that instance (tweet). We then use the score to rank instances for labeling and updating the NER model. Our approach is flexible as it can be used in combination with any NER model architecture.

3 Experiments

We empirically study the impact of retraining NER models on trending data in two different scenarios. In **Scenario 1**, we retrain the model in an incremental manner with N instances from a newer batch of data in the following year at every iteration. In **Scenario 2**, we retrain the model incrementally as well, but the pool of data we used to select instances includes all years available in the training partitions. In both cases, instances are selected based on their trend scores.

We use the Temporal Twitter Dataset from Rijhwani and Preotiuc-Pietro (2020) for all experiments. This dataset is temporally distributed and balanced with a variety of topics. It has 12K tweets collected from 2014 to 2019, with 2K samples from each year. In our experiments, the training set comprises of splits from 2014 to 2018. The validation set and test set have a random sample of 500 (25%) and 1,500 (75%) tweets from 2019, respectively.

3.1 Neural Architectures

As mentioned earlier, our approach is model agnostic. We validate this claim by experimenting with different NER neural architectures used in the prior art. The main difference between these models is the representation fed into a Conditional Random Field (CRF) (Lafferty et al., 2001) for prediction. The implementation and hyperparameters are described in Appendix A.

BiLSTM + CRF Following Ma and Hovy (2016), we use the GloVe (Pennington et al., 2014) word embeddings for word representations and Convolution Neural Networks (CNNs) for character representations. Then a bidirectional LSTM (Graves and Schmidhuber, 2005) takes both word representations and character representations as input and encodes sentences.

BERT + CRF BERT is a transformer-based model proposed by Devlin et al. (2019). It is pretrained using masked language modeling and next sentence prediction objectives on the corpora from the general domain. BERT takes subwords as input

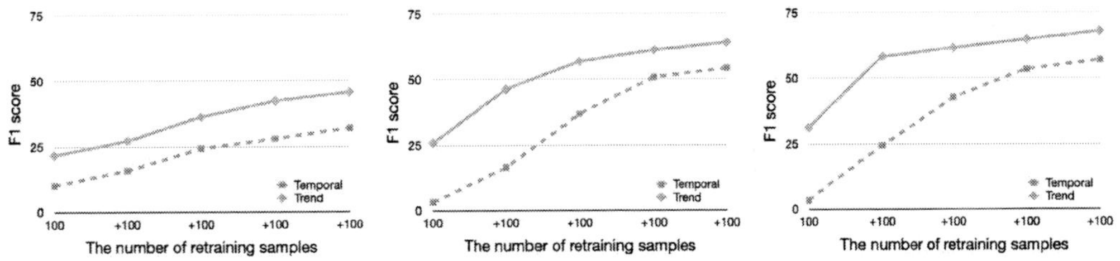

(a) BiLSTM + CRF (b) BERT + CRF (c) BERTweet + CRF

Figure 2: **Data can only be accessed year by year -** Each step represents a year from 2014 to 2018. At each step, we add instances from its respective year to the training set. For Temporal, we randomly select instances from that given year. For Trend, we rank instances based on their trending score. We experiment with 50 (Appendix B), 100 and 200 (Appendix B) instances per step to show the impact of training size.

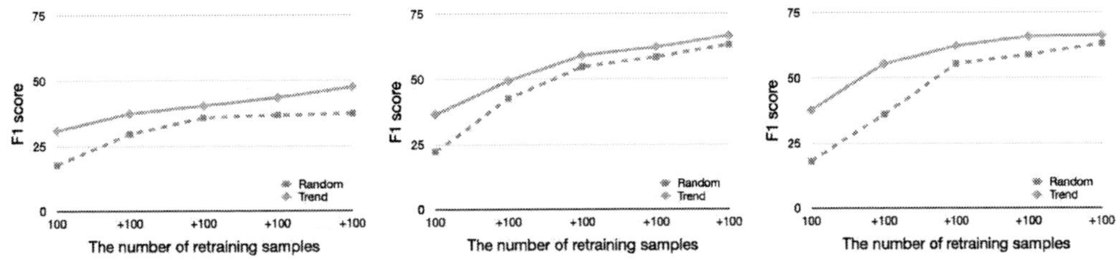

(a) BiLSTM + CRF (b) BERT + CRF (c) BERTweet + CRF

Figure 3: **Data from all years is available -** At each step, we add new instances to our training set. For Random, we randomly select instances from the available data. For Trend, we rank all available instances from most trending to less trending based on their trending scores. We then use this ranking to select the instances. At each step, we choose the instances with the highest trending scores that have not yet been added to the training set. We experiment with 50 (Appendix B), 100 and 200 (Appendix B) instances per step to show the impact of training size.

and generates contextualized word representations for each sentence.

BERTweet + CRF Similar to BERT, BERTweet (Nguyen et al., 2020) is a large-scale language model with the same configuration as BERT. It is pre-trained on the corpora from the social media domain and achieves state-of-the-art results on many downstream Twitter NER tasks.

3.2 Results

We empirically examine the performance of models under the influence of data evolution and temporal drift. We start with doing experiments on trending bi-grams and use the same amount of training samples at each step to eliminate the influence of training data size. Below we discuss the results of the two evaluation scenarios.

Scenario 1 In this scenario, we assume that the data can only be accessed chronologically by year. For each new batch of data selected based on the trendiness score (**trend**), we take the model as trained on the previous batch and retrain on the newest data. In other words, we consider the model from the previous iteration as a pre-trained model and fine-tune that model on the newest data. For comparison purposes, we run a **temporal** version, where the model is fine-tuned with newer data every time, but the instances are selected randomly for the corresponding year. Due to the randomness in this approach, we run each model five times, and then we report the average of the five runs as the final F1 score.

The results are shown in Figure 2. We observe that both temporal and trend F1 scores increase as we move temporally closer to the target data. However, in all cases, the trend-based models always reach a higher score.

Scenario 2 In this scenario, we assume the data can be accessed from all years at once. We merge the training data from all years and form a single pool of data. However, we still fine-tune models at each iteration using the same number of new instances each time. For the trend models, we select instances based on their trend scores, regardless of the year, whereas for the random model, we select instances at random from the merged pool of data. Similar to what we did in scenario 1, we run each model 5 times and report the averaged results.

The results are shown in Figure 3. Similar to scenario 1, the F1 scores of the models trained on instances selected based on their trend scores are always higher than random sampling F1 scores. In addition, scenario 2, on average, works better than scenario 1, which is consistent with Rijhwani and Preotiuc-Pietro (2020). However, this setting requires the data available from all years from the very beginning. Compared to scenario 2, scenario 1 is far more realistic because it can be more easily applied in practice.

3.3 Analysis

Impact of training data size We ran additional experiments where we add different amounts of training data at each iteration (50 and 200). With less training data available, the benefits of selecting instances based on trend scores are amplified. Even if more data is available, using trend scores to select which instances to add always results in better performance than randomly choosing instances. Due to space limitations, the plots are in Appendix B figures 4, 5, 6 and 7.

Impact of pre-trained knowledge From figures 2 and 3, we observe that, in general, pre-trained models (BERT and BERTweet) tend to perform closer to that of the trend-based models. Apart from the well-documented advantages of contextualized representations, we believe that higher performance here is due to these models' pre-trained knowledge. We suspect that if we had the ability to control the data, and in particular, the year of the data used in pre-training, the results would be different, and we would observe a larger gap between pre-trained transformer models and the trend-based approach.

Entity-wise Model Performance We investigate whether our approach affects named entity types differently. To this end, we create random data and trending data. The random data is randomly selected, while the trending data is selected based on the trend scores. Each data has 1,000 samples. Table 1 shows the model performance on the random data, versus the trending data. We notice that all three models overall benefit from trend detection with an improvement from 2.70% 5.71% on F1 metric, indicating that the models can adequately learn the context of named entities.

Model	Random data			Trending data		
	P	R	F1	P	R	F1
BiLSTM + CRF	59.38	48.02	53.10	63.42	54.83	58.81
BERT + CRF	62.26	73.23	67.30	70.07	69.93	70.00
BERTweet + CRF	60.64	64.84	62.67	65.45	70.46	67.86

Table 1: Performance comparison on random data and trending data, including persc.

To better understand the high model performance on trending data, Table 2 shows the distribution of random and trending data. By selecting training samples based on our approach, the number of entities in the trending data is 77% more than the number of entities in the random data, including 92% more PER, 38% more LOC, and 91% more ORG. In the token level, there are more 108% entity tokens in the trending data than in the random data. The higher ratio of named entities in the trending data increases the diversity of each entity type, and therefore, decreases the test error.

Entity Type	Random data		Trending data	
	Entity-level	Token-level	Entity-level	Token-level
PER	225	340	432	755
LOC	178	226	245	362
ORG	281	379	537	848
Total	684	945	1,214	1,965

Table 2: The distribution of random data and trending data, including entity-level distribution (entity spans) and token-level distribution (entity tokens).

4 Related Work

Previous work has studied trend detection in online social media platforms such as Twitter and Facebook (Benhardus and Kalita, 2013; Mathioudakis and Koudas, 2010; Miot and Drigout, 2020). Benhardus and Kalita (2013) outlined the methodologies for using the data from online platforms and proposed criteria based on the frequency of words to identify trending topics in Twitter. Mathioudakis and Koudas (2010) presented a system to detect bursty keywords that suddenly appear in tweets at an unusually high rate. Recently, Miot and Drigout (2020) investigated the efficiency of deep neural networks to detect trends. However, these techniques are applied without taking named entities into consideration.

Towards emerging named entities, recent work has mainly focus on identification and classification of unusual and previously unseen named entities. Derczynski et al. (2015) investigated the effects of data drift and the evaluation of the NER models on temporally unseen data. Agarwal et al. (2018) studied the disambiguation of named entities with explicit consideration of temporal background. Rijhwani and Preotiuc-Pietro (2020) reported improvements on performance for overlapping named entities under the impact of temporal drift. Due to the limitation of resources and lack of annotated data from social media, these NER models tend to have lower performances on emerging named entities.

5 Conclusion

In this work, we propose a simple approach to update model parameters and prevent degradation performance from temporal drifts. Our approach is inspired by our observations of how Twitter data follows trends in topics that can change very quickly. Experimentally, we show that leveraging emerging trends can benefit the recognition of named entities and reduce performance degradation, especially in low-resource scenarios. Our proposal is model agnostic, and can potentially be adapted to other NLP tasks that target social media and face the same problems of data evolution and temporal drift.

Acknowledgements

This work was partially supported by the National Science Foundation (NSF) under grant #1910192. We would like to thank the members from the RiTUAL lab at the University of Houston for their invaluable feedback. We also thank the anonymous reviewers for their valuable suggestions.

References

Prabal Agarwal, Jannik Strötgen, Luciano del Corro, Johannes Hoffart, and Gerhard Weikum. 2018. diaNED: Time-aware named entity disambiguation for diachronic corpora. In *Proceedings of the 56th Annual Meeting of the Association for Computational Linguistics (Volume 2: Short Papers)*, pages 686–693, Melbourne, Australia. Association for Computational Linguistics.

James Benhardus and J. Kalita. 2013. Streaming trend detection in twitter. *Int. J. Web Based Communities*, 9:122–139.

Leon Derczynski, Isabelle Augenstein, and Kalina Bontcheva. 2015. USFD: Twitter NER with drift compensation and linked data. In *Proceedings of the Workshop on Noisy User-generated Text*, pages 48–53, Beijing, China. Association for Computational Linguistics.

Jacob Devlin, Ming-Wei Chang, Kenton Lee, and Kristina Toutanova. 2019. BERT: Pre-training of deep bidirectional transformers for language understanding. In *Proceedings of the 2019 Conference of the North American Chapter of the Association for Computational Linguistics: Human Language Technologies, Volume 1 (Long and Short Papers)*, pages 4171–4186, Minneapolis, Minnesota. Association for Computational Linguistics.

Hege Fromreide, Dirk Hovy, and Anders Søgaard. 2014. Crowdsourcing and annotating NER for Twitter #drift. In *Proceedings of the Ninth International Conference on Language Resources and Evaluation (LREC'14)*, pages 2544–2547, Reykjavik, Iceland. European Language Resources Association (ELRA).

A. Graves and J. Schmidhuber. 2005. Framewise phoneme classification with bidirectional lstm networks. *Proceedings. 2005 IEEE International Joint Conference on Neural Networks, 2005.*, 4:2047–2052 vol. 4.

William L. Hamilton, Jure Leskovec, and Dan Jurafsky. 2016. Cultural shift or linguistic drift? comparing two computational measures of semantic change. In *Proceedings of the 2016 Conference on Empirical Methods in Natural Language Processing*, pages 2116–2121, Austin, Texas. Association for Computational Linguistics.

Andreas Kirsch, Joost R. van Amersfoort, and Y. Gal. 2019. Batchbald: Efficient and diverse batch acquisition for deep bayesian active learning. In *NeurIPS*.

J. Lafferty, A. McCallum, and Fernando Pereira. 2001. Conditional random fields: Probabilistic models for segmenting and labeling sequence data. In *ICML*.

Ilya Loshchilov and Frank Hutter. 2017. Decoupled weight decay regularization. *arXiv preprint arXiv:1711.05101*.

Xuezhe Ma and Eduard Hovy. 2016. End-to-end sequence labeling via bi-directional LSTM-CNNs-CRF. In *Proceedings of the 54th Annual Meeting of the Association for Computational Linguistics (Volume 1: Long Papers)*, pages 1064–1074, Berlin, Germany. Association for Computational Linguistics.

M. Mathioudakis and N. Koudas. 2010. Twittermonitor: trend detection over the twitter stream. In *SIGMOD Conference*.

Alexandre Miot and Gilles Drigout. 2020. An empirical study of neural networks for trend detection in time series. *SN Comput. Sci.*, 1:347.

Dat Quoc Nguyen, Thanh Vu, and Anh Tuan Nguyen. 2020. BERTweet: A pre-trained language model for English tweets. In *Proceedings of the 2020 Conference on Empirical Methods in Natural Language Processing: System Demonstrations*, pages 9–14, Online. Association for Computational Linguistics.

Jeffrey Pennington, Richard Socher, and Christopher Manning. 2014. GloVe: Global vectors for word representation. In *Proceedings of the 2014 Conference on Empirical Methods in Natural Language Processing (EMNLP)*, pages 1532–1543, Doha, Qatar. Association for Computational Linguistics.

Shruti Rijhwani and Daniel Preotiuc-Pietro. 2020. Temporally-informed analysis of named entity recognition. In *Proceedings of the 58th Annual Meeting of the Association for Computational Linguistics*, pages 7605–7617, Online. Association for Computational Linguistics.

Alex Rosenfeld and Katrin Erk. 2018. Deep neural models of semantic shift. In *Proceedings of the 2018 Conference of the North American Chapter of the Association for Computational Linguistics: Human Language Technologies, Volume 1 (Long Papers)*, pages 474–484, New Orleans, Louisiana. Association for Computational Linguistics.

Samarth Sinha, S. Ebrahimi, and Trevor Darrell. 2019. Variational adversarial active learning. *2019 IEEE/CVF International Conference on Computer Vision (ICCV)*, pages 5971–5980.

A Details for Experimental Setup

For BiLSTM-CRF model, we use GloVe Twitter embeddings. The dimensions of character embeddings and word embeddings are 50 and 100 respectively. We then use 2-layer LSTM with 300 hidden units to encode sentences. The dropout rate is 0.5. During training, we use stochastic gradient descent (SGD) with learning rate 0.1, batch size 20, and momentum 0.9. The L2 regularization is set to 0.001. For BERT and BERTweet, we do fine-tuning using AdamW optimizer (Loshchilov and Hutter, 2017) with learning rate 5e-5, batch size 32, and weight decay 0.01. We also use a gradient clipping of 1.0 and the dropout rate is 0.1. In scoring function, k is set as 0.1 for sample selection.

B Experiment with more data

In Figure 4 and Figure 5, we use 50 instances at each step. In Figure 6 and Figure 7, we use 200 instances at each step. We repeat our experiment with using different number of instances at each training step to study the impact of dataset size.

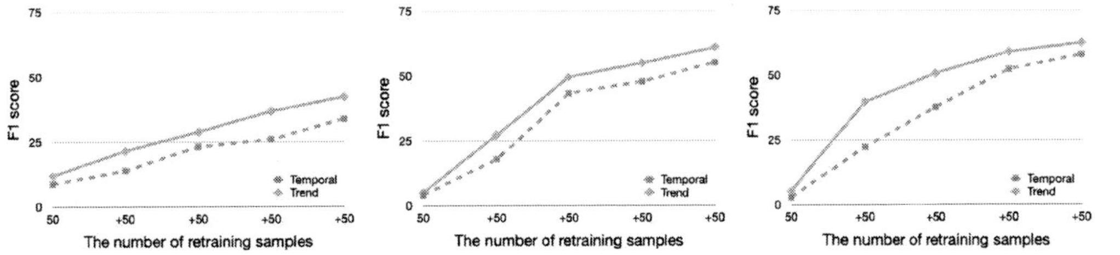

(a) BiLSTM + CRF (b) BERT + CRF (c) BERTweet + CRF

Figure 4: **Data can only be accessed year by year -** Each step represents a year from 2014 to 2018. At each step, we add instances from its respective year to the training set. For Temporal, we randomly select instances from that given year. For Trend, we rank instances based on their trending score. We experiment with 50 (Appendix B), 100 and 200 (Appendix B) instances per step to show the impact of training size.

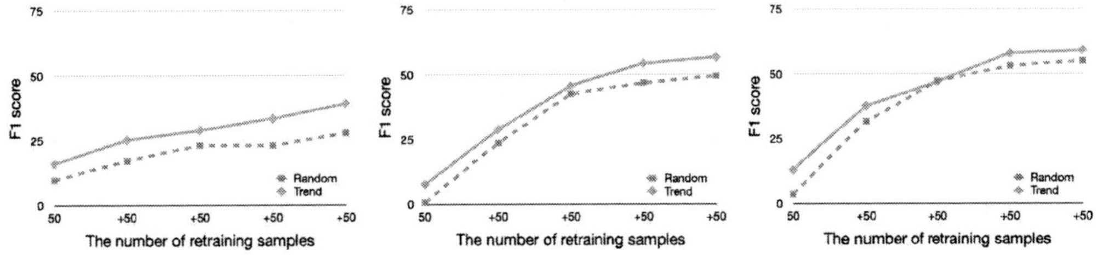

(a) BiLSTM + CRF (b) BERT + CRF (c) BERTweet + CRF

Figure 5: **Data from all years is available -** At each step, we add new instances to our training set. For Random, we randomly select instances from the available data. For Trend, we rank all available instances from most trending to less trending based on their trending scores. We then use this ranking to select the instances. At each step, we choose the instances with the highest trending scores that have not yet been added to the training set. We experiment with 50 (Appendix B), 100 and 200 (Appendix B) instances per step to show the impact of training size.

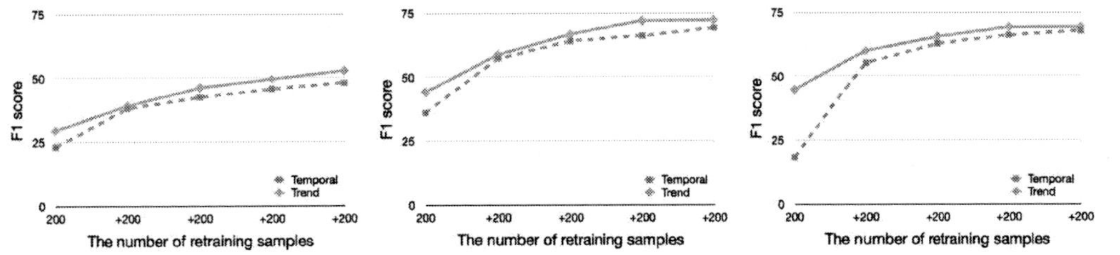

(a) BiLSTM + CRF (b) BERT + CRF (c) BERTweet + CRF

Figure 6: **Data can only be accessed year by year -** Each step represents a year from 2014 to 2018. At each step, we add instances from its respective year to the training set. For Temporal, we randomly select instances from that given year. For Trend, we rank instances based on their trending score. We experiment with 50 (Appendix B), 100 and 200 (Appendix B) instances per step to show the impact of training size.

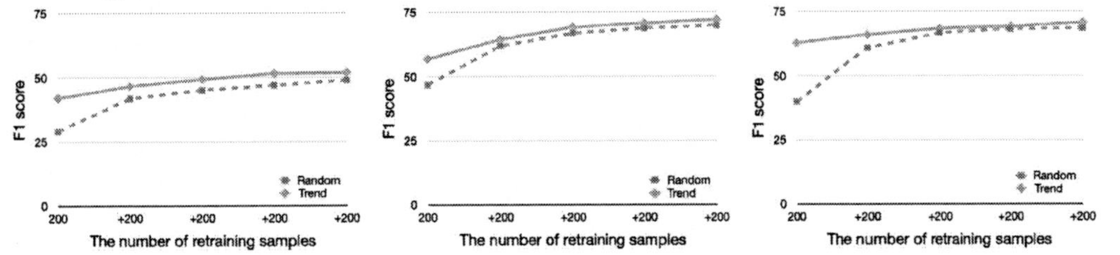

(a) BiLSTM + CRF (b) BERT + CRF (c) BERTweet + CRF

Figure 7: **Data from all years is available -** At each step, we add new instances to our training set. For Random, we randomly select instances from the available data. For Trend, we rank all available instances from most trending to less trending based on their trending scores. We then use this ranking to select the instances. At each step, we choose the instances with the highest trending scores that have not yet been added to the training set. We experiment with 50 (Appendix B), 100 and 200 (Appendix B) instances per step to show the impact of training size.

Jujeop: Korean Puns for K-pop Stars on Social Media

Soyoung Oh[*]
Sungkyunkwan University, Korea
sori424@g.skku.edu

Jisu Kim[*]
Sungkyunkwan University, Korea
rlawltn908@g.skku.edu

Seungpeel Lee[*]
Sungkyunkwan University, Korea
Sahoipyoungnon Publishing, Korea
leepeel@g.skku.edu

Eunil Park[†]
Sungkyunkwan University, Korea
and Raon Data, Korea
eunilpark@skku.edu

Abstract

Jujeop is a way for K-pop fans to express their love for the K-pop stars they adore by creating a type of Korean pun through unique comments in *Youtube* videos that feature those K-pop stars. One of the unique characteristics of *Jujeop* is its use of exaggerated expressions to compliment K-pop stars, which contain or lead to humor. Based on this characteristic, *Jujeop* can be separated into four distinct types, with their own lexical collocations: (1) Fragmenting words to create a twist, (2) Homophones and homographs, (3) Repetition, and (4) Nonsense. Thus, the current study defines the concept of *Jujeop* and manually annotates the 8.6K comments into one of the four *Jujeop* types. With the given annotated corpus, this study presents distinctive characteristics of *Jujeop* comments compared to the other comments by classification task. Moreover, with the clustering approach, we proposed a structural dependency within each *Jujeop* type. We have made our dataset publicly available for future research of *Jujeop* expressions.

1 Introduction

With the rapid improvement of information and telecommunication technologies, people have become not only consumers, but also producers of media content (Jenkins and Deuze, 2008). With this trend, there are a number of online media platforms that allow people to interact with other users anywhere and anytime (Burgess and Green, 2018). On these platforms, users actively create and share their contents, and express their thoughts and opinions on other users' contents (Van Dijck, 2013). In particular, online fan communities, where fans interact with each other, tend to use such platforms to share their contents and opinions on their favorite stars (e.g., Ariana Grande[1], BTS[2]; Baym (2007); Littlejohn and Foss (2009)).

With this vitalization of the communities on the platforms, several novel interaction patterns have been observed among South Korean users. Among these patterns, *Jujeop* in online environments is one of the notable phenomena presented by South Korean fans (Figure 1). Although the dictionary definition of the Korean word *Jujeop* refers to a disgraceful or silly behavior of a person, the term has evolved into a facetious expression with an implicit sense of humor in the online K-pop community; in South Korean culture, *Jujeop* is a punning activity that makes conversations enjoyable and allows users to engage on platforms (Yu et al., 2018).

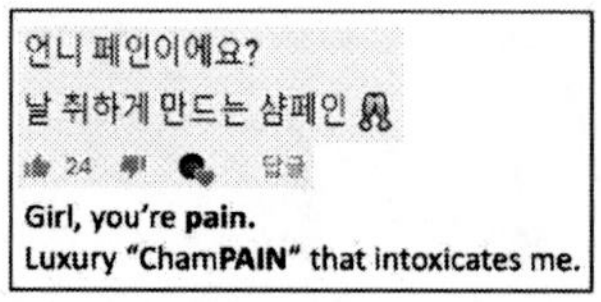

Figure 1: An example of *Jujeop* comments on *Youtube*

Miller and his colleagues (Miller et al., 2017) defined a pun as "*a form of wordplay in which a word suggests two or more meanings by exploiting polysemy, homonymy, or phonological similarity to another word, for an intended humorous or rhetorical effect.*" Based on this definition, the majority of recent studies have proposed several pun generation models using machine learning approaches (He et al., 2019; Luo et al., 2019).

However, compared to a huge body of prior research on English puns (Yu et al., 2018, 2020), only a few studies have been conducted on Korean puns in online environments. Because of some obstacles including the unique linguistic and cultural aspects of South Korea, there are several limitations in studying users' punning activities (Choi, 2018).

Thus, we propose the first Korean corpus, annotated for *Jujeop* comments, and categorize them into four different types. We have made the dataset

[*] Equally contributed first authors
[†] Corresponding author
[1]https://rb.gy/mzllvq
[2]https://rb.gy/0dfcdl

Proceedings of the Ninth International Workshop on Natural Language Processing for Social Media, pages 170–177
Online Workshop, June 10, 2021.

publicly available.[3]

2 *Jujeop* Data

2.1 Data Collection

As *Jujeop* comments are frequently observed in *Youtube* channels of K-pop stars, we assumed that high number of views in a channel guarantees the presence of the *Jujeop* comments. Based on this assumption, we collected 281,968 users' comments on K-pop stars from 285 *Youtube* channels[4], which have the number of views between 5,177 and 38,039,597. Then, we conducted the pre-processing procedures for the remaining Korean words (i.e., excluding words used for commercial purposes).

We sorted the comments based on the number of likes a *Jujeop* comment received. The comments that had more than the average number of likes in the collected comments (i.e., 167) were employed. With this approach, 8,650 comments were selected for annotation.

2.2 Annotation

Ten annotators who has been enthusiastic fans of their K-pop stars for at least 2 to 15 years (Mean: 9.3 SD: 4.2) and has been frequently exposed to *Jujeop* comments were employed for the annotation process. After explaining the definition and examples of *Jujeop* comments, each annotator was asked to respond to the following question to classify, whether each comment is a *Jujeop* comment:

- Is this a *Jujeop* comment, which has a sense of humor by praising K-pop stars with exaggerations and flashy modifiers?

Then, each annotator was asked to classify the *Jujeop* comment into one of the following types.

2.2.1 Fragmenting words to create a twist

The comments in this type intentionally fragment a specific word and extract/concentrate a single character from the word to disguise the word's full meaning (e.g., 'pretty' to 't'), in order to create a twist in the sentence meaning.

When one of the characters is included in both a specific word and sentence with the same pronunciation, the word and sentence are linked. This means that there are two steps in a *Jujeop* comment. After the sentence with hidden or sarcastic meanings is first presented, the word with complimentary meanings is then provided. For instance, 't' can mean 'tee' (t-shirt) as it has the same Korean pronunciation. Moreover, the fragmented word (e.g., 'T') usually carries a neutral connotation, while the complete word (e.g., 'Pretty') carries a positive connotation.

Because two words are linked and combined to make a sentence ('t' (t-shirt) and 'pretty'), it creates a pun in Korean:

언니. 왜 맨날 똑같은 **티**만 입어? **프리티!**
Sis, Why do you always wear the same **Tee**? **pretTee!**

The first sentence asks why she always wears the same t-shirt, which is pronounced [ti:]. Then, the following word changes the whole sentence meaning, which makes the initial meaning of the sentence a compliment about her prettiness [prti], thus creating a humorous twist.

2.2.2 Homophones and Homographs

Both homophones and homographs are sometimes employed to create pun expressions.

Homophones are defined as follows: "*when two or more words, different in origin and signification, are pronounced alike, whether they are alike or not in their spelling, they are said to be homophones*" (Bridges, 2018). The definition of homographs is "*words that have more than one meaning but share the same orthography*" (Twilley et al., 1994).

Users can employ specific lexical features of homophones and homographs to make a *Jujeop* comment. After a user makes his/her first sentence with the original meanings of words, they employ other word meanings in the second sentence to compliment the K-pop stars while allowing other users to enjoy the fun.

For example, George Bush, the former US president, has the same pronunciation in Korean and English (Korean: '조지 부시'), when George Bush is employed as a big name. The South Korean pronunciations of George is identical to the phrase 'to beat somebody/something' (Korean: '조지(다)'), while the pronunciation of Bush is identical to 'to break something' (Korean: '부시(다)'). Thus, the pronunciations of George Bush and 'to beat somebody/something + to break something' can be the same in Korean, although the meanings of the words differ depending on whether they are employed as a big name or as verbs.

너 영어이름을 **조지 부시**로 해줘...
내 마음을 **조지고 부시**니까.
Change your English name to **George Bush**...
because you **beat and break** my heart.

[3]https://github.com/merry555/Jujeop

[4]https://github.com/merry555/Jujeop/blob/main/dataset/channels.txt

2.2.3 Repetition

This is a type of repetition of the same phrase. As presented in the following example, the comments in this type employ repetition to emphasize the complimentary meanings on the K-pop stars.

아 진짜.. 그거 알아요? 잘생긴 사람을 보면 기억을 잃는대요.
아 진짜.. 그거 알아요? 잘생긴 사람을 보면 기억을 잃는대요.
Gosh... you know what? They say you lose your memory when you see a handsome person.
Gosh... you know what? They say you lose your memory when you see a handsome person.

2.2.4 Nonsense

The comments in this type include the K-pop stars within fictions. The majority of such comments flatter the stars by using exaggerated and almost nonsensical, over-the-top expressions. One representative example is presented below:

그녀가 예쁘다고 생각하는 사람 일어나! 라고 했더니 **지구가 일어나서 태양계 순서가 바뀌었잖아.**
I said, **Anybody who thinks she's pretty, get up!** and then **the whole Earth got up and the order of the solar system changed.**

There is no way that the Earth can 'get up' like a human being, nor could the order of the solar system change due to a person's prettiness. Such ridiculous and exaggerated expressions create humor and a profound expression with which fans can express admiration for their favorite celebrities.

2.3 Corpus Description

Among 8,650 comments, 1,867 (21.58%) were annotated as *Jujeop* comments. Then, three experts in natural language processing (NLP) manually validated whether or not each comment is a *Jujeop* comment. With these procedures, 7,077 non-*Jujeop* (81.82%), and 1,573 *Jujeop* (18.18%) comments were labeled with four separate *Jujeop* types (Table 1). We measured Krippendorff's alpha on four types of *Jujeop* comments (Krippendorff, 2011), and met inter-annotator agreement (0.532).

Type	Count
Fragmenting words to create a twist	39
Homophones and Homographs	57
Repetition	41
Nonsense	1436

Table 1: Descriptive analysis of *Jujeop* comments.

3 Experiments

We conducted two NLP tasks to investigate whether the labeled data can be significant in understanding *Jujeop* comments. First, we proposed several deep learning models to verify the annotated *Jujeop* comments. Then, we clustered *Jujeop* comments to figure out specific linguistic structures.

3.1 *Jujeop* Classification

At first, for the *Jujeop* classification, we applied three baseline classifiers for the experiment: Convolutional Neural Network (CNN; Kalchbrenner et al. (2014)), Bidirectional Long Short-Term Memory (BiLSTM; Schuster and Paliwal (1997)), and KoBERT[5]. All model configurations are presented in Appendix A.

Because more than 80% of the annotated comments in the dataset are non-*Jujeop* comments, we randomly selected 1,573 non-*Jujeop* comments, which is the same number of *Jujeop* comments to address the data imbalance issue. Then, we randomly divided the collected comments into training (2,256, 72%), validation (260, 8%), and testing (630, 20%) sets. We tokenized each comment with the *Mecab* tokenizer of *KoNLPy* package[6]. The maximum word counts of the comments and total vocabulary size are 58 and 6,536, respectively.

Classifier	Class	Precision	Recall	F1-score	Accuracy
CNN	*Jujeop*	75.41%	72.44%	73.90%	69.05%
	non-*Jujeop*	60.23%	63.86%	61.99%	
BiLSTM	*Jujeop*	77.59%	72.70%	75.07%	70.79%
	non-*Jujeop*	61.90%	67.87%	64.75%	
KoBERT	*Jujeop*	**80.45%**	**74.54%**	**77.38%**	**73.65%**
	non-*Jujeop*	**64.98%**	**72.29%**	**68.44%**	

Table 2: Results of the binary classification task (*Jujeop* and non-*Jujeop* comments).

F1-score	*Jujeop* (*2-ary*)	*Jujeop* type (*4-ary*)
CNN	67.94%	62.63%
BiLSTM	69.91%	56.96%
KoBERT	**72.91%**	**77.18%**

Table 3: Results of the macro f1-score; *2-ary*: binary classification of *Jujeop* and non-*Jujeop*, *4-ary*: multi-class classification of *Jujeop* types.

Table 2 presents the classification results with four evaluation metrics. In general, the KoBERT showed the greatest levels of all evaluation metrics. In particular, the accuracy of the KoBERT (73.65%) was higher than those of the CNN (69.05%) and BiLSTM (70.79%). In case of the recall level of

[5]https://github.com/SKTBrain/KoBERT
[6]https://konlpy.org/ko/v0.4.3/api/konlpy.tag/

Jujeop comments, it can be explained by the potentiality of misclassifying *Jujeop* to non-*Jujeop* comments. Moreover, we measured macro F1-score for the binary classification task (Table 3). Compared to the other benchmark models, KoBERT showed the best performance (72.91%).

Furthermore, we computed macro F1-score for the *Jujeop* classification task as each type of comment had a skewed distribution (Tran et al., 2018). The details of configurations are attached on Appendix A. Table 3 shows KoBERT with the highest performance of 77.18% followed by CNN (62.63%) and BiLSTM (56.96%). The implemented models are publicly available[7].

3.2 *Jujeop* Clustering

Pun usually relies on specific linguistic structure that can be classified based to patterns of the syllable, word, or phrase similarity (Binsted and Ritchie, 1997; Ritchie et al., 2007). Since, *Jujeop* comments share the characteristic of the pun, we assumed that *Jujeop* comments within the same type would share similar dependency relations.

Based on the assumption, we employed part-of-speech (pos) tagging to analyze the distinctive linguistic structure of each *Jujeop* type. Then, the tagged sentences were used as the input for the unsupervised learning algorithm, which allows identification of data into similar groups or clusters (Likas et al., 2003).

We utilized *Okt* pos tagger, which is commonly used to analyze the social media data analyses (Park and Cho, 2014). First, to balance the number of each type in *Jujeop* comments, we randomly selected 50 samples from type 4. Then, we vectorized each pos tag of the sentence as an input to the K-means clustering with K as 4, which represents 4 types of *Jujeop* comments.

Figure 2 represents the confusion matrix of the true and the predicted data points. The total accuracy of the K-means clustering was 32%, where the most correctly predicted type was type 2 with the 34 out of 57 correct predictions (59.65%).

Whereas most of type 1 were classified into type 3 (23 out of 39), which indicates that two types might share similar dependency relations. The single word appeared at the beginning of the sentence that was used again at the later part might have been characterized as a repetition. Type 3 was classified with 48.78% accuracy (20 out of 51), which indicates that type 3 might have been differentiated by syntactic features with the other types.

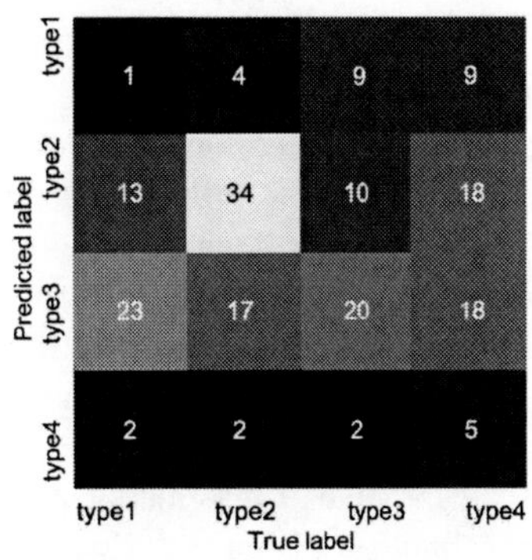

Figure 2: Confusion matrix on the clustering results of *Jujeop* types; x-axis indicates the true *Jujeop* types and y-axis indicates the predicted *Jujeop* types

Moreover, type 4 showed the lowest clustering accuracy with 10% (5 out of 50). This indicates that nonsense might be interpreted as semantic feature rather than syntactic feature. The further explanations and visual supplements are attached in Appendix B.

4 Conclusion

The current study first conceptualized the construct of *Jujeop*, which is one of the Korean pun interaction patterns on social media and annotated 8,650 comments. To provide a better understanding of *Jujeop* comments, four separate *Jujeop* types were proposed and labeled. Then, the presented NLP tasks results imply that *Jujeop* comments and each type of *Jujeop* has semantic and syntactic distinctiveness compared to the other comments.

Although we provide several findings on *Jujeop* comments, notable limitations remain. First, there are limited number of each type of *Jujeop* comments. Moreover, there might be other *Jujeop* types that were not observed in this study. The presented limitations might have occurred from the fact that the examples of *Jujeop* may be hard to collect in the wild. Thus, future study should aim to overcome the presented limitations with a crowd sourcing experiment or sentence generation based on the given definition to make a corpora of various *Jujeop* comments.

[7] `https://github.com/merry555/Jujeop/tree/main/models/multiclass`

Acknowledgements

Special thanks to Eun Been Choi and Jihwan Aum for their helpful comments. We would also like to thank "사회평론" (Sahoipyoungnon Publishing) for providing financial support with annotation. This research was supported by the MSIT(Ministry of Science and ICT), Korea, under the ICAN(ICT Challenge and Advanced Network of HRD) program (IITP-2020-0-01816) supervised by the IITP(Institute of Information & Communications Technology Planning & Evaluation). This research was also supported by the National Research Foundation of Korea funded by the Korean Government (NRF-2020R1C1C1004324).

References

Nancy K Baym. 2007. The new shape of online community: The example of swedish independent music fandom. *First Monday*, 12(8).

Kim Binsted and Graeme Ritchie. 1997. Computational rules for generating punning riddles. *Humor: International Journal of Humor Research*, 10(1):25–76.

Robert Bridges. 2018. *On English Homophones*. Litres.

Jean Burgess and Joshua Green. 2018. *YouTube: Online video and participatory culture*. John Wiley & Sons, Cambridge, United Kingdom.

Jinsook Choi. 2018. A linguistic anthropological study of the typification of middle-aged men in korea: An examination of ajae joke data. *Korean cultural anthropology*, 2:109–139.

He He, Nanyun Peng, and Percy Liang. 2019. Pun generation with surprise. In *Proceedings of the 2019 Conference of the North American Chapter of the Association for Computational Linguistics: Human Language Technologies, Volume 1 (Long and Short Papers)*, pages 1734–1744.

Henry Jenkins and Mark Deuze. 2008. *Convergence culture*. Sage Publications, London, United Kingdom.

Nal Kalchbrenner, Edward Grefenstette, and Phil Blunsom. 2014. A convolutional neural network for modelling sentences. In *Proceedings of the 52nd Annual Meeting of the Association for Computational Linguistics (Volume 1: Long Papers)*, pages 655–665.

Klaus Krippendorff. 2011. Computing krippendorff's alpha-reliability. `https://repository.upenn.edu/asc_papers/43/`.

Friedrich Leisch. 2006. A toolbox for k-centroids cluster analysis. *Computational statistics & data analysis*, 51(2):526–544.

Aristidis Likas, Nikos Vlassis, and Jakob J Verbeek. 2003. The global k-means clustering algorithm. *Pattern recognition*, 36(2):451–461.

Stephen W Littlejohn and Karen A Foss. 2009. *Encyclopedia of communication theory*, volume 1. Sage Publications, London, United Kingdom.

Fuli Luo, Shunyao Li, Pengcheng Yang, Lei Li, Baobao Chang, Zhifang Sui, and SUN Xu. 2019. Pun-gan: Generative adversarial network for pun generation. In *Proceedings of the 2019 Conference on Empirical Methods in Natural Language Processing and the 9th International Joint Conference on Natural Language Processing (EMNLP-IJCNLP)*, pages 3379–3384.

Tristan Miller, Christian F Hempelmann, and Iryna Gurevych. 2017. Semeval-2017 task 7: Detection and interpretation of english puns. In *Proceedings of the 11th International Workshop on Semantic Evaluation (SemEval-2017)*, pages 58–68.

Eunjeong L. Park and Sungzoon Cho. 2014. Konlpy: Korean natural language processing in python. In *Proceedings of the 26th Annual Conference on Human & Cognitive Language Technology*, Chuncheon, Korea.

Graeme Ritchie, Ruli Manurung, Helen Pain, Annalu Waller, Rolf Black, and Dave O'Mara. 2007. A practical application of computational humour. In *Proceedings of the 4th International Joint Conference on Computational Creativity*, pages 91–98.

Mike Schuster and Kuldip K Paliwal. 1997. Bidirectional recurrent neural networks. *IEEE transactions on Signal Processing*, 45(11):2673–2681.

Duc Tran, Hieu Mac, Van Tong, Hai Anh Tran, and Linh Giang Nguyen. 2018. A lstm based framework for handling multiclass imbalance in dga botnet detection. *Neurocomputing*, 275:2401–2413.

Leslie C Twilley, Peter Dixon, Dean Taylor, and Karen Clark. 1994. University of alberta norms of relative meaning frequency for 566 homographs. *Memory & Cognition*, 22(1):111–126.

José Van Dijck. 2013. *The culture of connectivity: A critical history of social media*. Oxford University Press, Oxford, United Kingdom.

Zhiwei Yu, Jiwei Tan, and Xiaojun Wan. 2018. A neural approach to pun generation. In *Proceedings of the 56th Annual Meeting of the Association for Computational Linguistics (Volume 1: Long Papers)*, pages 1650–1660.

Zhiwei Yu, Hongyu Zang, and Xiaojun Wan. 2020. Homophonic pun generation with lexically constrained rewriting. In *Proceedings of the 2020 Conference on Empirical Methods in Natural Language Processing (EMNLP)*, pages 2870–2876.

A Model Configuration

A.1 CNN

A.1.1 Binary classification

To employ a CNN-based classifier, we created a sequence of the tokenized words by embedding a layer with 128 units. The sequence was then sent to the CNN layer with 64 units. The max pooling layer was used to extract the prominent features of the given data. The final output was computed by sigmoid function to classify whether or not the given comment is a *Jujeop* comment. Ten epochs were employed in the training sessions with 32 batch size.

A.1.2 Quaternary classification

We used the the same configurations with the binary classification task except optimizer, loss and activation functions of the last layer. For the multi-class classifiction task, we employed the softmax activation function for the last layer and sparse categorical crossentropy for the loss function with adam optimizer. Also, we compiled the model with class weights by scikit-learn package[8] to handle the class imbalance problem.

A.2 BiLSTM

A.2.1 Binary classification

The tokenized words of the comments were outputted to the embedding layer with 128 units. The representation of the input data was then sent to the bi-directional LSTM layer with 64 units. The final output of the BiLSTM was calculated through sigmoid function. We trained the model with 10 epochs with 256 batch size.

A.2.2 Quaternary classification

We changed the optimizer, loss and activation functions of the last layer as in a CNN classifier for the multi-class classification. We also compiled the model with same class weights as in the CNN classifier.

A.3 KoBERT

A.3.1 Binary classification

To employ a KoBERT model, we adopted a built in SentencePiece tokenizer. We set embedding size as 128 and trained the model with 10 epochs. We set the batch size as 32 and learning rate as 0.00002.

[8] `https://scikit-learn.org/stable/modules/generated/sklearn.utils.class_weight.compute_class_weight.html`

A.3.2 Quaternary classification

We used same configurations as in the binary classification task. For the multi-class classification task, we modified the class number of the KoBERT classifier to 4.

B Jujeop Clustering

B.1 K-means Clusters Visualization

As shown in Figure 3, we visualized each type of *Jujeop* clusters with predicted data types and true data types. The predicted clusters are the results from K-means clustering with pos tagged *Jujeop* comments.

B.2 Centroids of the clusters from all types

Based on the K-means clustering results, we analyzed the dependency trees of centroids which are the representative data points to separate each cluster (Leisch, 2006). The structure of the type 1 centroid presents as below:

언니 다 좋은데 자꾸 **벽**이 느껴져요 **완벽**.
Sis, you make a **wall**. A **Perfection**.

[(NP<언니, Noun>) (AP <다, Adverb> <좋은데, Adjective>) (NP <자꾸, Noun> <벽,Noun>) 이,Josa (VP<느껴져요,Verb>) (NP<완벽,Noun>)]

which fragments word "벽" to make the word "완벽" to convert the meaning of the word "wall" into "perfection".

Moreover, the center data point of the type 2 is proposed as below:

언니 경**마**장 가지마요 언니가 경마장가면 **말**이 안나와.
Sis, don't go to **horse-racing**. Because you are **horse-less**.

[(NP<언니,Noun> <경마장,Noun> <가지,Noun> <마,Noun>) 요,Josa (NP<언니,Noun>) 가,Josa (NP<경마장,Noun> <가면,Noun> <말,Noun>) 이,Josa (NP<안나,Noun>) 와,Josa]

where the English word "horse" has the same pronunciation as "speech" in Korean as "말". Based on this homophone effect of word "말" in Korean, the horse-less can be interpreted as speechless.

The centroid of the type 3 is represented as below:

듣다 눈물날것같음 전남친이 저렇게 날 예쁘게 회상해준다면... 난 사실 **전남친 없어요, 남친도 없어요, 없어요, 아니 없어요, 그냥 없어요**.

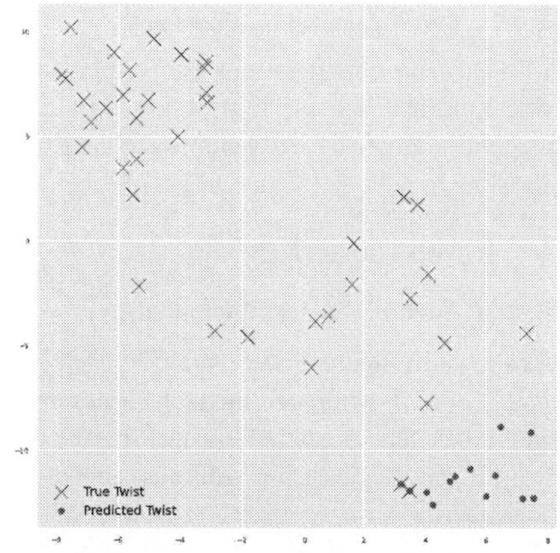

(a) Clusters of Type 1: Fragmenting words to create a twist

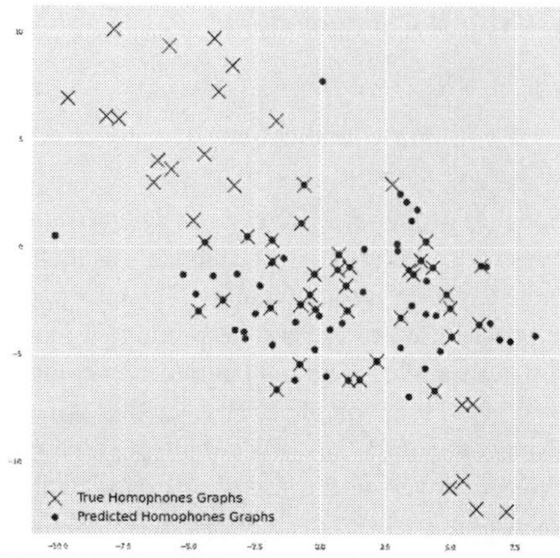

(b) Clusters of Type 2: Homophones and Homographs

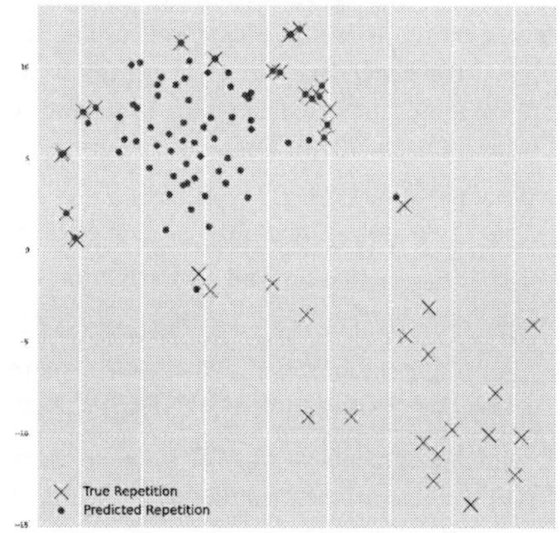

(c) Clusters of Type 3: Repetition

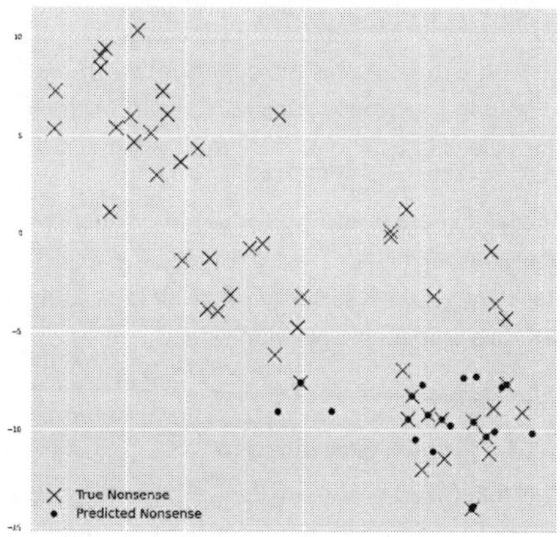

(d) Clusters of Type 4: Nonsense

Figure 3: K-means clustering results of each type of *Jujeop* comments where K as 4; Marker ○ as predicted data points and Marker × as true data points

I'm going to cry if my ex-boyfriend recalls me so beautifully... Actually I have **no ex, no boyfriend, nothing, nothing, nothing, just nothing**.

[(VP <듣다,Verb> <눈물날것,Verb>) (AP < 같음,Adjective>) (NP <전남친,Noun>) 이,Josa (AP <저렇게,Adverb>) (NP <날,Noun>)(AP < 예쁘게,Adjective>)(NP <회상,Noun>) (VP < 해준다면,Verb>) (NP <난,Noun> <사실,Noun> < 전남친,Noun>) (AP <없어요,Adjective>) (NP < 남친,Noun>) 도,Josa (AP <없어요,Adjective> < 없어요,Adjective> <아니,Adjective> < 없어요,Adjective>) (NP <그냥,Noun>) (AP < 없어요,Adjective>)]

which repeats the same word of "nothing" to make humor with emphasizing the attraction of the K-pop stars, simultaneously.

Moreover, the most representative data point of type 4 is given as below:

어이없네 이런걸 노래라구 낸건가. 그냥 이나은 인생 주제곡이잖아. 요즘 아이돌들 참 쉽다. 성의 없네. 그냥 이 노래 자체가 이나은인디.

It is ridiculous that this can be called as a song. It's just a life of "Naeun Lee". How easy to become star these days. This song is as "Naeun Lee" itself.

[(AP<어이없네,Adjective>) 이런,Modifier (NP < 걸,Noun> <노래,Noun>) 라,Josa (NP <구,Noun>) (VP <낸,Verb>) (NP <건가,Noun> <그냥,Noun>) 이,Determiner (NP <나은,Noun> <인생,Noun> < 주제곡,Noun>) 이,Josa (VP <잖아,Verb>) (NP < 요즘,Noun> <아이돌,Noun> <들,Suffix>) (VP < 참,Verb> <쉽다,Verb>) (NP <성의,Noun>) (AP< 없네,Adjective>) (NP <그냥,Noun> <이,Noun> <

노래,Noun> <자체,Noun>) 가,Josa 이,Determiner (NP <나은,Noun>) 인,Josa (NP <디,Noun>)]

which is far from the defined nonsense comments as it doesn't contain any of the nonsensical features. Rather, the presented centeroid comment uses critical note to paradoxically emphasize the coolness of the k-pop star. Considering the fallacious unsupervised classification results of type 4 (Figure 2), the given type would be interpret with semantic meanings rather than syntactic relations.

Identifying Distributional Perspective Differences from Colingual Groups

Yufei Tian[1], Tuhin Chakrabarty[2], Fred Morstatter[3] and Nanyun Peng[3,4]
[1] Department of Computer Science, University of Southern California
[2] Department of Computer Science, Columbia University
[3] Information Sciences Institute, University of Southern California
[4] Department of Computer Science, University of California Los Angeles
yufeit@usc.edu, tuhin.chakr@cs.columbia.edu,
fredsmors@isi.edu, violetpeng@cs.ucla.edu

Abstract

Perspective differences exist among different cultures or languages. A lack of mutual understanding among different groups about their perspectives on specific values or events may lead to uninformed decisions or biased opinions. Automatically understanding the group perspectives can provide essential background for many downstream applications of natural language processing techniques. In this paper, we study colingual groups[1] and use language corpora as a proxy to identify their *distributional perspectives*. We present a novel computational approach to learn shared understandings, and benchmark our method by building culturally-aware models for the English, Chinese, and Japanese languages. On a held out set of diverse topics including *marriage*, *corruption*, *democracy*, our model achieves high correlation with human judgements regarding intra-group values and inter-group differences.

1 Introduction

Sociologists have defined culture as a set of shared understandings, herein called *perspectives*, adopted by the members of that culture (Bar-Tal, 2000; Sperber and Hirschfeld, 2004). Languages and cultures have radical correlations (Khaslavsky, 1998; Bracewell and Tomlinson, 2012; Gelman and Roberts, 2017), because individuals communicate with each other by language, which carries the aspects of their cultures, experiences, beliefs, and values, thus will shape their perspectives. Lacking of understanding for these perspective differences could lead to biased predictions. Selection bias (Heckman, 1977) can often lead to misinformation as it sometimes ignores facts that do not reflect the entire population intended to be analyzed. For example, to verify a controversial statement like *"The free market causes fraud and corruption."*, we need to consider the perspectives from various groups (shown in Table 1). Similarly, a sentiment analysis model may fail to capture the correct emotions towards a debatable claim if the claim is viewed differently across different groups, such as the dispute

Claim	The free market does a much worse job than the government in providing essential services and the fraud and corruption part only gets worse.
CN Persp	Human: 72% support, Model: 79% support
JP Persp	Human: 17% support, Model: 15% support

(a) A claim about free market and government intervention from our test data, with the distributional perspectives of the Chinese (CN) and Japanese (JP) colingual groups. Human opinions and model predictions are highly correlated.

CN Wikipedia	中国特色的社会主义现阶段有如下特点：以国家的手段控制国内的要害经济部门和大量的企业，通过"国有资产"的概念以股份或者非股份形式保护国民经济的相当重要的部分。
	The current stage of socialism with Chinese characteristics has the following characteristics: the government *control the vital economic sectors* and a large number of enterprises in the country *by state means*, and protect a very important part of the national economy in the form of shares or non-shares through the concept of *"state-owned assets"*. [Translated]
JP Wikipedia	1930年以降、社会的市にして人の自由や市原理を再し、政府による人や市への介入は最低限とすべきと提唱する。... 日本では1950年の事再成以来、民の力会社が地域ごとに1社ずつ合10社あり。
	Since 1930, Japan reassessed the liberty and market principles of the individual for the social market economy, *advocating that government intervention* in the individual and *the market should be minimized*. ... In Japan, since the restructuring of the electric power business in 1950, *there are 10 private electric power companies, one in each region*. [Translated]

(b) Evidence from Wikipedia pages from the colingual groups (CN and JP), that potentially are for or against the claim shown in Table 1a. These are included in our training data after variation (discussed in Section 4.2). The two examples in the JP corpus are selected out from different articles.

Table 1: An example claim from our test data (1a), and possible evidences from wikipedia pages included in our colingual group training corpora (1b).

[1]A group of people that share the same language (https://www.merriam-webster.com/dictionary/colingual).

Proceedings of the Ninth International Workshop on Natural Language Processing for Social Media, pages 178–190
Online Workshop, June 10, 2021.

between India and Pakistan regarding Kashmir.

In this paper, we focus on *distributional differences* on controversial topics across groups. For example, within the United States, people have split views (approximately half-half) regarding gun control and abortion, while in China, people generally against the possession of guns and pro-choice for abortion. Hence, building a culture-aware model that considers groups' *distributional* perspectives will help improve comprehension and consequentially mitigate biases in decision making.

We aim to identify colingual groups' distributional perspectives towards a given claim, and spot claims that provoke such divergence. As colingual groups are naturally identifiable by the usage of language, we can obviate group detection and associated errors in the process of group identification.[2] Wikipedia, despite its overall goal of objectivity, has been shown to embed latent cultural biases (Callahan and Herring, 2011). Following these cues, we believe Wikipedia is an ideal source to study diverse perspectives among various colingual groups. Table 1a shows an example claim for which the Chinese and Japanese may have different opinions. Specifically, the Chinese-speaking group tends to support the claim (72% support) while the Japanese-speaking group tends to oppose it (17% support), which is likely due to the different economic/government environments. As shown in Table 1b, we can find evidences from wikipedia pages that support or oppose the claim in Table 1a.

We learn a perspective model for each colingual groups using a collection of Wikipedia pages for English, Chinese and Japanese, and then use these models to identify diverging perspectives for a separate set of claims that are manually curated and are *not* from Wikipedia.

Our contributions are as follows. **1)** We propose **CLUSTER** (**C**o**L**ing**U**al Per**S**pec**T**ive Identifi**ER**), a module that learns distributional perspectives of colingual groups based on Wikipedia articles. Towards this, we develop a novel procedure to algorithmically generate negative examples (introduced in Section 3.1) based on Wikipedia to train our group models (Section 4.1). **2)** We design an evaluation framework to systematically study the effectiveness of the proposed approach by testing our models on self-labeled claims from diverse topics including *cuisine, festivals, marriage, corruption, democracy, privacy*, etc. (Section 3.2, 3.3 and 4.3) **3)** Comprehensive quantitative and qualitative studies in Chinese, Japanese, and English show that our model outperforms multiple well-crafted baselines and achieves strong correlation with human judgements.[3] (Section 6 and 7)

2 Task Definition

In this paper, we focus on predicting a group's distributional perspective towards a *claim* and identifying claims that reflect *contrasting perspectives* from different groups on a particular topic. We further focus on English, Chinese and Japanese as the targeted colingual groups. Here, we define several key concepts and the task. We also explain why our task is different from stance detection.

Claim. A claim s_i, is a sentence that expresses opinions toward a certain topic (E.g Row 1 , Table 1) regardless of its language. We then translate and have a set of multi-lingual claims $\mathcal{S} = (\mathcal{S}^{en}, \mathcal{S}^{cn}\, \mathcal{S}^{jp})$, where $\mathcal{S}^{en}$ (English), $\mathcal{S}^{cn}$ (Chinese), $\mathcal{S}^{jp}$ (Japanese) are translations of each other.

Group Perspective Model and Score. Group Perspective Model is a probabilistic model that mirrors the group's distributional perspective on a claim - the model gives a score that reflects a group's likelihood of agreeing with that claim. For any claim s and its translations (s^{en}, s^{cn}, s^{jp}), a machine-generated score $P^l(s^l) \in [0, 1]$ is assigned to estimate the probability of s^l (l denoting language) being supported by the corresponding group. A distributional perspective score closer to 1 (fully support) and 0 (fully reject) indicates unanimity, while a score closer to 0.5 implies split within group. Similarly, a human-annotated perspective score $H^l(s^l) \in [0, 1]$ is assigned and considered as the ground truth of the likelihood that s^l is supported by its corresponding group.

Distributional Perspective Difference. Finally, we define (distributional) perspective difference. Let $\mathcal{D}^{l_1-l_2}_{model_i} \in [-1, 1]$ be the difference of perspective scores predicted by two models (for group l_1 and l_2) of s, where

$$\mathcal{D}^{l_1-l_2}_{model} = P^{l_1}(s^{l_1}) - P^{l_2}(s^{l_2}), l_1 \neq l_2. \quad (1)$$

[2]The only caveat is that such simplification ignores finer-grained cultural distinctions across subgroups speaking the same language, especially for English as a global language spoken by many nations; we leave those studies of more fine-grained groups for future work.

[3]We use these three languages as examples throughout the paper, but our algorithm is naturally applicable to other languages. Data and code are available at https://github.com/PlusLabNLP/CLUSTER

Here l_1 and l_2 each denotes a language such as 'cn' and 'jp'. A positive $\mathcal{D}^{cn-jp}_{model}$ indicates that the Chinese model agrees more with the claim s than the Japanese model. Similarly, we denote $\mathcal{D}^{l_1-l_2}_{human} \in [-1, 1]$ as the quantity of perspective difference reported by human annotators:

$$\mathcal{D}^{l_1-l_2}_{human} = H^{l_1}(s^{l_1}) - H^{l_2}(s^{l_2}), l_1 \neq l_2. \quad (2)$$

In Table 1, $\mathcal{D}^{cn-jp}_{model} = 0.79 - 0.15 = 0.64$, and $\mathcal{D}^{cn-jp}_{human} = 0.55$. A higher absolute value of $\mathcal{D}$ indicates bigger distributional differences.

Comparison With Stance Detection. Stance detection aims at detecting if a piece of text (usually a sentence or a document) supports or opposes a given claim (Hasan and Ng, 2014). Unlike stance detection, we do not have a given text associated with our claims. Instead, we learn representations of *group* perspectives through training on language corpora so that we can identify if a claim is likely to be supported or opposed by *a group*.

3 Data Preparation

In this section, we describe the procedure of composing our training data from multi-lingual Wikipedia articles. We then introduce an out-of-domain test dataset retrieved from Reddit that contain opinions regarding wide range of topics and the procedure of collecting human annotations on the test set.

3.1 Training Data

Topic Selection. We leverage the category hierarchy provided by Wikipedia to retrieve a list of child topics that belong to a few parent categories, including *politics*, *foods*, *sport*, *history*,*social issues*, etc. The selected root categories in English, Chinese and Japanese are aligned entities obtained from Wikipedia language links, and their sub-tree structures are only partially aligned. In this way, sub-topics obtained in the three languages have considerable overlap but are not identical. Hence we have different numbers of subtopics and training samples as seen in Table 2. We then retrieve all the articles under the selected subtopics separately[4], so that different claims that potentially reflect the cultural bias are included in our training data.

[4]https://en.wikipedia.org/wiki/Special:CategoryTree, https://zh.wikipedia.org/w/title=Special:分 类 树, https://ja.wikipedia.org/wiki/特別:カテゴリツリ

	Topics	Positive Samples	Negative Samples
English	4,245	292,444	292,444
Chinese	1,563	57,904	57,904
Japanese	1,266	25,039	25,039

Table 2: Statistics of Our Training Dataset. We deliberately balance the number of positive and negative samples so that no priori probability will intervene with the learning step.

Training Dataset Creation. Upon observing many examples similar to the economics pages in Table 1, we form our fundamental assumption that the *collection* of sentences extracted from Wikipedia in a certain language represent the corresponding *distributional* perspective of that colingual group. Therefore, we label each sentence extracted from the Wikipedia articles as ***positive examples***, as illustrated in part A of Figure 1.

Although positive examples mirror their corresponding perspective, we also need to compose ***negative samples*** — the claims that the corresponding colingual groups will disagree with. An intuitive approach is to flip the semantic meaning of the positive examples. This could be achieved by replacing the adjectives in a sentence with their antonyms. As shown in Figure 1.A, there are four adjectives in the original text: *'Making **safe** abortion **legal** and **accessible** reduces **maternal** deaths'*. We can obtain four negative examples by replacing each of the adjectives with its antonym (note that we do not flip multiple adjectives simultaneously). Each of the fabricated negative samples (in Figure 1.B) is ideal because it expresses conflicting viewpoints compared to the original text.

However, certain collocations such as *New York* and *legal systems* are also converted. Since bigrams such as *Old York* and *illegal systems* seldom appear in real sentences, we use a statistical n-gram model to avoid those poorly constructed negative samples. So far, we've obtained all data to train the perspective models. We list the number of topics, retrieved sentences, and training samples in Table 2.

3.2 Out-of-domain Test Data

While training and testing on the same Wikipedia data is a possible choice, a more ideal scenario is to test on different domains to see if the distributional representation learned by the model generalizes to other datasets, not merely representing the style of Wikipedia. Hence, selecting a good held-out set to test the performance of our models is important.

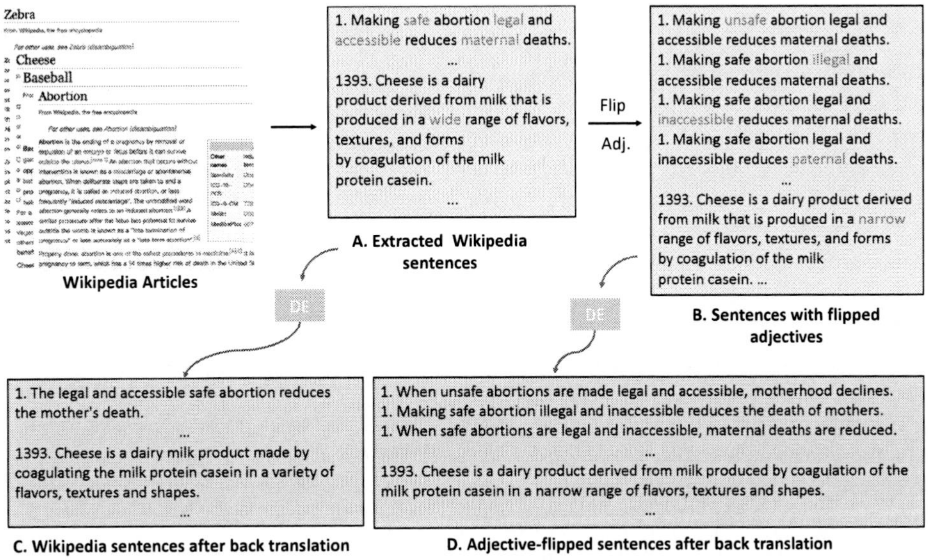

Figure 1: An illustration of the creation of the English training data. We first extract sentences from the retrieved Wikipedia articles to form the positive samples, and then replace adjectives with their antonyms as negative samples. *Back-translation* (discussed in 4.2) is then used to resolve pattern bias among negative samples. Note that we do not flip multiple adjectives simultaneously.

IMHO, what I find strange, and this is totally, some Chinese people have dogs as both pets and as dinner. [6]
IMO, in an utopia Communism is the best system to live by.

Table 3: Sentence from the IMO dataset expressing opinions about which differ between cultures.

We are motivated by the fact that people always express personal opinions on social media such as Reddit, where many opinionated claims are included. We leverage a previous work (Chakrabarty et al., 2019) which collects a distant supervision-labeled corpus of 5.5 million opinionated claims covering a wide range of topics using sentences containing the acronyms IMO (in my opinion) or IMHO (in my humble opinion) from Reddit. Table 3 shows two examples from the IMO dataset that may reveal contrasting perspectives between two different colingual groups. As this dataset is only in English, to obtain scores from the Chinese and Japanese cultural models, we translate each sentence into the target language using the Youdao and Google Translate API[5].

Test Data Selection. We first automatically extract claims that contain certain topical keywords, such as *free market* and *democracy*, and then remove the candidates which are out-of-context. Then we ask the English and Chinese volunteers to jointly select high-quality statements. Finally, for human annotation, we select out 128 high-quality claims from over 2,000 candidates in the IMO/IMHO dataset. The topics include personal life, social and political views, etc.

[5]https://ai.youdao.com, https://translate.google.com

[6]This does not reflect the opinion of the authors.

3.3 Human Annotations for Test Data

For each test sample, we collect 20 annotations from annotators living in the United States using the Amazon Mechanical Turk platform (MTurk). We then collect another 20 annotations from Chinese/Japanese netizens using the SurveyHero/Crowdworks[7] platform because MTurk is less used by the local people. The annotations are binarized, with 1 indicating agreement and 0 indicating disagreement. The average scores are viewed as the distributional scores.

For instance, for a given claim s^{en_i}, if 13 out of 20 English annotators give scores of 1, and the other 7 give scores of 0, then the human-annotated score $H^{en}(s^{en_i})$ equals $13/20 = 0.65$. In this way, we ensure that human annotation is of the same scale and meaning as the model prediction, and thus prove the validity of using the correlation between model predictions and human annotations as a measurement of effectiveness.

[7]https://www.surveyhero.com, https://crowdworks.jp

4 Methodology

In this section, we present the procedure of training our CLUSTER model. We explain how to learn group perspective models for English, Chinese, and Japanese colingual groups. We then raise the issue of pattern bias in negative samples and provide our corresponding solution. Lastly, we introduce the inference process.

4.1 Training Process

In the training stage, we leverage the pretrained multilingual BERT (Devlin et al., 2018) and fine-tune it for the perspective-specific classification task on the labeled data that is obtained in 3.1.

To enable the whole system to capture as much cultural discrepancy as possible, we separately fine-tune a BERT model for each language corpora despite the multilingualism of BERT. In other words, the learning steps of English, Chinese and Japanese systems have exactly the same structure but are completely isolated from each other in terms of training data and model parameters.

4.2 Pattern Bias in Negative Samples and Targeted Improvements

While flipping adjectives to create negative samples appears as an obvious approach, it ends up introducing certain style biases. Since the placeholders for adjectives are the only difference between positive and negative samples in training data, most classifiers would be able to identify this.

Niven and Kao (2019) show that high performance obtained from pre-trained language models such as BERT (Devlin et al., 2018) are often achieved by exploiting spurious statistical cues in the dataset. We face a similar problem in our preliminary study when evaluating on a test set from a different domain. While the quantitative results of our models trained on Wikipedia data are extremely high, we observe a huge drop when testing on out-of-domain data. This motivates us to mitigate statistical cues in our data.

Inspired by *back-translation* (Hoang et al., 2018), we generate paraphrases of our training data by introducing a pivot language and then translating the sentences back. This retains the semantics of the statements while removing existing stylistic biases. We back-translated both original Wikipedia sentences (i.e., positive samples) and the fabricated ones (i.e., negative samples). Part C and D of Figure 1 show the back-translated versions of our positive and negative samples respectively.

English (EN)	Chinese (CN)	Japanese (JP)
0.53	0.61	0.58

Table 4: Inter-rater agreement for English, Chinese and Japanese annotators using Krippendorff's alpha, with p-value $<$1e-10. All annotators show moderate agreement within their own group.

	Pearson correlation	Spearman correlation
English-Chinese (E-C)	0.26 (3e-3)	0.27(2e-3)
Chinese-Japanese (C-J)	0.49(5e-9)	0.50(2e-9)
Japanese-English (J-E)	0.29(7e-4)	0.30(6e-4)

Table 5: Cross-group rater agreement, in terms of *corr (p-value)*. We measure the correlation between collective judgements on 128 claims by raters from each pair of the colingual groups: {E-C, C-J, J-E}.

4.3 Inference Process

The framework of our inference stage is similar to the training procedure except that we also test on out-of-domain data. For each claim s_i in test data, three model predictions $\{P^{en}(s^{en_i}), P^{cn}(s^{cn_i}), P^{jp}(s^{jp_i})\}$ are generated. We then compute the colingual perspective difference of s_i based on Equation 1. Finally, we compute the correlation between model-predicted scores and human annotations.

5 Experiments

5.1 Experimental Setup

For all classifiers, we start the sentence representations with BERT-base (Devlin et al., 2018) model, and then fine-tune them during training. We set sequence length as 128, batch size as 64 and learning rate as 2e−5. We also study the efficiency of back-translation on reducing stylistic biases. Specifically, we train BERT models using data from 3 different settings: 1) no back-translation, 2) back-translate only negative samples, and 3) back-translate both positive and negative samples.

5.2 Binarization

We binarize the ground truth (with 0.5 as threshold) for the simplicity of data collection. Here 0 represents that a colingual group tends to maintain an opposite perspective, while 1 indicates a group tends to agree with the claim. For Wikipedia sentences, which we use for training and in-domain evaluation, the sentences originally selected from

Training \ Testing	No back-translation		Translate only negative		Back-translate both	
	Negative	Positive	Negative	Positive	Negative	Positive
No back-translation	85.15	88.74	65.23	72.55	67.82	64.61
Translate only negative	79.78	87.11	92.06	94.53	77.26	76.31
Back-translate both	**92.56**	**94.88**	**92.17**	**95.69**	**87.10**	**91.92**

Table 6: F1 scores of positive and negative class respectively, with models trained under three different settings: 1) neither the positive or the negative samples are back-translated, 2) only negative samples are back-translated, and 3) both positive and negative samples are back-translated. We then test them on the same held-out dataset.

Wikipedia are positive (1) while the one we modified algorithmically are negative (0).

5.3 Inter and cross-group rater agreement

To show how the annotators within a colingual group agree with each other, we calculate the inter-annotator agreement (IAA) using Krippendorff's alpha. We also leverage attention questions to remove irresponsible annotators. The final IAAs are listed in Table 4. For all three languages, the correlation within a culture is above 0.5, demonstrating that the annotators are moderately correlated.

We also investigate how cross-group raters agree with each other, and calculate their Pearson and Spearman correlation (as listed in Table 5). The Chinese and Japanese raters have higher correlation with each other than they are with English raters.

5.4 Baselines

We compare our proposed Colingual Perspective Identifier (CLUSTER) with these baselines:

Random: Random numbers within $[0, 1]$ are generated to simulate model predictions of all perspective classifiers.

LM: We regard the average of word-level log probability (sentence log probability divided by length) generated by multi-lingual GPT2 (Radford et al., 2019; Zhang, 2019; Sakamoto, 2019) as model predictions. We then use the min-max method to normalize the log probabilities.

Weak CLUSTER: Our proposed Colingual Perspective Identifier, trained on Wikipedia sentences *without back-translation*.

6 Results

6.1 The Effects of Back-translation

Table 6 shows that models trained with *no back-translation* and *translate only negative* work well under their own respective setting, but does not transfer well to other scenarios. On the other hand, we obtain best and most robust results when the model is trained on data being back-translated for both positive and negative samples. Hence, back-translation (for both positive and negative samples) is ideal to be used for inference in other domains.

6.2 Agreement between Model Prediction and Human Annotation

Table 7 reports the the correlations between the CLUSTER and baseline models with human annotations. We observe that the Random method does not capture any perspective representations at all. A competitive language model such as GPT-2 can bring significant improvements over Random because it is trained on a very large NLP corpus (including English Wikipedia), where group perspectives are implicitly included.

Moreover, the performance of Weak CLUSTER is partially better then language models, but still rather limited, probably due to style bias in negative samples. Finally, we can find that CLUSTER consistently outperforms all its competitors, and obtains $0.10 \sim 0.22$ performance gains over the second best model for all three colingual groups.

Last, we want to point out that unlike many other NLP tasks, the IAA (or human performance) should not be viewed as golden or an upper-bound in our evaluation. The IAA is just an indicator of how unanimous the annotators are on diverse concepts, including very controversial topics such as abortion. Therefore, machine-human correlation can reasonably be higher than within-human correlation.

6.3 Binary Accuracy

To further investigate the performance of our model and the baselines, we calculate the number of instances where binarized predictions and ground truths match with each other. The results are shown in Table 8. Again, our CLUSTER model achieved the best performance in all aspects.

7 Qualitative Analysis

While section 6 shows quantitative results and correlation values, we want to understand the advan-

Model	Correlation Type	English (EN)	Chinese (CN)	Japanese (JP)	Cross-culture (E-C)	Cross-culture (C-J)	Cross-culture (J-E)
Random	Pearson	0.00(0.5)	0.00(0.5)	0.00(0.5)	0.00(0.5)	0.00(0.5)	0.00(0.5)
	Spearman	0.00(0.5)	0.00(0.5)	0.00(0.5)	0.00(0.5)	0.00(0.5)	0.00(0.5)
LM	Pearson	0.17 (0.05)	0.07 (0.42)	0.12(0.19)	0.11 (0.23)	0.08(0.36)	0.15(0.09)
	Spearman	0.16 (0.08)	0.08 (0.35)	0.11(0.22)	0.09 (0.30)	0.09(0.33)	0.13(0.14)
Weak CLUSTER	Pearson	0.22 (0.01)	0.19 (0.03)	0.18(0.05)	0.03 (0.73)	0.05(0.61)	0.15(0.09)
	Spearman	0.11 (0.23)	0.13 (0.14)	0.10(0.28)	0.07 (0.42)	0.06(0.51)	0.11(0.23)
CLUSTER	Pearson	**0.37 (1e-5)**	**0.41 (1e-6)**	**0.40(3e-6)**	**0.25 (4e-3)**	**0.20(0.02)**	**0.35(4e-5)**
	Spearman	0.32 (2e-4)	0.34 (5e-4)	0.39(6e-6)	0.21 (0.01)	0.18(0.04)	0.31(4e-4)

Table 7: Agreement between model predictions and human annotations, in the format of *correlation (p-value)*. A higher value on Pearson correlation over Spearman correlation indicates that linear correlation is more significant than the rank correlation, and vice versa.

Model	EN	CN	JP	E-C	C-J	J-E
Random	0.50	0.50	0.50	0.50	0.50	0.50
LM	0.60	0.50	0.54	0.53	0.55	0.56
Weak CLUSTER	0.70	0.55	0.56	0.45	0.53	0.52
CLUSTER	**0.73**	**0.64**	**0.66**	**0.58**	**0.60**	**0.63**

Table 8: The binary accuracy. We test both within {EN, CN, JP} and across {E-C, C-J, J-E} groups. For scores within a culture($\in [0, 1]$), the threshold is set to 0.5. For cross-group perspective scores ($\in [-1, 1]$), the threshold is set to 0.

tages of our model on a qualitative basis. To this end, we select 50 claims from five particular topics: *marriage*, *corruption*, *cuisine*, *christmas* and *baseball*, and then obtain CLUSTER model predictions on these claims. We do not collect human annotations for these sentences, but use them only for qualitative analysis and visualization purposes detailed below.

For each colingual group pair in {E-C, C-J, J-E} and a given topic, we report the visualization of 50 claim pairs in Figure 2 and 3. Here, each dot (or triangle) represents one of the 50 claims which are randomly selected from IMHO, with the x-y axis representing the {E-C, C-J, J-E} model predictions. The blue dots that fall along the diagonals are where the two models agree. On the contrary, dots that fall on the upper left or the lower right part are where the models do not agree with each other. For example, sentence 1 in Figure 2 is closer to the Chinese culture (upper left corner), while English speakers tend to agree more with sentence 2 (lower right corner). We select representative examples in each region and list them in the captions.

First, from Figure 2 we observe that the model pairs have zero or negative correlation on three topics: *marriage*, *corruption* and *cuisine*, suggesting that the corresponding language speakers take contrasting stances towards these topics. Second, Figure 3 shows that 1) the English and Chinese speakers hold similar views on *baseball*, and 2) the Chinese and Japanese speakers share similar views on *christmas*. For example, Christmas, which is not a traditional holiday in East Asia, is adopted directly from the western world. The Chinese and Japanese speakers both follow the western customs and hence view Christmas likewise.

8 Related Work

Online Disagreement Most works about online disagreement focus on a single culture or language (Sridhar et al., 2015; Wang and Yang, 2015; Sridhar et al., 2015; Rosenthal and McKeown, 2015), thus are restricted to a single group. While these works try to computationally model disagreement or stance in debates, they do not target at finding cultural or cross-group differences. We, on the other hand, aim at understanding the disagreement in perspectives through different colingual groups according to their respective languages.

Cultural Study in Blogs or Social Media Nakasaki et al. (2009) present a framework to visualize the cross-cultural differences in multilingual blogs. Elahi and Monachesi (2012) show that using emotion terms as culture features is effective in analyzing cross-cultural difference in social media data. However, it is only restricted to a single topic (love and relationship). In contrast, we use Wikipedia to study cross-group differences in perspectives on a much larger scale and do not restrict ourselves to one single topic.

Cultural Difference in Word Usage Garimella et al. (2018) investigate the cross-cultural differences in word usages between Australian and American English through *socio-linguistic features* supervisedly. Garimella et al. (2016) use social network structures and user interactions, to study how to quantify the controversy of topics within a

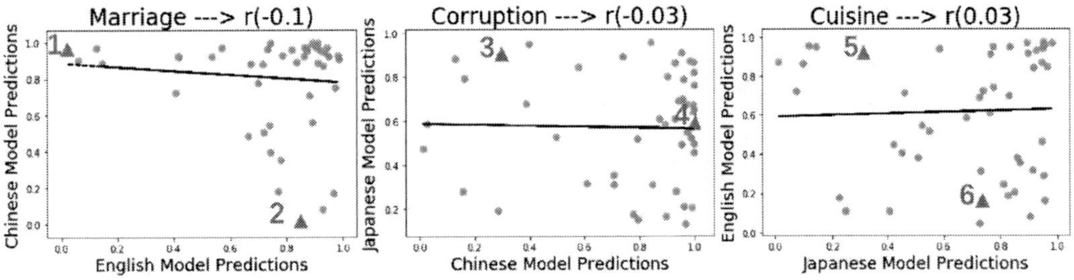

Figure 2: Model predictions on crosslingually disagreed topics: *marriage*, *corruption* and *cuisine* with their correlation values. Each dot (or triangle) represents one of the claims randomly selected from IMHO, with the x-y axis representing {E-C, C-J, J-E} predicted scores in sequence. Red triangular points are the following sentences: **1.** *Marriage is not about meeting someone you connect to, but both people being matured, and in the same headspace.* **2.** *If he cannot share his concerns with her, he is poor marriage material.* **3.** *If you don't reveal others' corruption you are culpable as well.* **4.** *There is plenty of corruption pulled out in the open these days, and that has been happening at a faster pace than ever before.* **5.** *Mexican, Mediterranean, Indian and Thai cuisines have the most delicious vegetarian dishes.* **6.** *Grilled fish is much better cooked at home and shared with friends.*

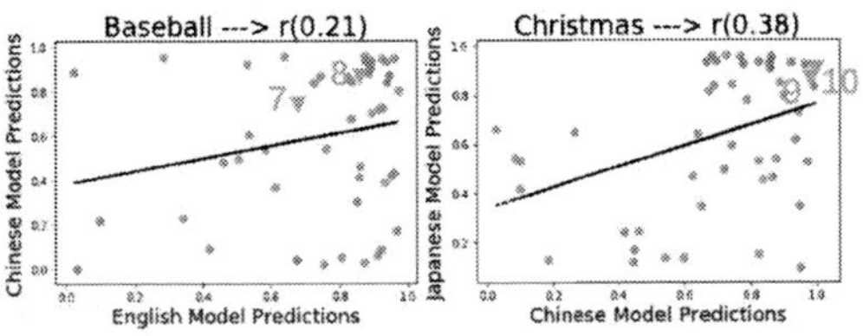

Figure 3: Model predictions on cross-lingually agreed topics: *baseball* and *christmas*, along with their correlation. The meaning of dots is the same as Figure 2. Orange triangles represent the following sentences: **7.** *Cricket is as fun to play as baseball if you limit the "innings" or overs.* **8.** *Things like basketball, baseball, tennis, golf, etc. are far more popular globally.* **9.** *Christmas, even minus the religious meanings, has good attributes in theory but has been too commercialized.* **10.** *I believe in giving gifts to kids because, Christmas is for children.*

culture and language. Gutiérrez et al. (2016) detect differences of word usage in the cross-lingual topics of multilingual topic modeling results. Lin et al. (2018) present distributional approaches to compute cross-cultural differences or similarities between two terms from different cultures focusing primarily on named entities. Our work is not limited to word usage or any particular topics. Instead, we focus on understanding cross-group differences of perspective at the sentence level.

Argumentation In argumentation, *Framing* is used to emphasize a specific aspect of a controversial topic. Ajjour et al. (2019) introduce frame identification, which is the task of splitting a set of arguments into non-overlapping frames. Chen et al. (2019) also release a dataset of claims, perspectives and evidence and propose the task of substantiated perspective discovery where, given a claim, a system is expected to discover a diverse set of well-corroborated perspectives that take a stance with respect to the claim. Different interests, cultural and cultural backgrounds diverge people from on taking a certain course of action. While both works deal with different perspectives about arguments in English, our work focuses on identifying the differences from a cross-lingual point of view.

9 Conclusion

We present CLUSTER, a computational method to identify distributional differences in cross-group perspectives, and evaluate it with human judgements. Through detailed experiments, we show that CLUSTER is straightforward and effective. Furthermore, we show CLUSTER generalizes well for out-of-domain scenarios by training the group perspective models on Wikipedia and test on claims collected from Reddit. This means that the proposed method learns the task, not the data. Besides, the general model of perspective difference identification can be useful in many NLP tasks such as fact checking, sentiment analysis, as well as cross-cultural studies in computational social science or multilingual debate forums.

As a first attempt towards automatic identification of cross-cultural differences, our work still has much room for improvement. Future directions include more complicated ways of composing negative samples, more well-crafted models, and extending our pipeline to fine-grained subgroups speaking the same language, especially for English as a global language spoken by many nations.

Acknowledgments

This work was supported by the Defense Advanced Research Projects Agency (DARPA) and Army Research Office (ARO) under Contract No. W911NF-21-C-0002. The views expressed do not reflect the official policy or position of the Department of Defense or the U.S. Government. The authors would like to thank the members of PLUSLab at the University of California Los Angeles and University of Southern California and the anonymous reviewers for helpful comments.

References

Yamen Ajjour, Milad Alshomary, Henning Wachsmuth, and Benno Stein. 2019. Modeling frames in argumentation. In *Proceedings of the 2019 Conference on Empirical Methods in Natural Language Processing and the 9th International Joint Conference on Natural Language Processing (EMNLP-IJCNLP)*, pages 2922–2932.

Daniel Bar-Tal. 2000. *Shared beliefs in a society: Social psychological analysis*. Sage Publications.

David Bracewell and Marc Tomlinson. 2012. The language of power and its cultural influence. In *Proceedings of COLING 2012: Posters*.

Ewa S Callahan and Susan C Herring. 2011. Cultural bias in wikipedia content on famous persons. *Journal of the American society for information science and technology*, 62(10):1899–1915.

Tuhin Chakrabarty, Christopher Hidey, and Kathleen McKeown. 2019. Imho fine-tuning improves claim detection. *arXiv preprint arXiv:1905.07000*.

Sihao Chen, Daniel Khashabi, Wenpeng Yin, Chris Callison-Burch, and Dan Roth. 2019. Seeing things from a different angle: Discovering diverse perspectives about claims. *arXiv preprint arXiv:1906.03538*.

Jacob Devlin, Ming-Wei Chang, Kenton Lee, and Kristina Toutanova. 2018. Bert: Pre-training of deep bidirectional transformers for language understanding. *arXiv preprint arXiv:1810.04805*.

Mohammad Fazleh Elahi and Paola Monachesi. 2012. An examination of cross-cultural similarities and differences from social media data with respect to language use. In *Proceedings of the Eighth International Conference on Language Resources and Evaluation (LREC-2012)*, pages 4080–4086, Istanbul, Turkey. European Languages Resources Association (ELRA).

Aparna Garimella, Rada Mihalcea, and James Pennebaker. 2016. Identifying cross-cultural differences in word usage. In *Proceedings of COLING 2016, the 26th International Conference on Computational Linguistics: Technical Papers*, pages 674–683, Osaka, Japan. The COLING 2016 Organizing Committee.

Kiran Garimella, Gianmarco De Francisci Morales, Aristides Gionis, and Michael Mathioudakis. 2018. Quantifying controversy on social media. *ACM Transactions on Social Computing*, 1(1):3.

Susan A Gelman and Steven O Roberts. 2017. How language shapes the cultural inheritance of categories. *Proceedings of the National Academy of Sciences*, 114(30):7900–7907.

E Dario Gutiérrez, Ekaterina Shutova, Patricia Lichtenstein, Gerard de Melo, and Luca Gilardi. 2016. Detecting cross-cultural differences using a multilingual topic model. *Transactions of the Association for Computational Linguistics*, 4:47–60.

Kazi Saidul Hasan and Vincent Ng. 2014. Why are you taking this stance? identifying and classifying reasons in ideological debates. In *Proceedings of the 2014 Conference on Empirical Methods in Natural Language Processing (EMNLP)*, pages 751–762, Doha, Qatar. Association for Computational Linguistics.

James J Heckman. 1977. Sample selection bias as a specification error (with an application to the estimation of labor supply functions). Technical report, National Bureau of Economic Research.

Vu Cong Duy Hoang, Philipp Koehn, Gholamreza Haffari, and Trevor Cohn. 2018. Iterative back-translation for neural machine translation. In *Proceedings of the 2nd Workshop on Neural Machine Translation and Generation*, pages 18–24, Melbourne, Australia. Association for Computational Linguistics.

Julie Khaslavsky. 1998. Integrating culture into interface design. In *CHI 98 conference summary on Human factors in computing systems*, pages 365–366. ACM.

Bill Yuchen Lin, Frank F. Xu, Kenny Zhu, and Seung-won Hwang. 2018. Mining cross-cultural differences and similarities in social media. In *Proceedings of the 56th Annual Meeting of the Association for Computational Linguistics (Volume 1: Long Papers)*, pages 709–719, Melbourne, Australia. Association for Computational Linguistics.

Hiroyuki Nakasaki, Mariko Kawaba, Sayuri Yamazaki, Takehito Utsuro, and Tomohiro Fukuhara. 2009. Visualizing cross-lingual/cross-cultural differences in concerns in multilingual blogs. In *Third International AAAI Conference on Weblogs and Social Media*.

Nathan Ng, Kyra Yee, Alexei Baevski, Myle Ott, Michael Auli, and Sergey Edunov. 2019. Facebook fair's wmt19 news translation task submission. *arXiv preprint arXiv:1907.06616*.

Timothy Niven and Hung-Yu Kao. 2019. Probing neural network comprehension of natural language arguments. *arXiv preprint arXiv:1907.07355*.

Alec Radford, Jeff Wu, Rewon Child, David Luan, Dario Amodei, and Ilya Sutskever. 2019. Language models are unsupervised multitask learners.

Sara Rosenthal and Kathy McKeown. 2015. I couldn't agree more: The role of conversational structure in agreement and disagreement detection in online discussions. In *Proceedings of the 16th Annual Meeting of the Special Interest Group on Discourse and Dialogue*, pages 168–177, Prague, Czech Republic. Association for Computational Linguistics.

Toshiyuki Sakamoto. 2019. Japanese gpt2 generation model. https://github.com/tanreinama/gpt2-japanese.

Dan Sperber and Lawrence A Hirschfeld. 2004. The cognitive foundations of cultural stability and diversity. *Trends in cognitive sciences*, 8(1):40–46.

Dhanya Sridhar, James Foulds, Bert Huang, Lise Getoor, and Marilyn Walker. 2015. Joint models of disagreement and stance in online debate. In *Proceedings of the 53rd Annual Meeting of the Association for Computational Linguistics and the 7th International Joint Conference on Natural Language Processing (Volume 1: Long Papers)*, pages 116–125, Beijing, China. Association for Computational Linguistics.

William Yang Wang and Diyi Yang. 2015. That's so annoying!!!: A lexical and frame-semantic embedding based data augmentation approach to automatic categorization of annoying behaviors using #petpeeve tweets. In *Proceedings of the 2015 Conference on Empirical Methods in Natural Language Processing*, pages 2557–2563, Lisbon, Portugal. Association for Computational Linguistics.

Zhibo Zhang. 2019. Gpt2-ml: Gpt-2 for multiple languages. https://github.com/imcaspar/gpt2-ml.

Appendix

A Hyper-parameters and other Experimental Settings

To train the classifiers, we start the sentence representations with the pre-trained BERT (Devlin et al., 2018) model, and then fine-tune them. For all models, we set sequence length as 128, batch size as 64 and learning rate as 2e−5. We train each CLUSTER model for 5 epochs and save the best model only.

1. **Number of parameters:** Each CLUSTER model, fine-tuned on the BERT-base model, has 102M trainable parameters.

2. **Runtime:** Our average training time is 2 to 5 hours, depending on the size of training data for each language (see Table 2).

3. **Hardware configuration:** We use three GeForce RTX 2080 GPUs.

4. **Hyper-parameter tuning:** We manually tune the hyper-parameters and report the configuration that has the best F1 score on our validation set.

B Topics and Visualization

The sixteen topics that are selected for evaluation, along with the Pearson correlations of culture model predictions on 50 randomly sampled sentences, are listed in Table 9. We highlight the topics with relatively high and low values of correlation coefficients in red and blue. Note that we do not collect human annotations for these sentences, but use them only for qualitative analysis and visualization purposes.

As can be seen, most topics have a positive correlation, meaning that the English, Chinese and Japanese colingual groups have a general agreements on most subjects such as *savings*, *baseball* and *cheese*. Christmas, which is not a traditional holiday in China or Japan, is adopted directly from the western world. That's why all the three models view Christmas likewise. In addition, the models have dispute on topics such as *bible*, *marriage*, *corruption*, and *abortion*. To get a more intuitive sense of the score distribution, we further visualize the model-predicted scores on more topics in Figure 4 and Figure 6.

Topics	E-C	C-J	J-E
Savings	0.09 (0.51)	0.40 (0.00)	0.31 (0.03)
Cuisine	0.01 (0.97)	0.21 (0.14)	0.03 (0.83)
Christmas	0.37 (0.01)	0.38 (0.01)	0.45 (0.00)
Bible	-0.02 (0.89)	0.16 (0.26)	0.16 (0.28)
Soup	0.26 (0.07)	0.15 (0.30)	0.22 (0.12)
Terrorism	0.09 (0.51)	0.07 (0.61)	0.20 (0.16)
Marriage	-0.10 (0.50)	0.21 (0.13)	0.04 (0.81)
Corruption	0.11 (0.44)	-0.04 (0.77)	-0.09 (0.54)
Baseball	0.21 (0.13)	0.13 (0.35)	0.11 (0.46)
Cheese	0.17 (0.23)	0.03 (0.83)	0.28 (0.05)
Communism	0.06 (0.67)	0.03 (0.83)	0.10 (0.48)
Democracy	0.09 (0.56)	-0.20 (0.16)	0.17 (0.23)
Russia	0.29 (0.04)	0.33 (0.02)	0.16 (0.27)
Abortion	-0.04 (0.77)	0.07 (0.65)	0.33 (0.02)
Racism	0.31 (0.03)	0.18 (0.20)	0.12 (0.40)
Gun control	0.07 (0.63)	0.15 (0.30)	0.19 (0.18)

Table 9: The sixteen topics that are selected for evaluation, along with the correlations between English-Chinese (E-C), Chinese-Japanese (C-J), and Japanese-English (J-E) culture model predictions on 50 randomly sampled sentences, in terms of *corr (p-value)*.

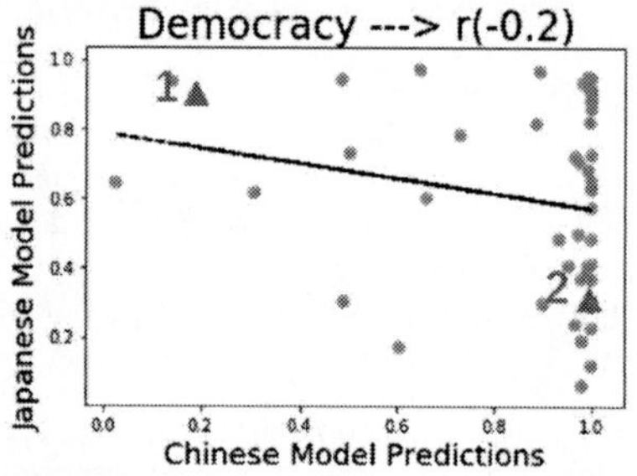

Figure 4: Model predictions on *democracy* of Chinese (x-axis) and Japanese (y-axis) models, and the correlation coefficient. The red triangles represent cross-lingually disagreed sentences: **1.** *Yeah, mandatory voting should be a required part of a democracy.* **2.** *The ideal system would be a merger of democracy and socialism (which we are slowly moving towards).*

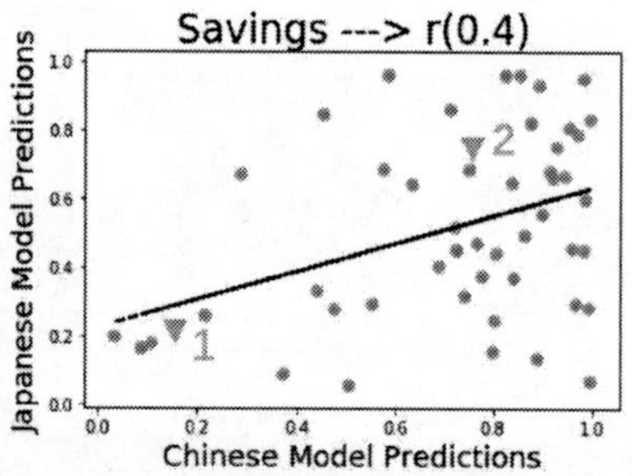

Figure 5: Model predictions on *savings* of Chinese (x-axis) and Japanese (y-axis) models, and the correlation coefficient. The orange triangles represent cross-lingually agreed sentences: **1.** *Higher risk-free interest is needed to stimulate savings and to avoid credit recessions.* **2.** *Life savings essentially means to me what you are gonna leave to your heirs.*

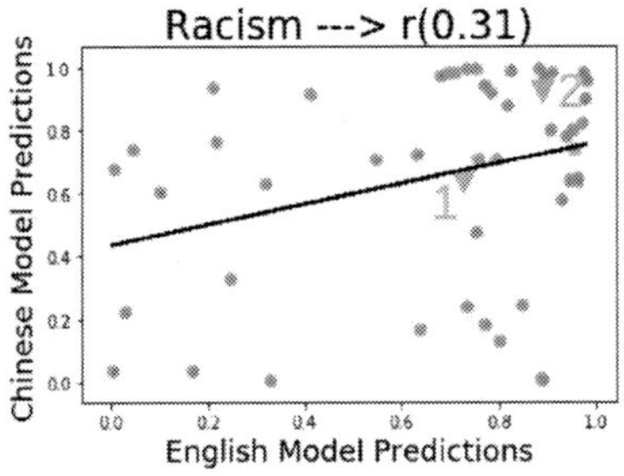

Figure 6: Model predictions on *racism* of English (x-axis) and Chinese (y-axis) models, and the correlation coefficient. The orange triangles represent cross-lingually agreed sentences: **1.** *Racism is the prejudice against other cultures through identification of physical appearance and cues.* **2.** *Fat shaming and/or body shaming can be just as bad as racism or homophobia.*

C Additional Details for Data Collection

C.1 Training Data

We have described the procedure of collecting our training data from multi-lingual Wikipedia articles in Section 3.1. In addition, for pre-processing details, we utilize Jieba[8] and Mecab[9] to tokenize Chinese and Japanese sentences.

Back-translation (discussed in Section 4.2) is the backbone of our CLUSTER model. Table 10 show the pivot languages as well as different translation systems used for our English, Chinese and Japanese models.

	Pivot language	Translation model
English	German	Fined-tuned transformer (Ng et al., 2019)
Chinese	Japanese	Youdao API
Japanese	Chinese	Google Translate

Table 10: The pivot languages and translation systems that we use for back-translation.

C.2 Questionnaire for Selecting Test Data

We design questionnaires to select out meaningful and high-quality claims from the original IMO/IMHO dataset (discussed in Section **??**), and collect three answers per claim. Figure 7 shows our instructions to the English annotators on the Amazon Mechanical Turk (MTurk) platform.

The turkers are asked to give a categorical score to each candidate sentence. The categorical score ranges from 1 to 3, with 1 indicating not meaningful, incoherent, or talking about facts, 2 indicating somewhat meaningful but few people have opinions on it, and 3 indicating highly meaningful. Because we extract single sentences from online discussion forums, we ask the turkers to ignore the out-of-context words such as 'and', 'also', and 'but', and focus on the opinion only. Finally, if all annotators agree that a given claim is meaningful enough so that other people will hold a stance (either agreement or disagreement) towards it, we regard this candidate claim as one of our test samples for the final human annotation step.

C.3 Questionnaire for Collecting Human Annotation

Figure 8 is an English demonstration of our survey to collect human annotations of the test data. The annotators as instructed to read each sentence carefully, and give a binary score to each sentence based on their personal opinions. The score is either 0 or 1, with 1 indicating they mostly agree with this statement, and 0 indicating they mostly do not agree with it, or don't know what this statement is talking about.

Besides, we adopt attention checks to control the quality of our collected annotations. To this end, we manually select 7 facts from Wikipedia as attention check statements, which are obviously true to the masses, such as *'Cheese is a dairy product derived from milk that is produced in a wide range of flavors, textures, and forms'*. We insert an attention check statement after every 9 test claims. If an annotator does not agree with one of our attention check statements, his entire HIT is rejected. Each annotator is allowed to annotate at most 20 sentences including the attention check statements.

[8]https://pypi.org/project/jieba/
[9]https://pypi.org/project/mecab-python3/

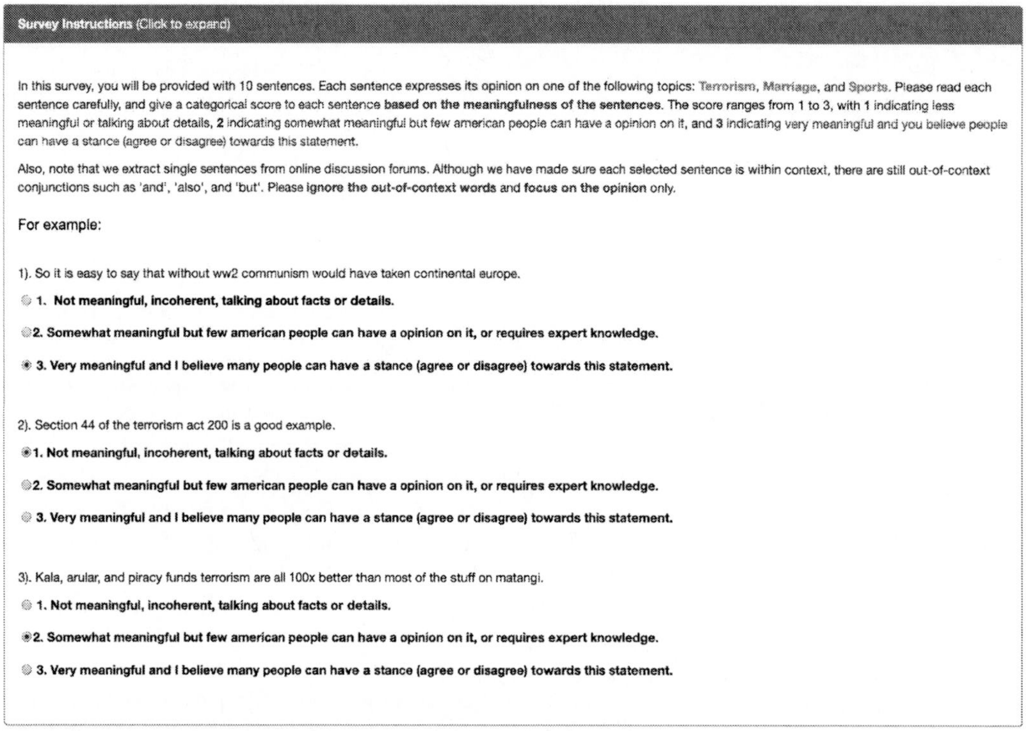

Survey Instructions (Click to expand)

In this survey, you will be provided with 10 sentences. Each sentence expresses its opinion on one of the following topics: Terrorism, Marriage, and Sports. Please read each sentence carefully, and give a categorical score to each sentence **based on the meaningfulness of the sentences**. The score ranges from 1 to 3, with **1** indicating less meaningful or talking about details, **2** indicating somewhat meaningful but few american people can have a opinion on it, and **3** indicating very meaningful and you believe people can have a stance (agree or disagree) towards this statement.

Also, note that we extract single sentences from online discussion forums. Although we have made sure each selected sentence is within context, there are still out-of-context conjunctions such as 'and', 'also', and 'but'. Please **ignore the out-of-context words** and **focus on the opinion** only.

For example:

1). So it is easy to say that without ww2 communism would have taken continental europe.

1. Not meaningful, incoherent, talking about facts or details.

2. Somewhat meaningful but few american people can have a opinion on it, or requires expert knowledge.

3. Very meaningful and I believe many people can have a stance (agree or disagree) towards this statement.

2). Section 44 of the terrorism act 200 is a good example.

1. Not meaningful, incoherent, talking about facts or details.

2. Somewhat meaningful but few american people can have a opinion on it, or requires expert knowledge.

3. Very meaningful and I believe many people can have a stance (agree or disagree) towards this statement.

3). Kala, arular, and piracy funds terrorism are all 100x better than most of the stuff on matangi.

1. Not meaningful, incoherent, talking about facts or details.

2. Somewhat meaningful but few american people can have a opinion on it, or requires expert knowledge.

3. Very meaningful and I believe many people can have a stance (agree or disagree) towards this statement.

Figure 7: The instructions of our survey to evaluate the meaningfulness of the IMO/IMHO sentences on the MTurk platform.

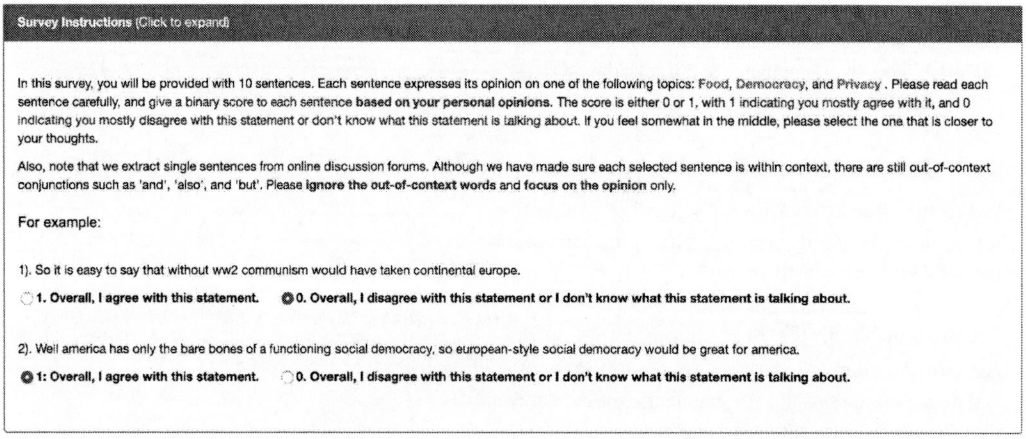

Survey Instructions (Click to expand)

In this survey, you will be provided with 10 sentences. Each sentence expresses its opinion on one of the following topics: Food, Democracy, and Privacy . Please read each sentence carefully, and give a binary score to each sentence **based on your personal opinions.** The score is either 0 or 1, with 1 indicating you mostly agree with it, and 0 indicating you mostly disagree with this statement or don't know what this statement is talking about. If you feel somewhat in the middle, please select the one that is closer to your thoughts.

Also, note that we extract single sentences from online discussion forums. Although we have made sure each selected sentence is within context, there are still out-of-context conjunctions such as 'and', 'also', and 'but'. Please **ignore the out-of-context words** and **focus on the opinion** only.

For example:

1). So it is easy to say that without ww2 communism would have taken continental europe.

1. Overall, I agree with this statement. **0. Overall, I disagree with this statement or I don't know what this statement is talking about.**

2). Well america has only the bare bones of a functioning social democracy, so european-style social democracy would be great for america.

1: Overall, I agree with this statement. **0. Overall, I disagree with this statement or I don't know what this statement is talking about.**

Figure 8: An example instruction page of our survey to collect the human annotations on the MTurk platform.

Author Index

Arendt, Dustin, 70
Arseniev-Koehler, Alina, 81
Ayton, Ellyn, 70

Bose, Tulika, 113
Bošnjak, Mihaela, 138
Brambilla, Marco, 14

Cao, Ivy, 36
Chakrabarty, Tuhin, 178
Chen, Shuguang, 163
Cosbey, Robin, 70

Di Giovanni, Marco, 14
Dong, MeiXing, 153
Dredze, Mark, 123

Escalante, Hugo Jair, 103

Fohr, Dominique, 113
Fujita, Soichiro, 24

Gjurković, Matej, 138
Glenski, Maria, 70
Goldwasser, Dan, 1
Gravano, Luis, 36
Groh, Georg, 91

Haskett, Breon, 81
Hsu, Daniel, 36

Illina, Irina, 113

Jarquín-Vásquez, Horacio, 103

Karamanolakis, Giannis, 36
Karan, Mladen, 138
Kennedy, Ian, 81
KIM, JISU, 170
Kobayashi, Hayato, 24
Kobayashi, Ken, 24
Koleejan, Chahine, 24

Larimore, Savannah, 81
Lee, Lillian, 61
Lee, Seungpeel, 170
Liu, Xiao, 123
Liu, Zizhou, 36

Masuyama, Takeshi, 24
Mihalcea, Rada, 153
Montes, Manuel, 103
Morstatter, Fred, 178
Mosca, Edoardo, 91
Murao, Kazuma, 24

Neves, Leonardo, 163

Oh, Soyoung, 170
Okumura, Manabu, 24

Park, Eunil, 170
Peng, Nanyun, 178

Roy, Shamik, 1

Sekine, Satoshi, 24
Smith, Ana, 61
Snajder, Jan, 138
Solorio, Thamar, 163
Stewart, Ian, 153

Tabuchi, Yoshimune, 24
Taguchi, Hiroaki, 24
Tian, Yufei, 178

Volkova, Svitlana, 70
Vukojević, Iva, 138

Wich, Maximilian, 91
Wood-Doughty, Zach, 123

Xu, Paiheng, 123
Xu, Xueming, 153

Yatsuka, Taichi, 24

Zhang, Yiwei, 153
Zhou, Karen, 61

Association for Computational Linguistics
209 N. Eighth Street
Stroudsburg, Pennsylvania 18360

ISBN 978-1-7138-3030-6

CURRAN ASSOCIATES INC.
proceedings.com